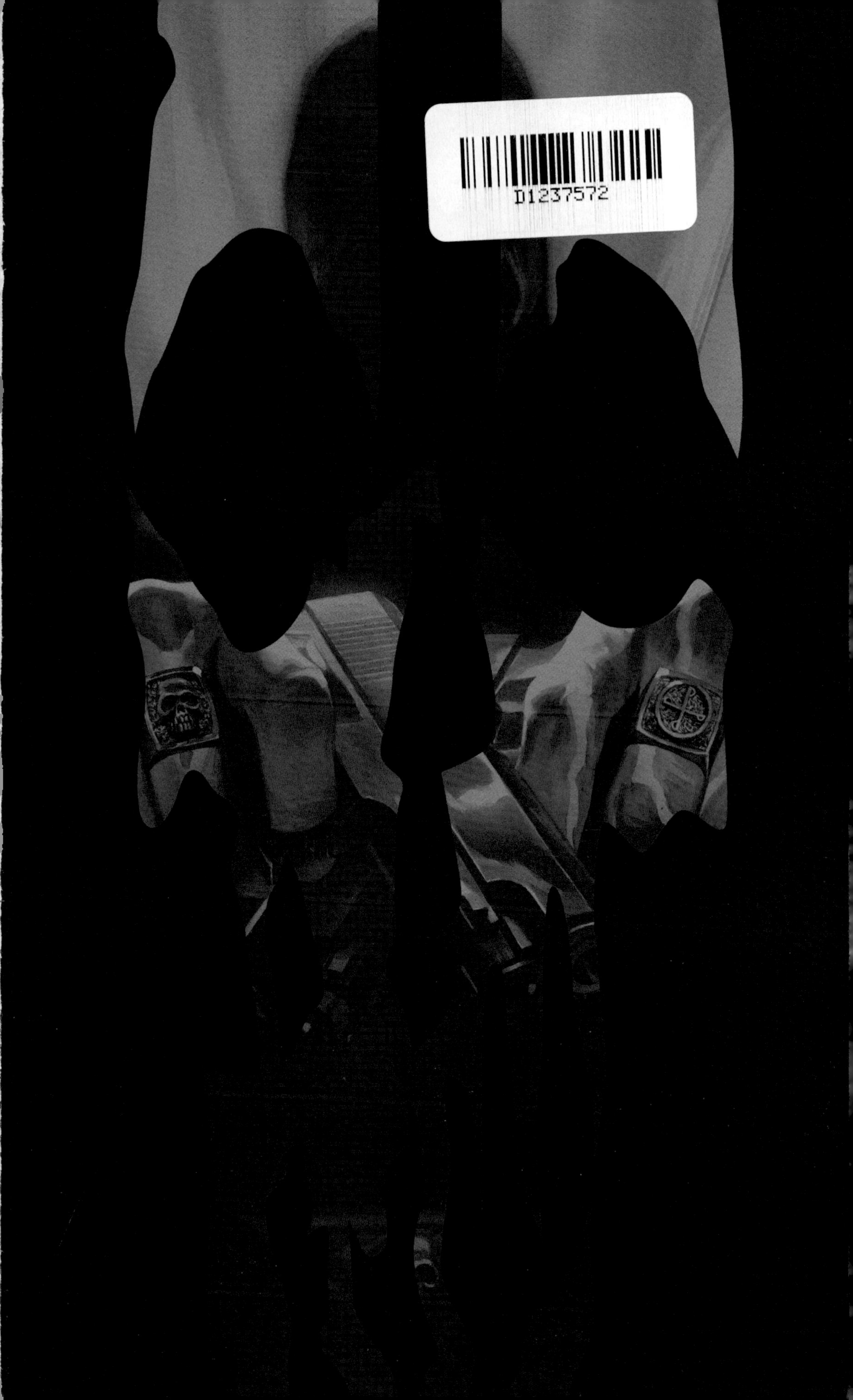

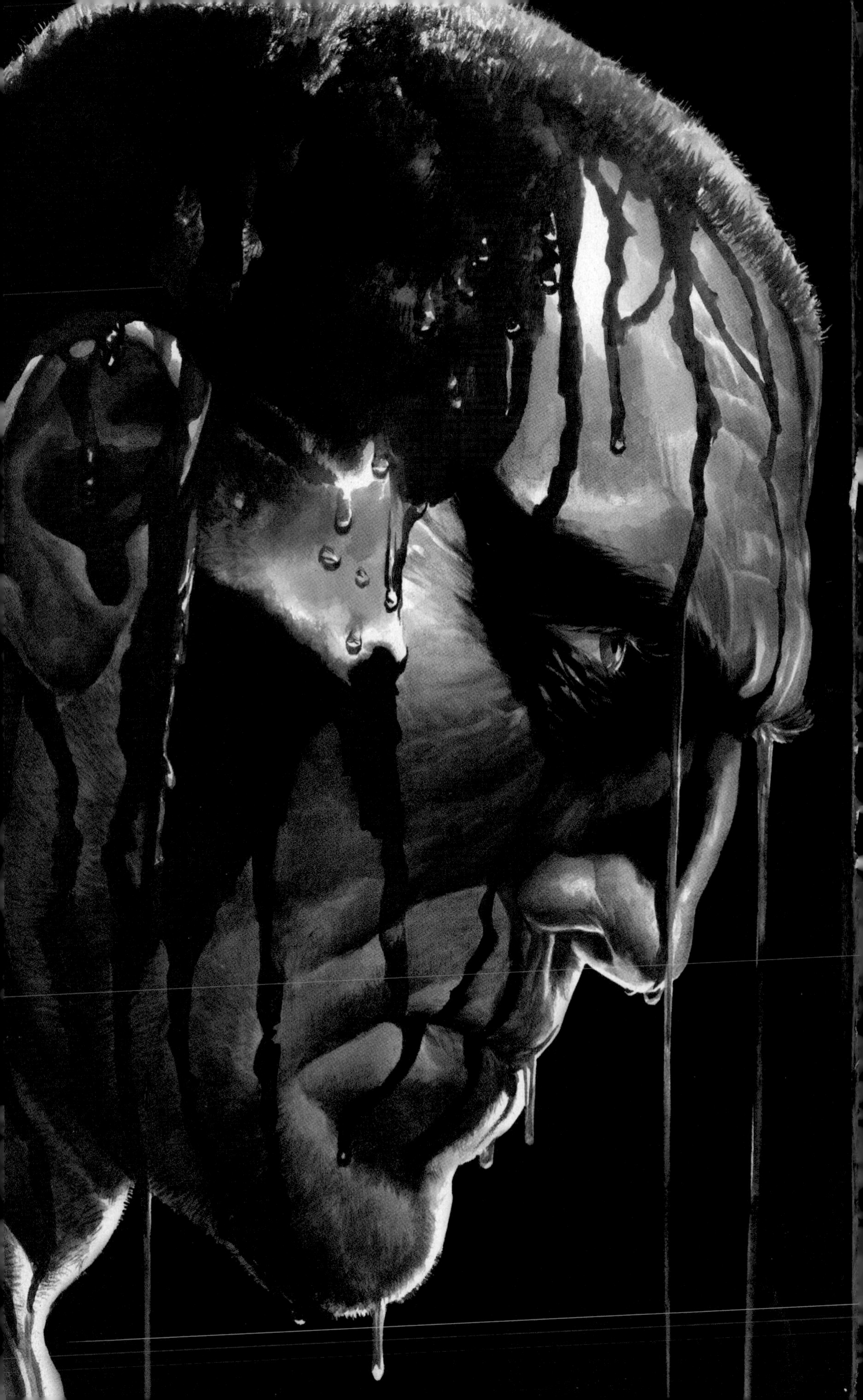

THE LAST PHANTOM

GHOSTWALK

written by SCOTT BEATTY

illustrated by EDUARDO FERIGATO

colored by VINICIUS ANDRADE

lettered by SIMON BOWLAND

collection cover by ALEX ROSS

The Phantom created by LEE FALK

collection design by JASON ULLMEYER

special thanks to DAVE ROMEO JR,
lifelong member of the Jungle Patrol

DYNAMITE® ENTERTAINMENT

WWW.DYNAMITE.NET

NICK BARRUCCI • PRESIDENT
JUAN COLLADO • CHIEF OPERATING OFFICER
JOSEPH RYBANDT • EDITOR
JOSH JOHNSON • CREATIVE DIRECTOR
RICH YOUNG • DIRECTOR OF BUSINESS DEVELOPMENT
JASON ULLMEYER • SENIOR DESIGNER

ISBN-10: 1-60690-201-6 ISBN-13: 978-1-60690-201-1 First Printing 10 9 8 7 6 5 4 3 2 1

THE LAST PHANTOM VOLUME ONE: GHOSTWALK. First printing. Contains materials originally published in The Last Phantom #1-6. Published by Dynamite Entertainment. 155 Ninth Ave. Suite B, Runnemede, NJ 08078. Printed in Canada.

For media rights, foreign rights, promotions, licensing, and advertising: marketing@dynamite.net

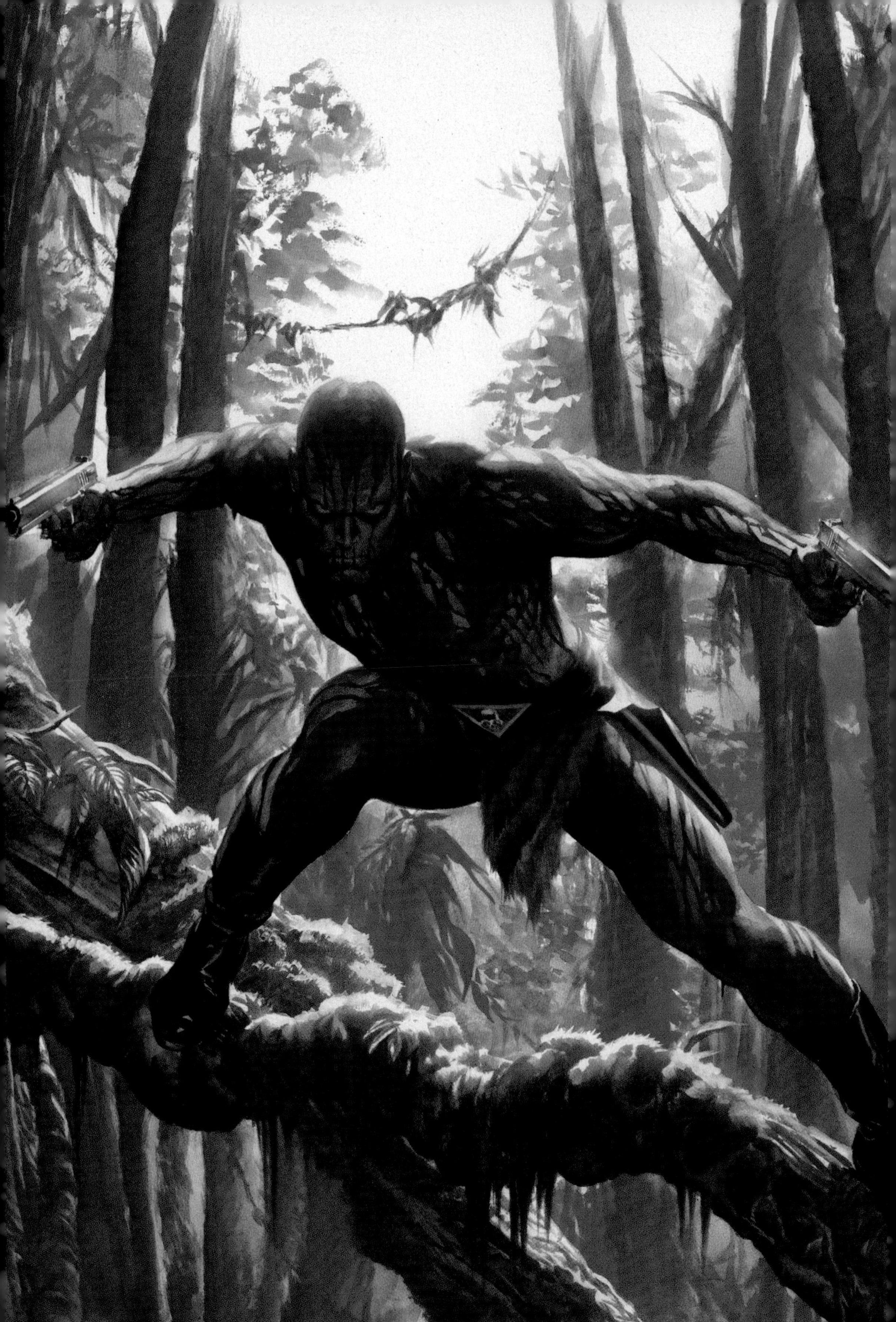

issue one cover by ALEX ROSS

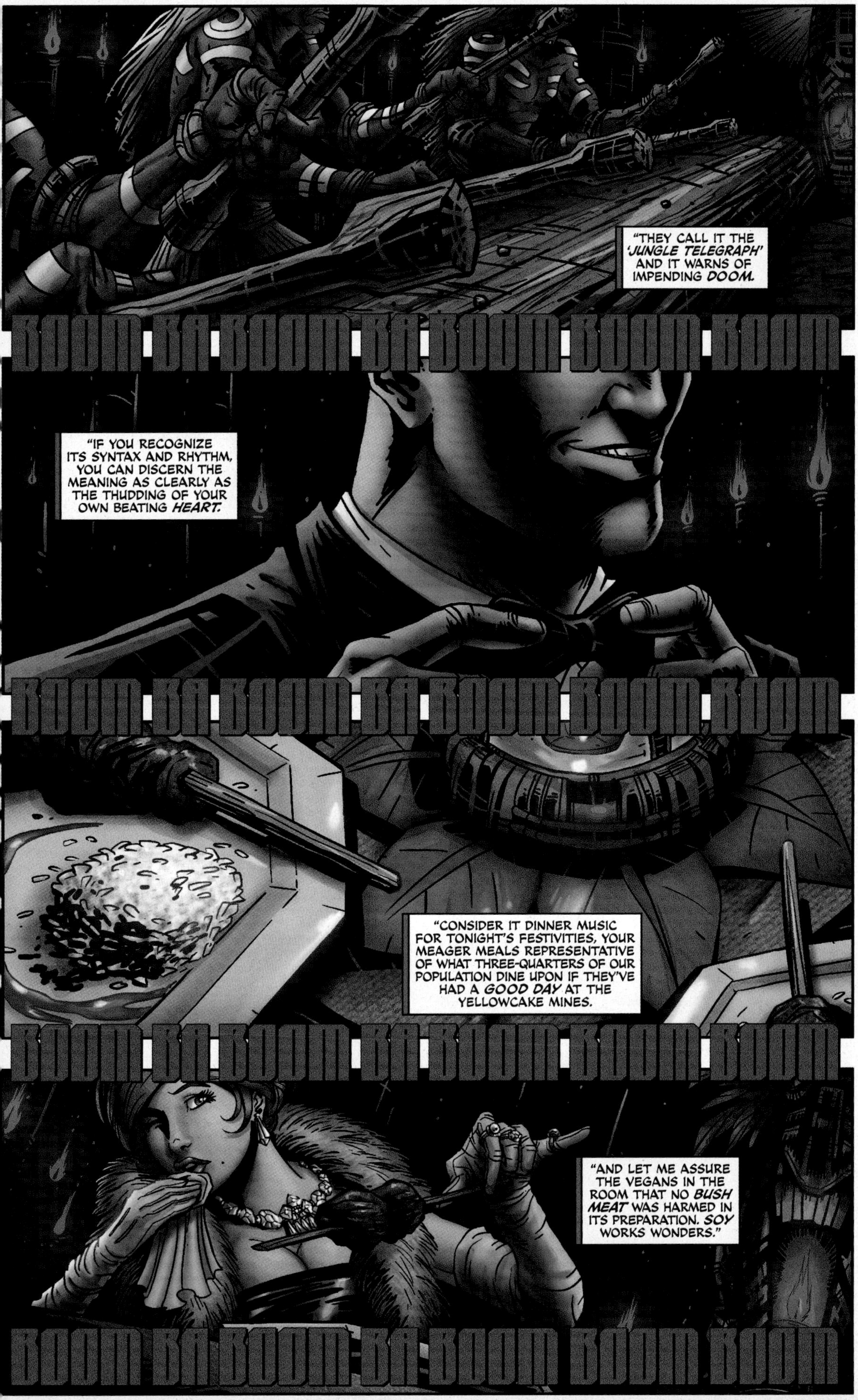
"THEY CALL IT THE 'JUNGLE TELEGRAPH' AND IT WARNS OF IMPENDING DOOM.
BOOM BA BOOM BA BOOM BOOM BOOM
"IF YOU RECOGNIZE ITS SYNTAX AND RHYTHM, YOU CAN DISCERN THE MEANING AS CLEARLY AS THE THUDDING OF YOUR OWN BEATING HEART.
BOOM BA BOOM BA BOOM BOOM BOOM
"CONSIDER IT DINNER MUSIC FOR TONIGHT'S FESTIVITIES, YOUR MEAGER MEALS REPRESENTATIVE OF WHAT THREE-QUARTERS OF OUR POPULATION DINE UPON IF THEY'VE HAD A GOOD DAY AT THE YELLOWCAKE MINES.
BOOM BA BOOM BA BOOM BOOM BOOM
"AND LET ME ASSURE THE VEGANS IN THE ROOM THAT NO BUSH MEAT WAS HARMED IN ITS PREPARATION. SOY WORKS WONDERS."
BOOM BA BOOM BA BOOM BOOM BOOM

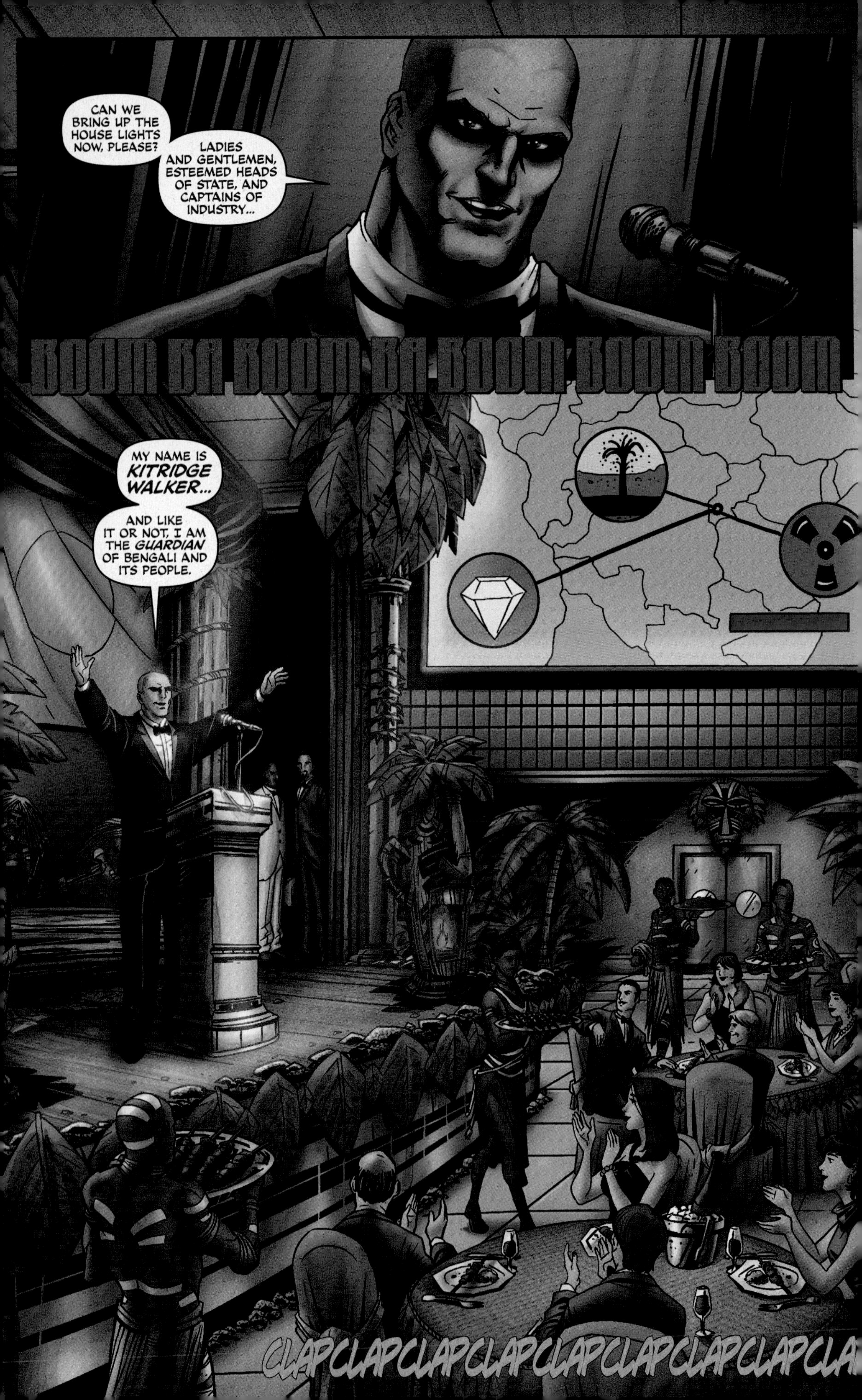
CAN WE BRING UP THE HOUSE LIGHTS NOW, PLEASE?
LADIES AND GENTLEMEN, ESTEEMED HEADS OF STATE, AND CAPTAINS OF INDUSTRY...
BOOM BA BOOM BA BOOM BOOM BOOM
MY NAME IS *KITRIDGE WALKER*...
AND LIKE IT OR NOT, I AM THE *GUARDIAN* OF BENGALI AND ITS PEOPLE.
CLAPCLAPCLAPCLAPCLAPCLAPCLAPCLAPCLA

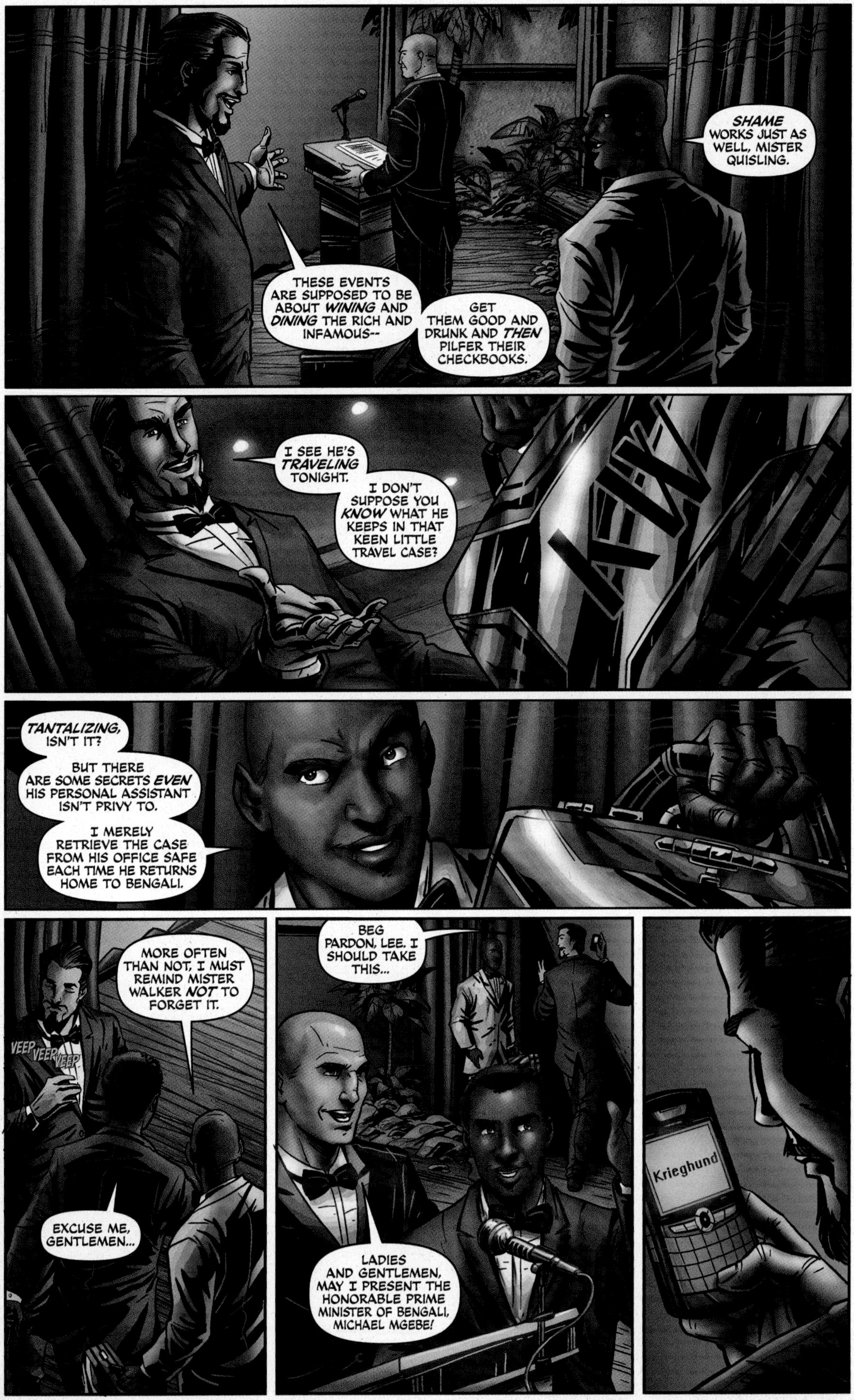
SHAME WORKS JUST AS WELL, MISTER QUISLING.
THESE EVENTS ARE SUPPOSED TO BE ABOUT WINING AND DINING THE RICH AND INFAMOUS--
GET THEM GOOD AND DRUNK AND THEN PILFER THEIR CHECKBOOKS.
I SEE HE'S TRAVELING TONIGHT.
I DON'T SUPPOSE YOU KNOW WHAT HE KEEPS IN THAT KEEN LITTLE TRAVEL CASE?
TANTALIZING, ISN'T IT?
BUT THERE ARE SOME SECRETS EVEN HIS PERSONAL ASSISTANT ISN'T PRIVY TO.
I MERELY RETRIEVE THE CASE FROM HIS OFFICE SAFE EACH TIME HE RETURNS HOME TO BENGALI.
MORE OFTEN THAN NOT, I MUST REMIND MISTER WALKER NOT TO FORGET IT.
VEEP VEEP VEEP
EXCUSE ME, GENTLEMEN...
BEG PARDON, LEE. I SHOULD TAKE THIS...
LADIES AND GENTLEMEN, MAY I PRESENT THE HONORABLE PRIME MINISTER OF BENGALI, MICHAEL MGEBE!
Krieghund

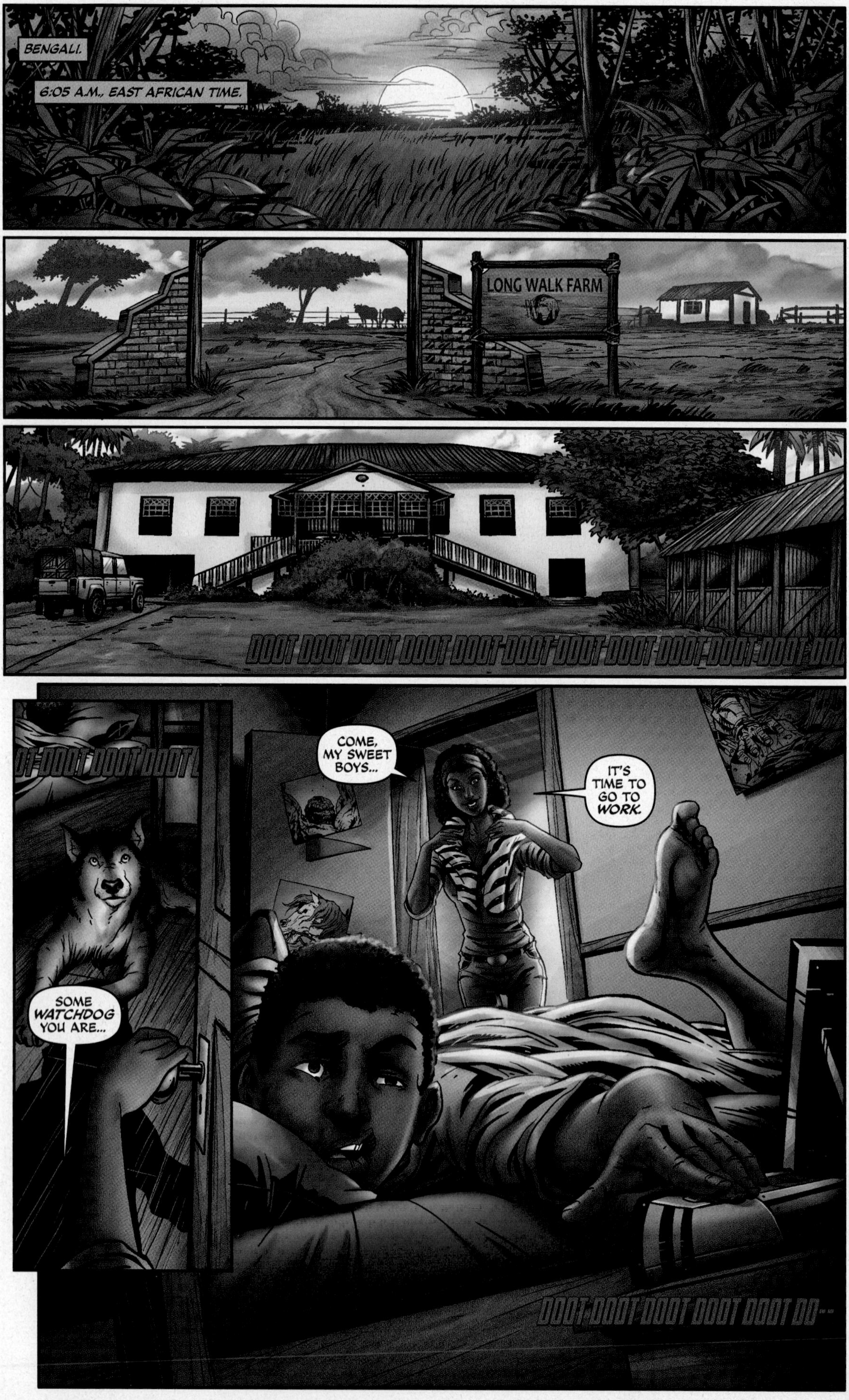
BENGALI.
6:05 A.M., EAST AFRICAN TIME.
LONG WALK FARM
DOOT DOOT DOOT DOOT DOOT DOOT DOOT DOOT DOOT DOOT DOO
DOOT DOOT DOOT DOOT
COME, MY SWEET BOYS...
IT'S TIME TO GO TO WORK.
SOME WATCHDOG YOU ARE...
DOOT DOOT DOOT DOOT DOOT DO

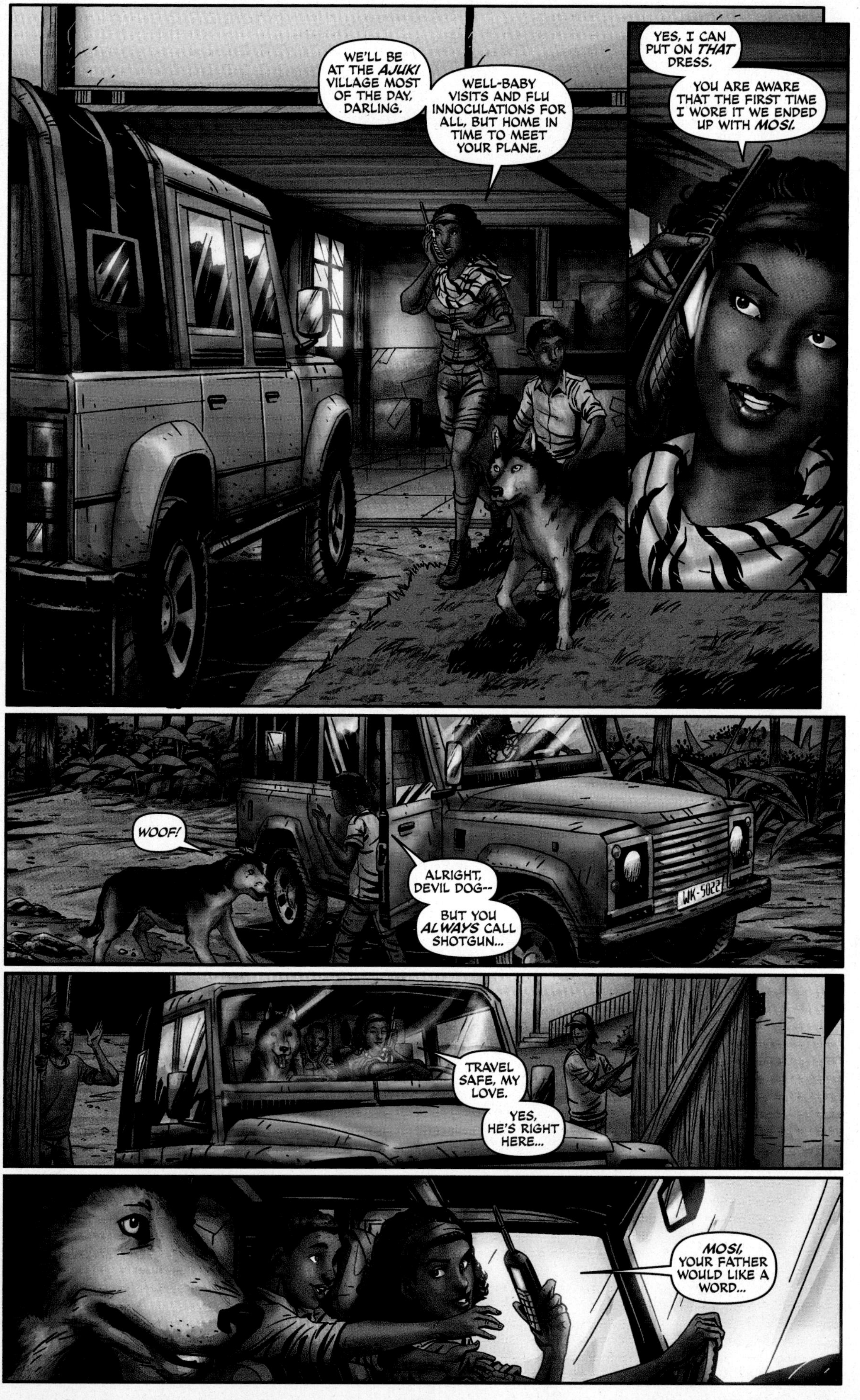
WE'LL BE AT THE AJUKI VILLAGE MOST OF THE DAY, DARLING.
WELL-BABY VISITS AND FLU INNOCULATIONS FOR ALL, BUT HOME IN TIME TO MEET YOUR PLANE.
YES, I CAN PUT ON THAT DRESS.
YOU ARE AWARE THAT THE FIRST TIME I WORE IT WE ENDED UP WITH MOSI.
WOOF!
ALRIGHT, DEVIL DOG--
BUT YOU ALWAYS CALL SHOTGUN...
WK-5022
TRAVEL SAFE, MY LOVE.
YES, HE'S RIGHT HERE...
MOSI, YOUR FATHER WOULD LIKE A WORD...

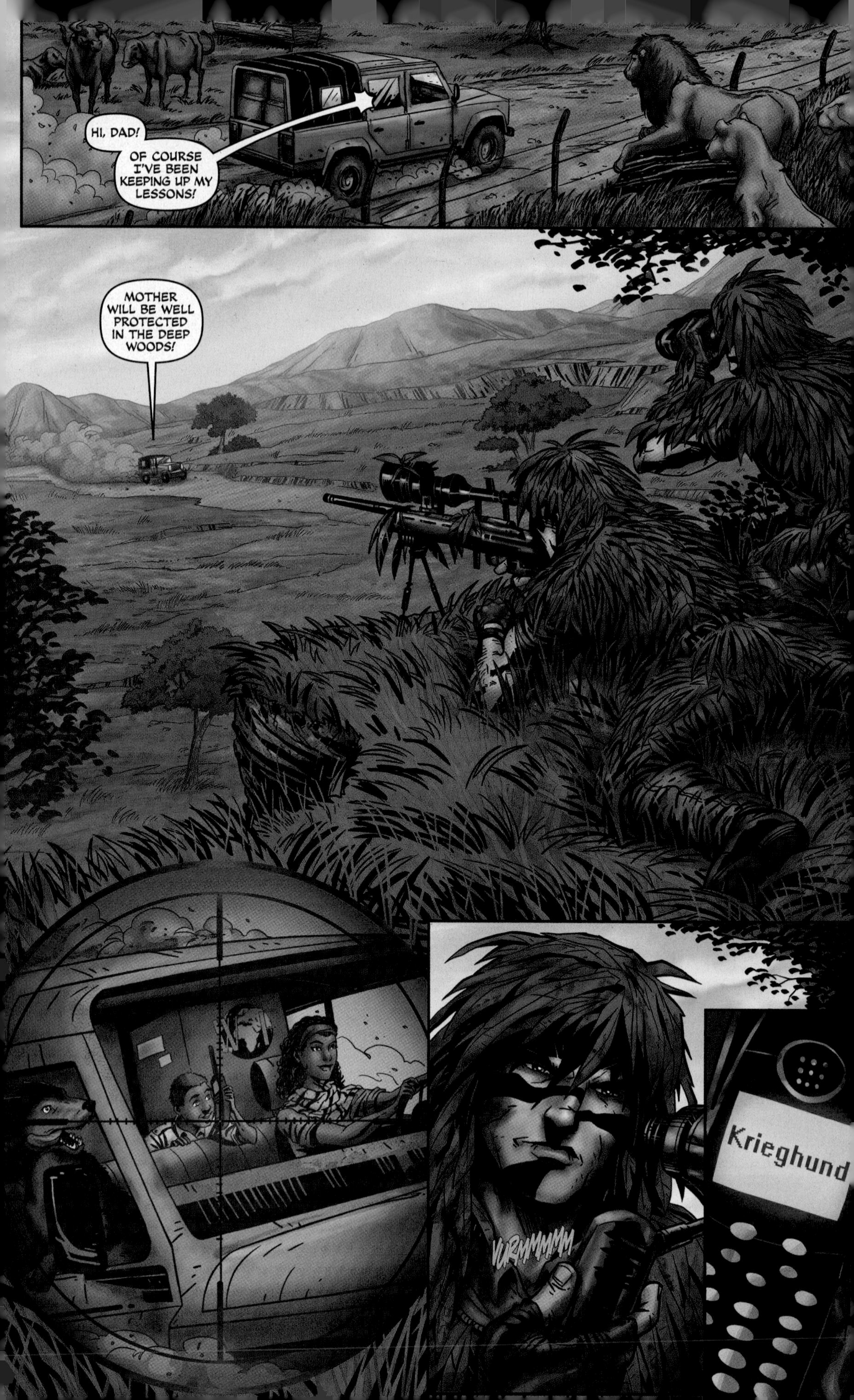
HI, DAD!
OF COURSE I'VE BEEN KEEPING UP MY LESSONS!
MOTHER WILL BE WELL PROTECTED IN THE DEEP WOODS!
Krieghund
VURMMMMM

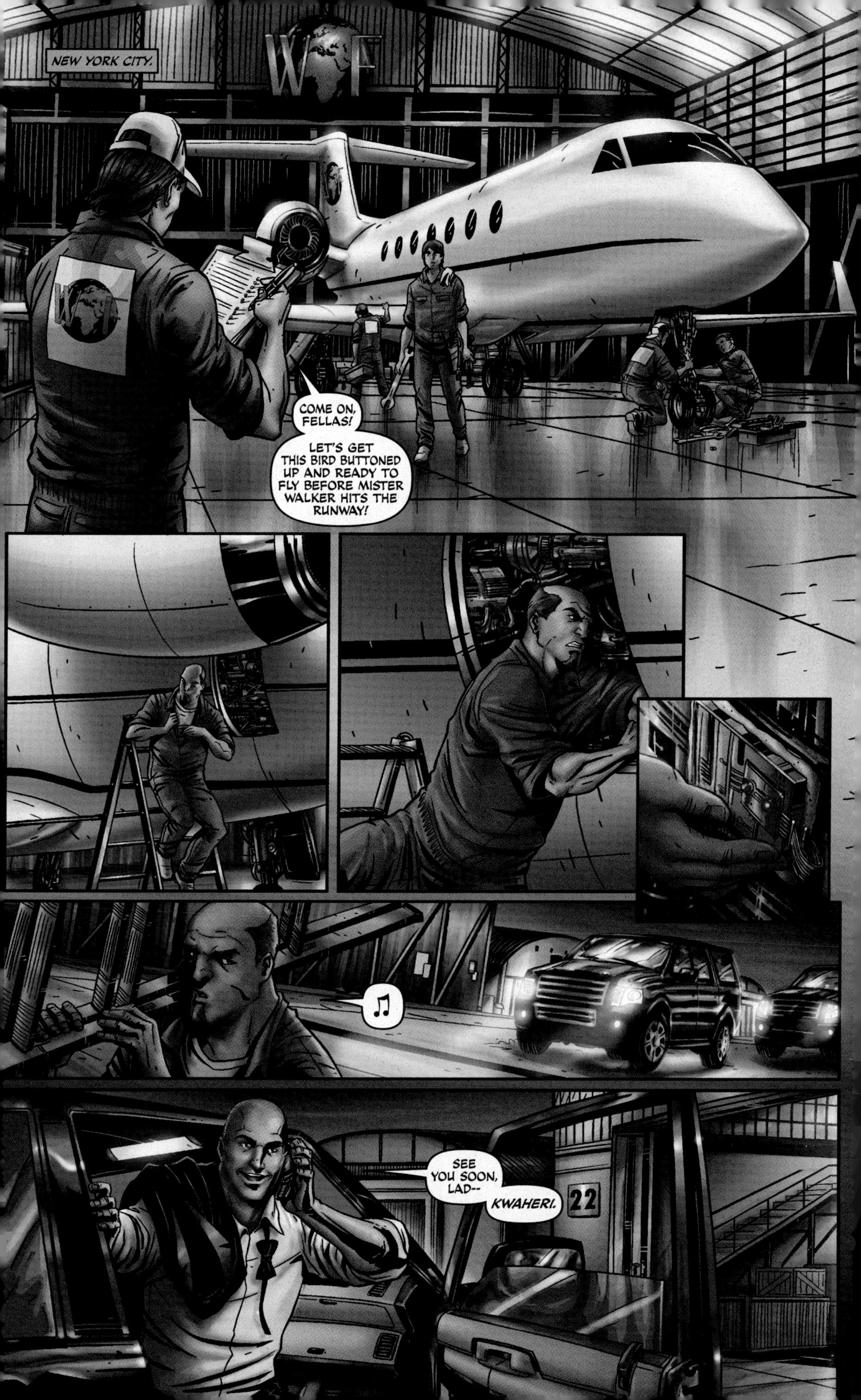
NEW YORK CITY.
COME ON, FELLAS!
LET'S GET THIS BIRD BUTTONED UP AND READY TO FLY BEFORE MISTER WALKER HITS THE RUNWAY!
♫
SEE YOU SOON, LAD--
KWAHERI.
22

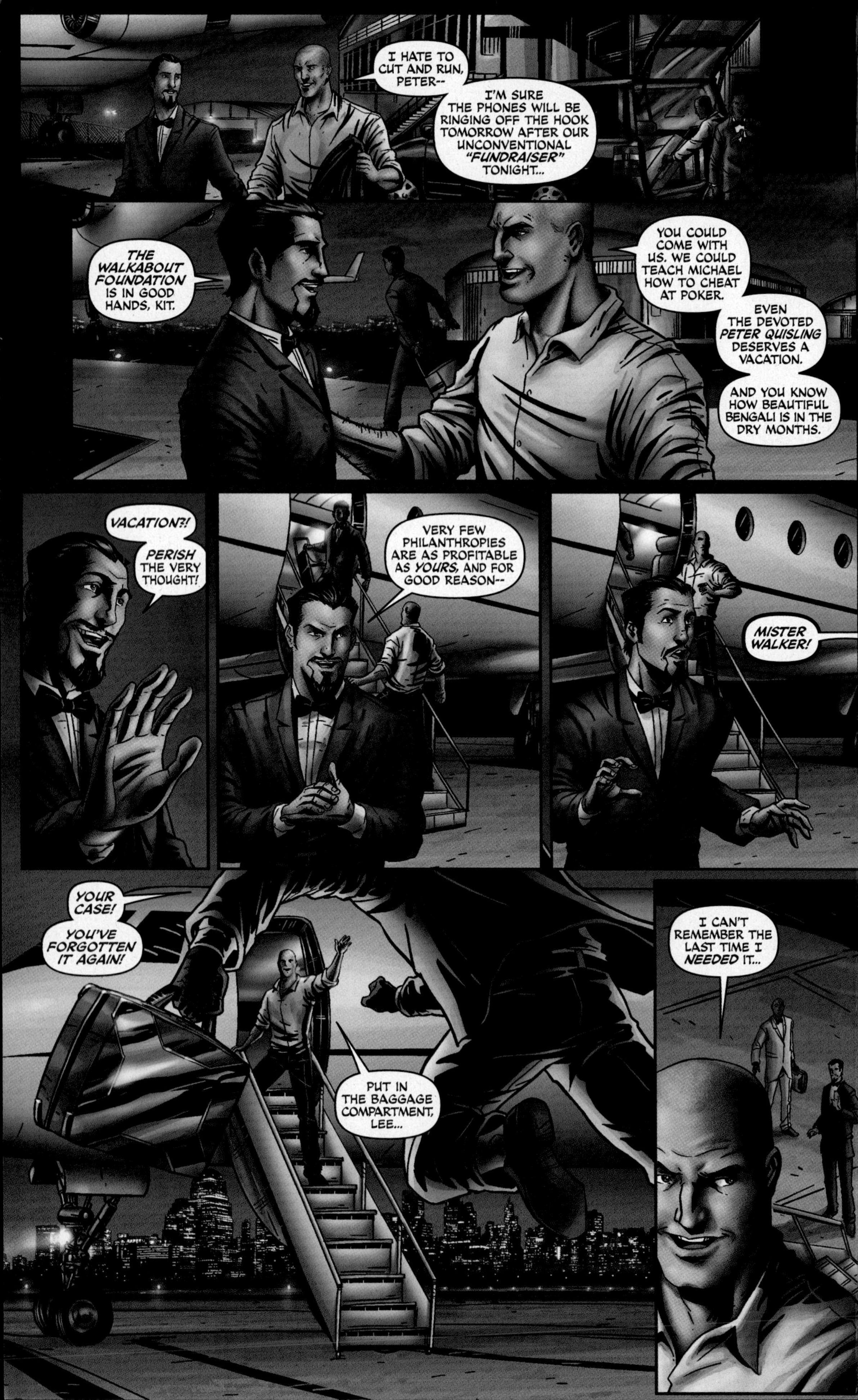
I HATE TO CUT AND RUN, PETER--
I'M SURE THE PHONES WILL BE RINGING OFF THE HOOK TOMORROW AFTER OUR UNCONVENTIONAL "FUNDRAISER" TONIGHT...
THE WALKABOUT FOUNDATION IS IN GOOD HANDS, KIT.
YOU COULD COME WITH US. WE COULD TEACH MICHAEL HOW TO CHEAT AT POKER.
EVEN THE DEVOTED PETER QUISLING DESERVES A VACATION.
AND YOU KNOW HOW BEAUTIFUL BENGALI IS IN THE DRY MONTHS.
VACATION?!
PERISH THE VERY THOUGHT!
VERY FEW PHILANTHROPIES ARE AS PROFITABLE AS YOURS, AND FOR GOOD REASON--
MISTER WALKER!
YOUR CASE!
YOU'VE FORGOTTEN IT AGAIN!
PUT IN THE BAGGAGE COMPARTMENT, LEE...
I CAN'T REMEMBER THE LAST TIME I NEEDED IT...

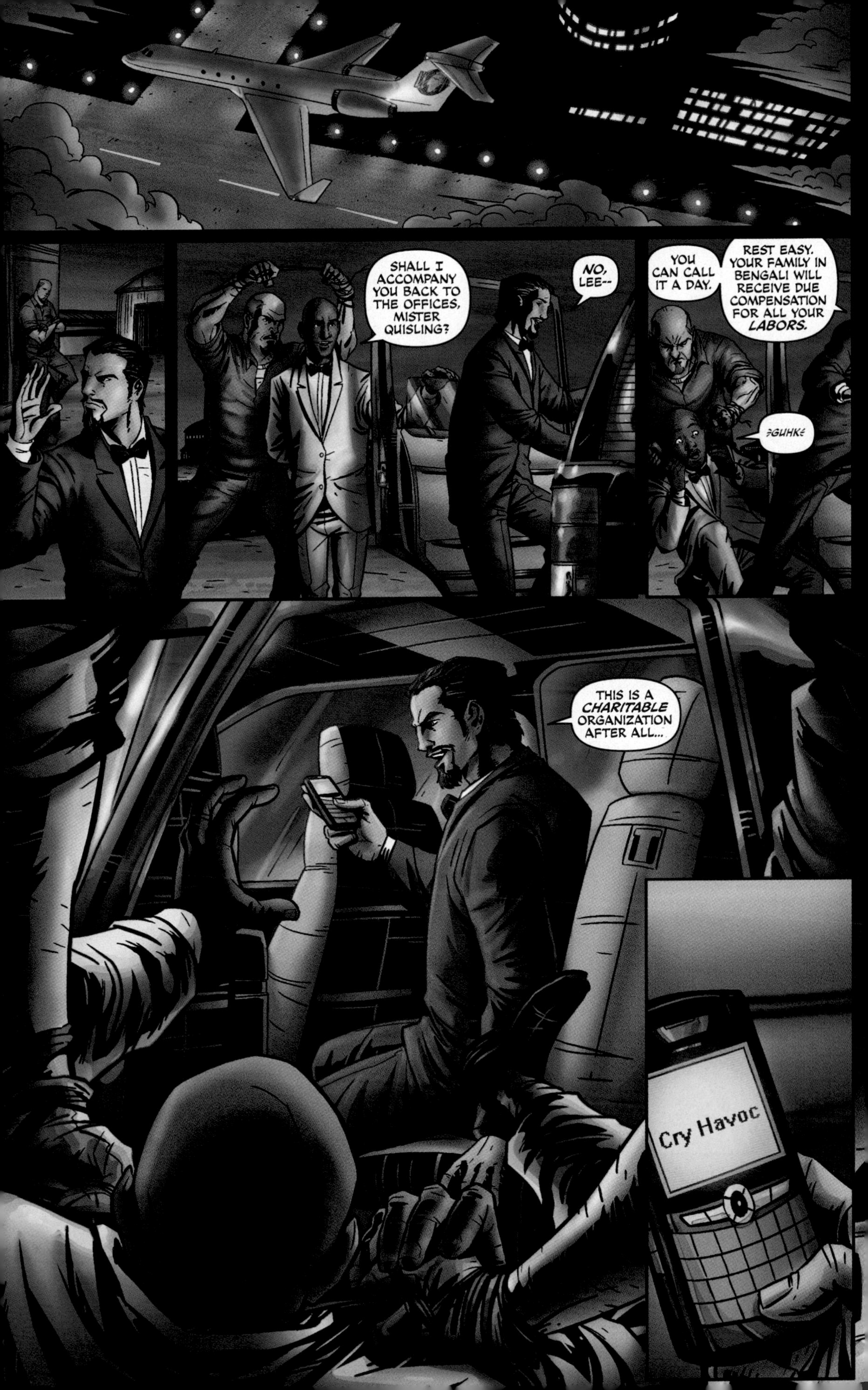

SHALL I ACCOMPANY YOU BACK TO THE OFFICES, MISTER QUISLING?
NO, LEE--
YOU CAN CALL IT A DAY.
REST EASY. YOUR FAMILY IN BENGALI WILL RECEIVE DUE COMPENSATION FOR ALL YOUR LABORS.
GUHK
THIS IS A CHARITABLE ORGANIZATION AFTER ALL...
Cry Havoc

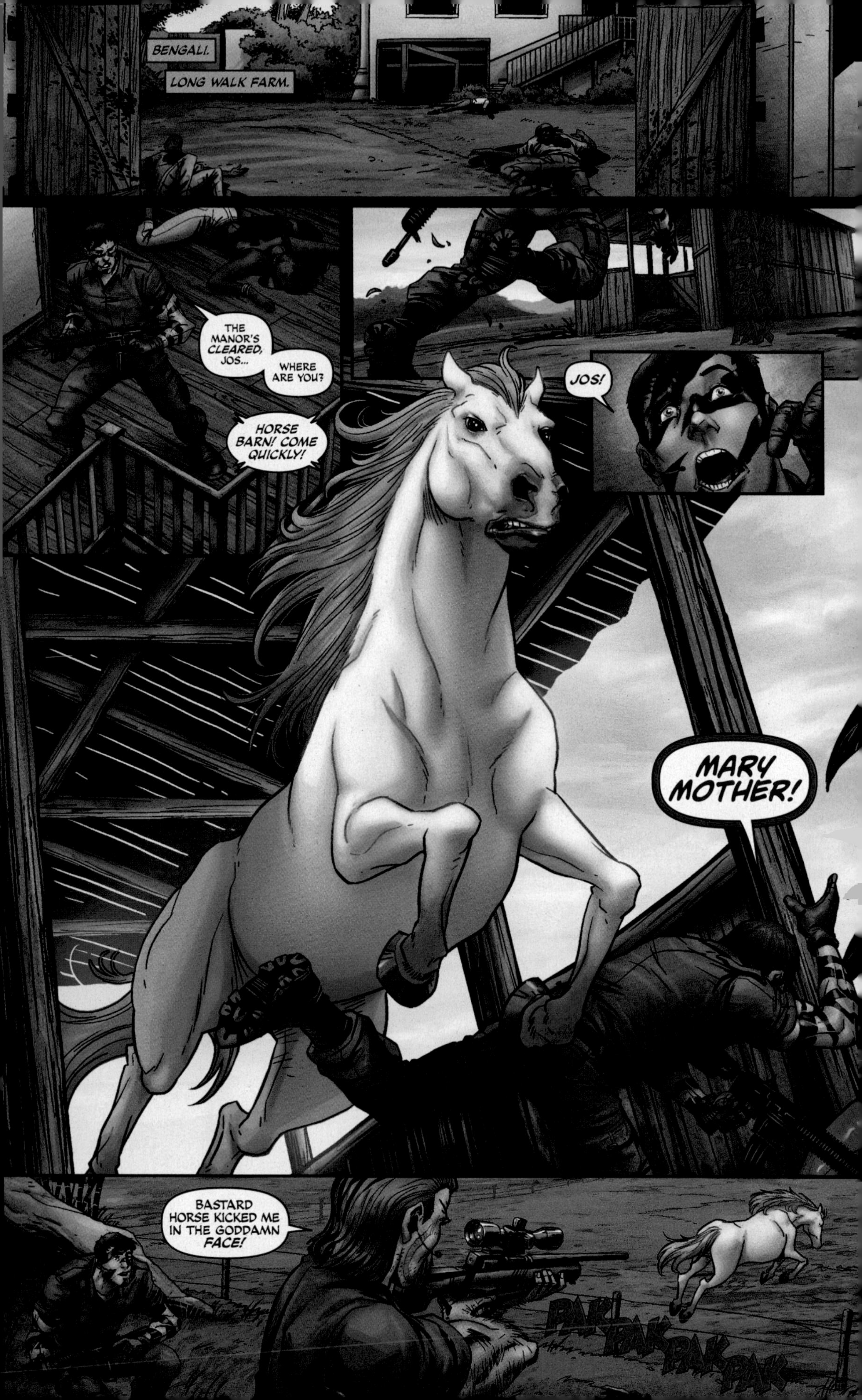

BENGALI.
LONG WALK FARM.
THE MANOR'S CLEARED, JOS...
WHERE ARE YOU?
HORSE BARN! COME QUICKLY!
JOS!
MARY MOTHER!
BASTARD HORSE KICKED ME IN THE GODDAMN FACE!
PAK PAK PAK PAK

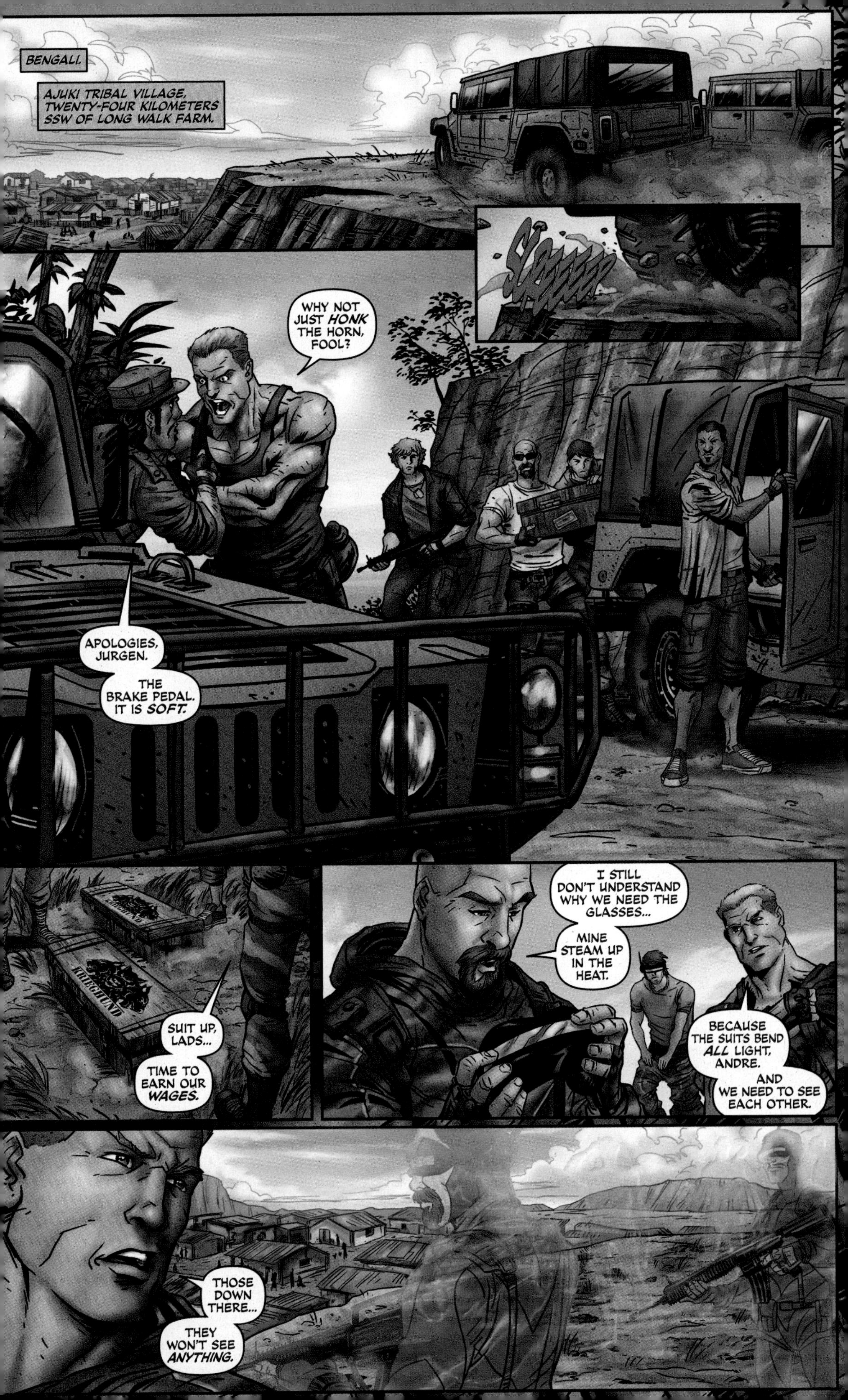
BENGALI.
AJUKI TRIBAL VILLAGE, TWENTY-FOUR KILOMETERS SSW OF LONG WALK FARM.
WHY NOT JUST HONK THE HORN, FOOL?
APOLOGIES, JURGEN.
THE BRAKE PEDAL. IT IS SOFT.
KRIEGHUND
KRIEGHUND
SUIT UP, LADS...
TIME TO EARN OUR WAGES.
I STILL DON'T UNDERSTAND WHY WE NEED THE GLASSES...
MINE STEAM UP IN THE HEAT.
BECAUSE THE SUITS BEND ALL LIGHT, ANDRE.
AND WE NEED TO SEE EACH OTHER.
THOSE DOWN THERE...
THEY WON'T SEE ANYTHING.

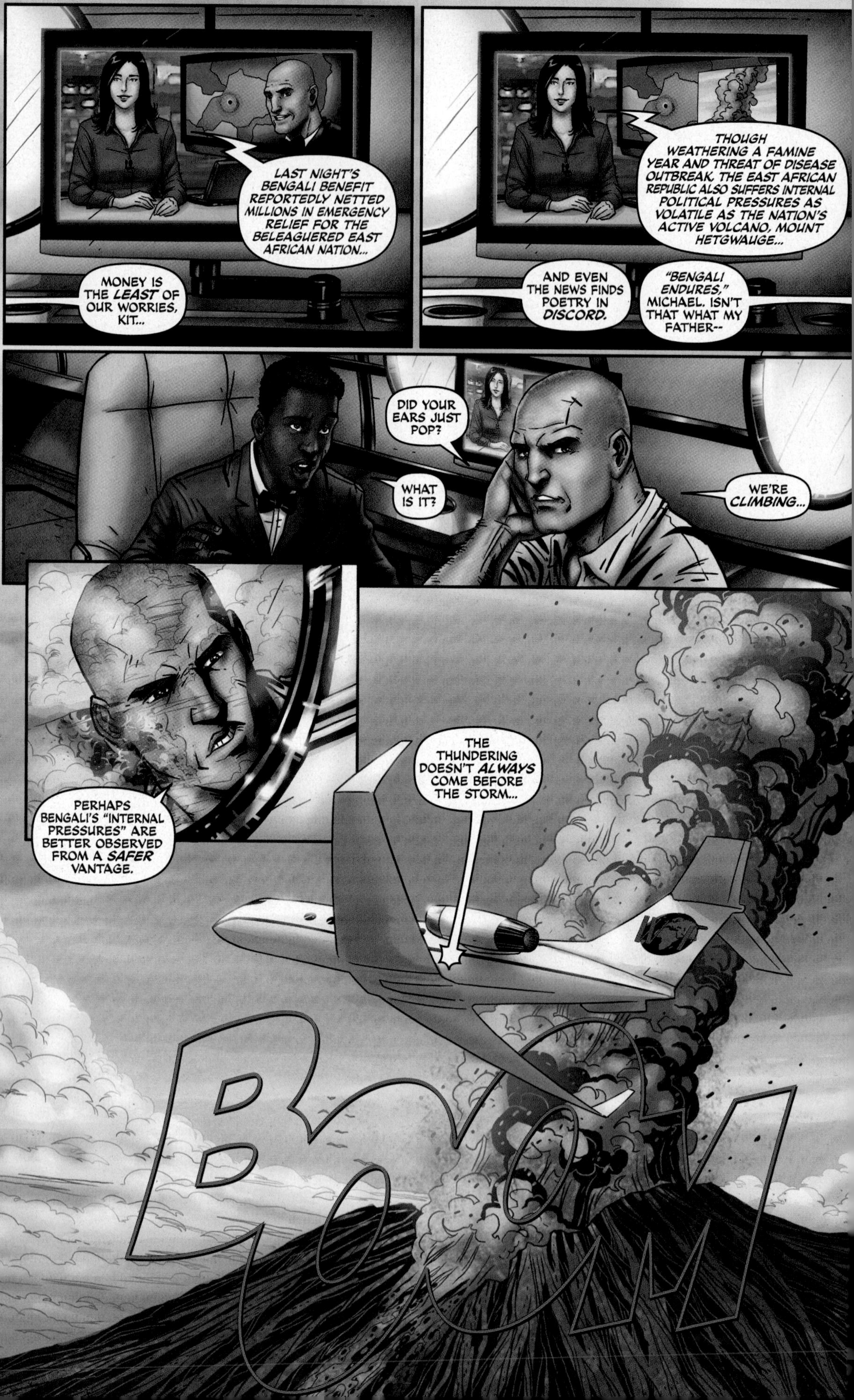
LAST NIGHT'S BENGALI BENEFIT REPORTEDLY NETTED MILLIONS IN EMERGENCY RELIEF FOR THE BELEAGUERED EAST AFRICAN NATION...
MONEY IS THE LEAST OF OUR WORRIES, KIT...
THOUGH WEATHERING A FAMINE YEAR AND THREAT OF DISEASE OUTBREAK, THE EAST AFRICAN REPUBLIC ALSO SUFFERS INTERNAL POLITICAL PRESSURES AS VOLATILE AS THE NATION'S ACTIVE VOLCANO, MOUNT HETGWAUGE...
AND EVEN THE NEWS FINDS POETRY IN DISCORD.
"BENGALI ENDURES," MICHAEL. ISN'T THAT WHAT MY FATHER--
DID YOUR EARS JUST POP?
WHAT IS IT?
WE'RE CLIMBING...
PERHAPS BENGALI'S "INTERNAL PRESSURES" ARE BETTER OBSERVED FROM A SAFER VANTAGE.
THE THUNDERING DOESN'T ALWAYS COME BEFORE THE STORM...
BOOOM

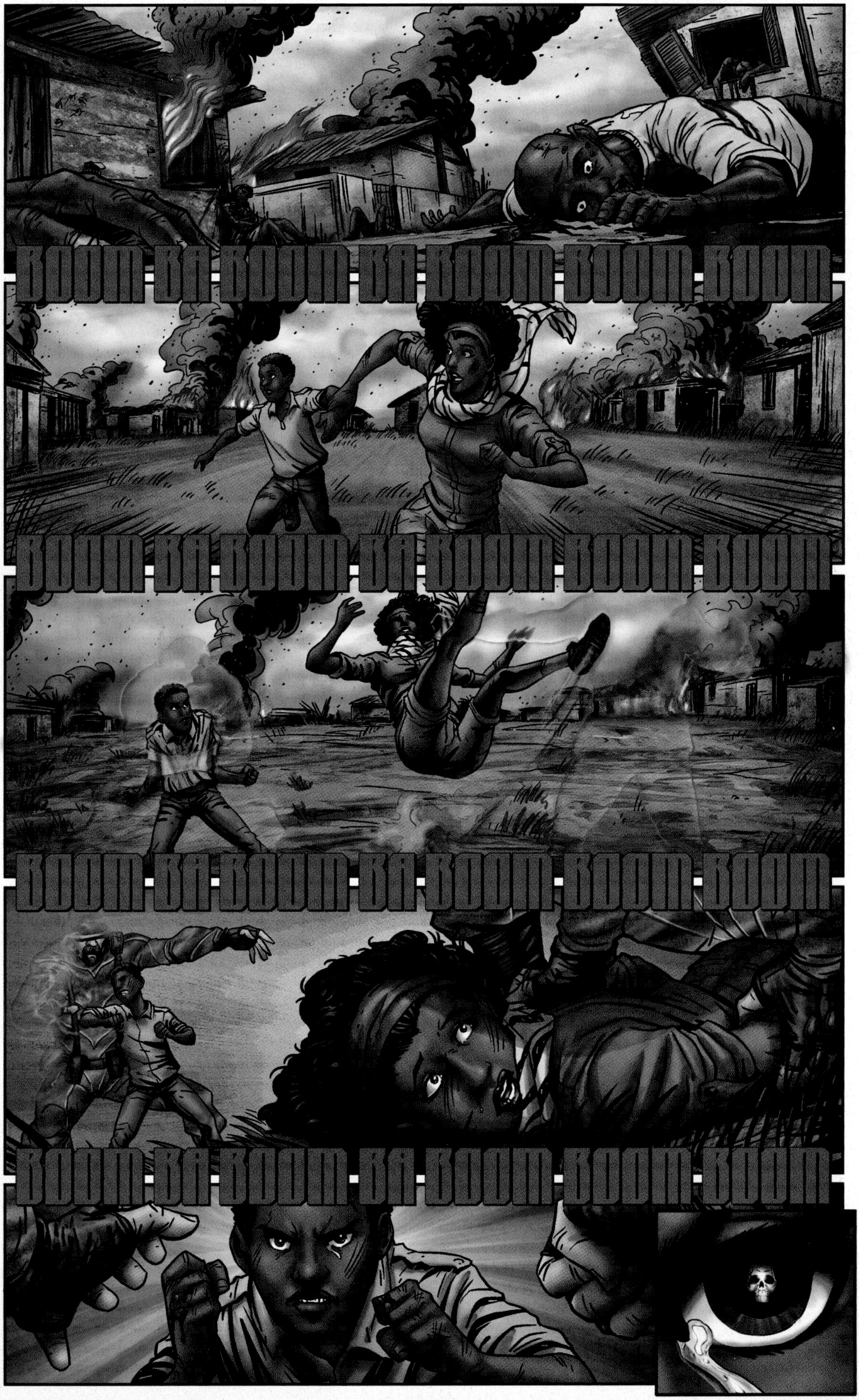
BOOM BA BOOM BA BOOM BOOM BOOM
BOOM BA BOOM BA BOOM BOOM BOOM
BOOM BA BOOM BA BOOM BOOM BOOM
BOOM BA BOOM BA BOOM BOOM BOOM

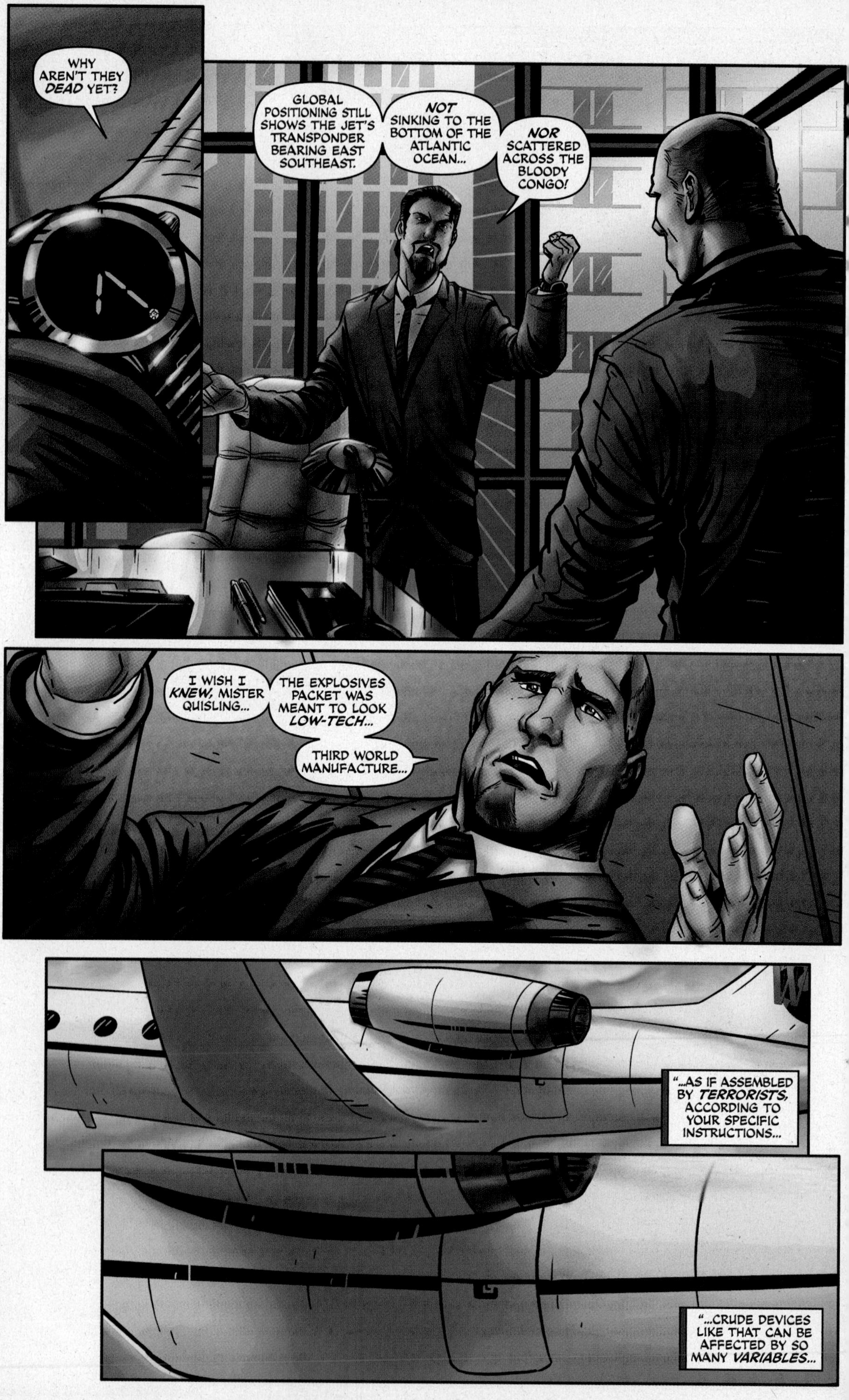
WHY AREN'T THEY DEAD YET?
GLOBAL POSITIONING STILL SHOWS THE JET'S TRANSPONDER BEARING EAST SOUTHEAST.
NOT SINKING TO THE BOTTOM OF THE ATLANTIC OCEAN...
NOR SCATTERED ACROSS THE BLOODY CONGO!
I WISH I KNEW, MISTER QUISLING...
THE EXPLOSIVES PACKET WAS MEANT TO LOOK LOW-TECH...
THIRD WORLD MANUFACTURE...
"...AS IF ASSEMBLED BY TERRORISTS, ACCORDING TO YOUR SPECIFIC INSTRUCTIONS...
"...CRUDE DEVICES LIKE THAT CAN BE AFFECTED BY SO MANY VARIABLES...

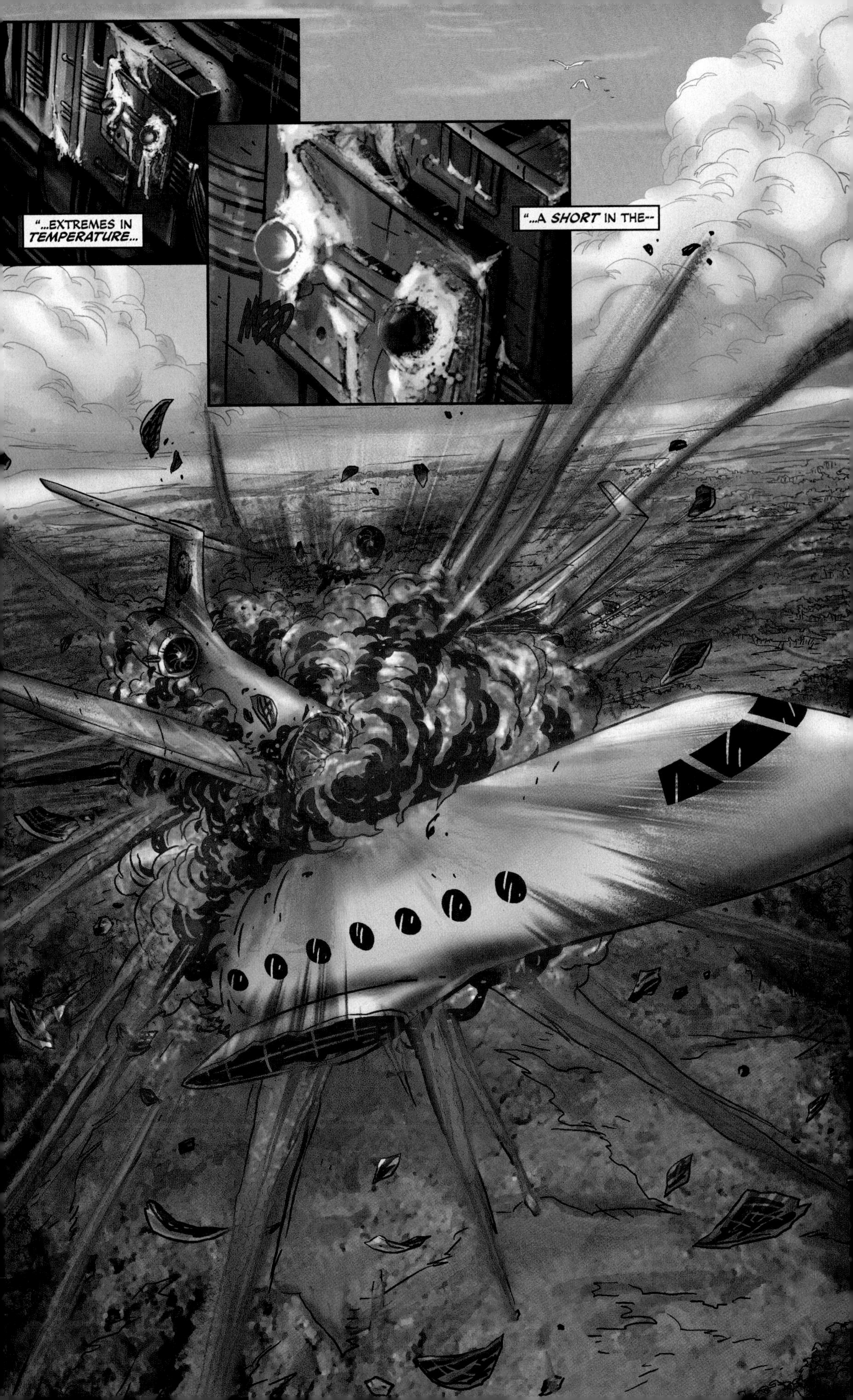
"...EXTREMES IN TEMPERATURE...
"...A SHORT IN THE--
MEEP

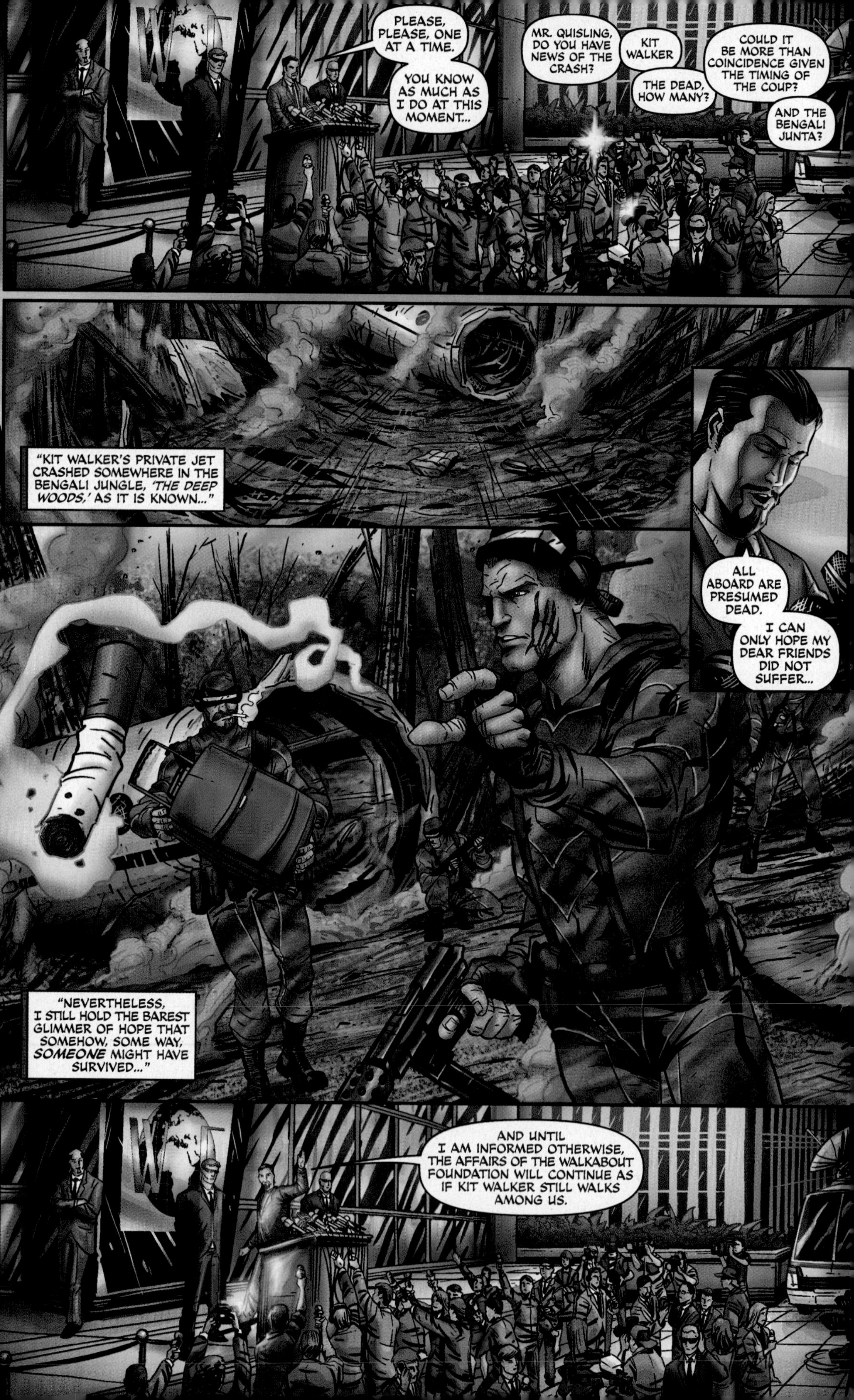
PLEASE, PLEASE, ONE AT A TIME.
YOU KNOW AS MUCH AS I DO AT THIS MOMENT...
MR. QUISLING, DO YOU HAVE NEWS OF THE CRASH?
KIT WALKER
THE DEAD, HOW MANY?
COULD IT BE MORE THAN COINCIDENCE GIVEN THE TIMING OF THE COUP?
AND THE BENGALI JUNTA?
"KIT WALKER'S PRIVATE JET CRASHED SOMEWHERE IN THE BENGALI JUNGLE, *'THE DEEP WOODS,'* AS IT IS KNOWN..."
ALL ABOARD ARE PRESUMED DEAD.
I CAN ONLY HOPE MY DEAR FRIENDS DID NOT SUFFER...
"NEVERTHELESS, I STILL HOLD THE BAREST GLIMMER OF HOPE THAT SOMEHOW, SOME WAY, ***SOMEONE*** MIGHT HAVE SURVIVED..."
AND UNTIL I AM INFORMED OTHERWISE, THE AFFAIRS OF THE WALKABOUT FOUNDATION WILL CONTINUE AS IF KIT WALKER STILL WALKS AMONG US.

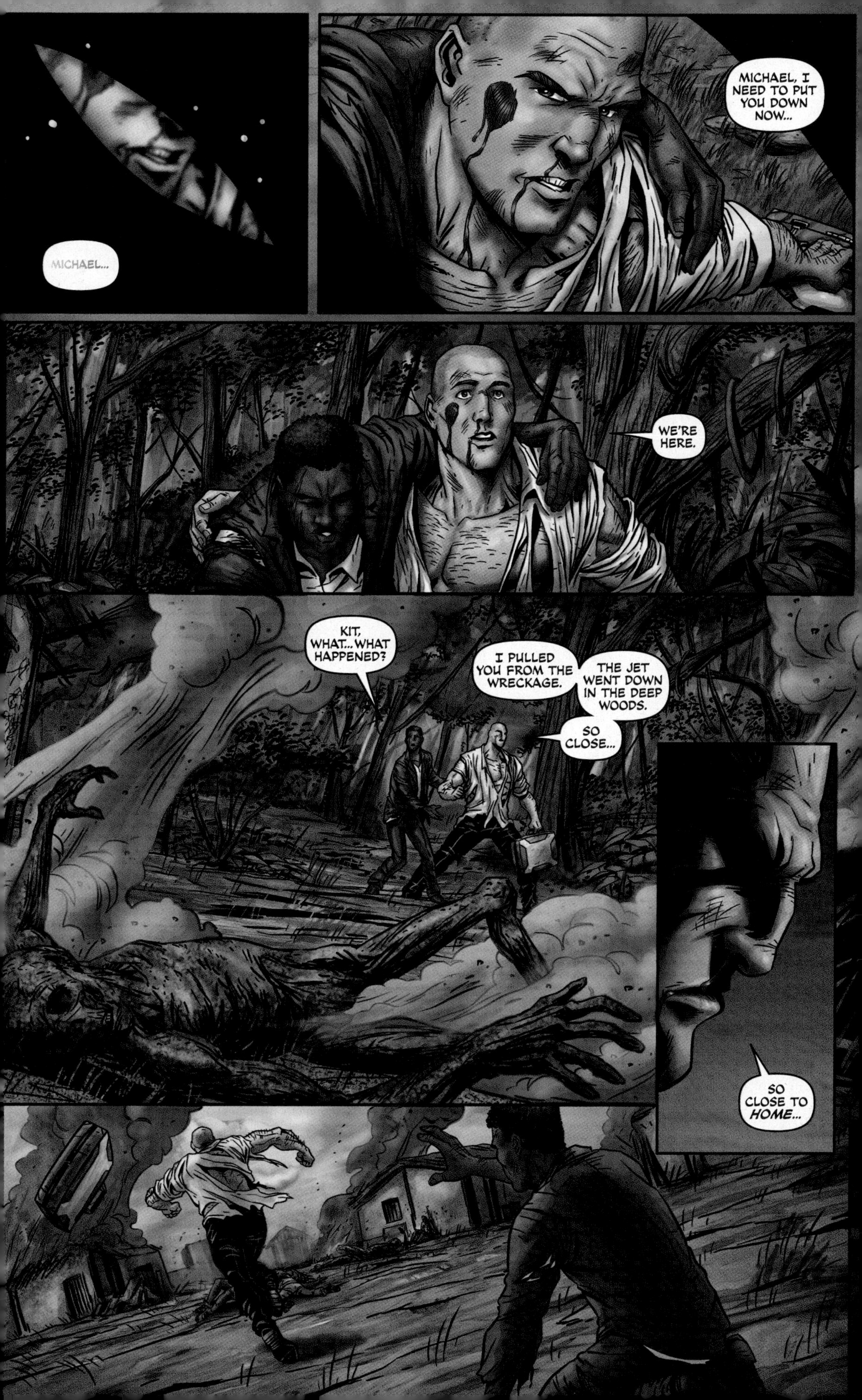
MICHAEL...
MICHAEL, I NEED TO PUT YOU DOWN NOW...
WE'RE HERE.
KIT, WHAT... WHAT HAPPENED?
I PULLED YOU FROM THE WRECKAGE.
THE JET WENT DOWN IN THE DEEP WOODS.
SO CLOSE...
SO CLOSE TO *HOME*...

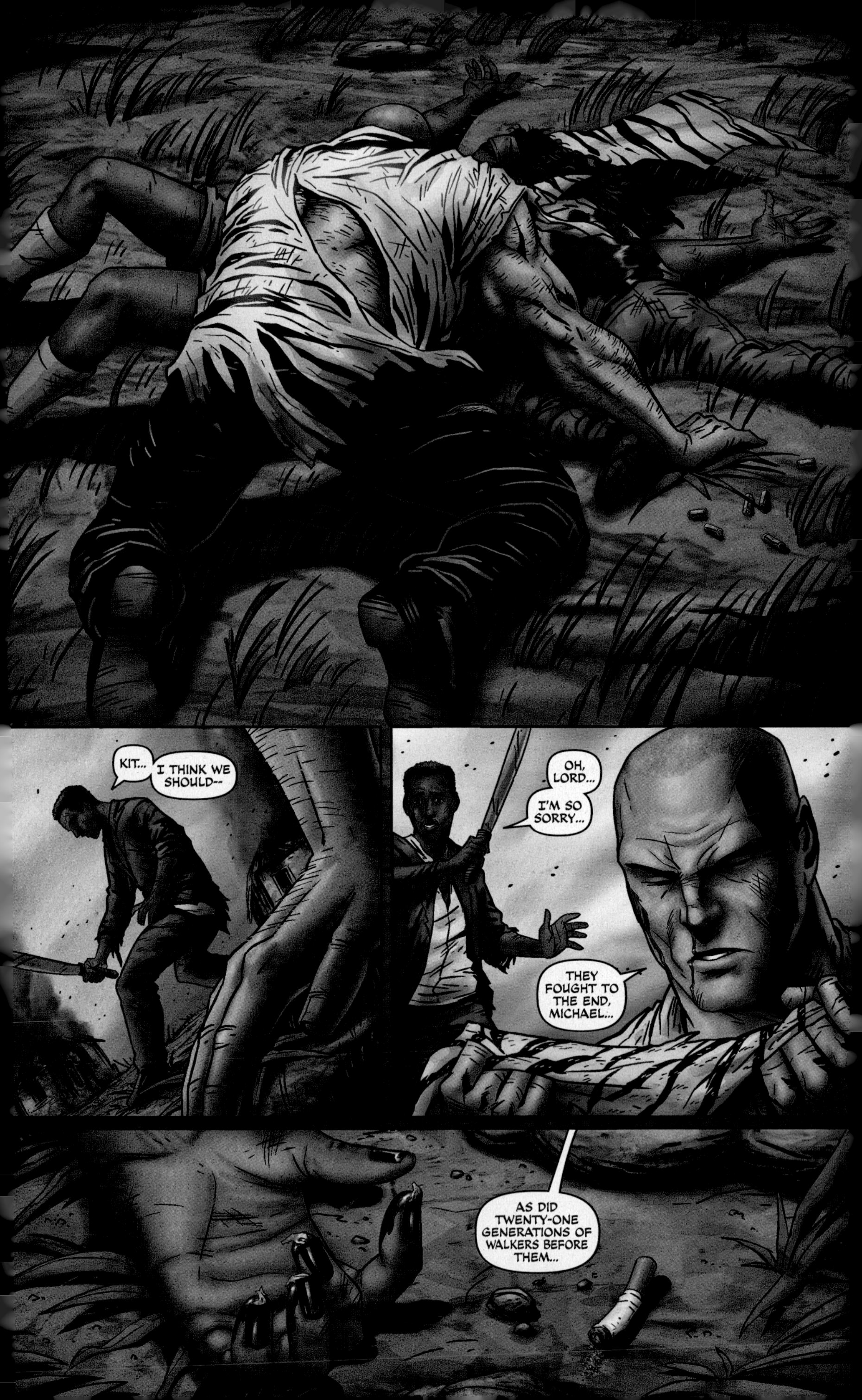
KIT...
I THINK WE SHOULD--
OH, LORD...
I'M SO SORRY...
THEY FOUGHT TO THE END, MICHAEL...
AS DID TWENTY-ONE GENERATIONS OF WALKERS BEFORE THEM...

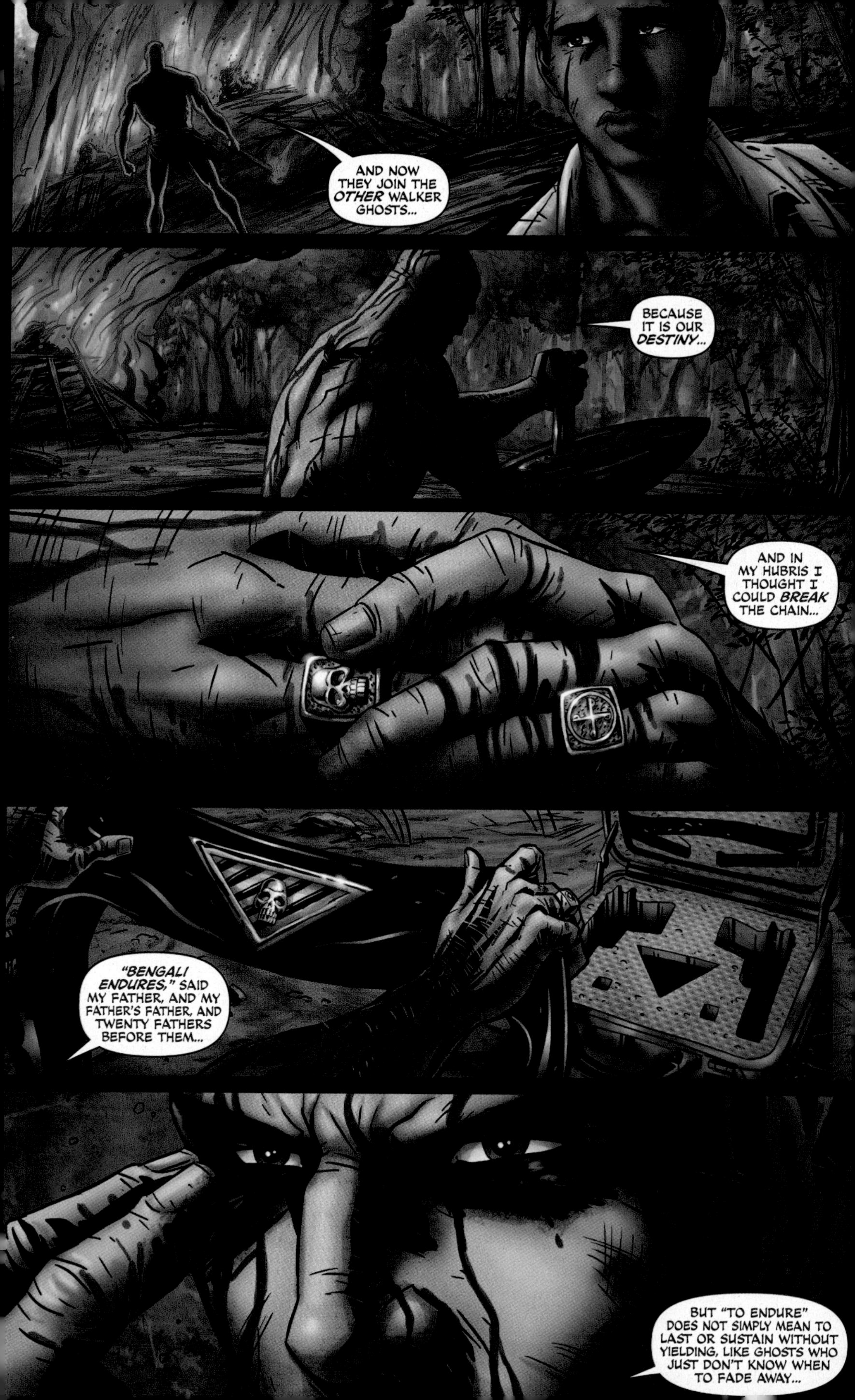
AND NOW THEY JOIN THE *OTHER* WALKER GHOSTS...
BECAUSE IT IS OUR *DESTINY*...
AND IN MY HUBRIS I THOUGHT I COULD *BREAK* THE CHAIN...
"BENGALI ENDURES," SAID MY FATHER, AND MY FATHER'S FATHER, AND TWENTY FATHERS BEFORE THEM...
BUT "TO ENDURE" DOES NOT SIMPLY MEAN TO LAST OR SUSTAIN WITHOUT YIELDING, LIKE GHOSTS WHO JUST DON'T KNOW WHEN TO FADE AWAY...

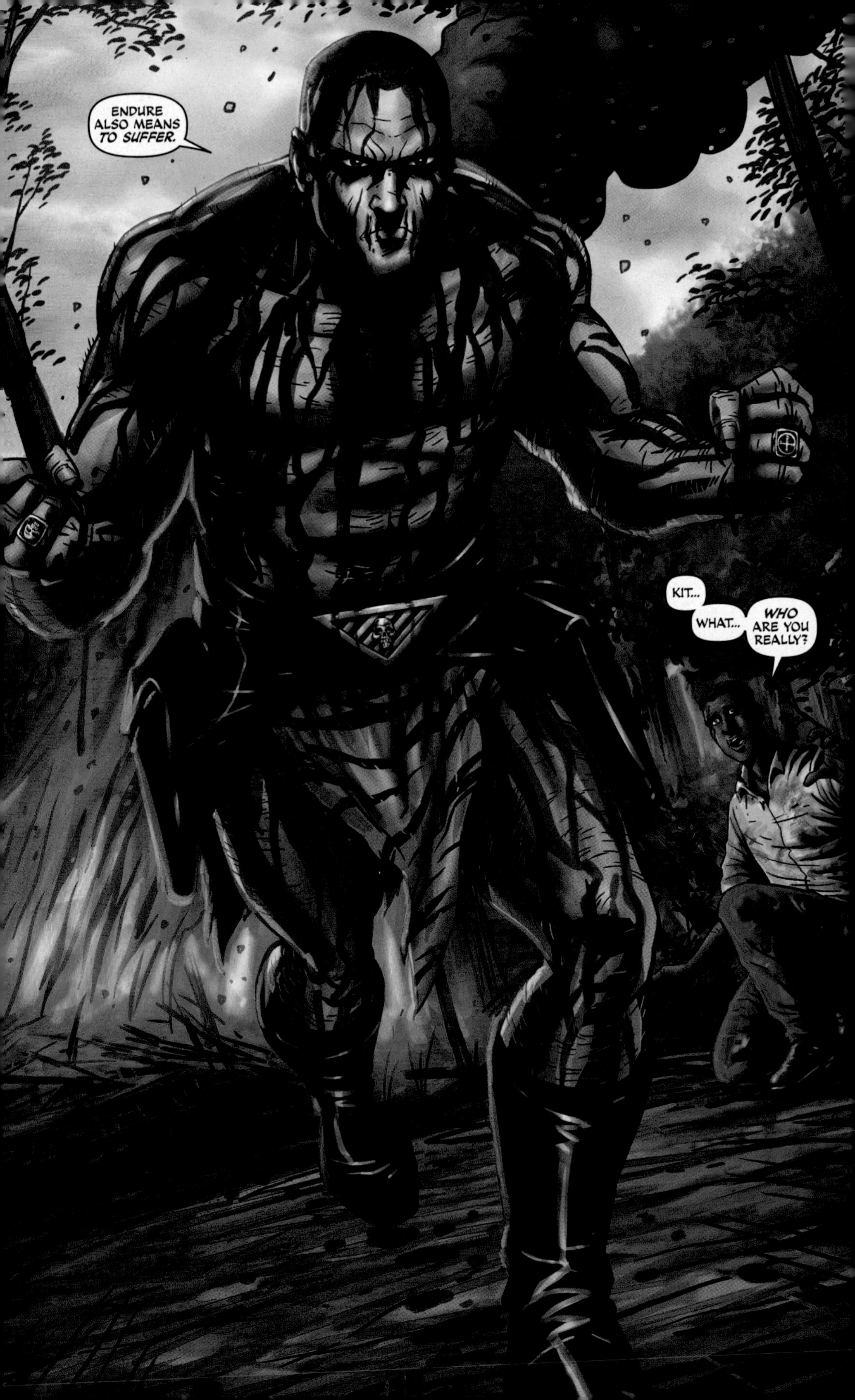
ENDURE ALSO MEANS TO SUFFER.
KIT...
WHAT...
WHO ARE YOU REALLY?

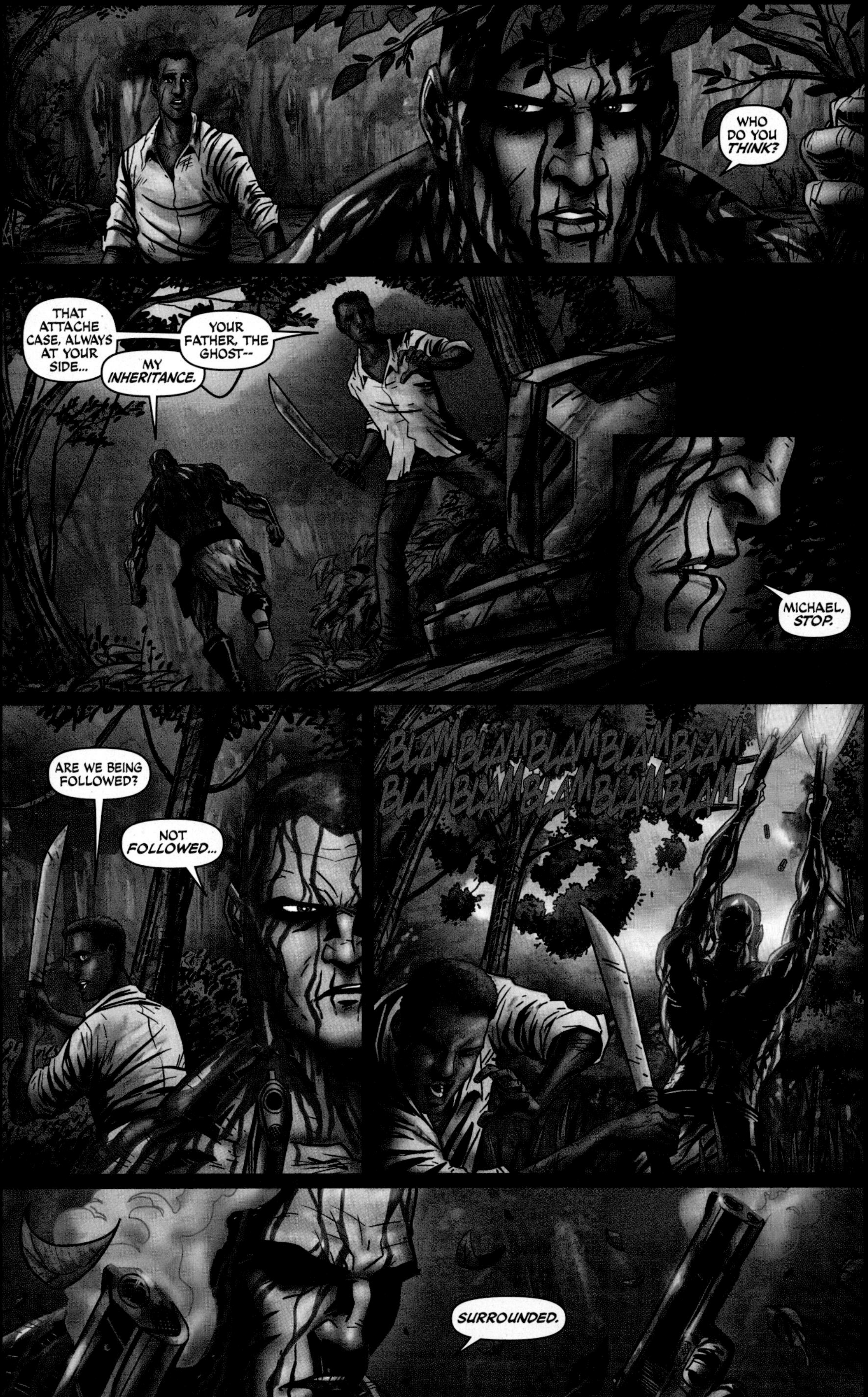
WHO DO YOU *THINK?*
THAT ATTACHE CASE, ALWAYS AT YOUR SIDE...
YOUR FATHER, THE GHOST--
MY *INHERITANCE.*
MICHAEL, *STOP.*
ARE WE BEING FOLLOWED?
NOT *FOLLOWED...*
BLAMBLAMBLAMBLAMBLAM
BLAMBLAMBLAMBLAMBLAM
SURROUNDED.

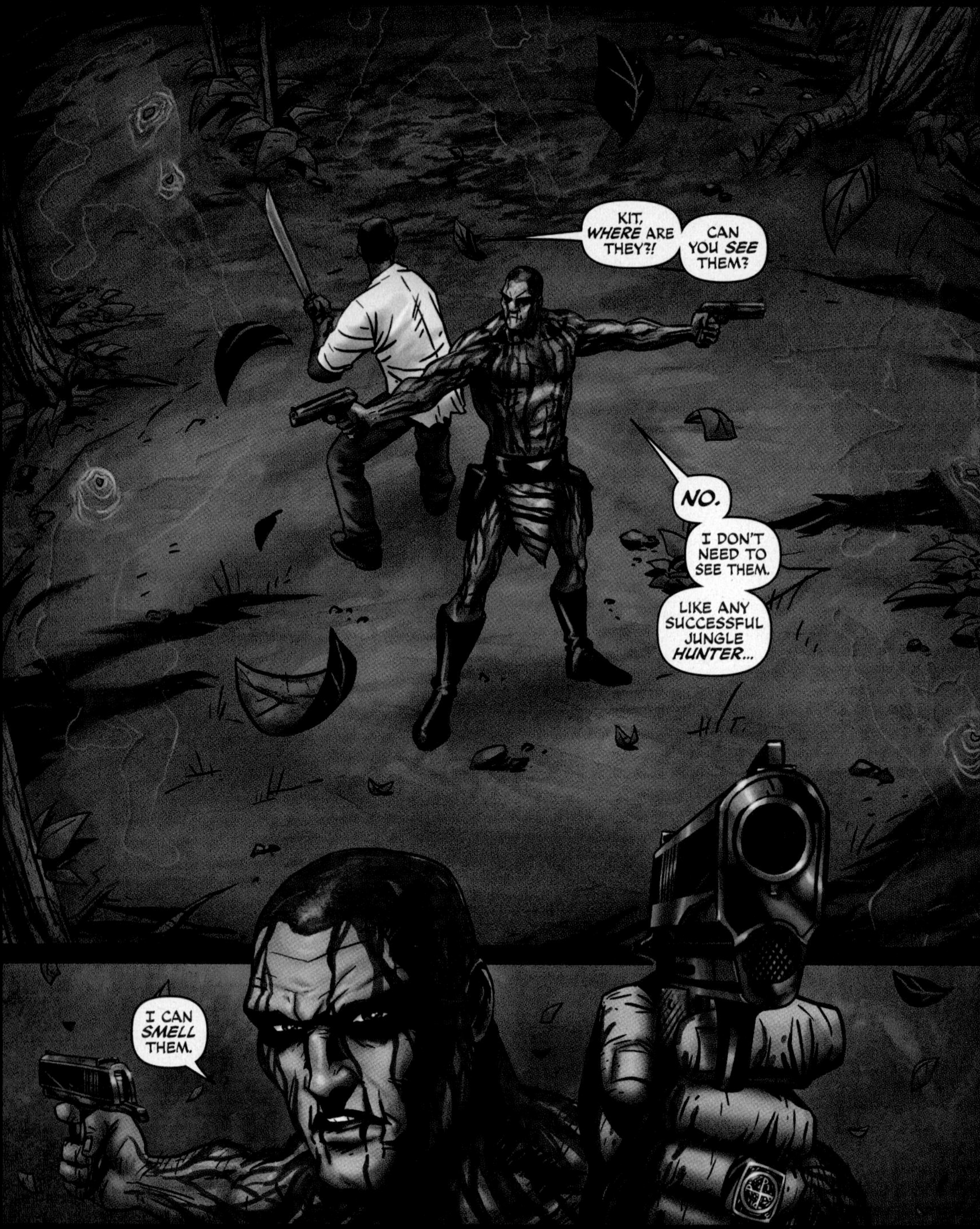
KIT, WHERE ARE THEY?!
CAN YOU SEE THEM?
NO.
I DON'T NEED TO SEE THEM.
LIKE ANY SUCCESSFUL JUNGLE HUNTER...
I CAN SMELL THEM.

GHOSTWALK

chapter one: PHANTOM LIVING

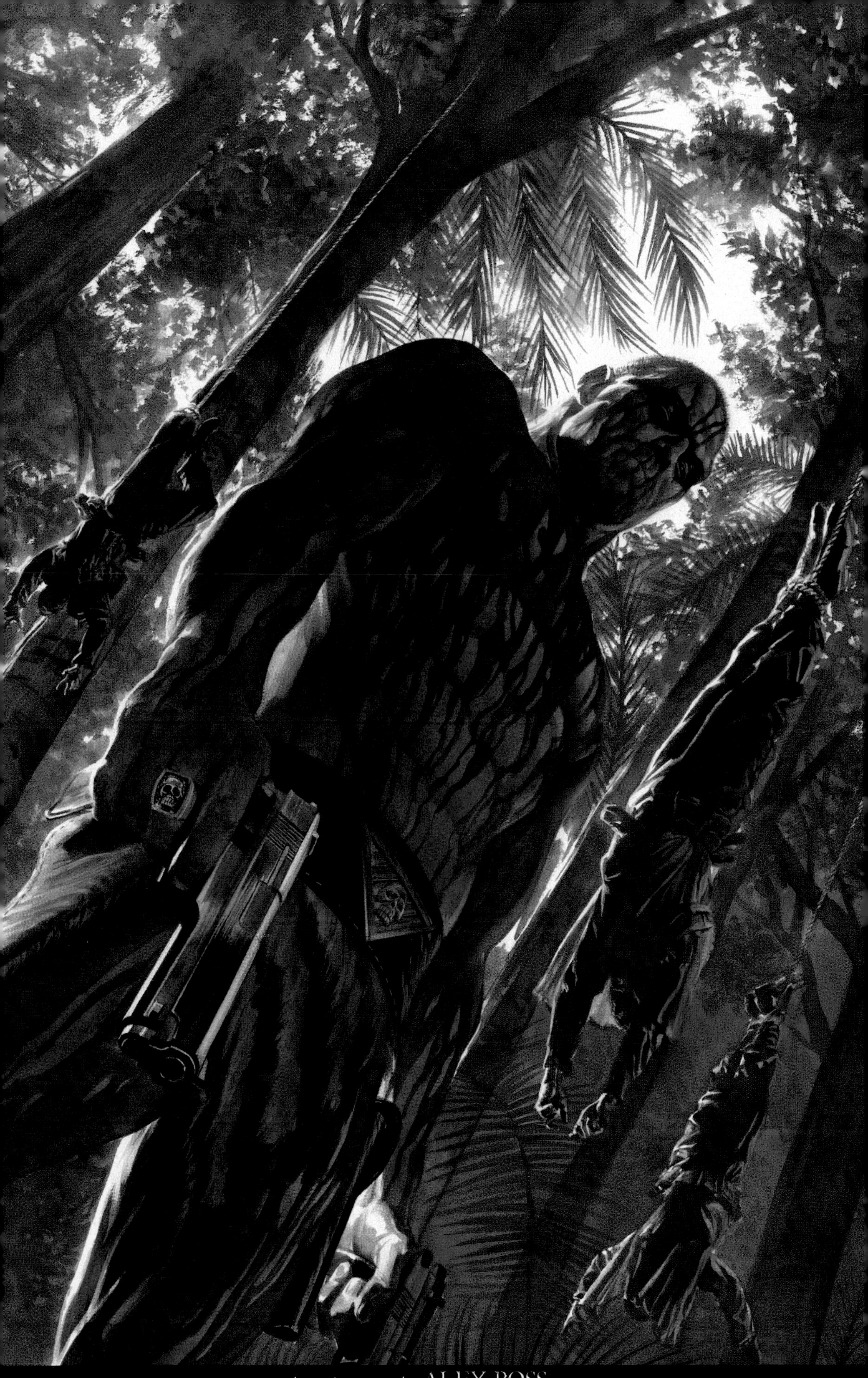

issue two cover by ALEX ROSS

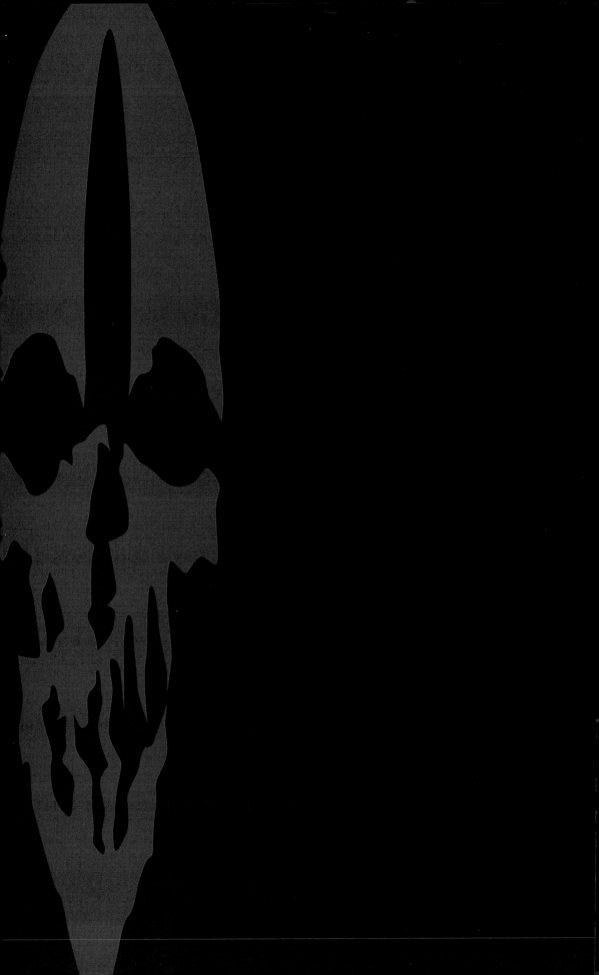

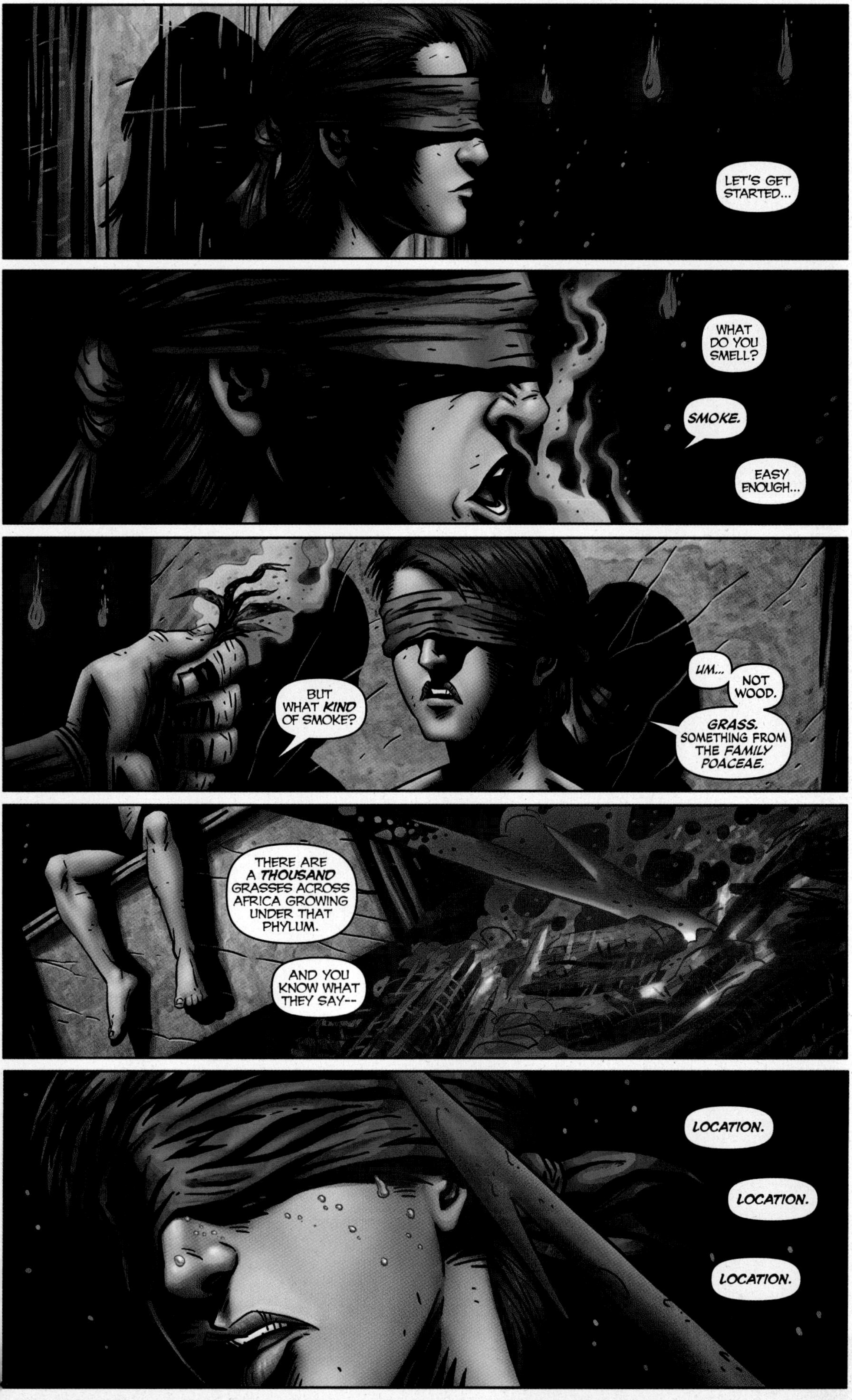
LET'S GET STARTED...
WHAT DO YOU SMELL?
SMOKE.
EASY ENOUGH...
BUT WHAT *KIND* OF SMOKE?
UM...
NOT WOOD.
GRASS. SOMETHING FROM THE *FAMILY POACEAE.*
THERE ARE A *THOUSAND* GRASSES ACROSS AFRICA GROWING UNDER THAT PHYLUM.
AND YOU KNOW WHAT THEY SAY--
LOCATION.
LOCATION.
LOCATION.

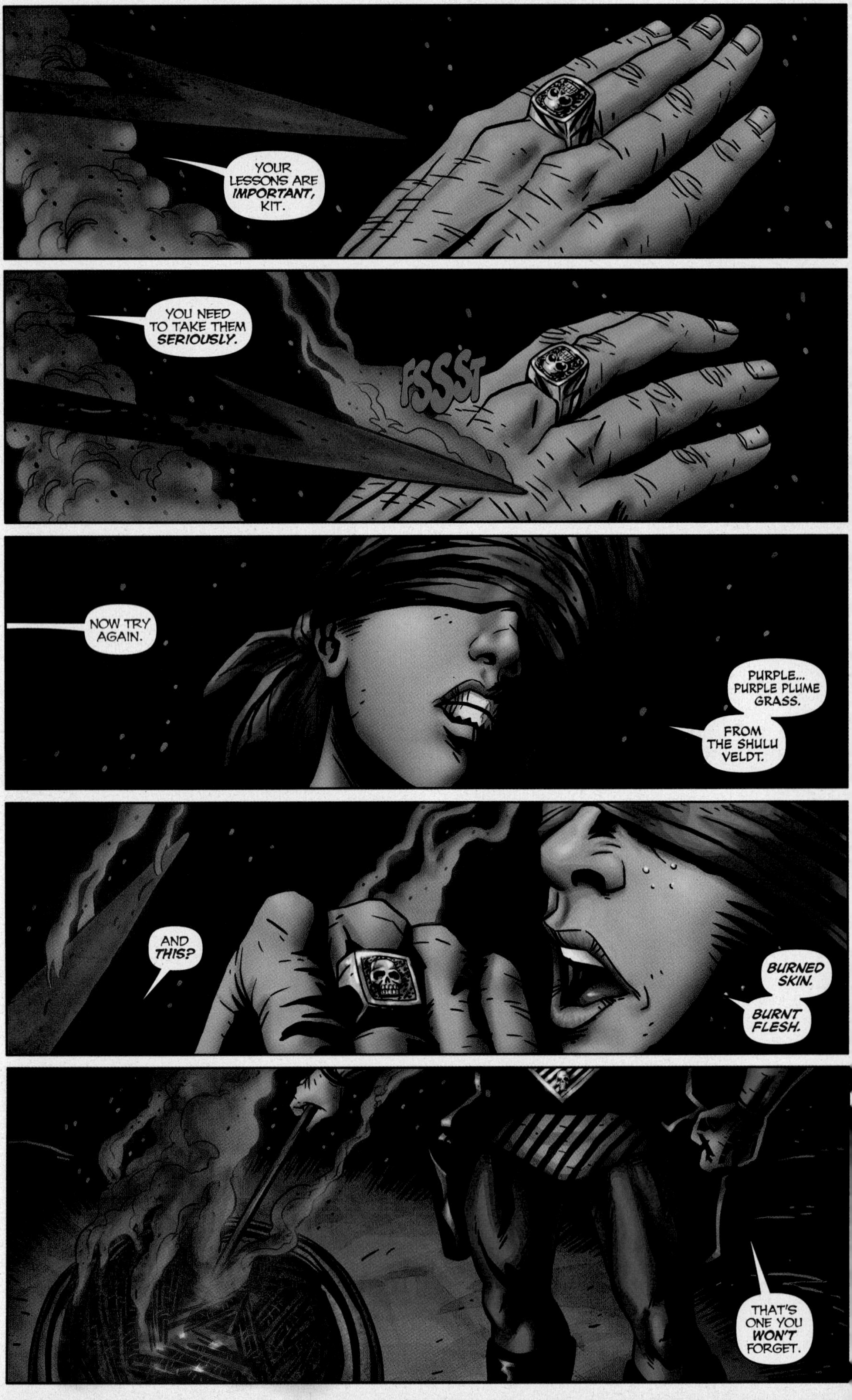
YOUR LESSONS ARE IMPORTANT, KIT.
YOU NEED TO TAKE THEM SERIOUSLY.
FSSST
NOW TRY AGAIN.
PURPLE... PURPLE PLUME GRASS.
FROM THE SHULU VELDT.
AND THIS?
BURNED SKIN.
BURNT FLESH.
THAT'S ONE YOU WON'T FORGET.

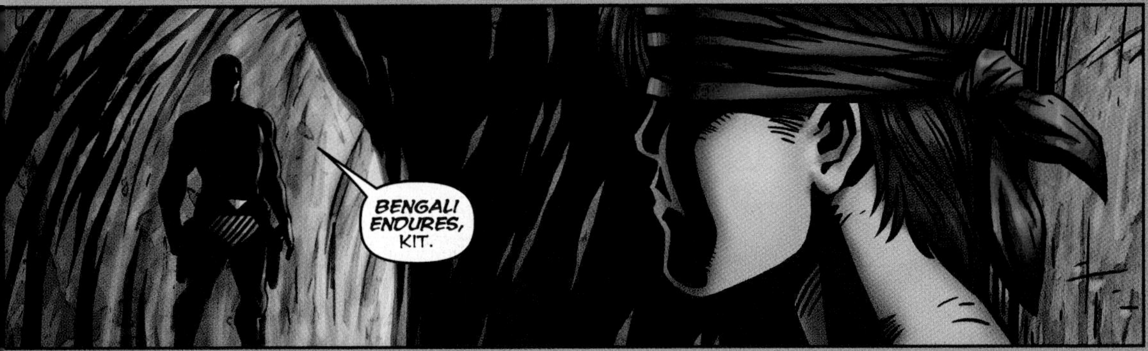
BENGALI ENDURES, KIT.

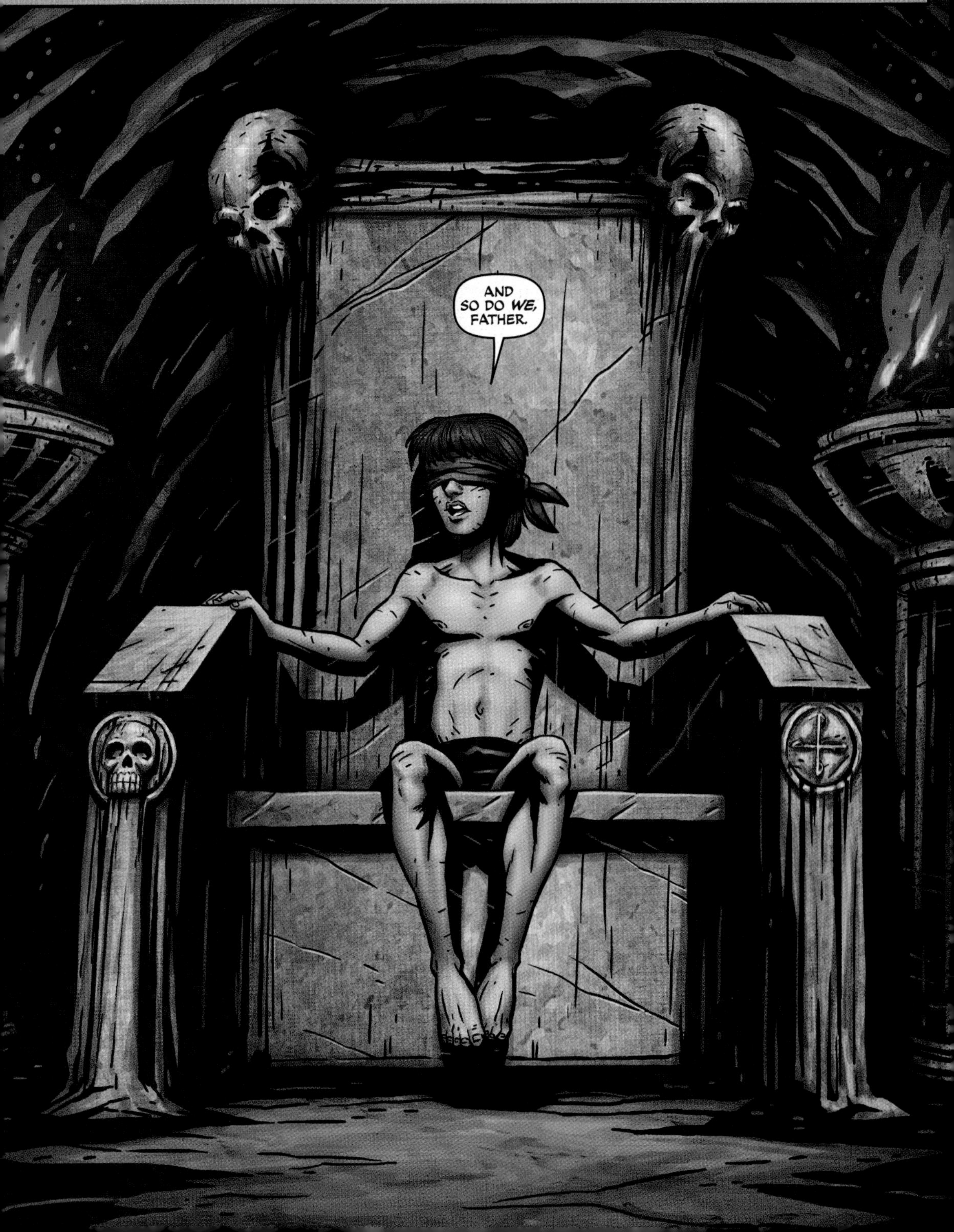
AND SO DO WE, FATHER.

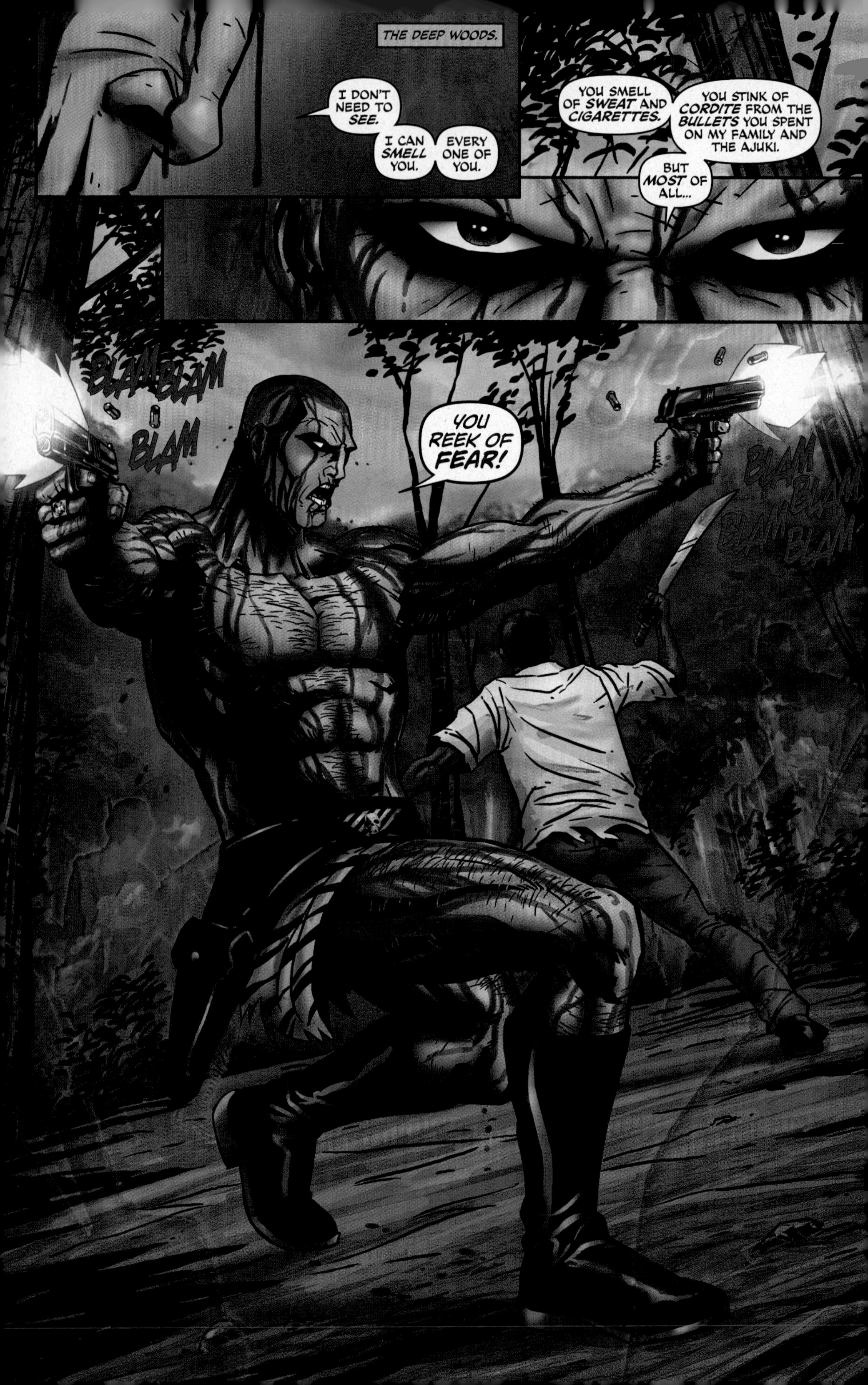
THE DEEP WOODS.
I DON'T NEED TO SEE.
I CAN SMELL YOU.
EVERY ONE OF YOU.
YOU SMELL OF SWEAT AND CIGARETTES.
YOU STINK OF CORDITE FROM THE BULLETS YOU SPENT ON MY FAMILY AND THE AJUKI.
BUT MOST OF ALL...
BLAM BLAM
BLAM
YOU REEK OF FEAR!
BLAM BLAM BLAM BLAM

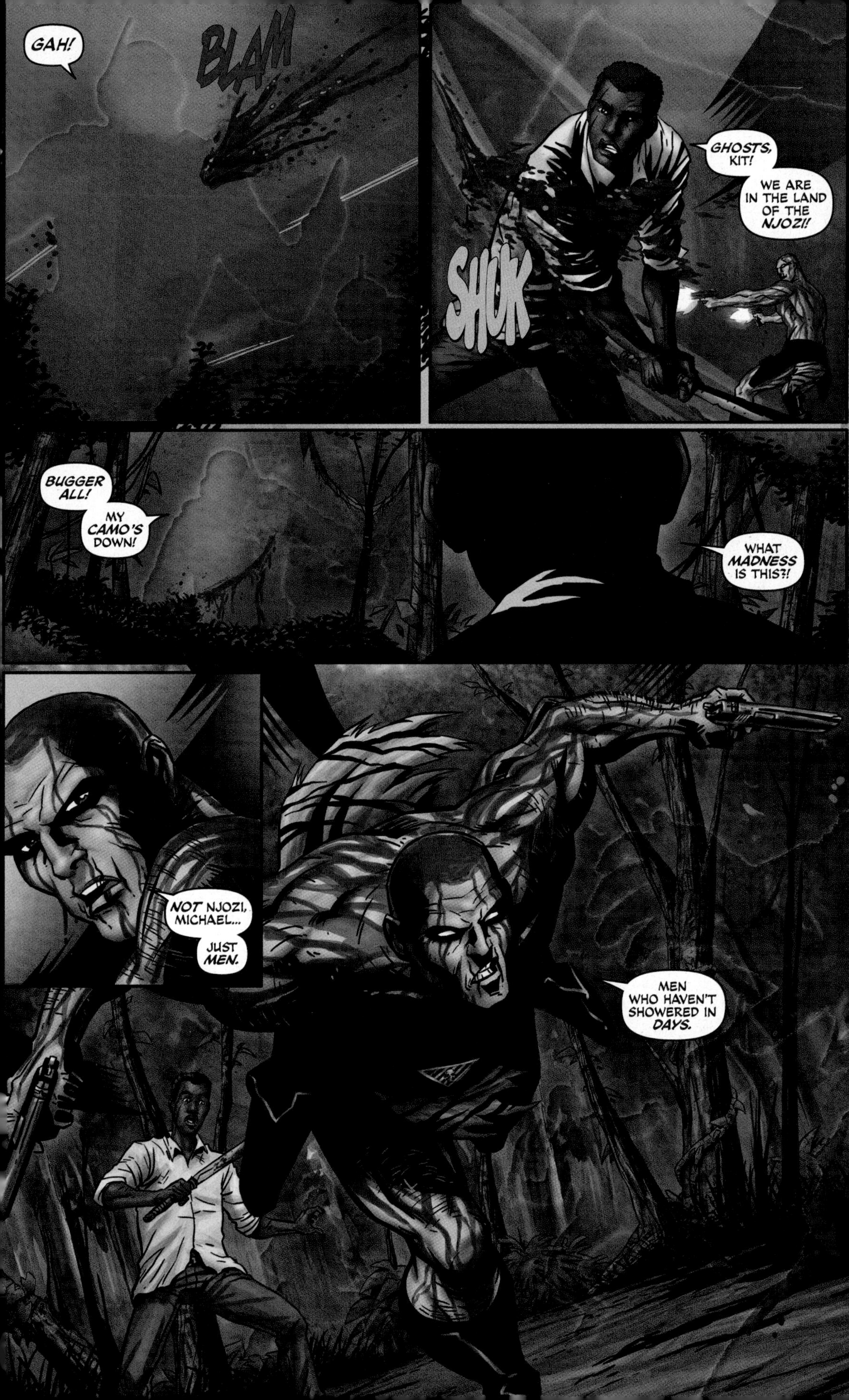
GAH!
BLAM
GHOSTS, KIT!
WE ARE IN THE LAND OF THE NJOZI!
SHUK
BUGGER ALL!
MY CAMO'S DOWN!
WHAT MADNESS IS THIS?!
NOT NJOZI, MICHAEL...
JUST MEN.
MEN WHO HAVEN'T SHOWERED IN DAYS.

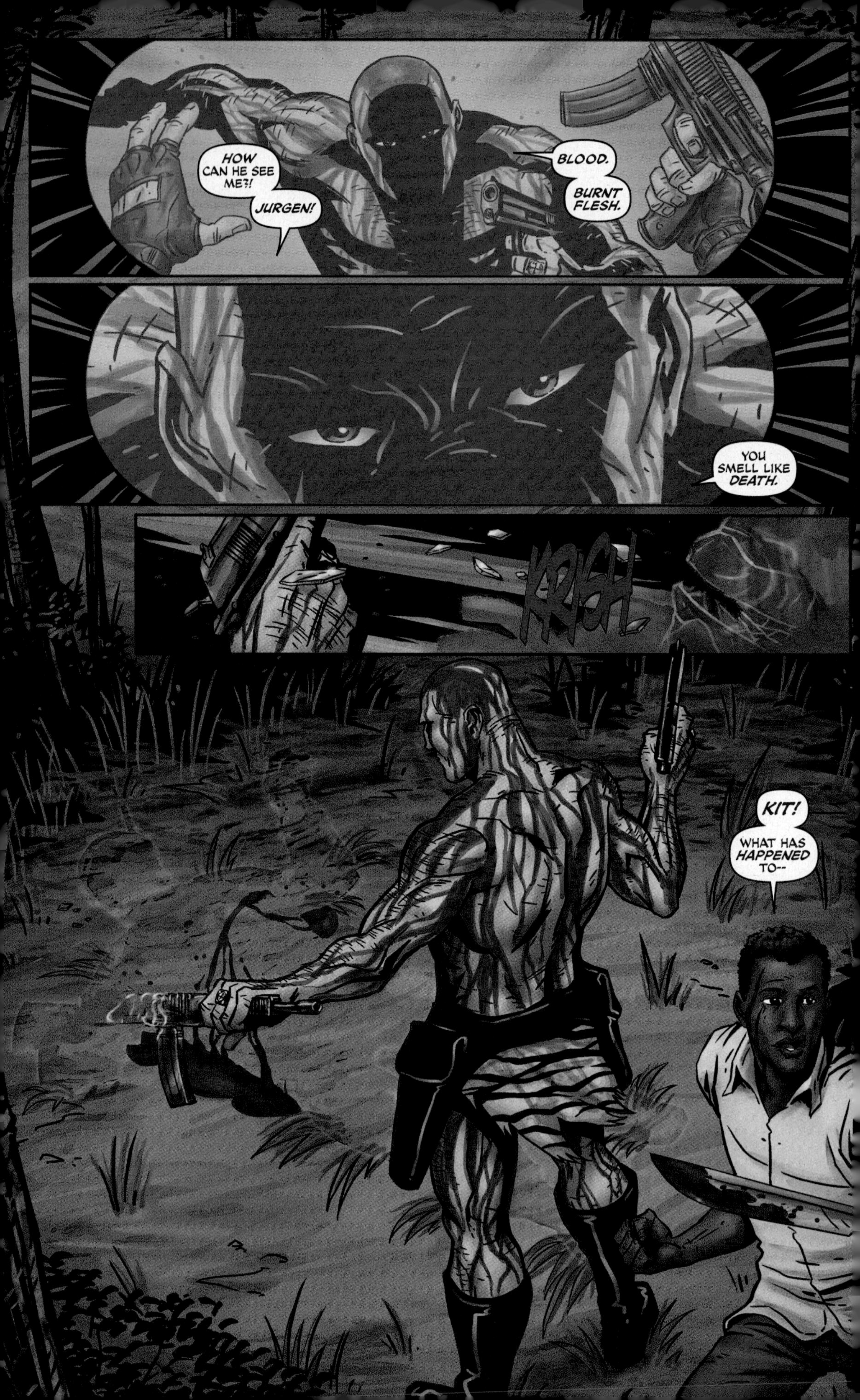
HOW CAN HE SEE ME?!
JURGEN!
BLOOD.
BURNT FLESH.
YOU SMELL LIKE DEATH.
KRISH
KIT!
WHAT HAS HAPPENED TO--

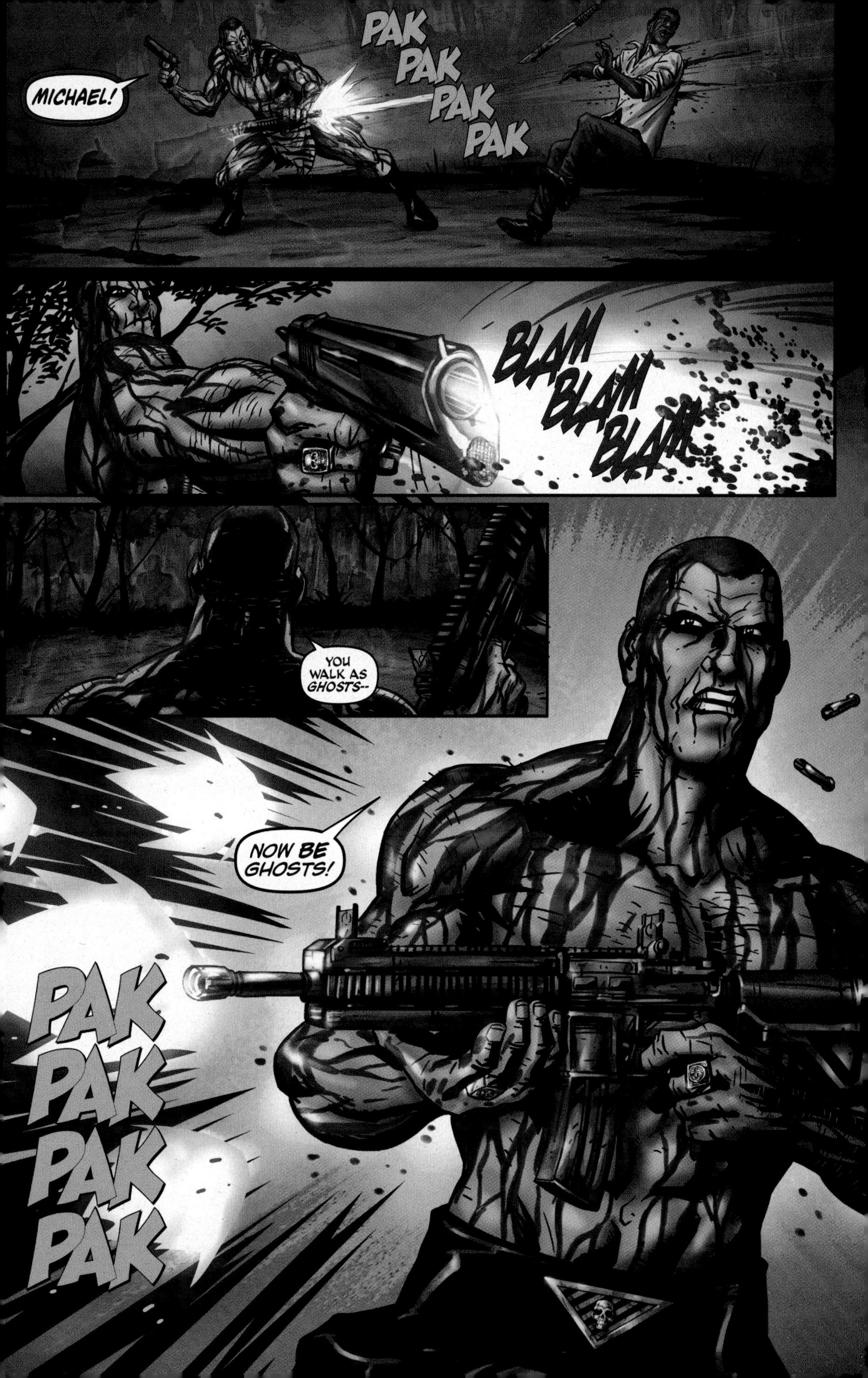
MICHAEL!
PAK
PAK
PAK
PAK
BLAM
BLAM
BLAM
YOU WALK AS GHOSTS--
NOW BE GHOSTS!
PAK
PAK
PAK
PAK

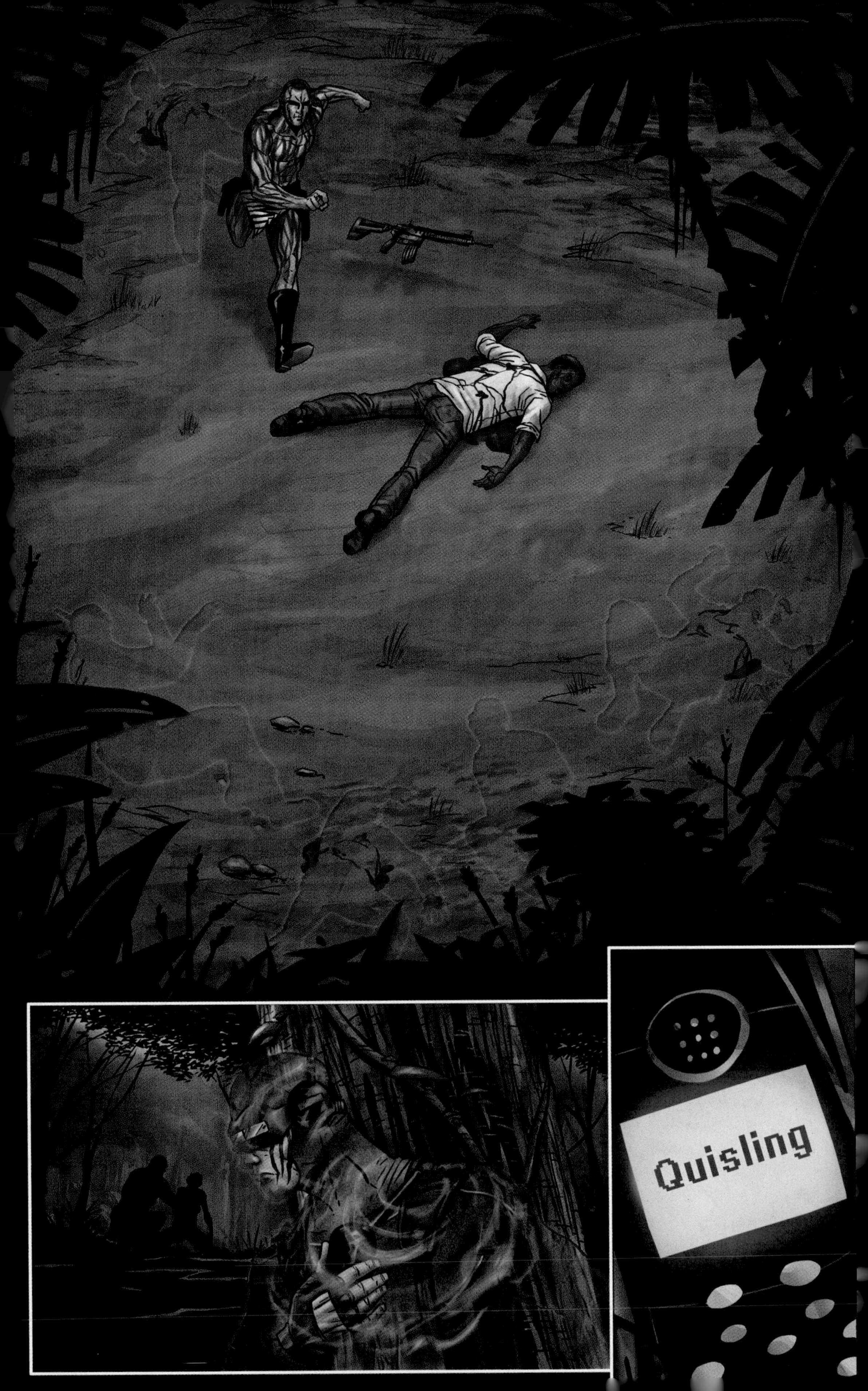
Quisling

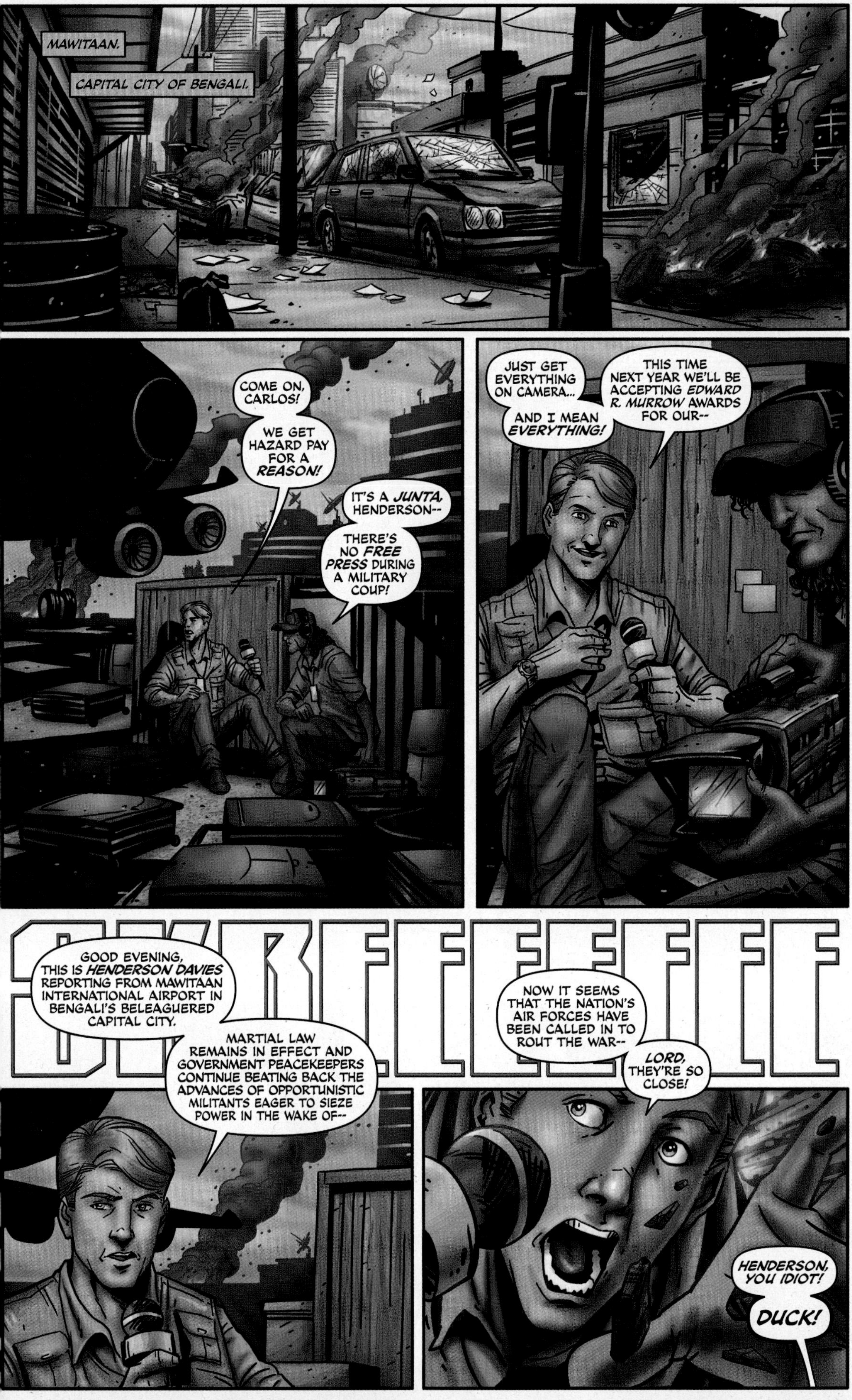
MAWITAAN.
CAPITAL CITY OF BENGALI.
COME ON, CARLOS!
WE GET HAZARD PAY FOR A REASON!
IT'S A JUNTA, HENDERSON--
THERE'S NO FREE PRESS DURING A MILITARY COUP!
JUST GET EVERYTHING ON CAMERA...
AND I MEAN EVERYTHING!
THIS TIME NEXT YEAR WE'LL BE ACCEPTING EDWARD R. MURROW AWARDS FOR OUR--
GOOD EVENING, THIS IS HENDERSON DAVIES REPORTING FROM MAWITAAN INTERNATIONAL AIRPORT IN BENGALI'S BELEAGUERED CAPITAL CITY.
MARTIAL LAW REMAINS IN EFFECT AND GOVERNMENT PEACEKEEPERS CONTINUE BEATING BACK THE ADVANCES OF OPPORTUNISTIC MILITANTS EAGER TO SIEZE POWER IN THE WAKE OF--
NOW IT SEEMS THAT THE NATION'S AIR FORCES HAVE BEEN CALLED IN TO ROUT THE WAR--
LORD, THEY'RE SO CLOSE!
HENDERSON, YOU IDIOT!
DUCK!

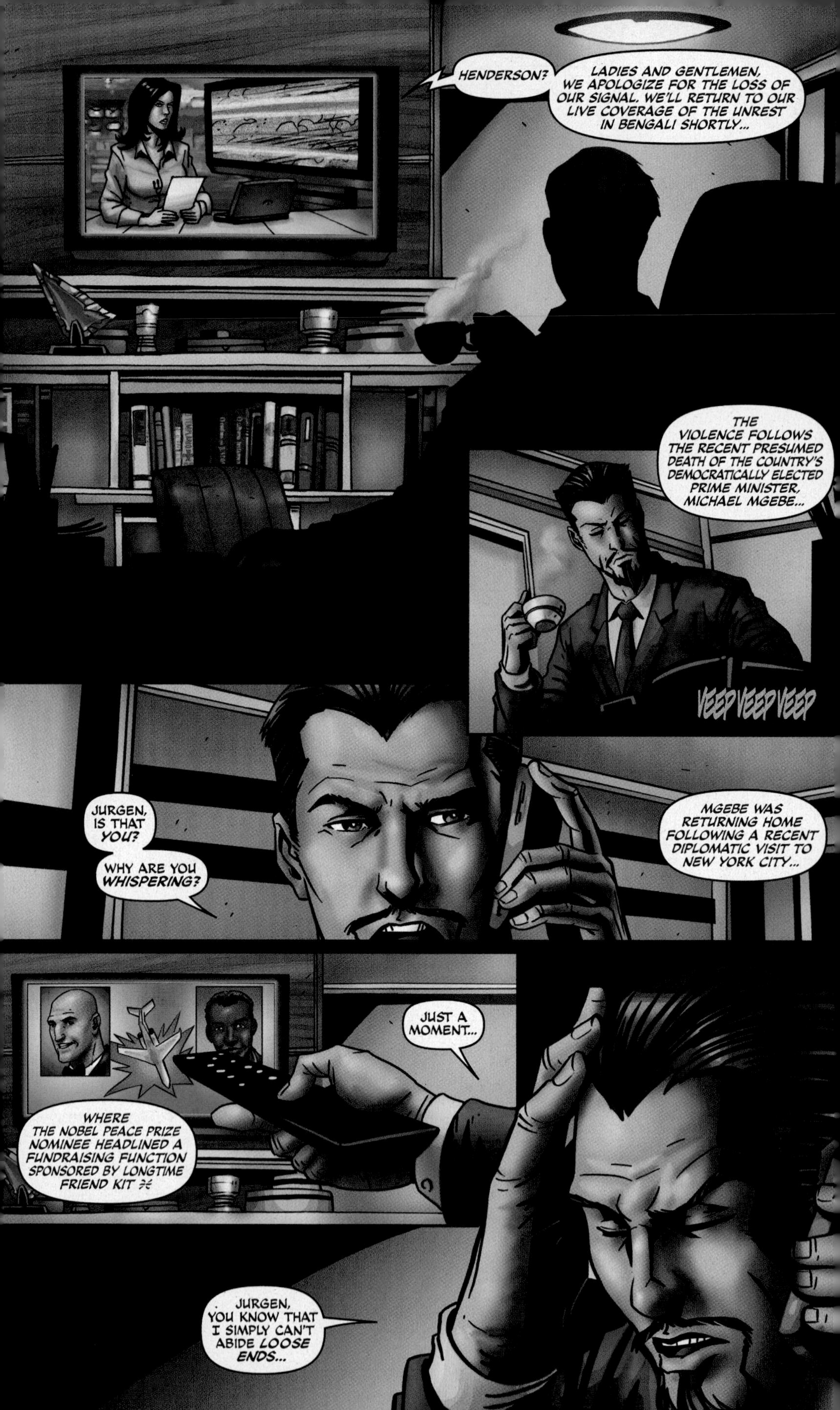
HENDERSON?
LADIES AND GENTLEMEN, WE APOLOGIZE FOR THE LOSS OF OUR SIGNAL. WE'LL RETURN TO OUR LIVE COVERAGE OF THE UNREST IN BENGALI SHORTLY...
THE VIOLENCE FOLLOWS THE RECENT PRESUMED DEATH OF THE COUNTRY'S DEMOCRATICALLY ELECTED PRIME MINISTER, MICHAEL MGEBE...
VEEP VEEP VEEP
JURGEN, IS THAT YOU?
WHY ARE YOU WHISPERING?
MGEBE WAS RETURNING HOME FOLLOWING A RECENT DIPLOMATIC VISIT TO NEW YORK CITY...
JUST A MOMENT...
WHERE THE NOBEL PEACE PRIZE NOMINEE HEADLINED A FUNDRAISING FUNCTION SPONSORED BY LONGTIME FRIEND KIT
JURGEN, YOU KNOW THAT I SIMPLY CAN'T ABIDE LOOSE ENDS...

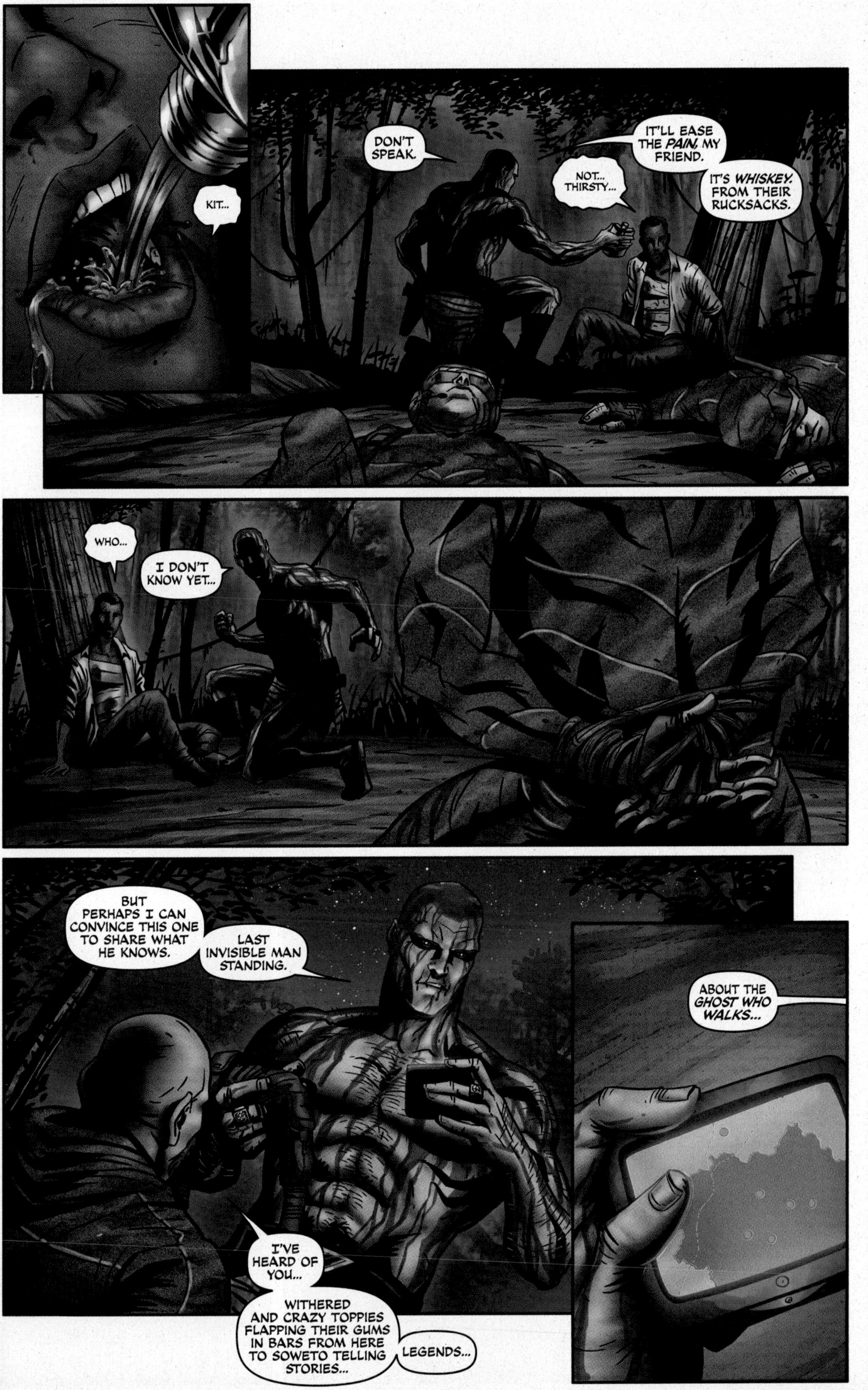
KIT...
DON'T SPEAK.
IT'LL EASE THE *PAIN,* MY FRIEND.
NOT... THIRSTY...
IT'S *WHISKEY.* FROM THEIR RUCKSACKS.
WHO...
I DON'T KNOW YET...
BUT PERHAPS I CAN CONVINCE THIS ONE TO SHARE WHAT HE KNOWS.
LAST INVISIBLE MAN STANDING.
ABOUT THE *GHOST WHO WALKS...*
I'VE HEARD OF YOU...
WITHERED AND CRAZY TOPPIES FLAPPING THEIR GUMS IN BARS FROM HERE TO SOWETO TELLING STORIES...
LEGENDS...

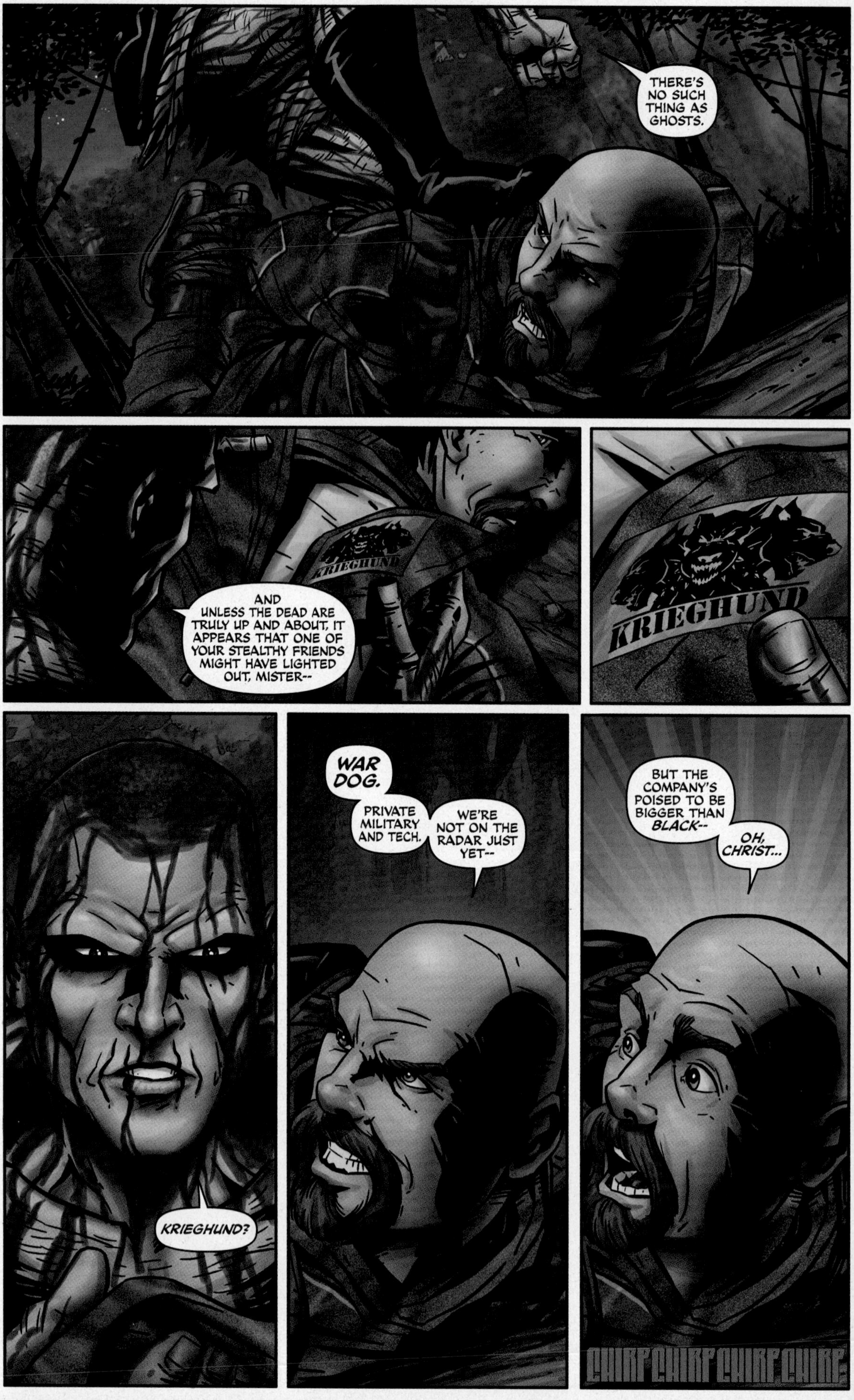
THERE'S NO SUCH THING AS GHOSTS.
AND UNLESS THE DEAD ARE TRULY UP AND ABOUT, IT APPEARS THAT ONE OF YOUR STEALTHY FRIENDS MIGHT HAVE LIGHTED OUT, MISTER--
KRIEGHUND
KRIEGHUND
KRIEGHUND?
WAR DOG.
PRIVATE MILITARY AND TECH.
WE'RE NOT ON THE RADAR JUST YET--
BUT THE COMPANY'S POISED TO BE BIGGER THAN BLACK--
OH, CHRIST...
CHIRP CHIRP CHIRP CHIRP

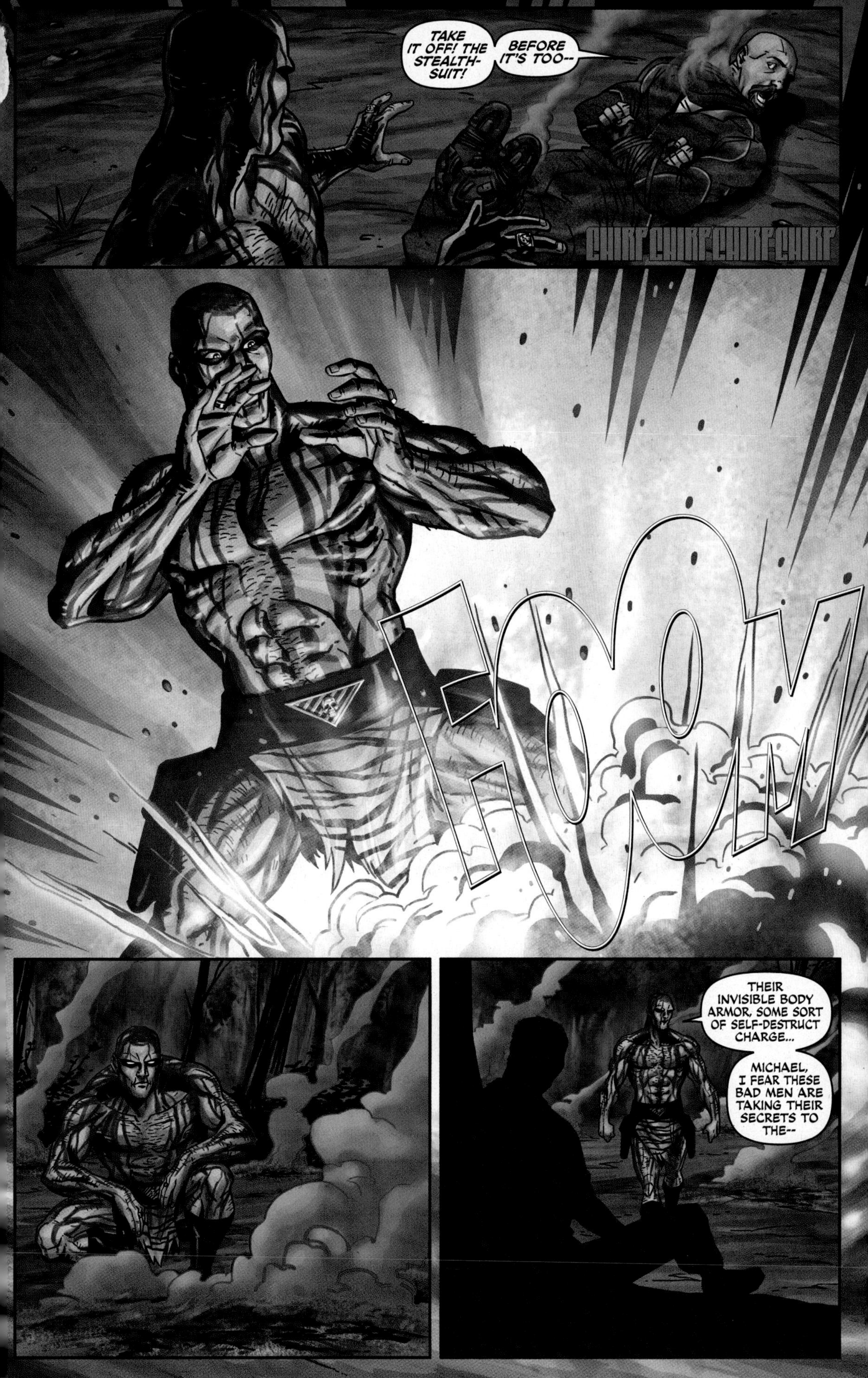
TAKE IT OFF! THE STEALTH-SUIT!
BEFORE IT'S TOO--
CHIRP CHIRP CHIRP CHIRP
FOOOM
THEIR INVISIBLE BODY ARMOR, SOME SORT OF SELF-DESTRUCT CHARGE...
MICHAEL, I FEAR THESE BAD MEN ARE TAKING THEIR SECRETS TO THE--

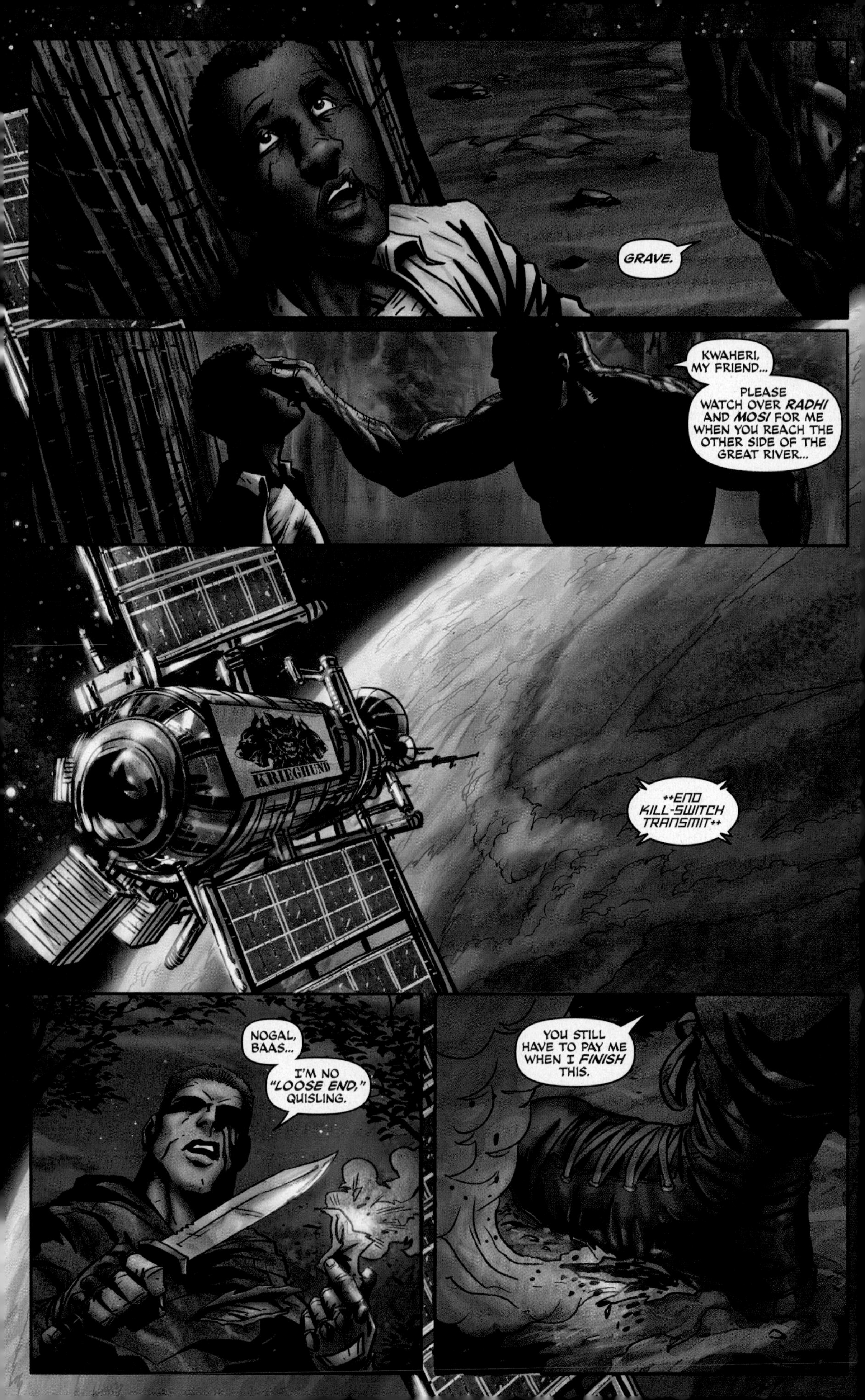
GRAVE.
KWAHERI, MY FRIEND...
PLEASE WATCH OVER RADHI AND MOSI FOR ME WHEN YOU REACH THE OTHER SIDE OF THE GREAT RIVER...
KRIEGHUND
++END KILL-SWITCH TRANSMIT++
NOGAL, BAAS...
I'M NO "LOOSE END," QUISLING.
YOU STILL HAVE TO PAY ME WHEN I FINISH THIS.

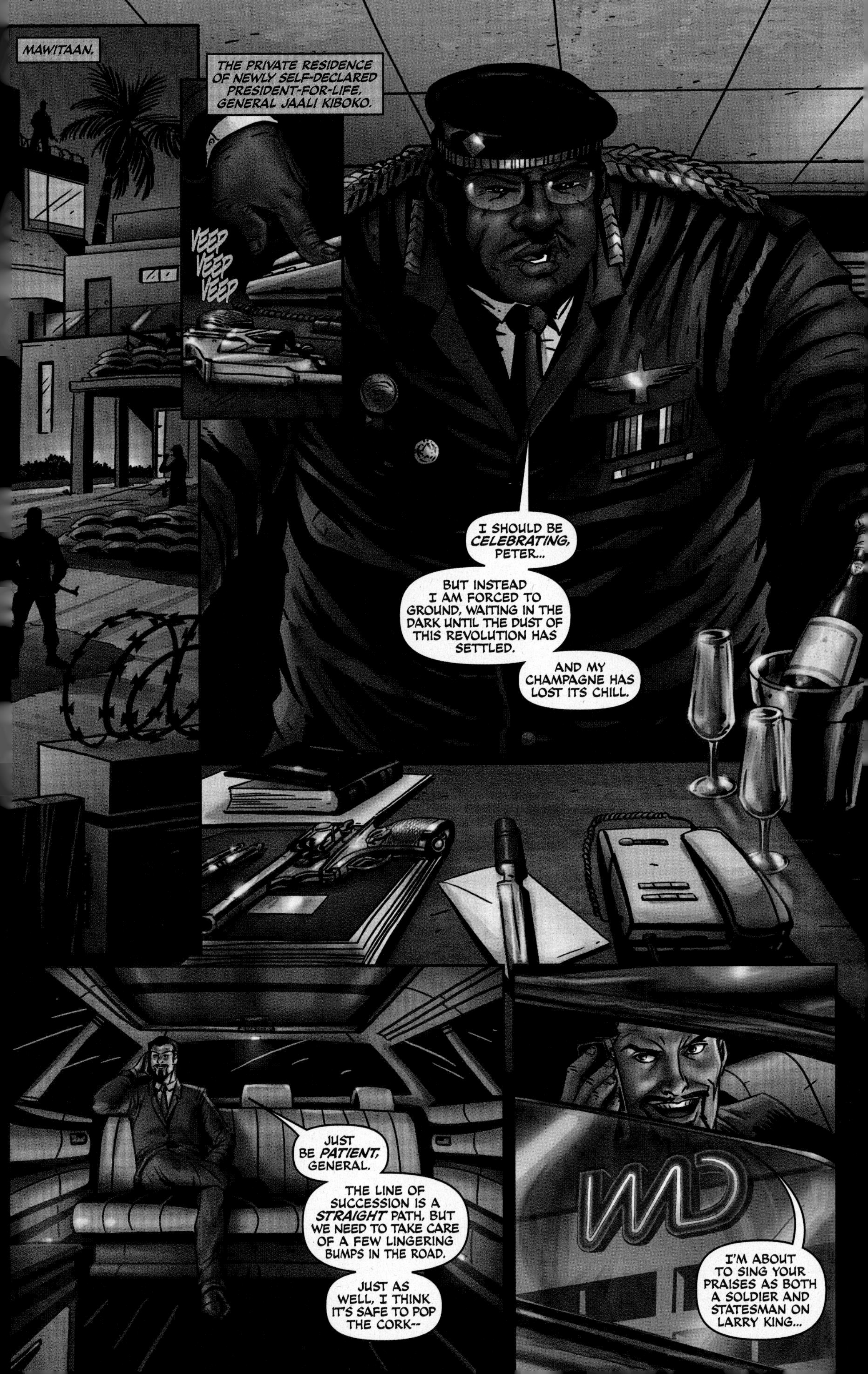
MAWITAAN.
THE PRIVATE RESIDENCE OF NEWLY SELF-DECLARED PRESIDENT-FOR-LIFE, GENERAL JAALI KIBOKO.
VEEP VEEP VEEP
I SHOULD BE CELEBRATING, PETER...
BUT INSTEAD I AM FORCED TO GROUND, WAITING IN THE DARK UNTIL THE DUST OF THIS REVOLUTION HAS SETTLED.
AND MY CHAMPAGNE HAS LOST ITS CHILL.
JUST BE PATIENT, GENERAL.
THE LINE OF SUCCESSION IS A STRAIGHT PATH, BUT WE NEED TO TAKE CARE OF A FEW LINGERING BUMPS IN THE ROAD.
JUST AS WELL, I THINK IT'S SAFE TO POP THE CORK--
I'M ABOUT TO SING YOUR PRAISES AS BOTH A SOLDIER AND STATESMAN ON LARRY KING...

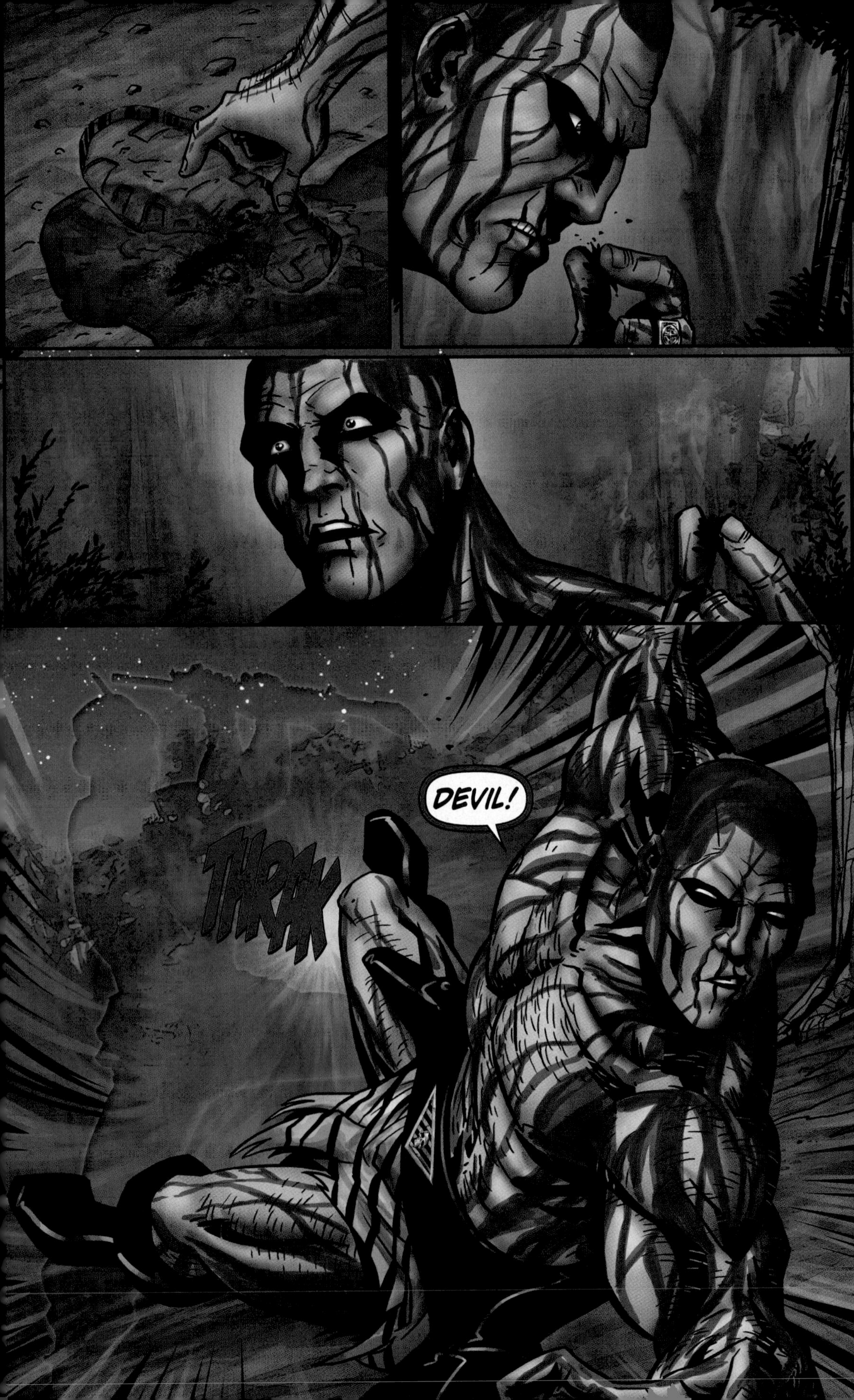
DEVIL!
THRAK

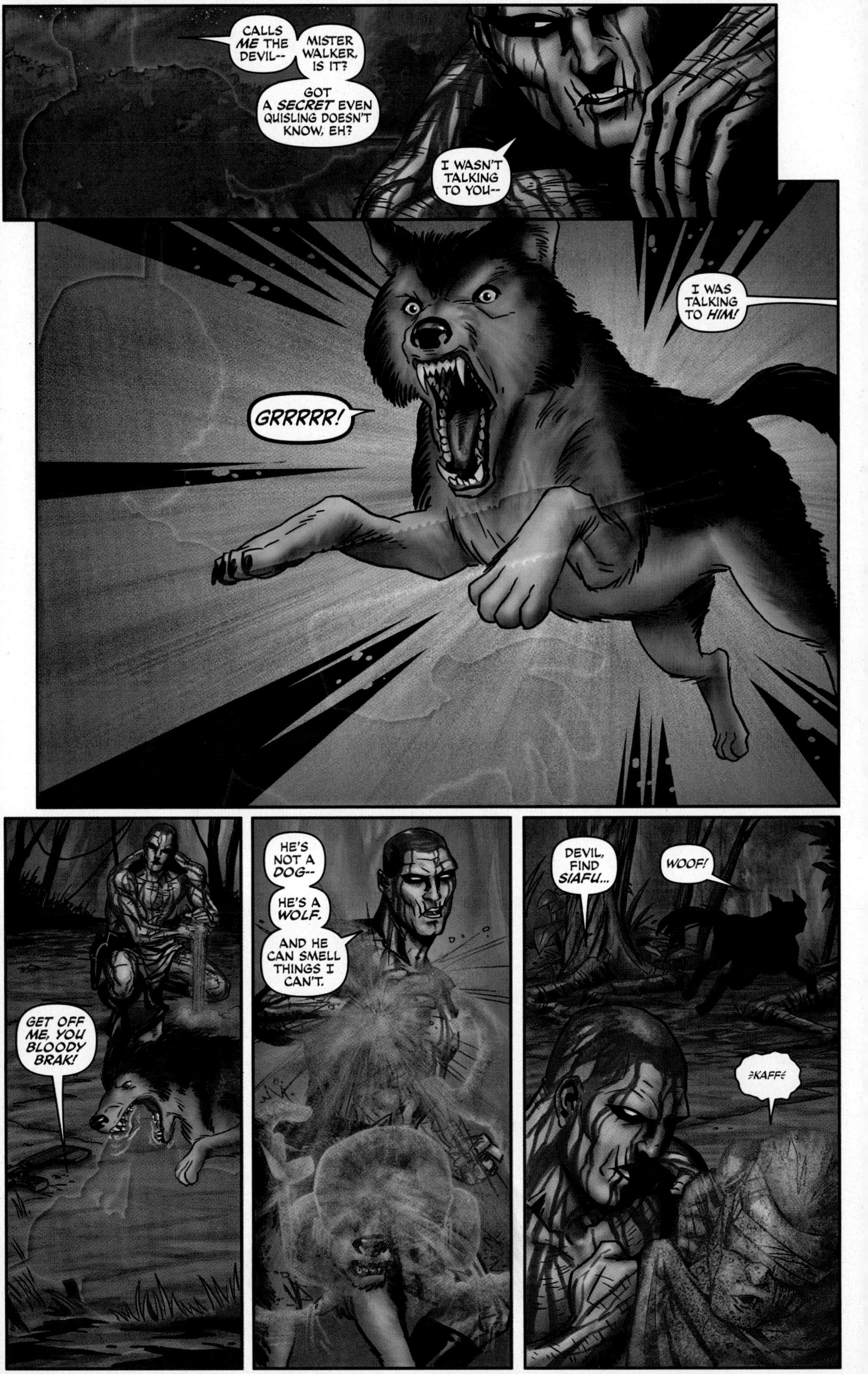

CALLS *ME* THE DEVIL--
MISTER WALKER, IS IT?
GOT A *SECRET* EVEN QUISLING DOESN'T KNOW, EH?
I WASN'T TALKING TO YOU--
I WAS TALKING TO *HIM!*
GRRRRR!
GET OFF ME, YOU BLOODY BRAK!
HE'S NOT A *DOG*--
HE'S A *WOLF.*
AND HE CAN SMELL THINGS I CAN'T.
DEVIL, FIND *SIAFU*...
WOOF!
KAFF

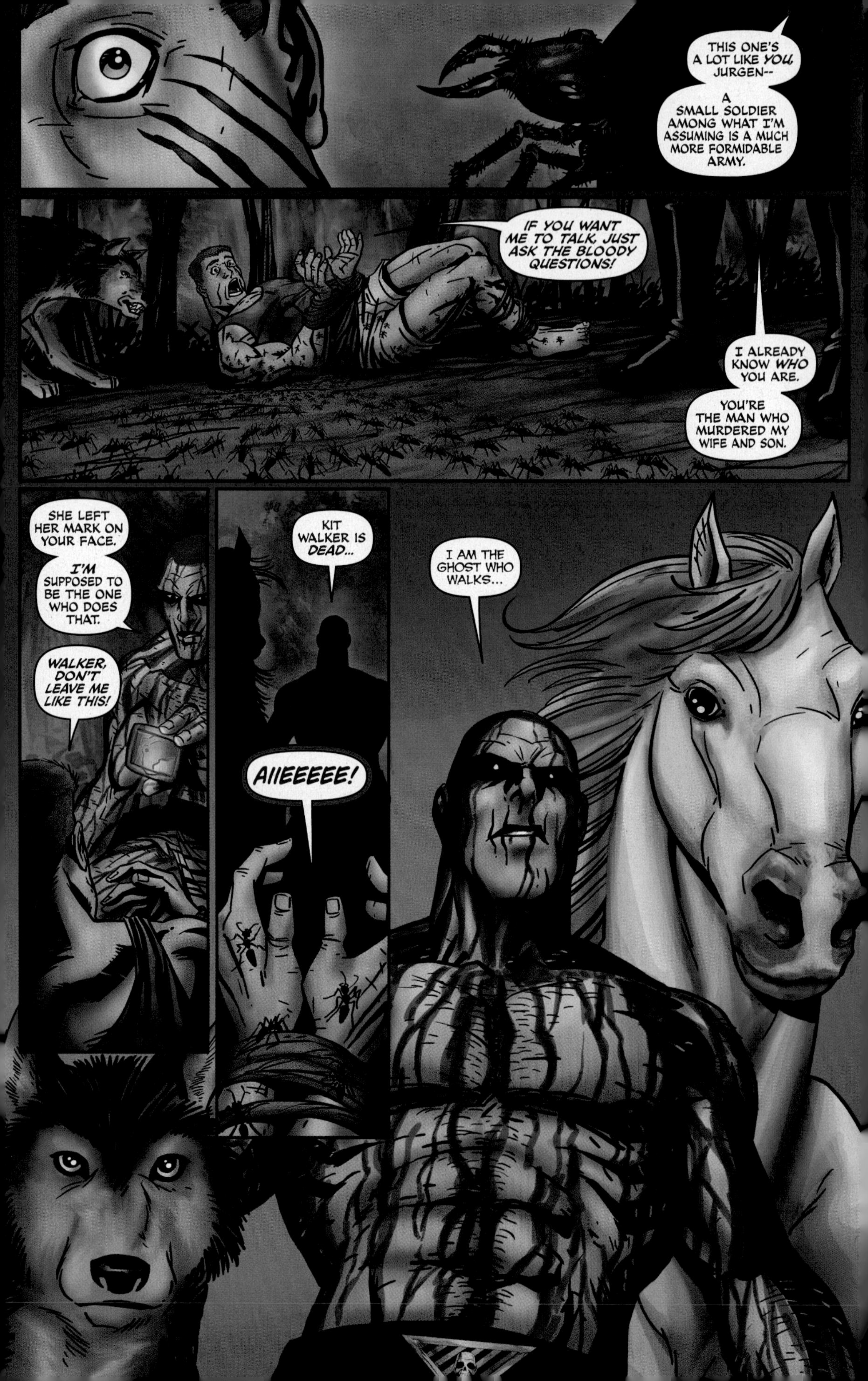

THIS ONE'S A LOT LIKE *YOU*, JURGEN--
A SMALL SOLDIER AMONG WHAT I'M ASSUMING IS A MUCH MORE FORMIDABLE ARMY.
IF YOU WANT ME TO TALK, JUST ASK THE BLOODY QUESTIONS!
I ALREADY KNOW *WHO* YOU ARE.
YOU'RE THE MAN WHO MURDERED MY WIFE AND SON.
SHE LEFT HER MARK ON YOUR FACE.
I'M SUPPOSED TO BE THE ONE WHO DOES THAT.
WALKER, DON'T LEAVE ME LIKE THIS!
KIT WALKER IS *DEAD*...
AIIEEEEE!
I AM THE GHOST WHO WALKS...

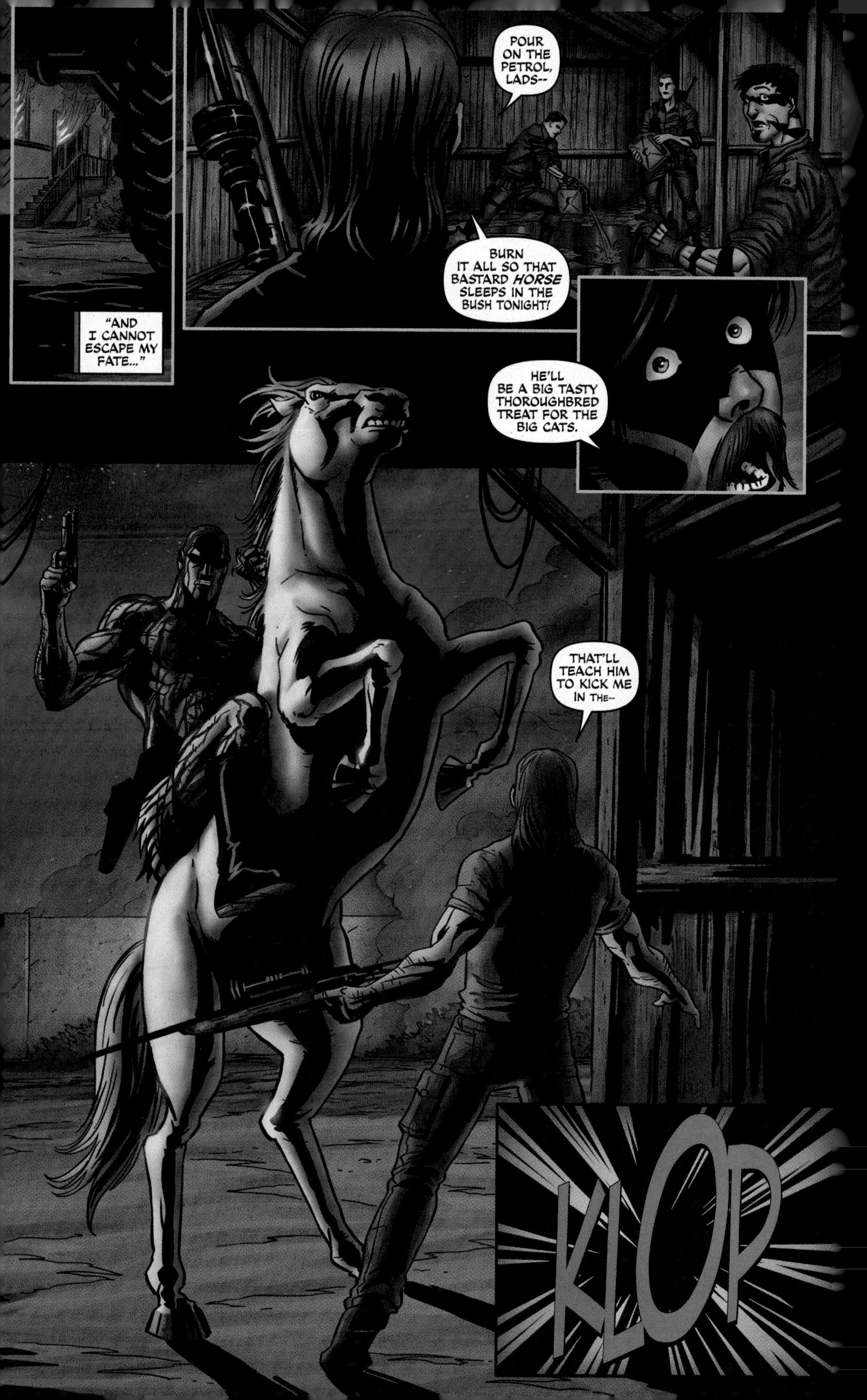

"AND I CANNOT ESCAPE MY FATE..."
POUR ON THE PETROL, LADS--
BURN IT ALL SO THAT BASTARD *HORSE* SLEEPS IN THE BUSH TONIGHT!
HE'LL BE A BIG TASTY THOROUGHBRED TREAT FOR THE BIG CATS.
THAT'LL TEACH HIM TO KICK ME IN THE--
KLOP

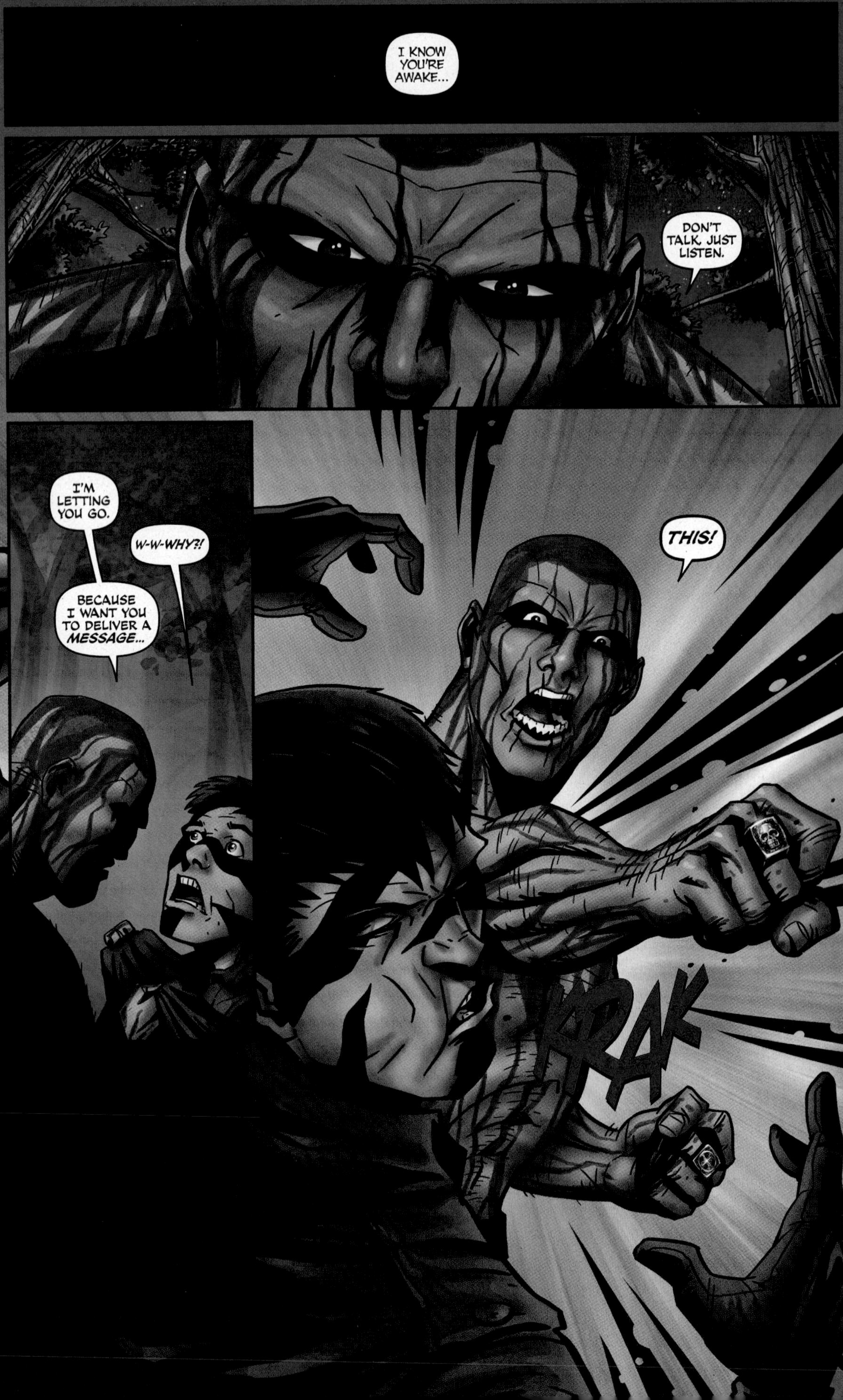
I KNOW YOU'RE AWAKE...
DON'T TALK, JUST LISTEN.
I'M LETTING YOU GO.
W-W-WHY?!
BECAUSE I WANT YOU TO DELIVER A MESSAGE...
THIS!
KRAK

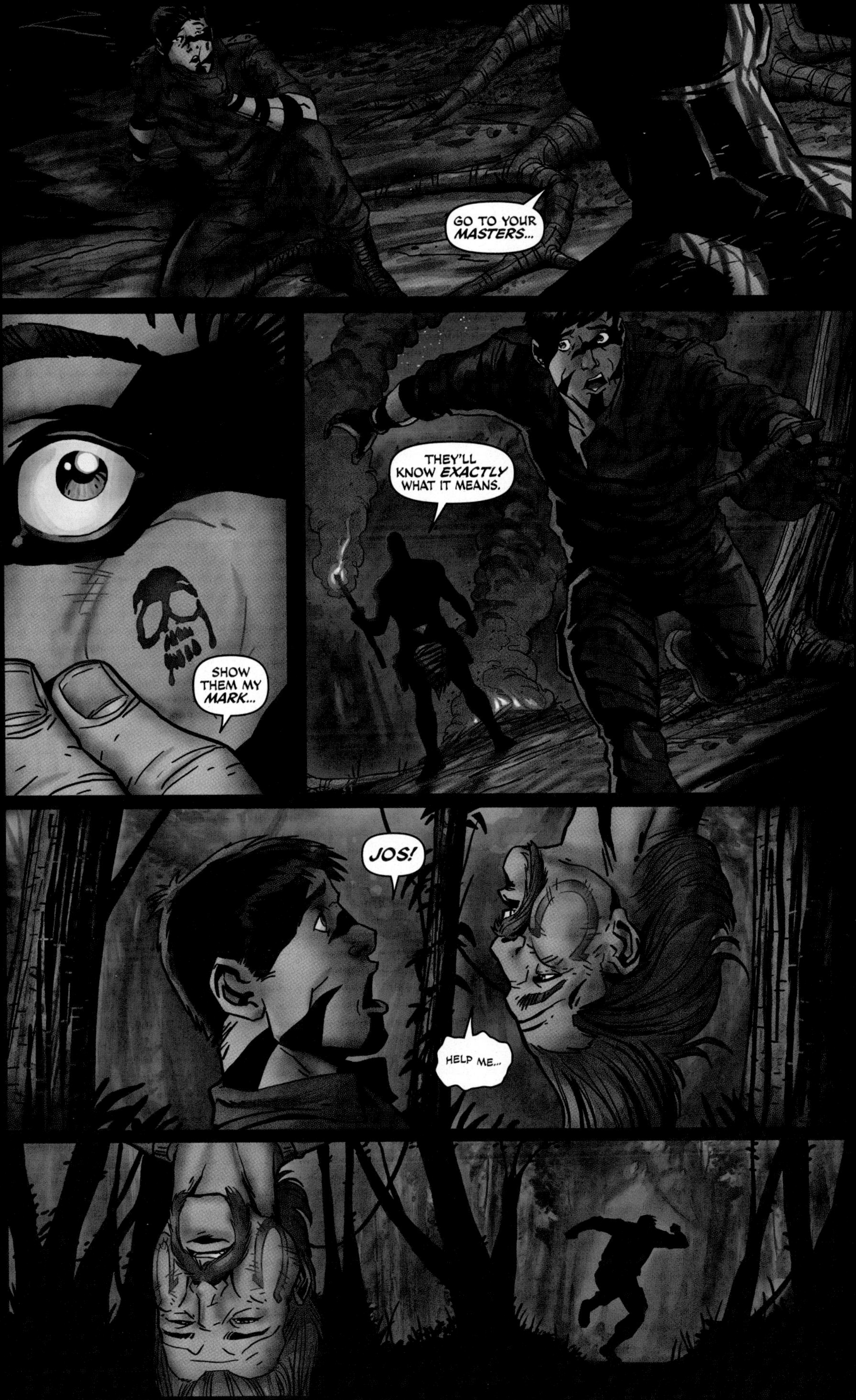
GO TO YOUR MASTERS...
SHOW THEM MY MARK...
THEY'LL KNOW EXACTLY WHAT IT MEANS.
JOS!
HELP ME...

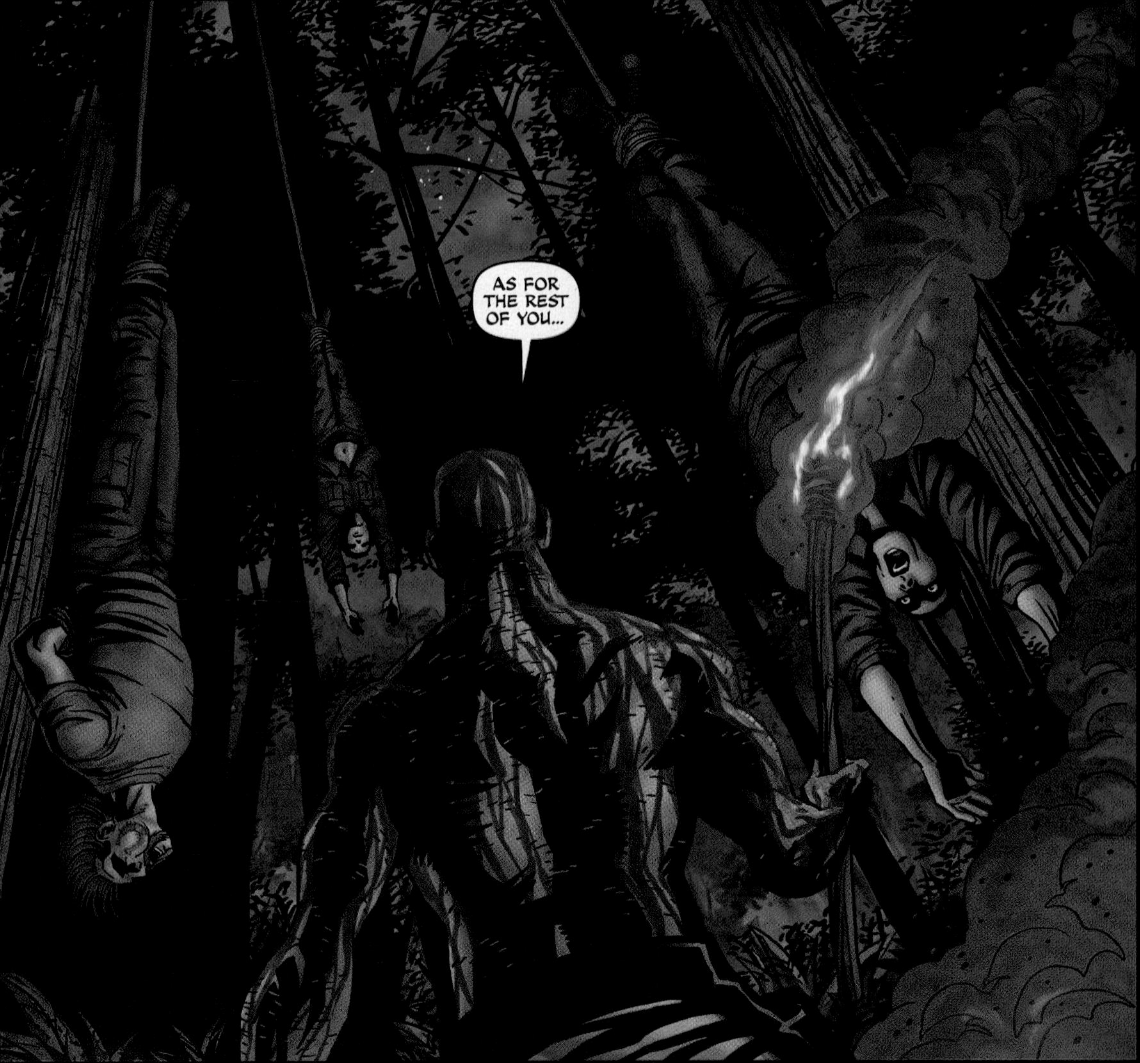
AS FOR THE REST OF YOU...

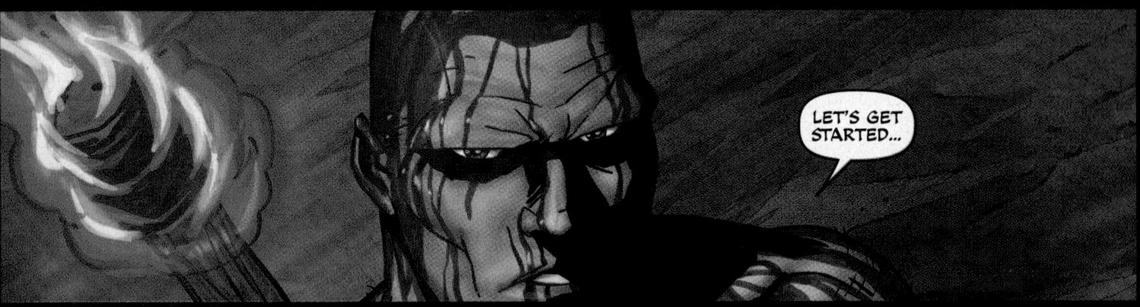
LET'S GET STARTED...

GHOSTWALK

chapter two: GHOST HUNTERS

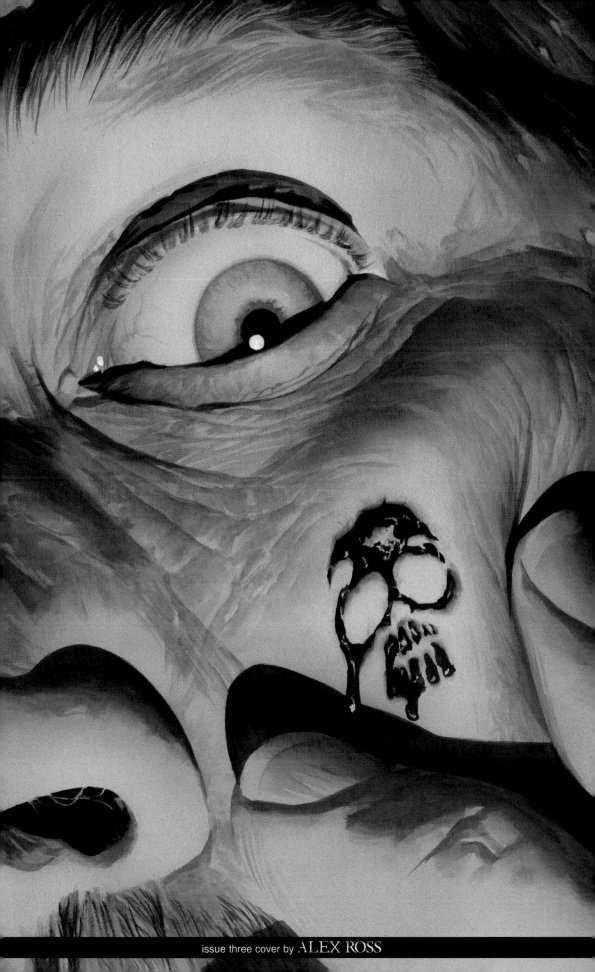

issue three cover by ALEX ROSS

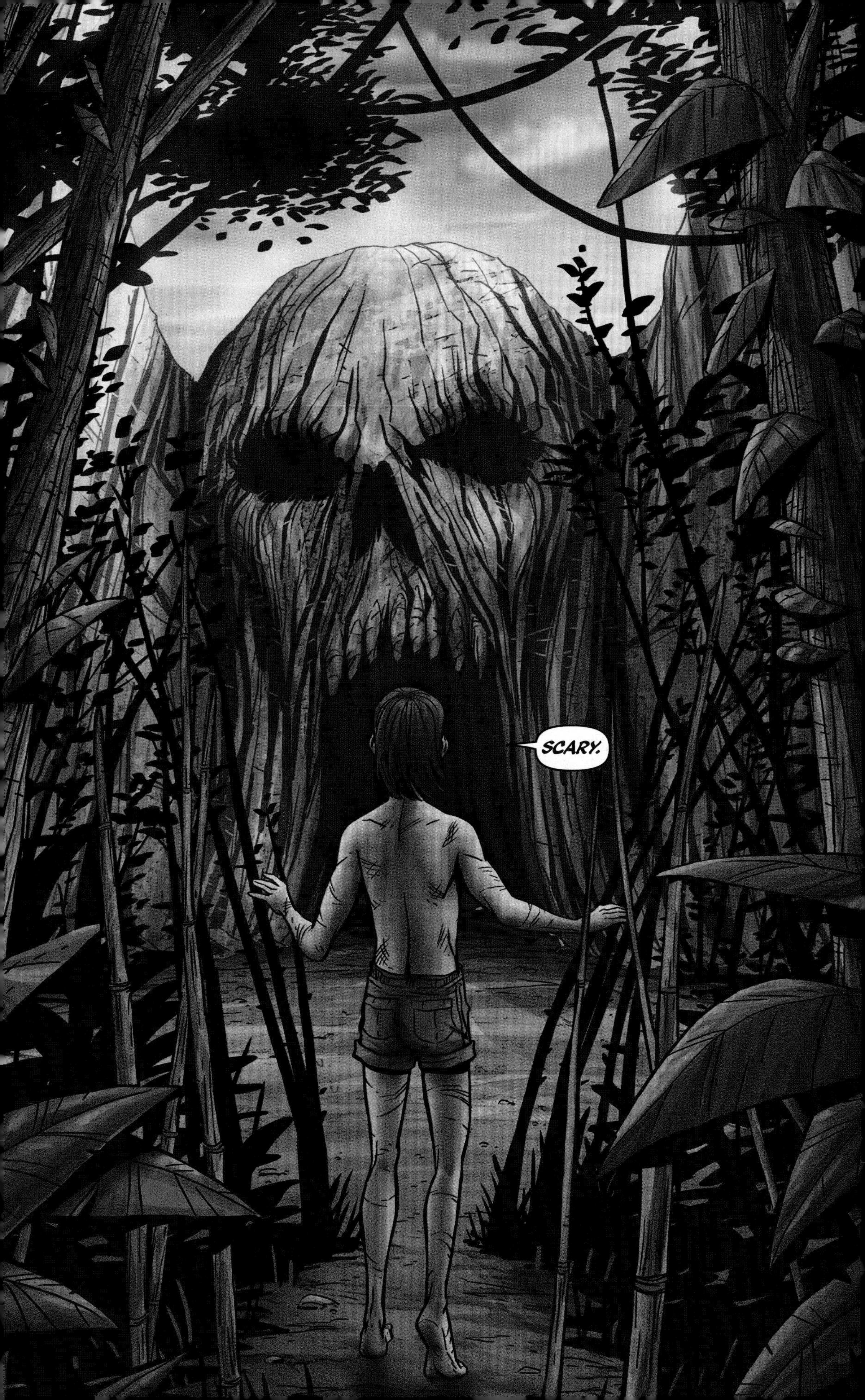
SCARY.

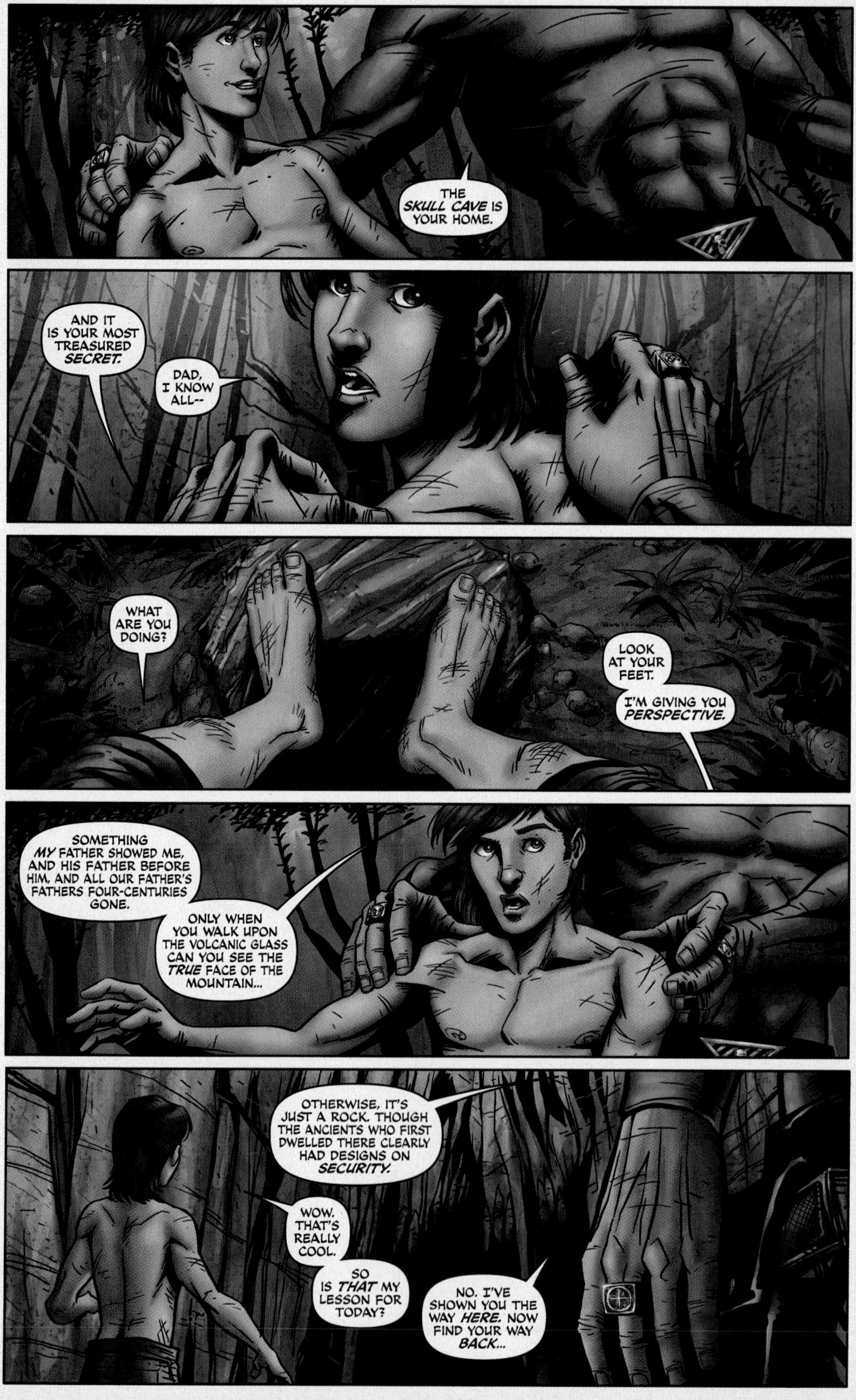
THE SKULL CAVE IS YOUR HOME.
AND IT IS YOUR MOST TREASURED SECRET.
DAD, I KNOW ALL--
WHAT ARE YOU DOING?
LOOK AT YOUR FEET.
I'M GIVING YOU PERSPECTIVE.
SOMETHING MY FATHER SHOWED ME, AND HIS FATHER BEFORE HIM, AND ALL OUR FATHER'S FATHERS FOUR-CENTURIES GONE.
ONLY WHEN YOU WALK UPON THE VOLCANIC GLASS CAN YOU SEE THE TRUE FACE OF THE MOUNTAIN...
OTHERWISE, IT'S JUST A ROCK. THOUGH THE ANCIENTS WHO FIRST DWELLED THERE CLEARLY HAD DESIGNS ON SECURITY.
WOW. THAT'S REALLY COOL.
SO IS THAT MY LESSON FOR TODAY?
NO. I'VE SHOWN YOU THE WAY HERE. NOW FIND YOUR WAY BACK...

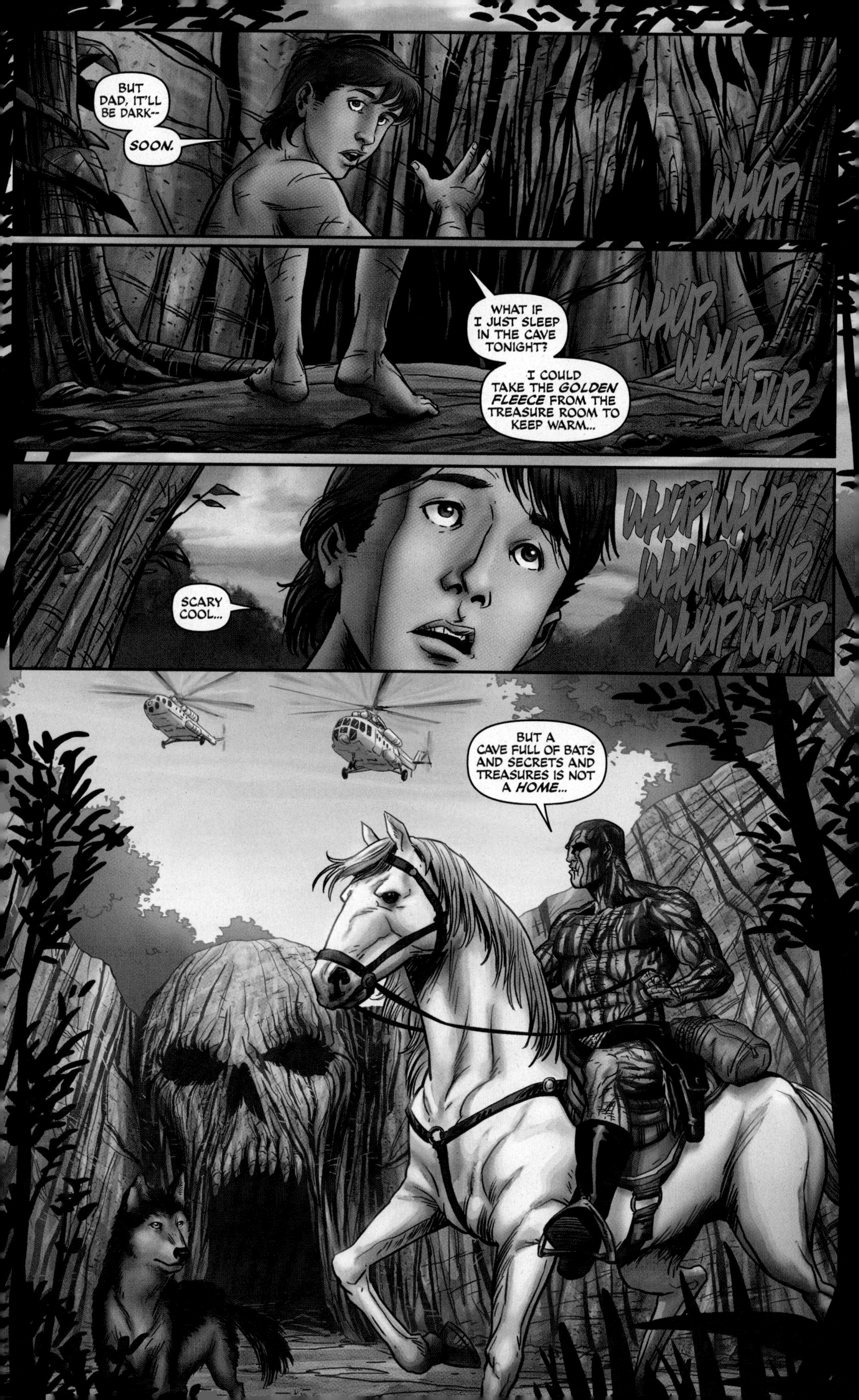
BUT DAD, IT'LL BE DARK--
SOON.
WHUP
WHAT IF I JUST SLEEP IN THE CAVE TONIGHT?
I COULD TAKE THE *GOLDEN FLEECE* FROM THE TREASURE ROOM TO KEEP WARM...
WHUP WHUP WHUP
SCARY COOL...
WHUP WHUP WHUP WHUP WHUP WHUP
BUT A CAVE FULL OF BATS AND SECRETS AND TREASURES IS NOT A *HOME*...

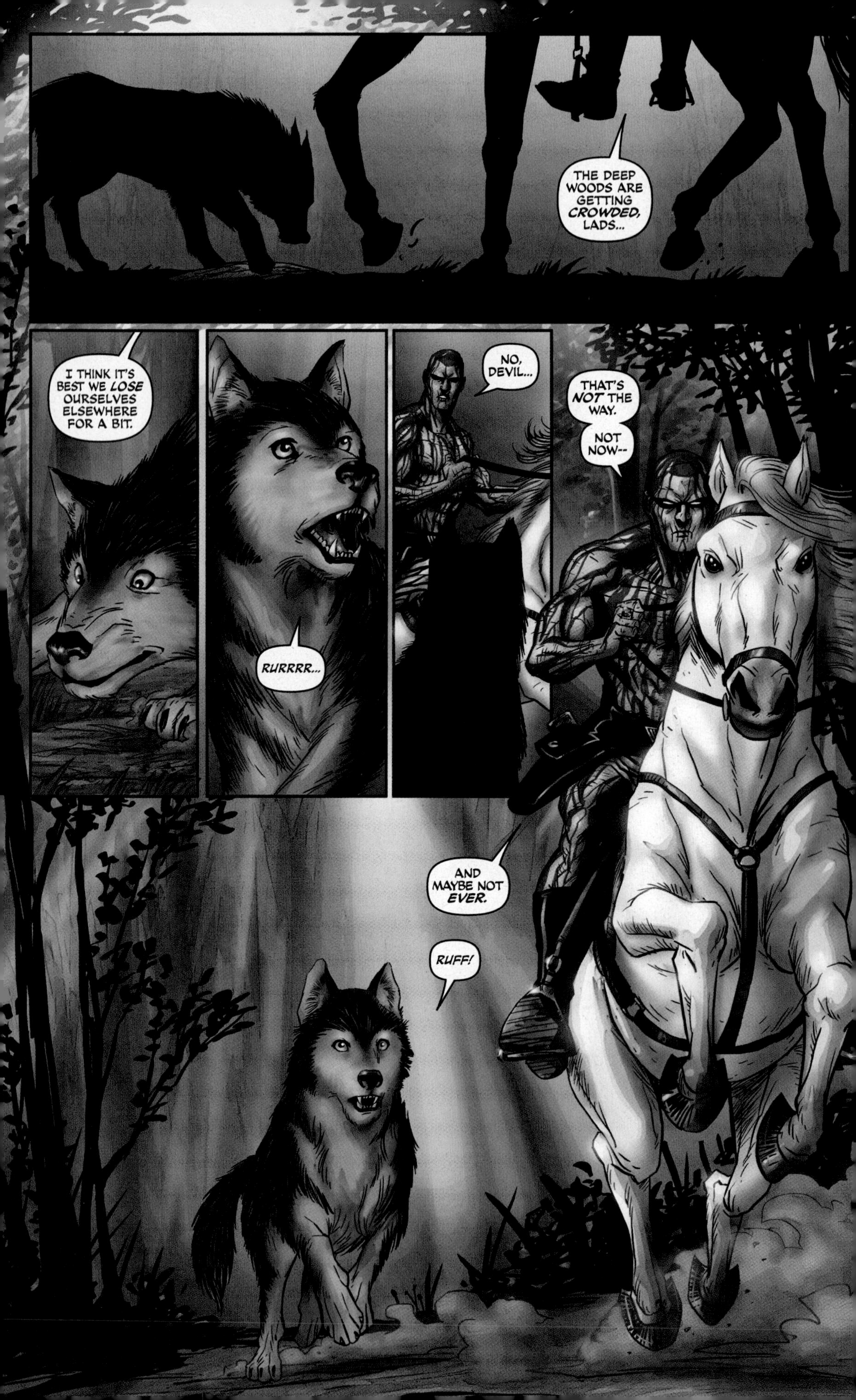
THE DEEP WOODS ARE GETTING *CROWDED,* LADS...
I THINK IT'S BEST WE *LOSE* OURSELVES ELSEWHERE FOR A BIT.
RURRRR...
NO, DEVIL...
THAT'S *NOT* THE WAY.
NOT NOW--
AND MAYBE NOT *EVER.*
RUFF!

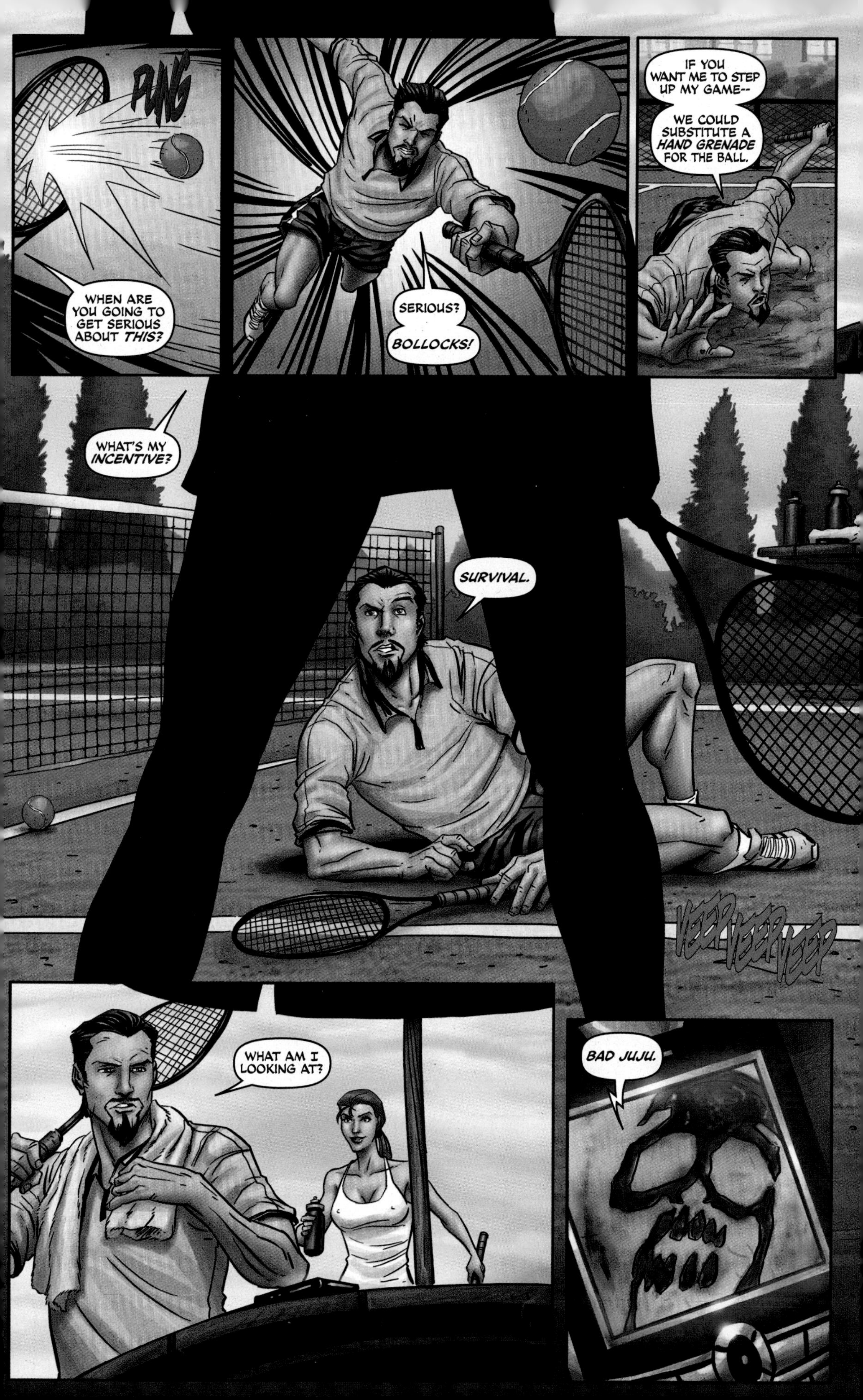
PUNG
WHEN ARE YOU GOING TO GET SERIOUS ABOUT *THIS*?
SERIOUS?
BOLLOCKS!
IF YOU WANT ME TO STEP UP MY GAME--
WE COULD SUBSTITUTE A *HAND GRENADE* FOR THE BALL.
WHAT'S MY *INCENTIVE*?
SURVIVAL.
VEEP VEEP VEEP
WHAT AM I LOOKING AT?
BAD JUJU.

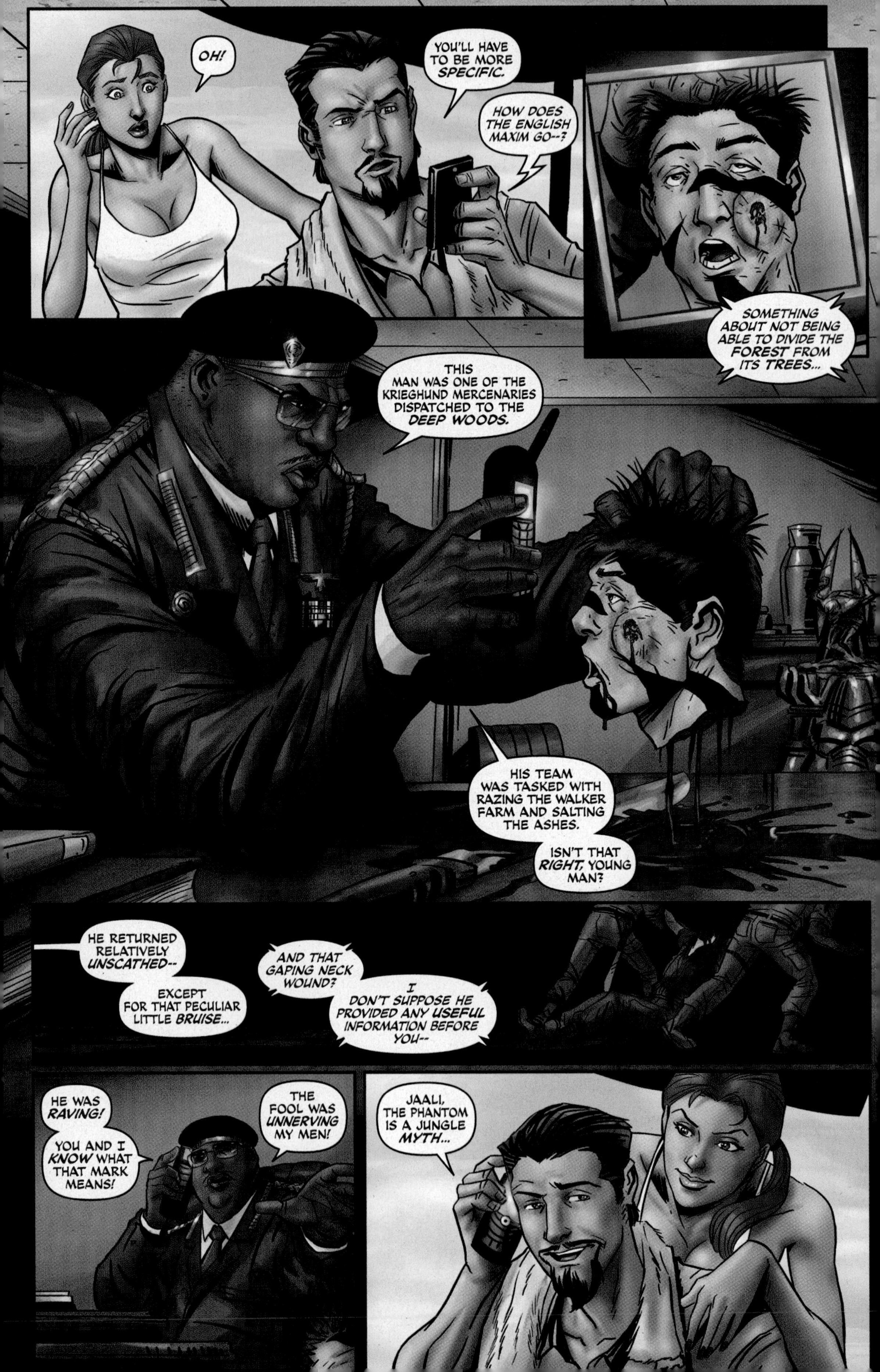
OH!
YOU'LL HAVE TO BE MORE SPECIFIC.
HOW DOES THE ENGLISH MAXIM GO--?
SOMETHING ABOUT NOT BEING ABLE TO DIVIDE THE FOREST FROM ITS TREES...
THIS MAN WAS ONE OF THE KRIEGHUND MERCENARIES DISPATCHED TO THE DEEP WOODS.
HIS TEAM WAS TASKED WITH RAZING THE WALKER FARM AND SALTING THE ASHES.
ISN'T THAT RIGHT, YOUNG MAN?
HE RETURNED RELATIVELY UNSCATHED--
EXCEPT FOR THAT PECULIAR LITTLE BRUISE...
AND THAT GAPING NECK WOUND?
I DON'T SUPPOSE HE PROVIDED ANY USEFUL INFORMATION BEFORE YOU--
HE WAS RAVING!
YOU AND I KNOW WHAT THAT MARK MEANS!
THE FOOL WAS UNNERVING MY MEN!
JAALI, THE PHANTOM IS A JUNGLE MYTH...

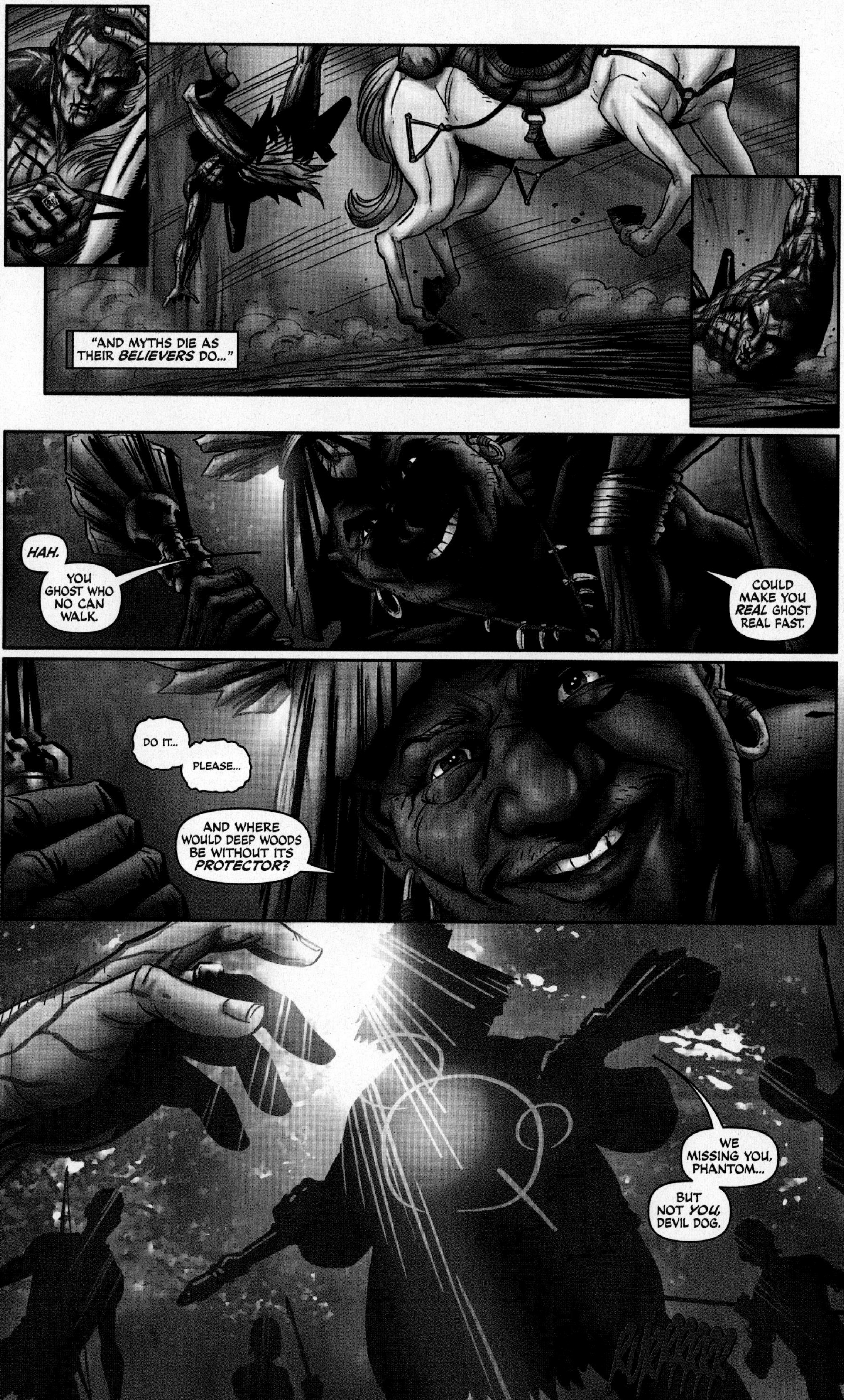
"AND MYTHS DIE AS THEIR BELIEVERS DO..."
HAH.
YOU GHOST WHO NO CAN WALK.
COULD MAKE YOU REAL GHOST REAL FAST.
DO IT...
PLEASE...
AND WHERE WOULD DEEP WOODS BE WITHOUT ITS PROTECTOR?
WE MISSING YOU, PHANTOM...
BUT NOT YOU, DEVIL DOG.

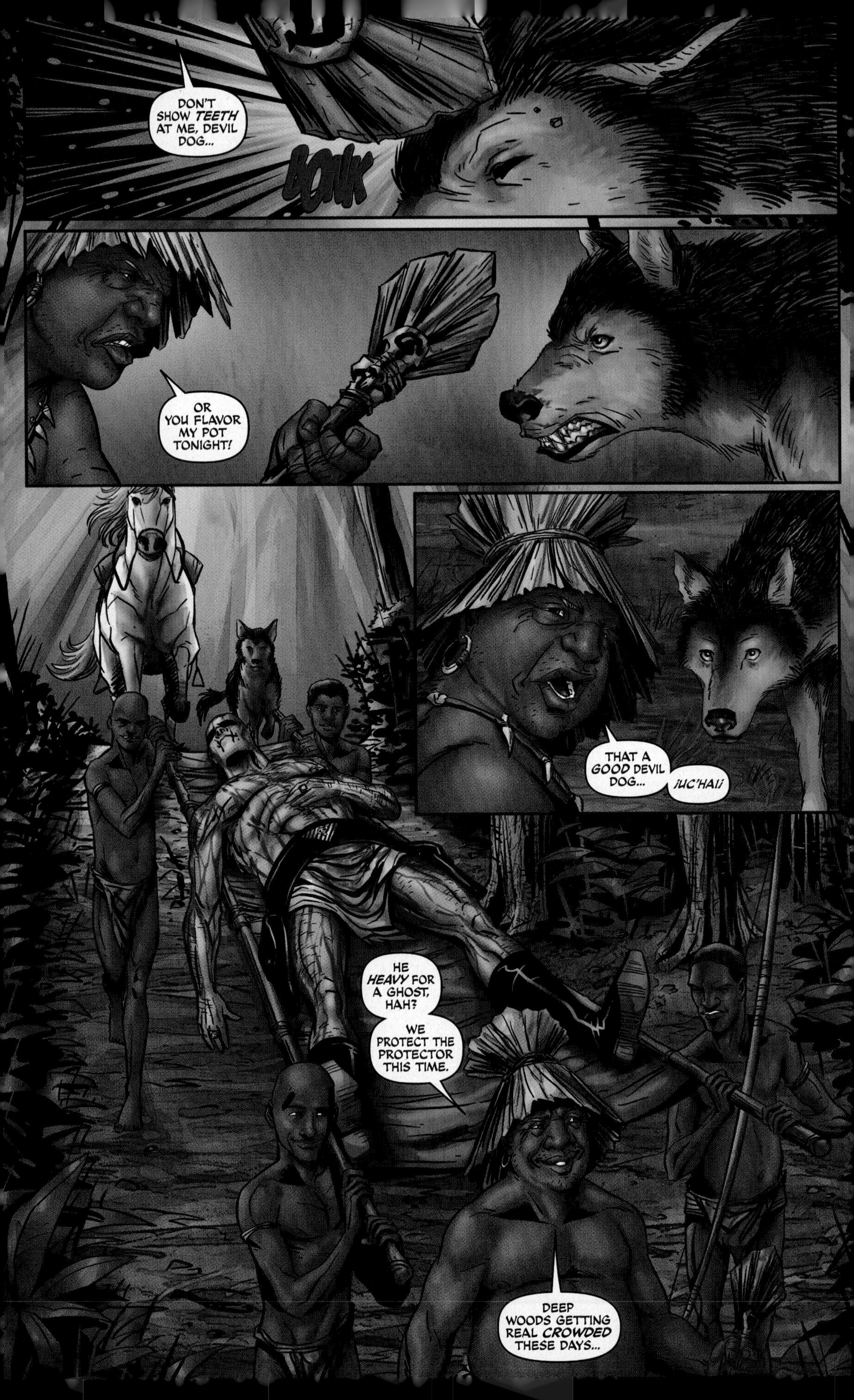
DON'T SHOW *TEETH* AT ME, DEVIL DOG...
BONK
OR YOU FLAVOR MY POT TONIGHT!
THAT A *GOOD* DEVIL DOG...
¡UC'HA!¡
HE *HEAVY* FOR A GHOST, HAH?
WE PROTECT THE PROTECTOR THIS TIME.
DEEP WOODS GETTING REAL *CROWDED* THESE DAYS...

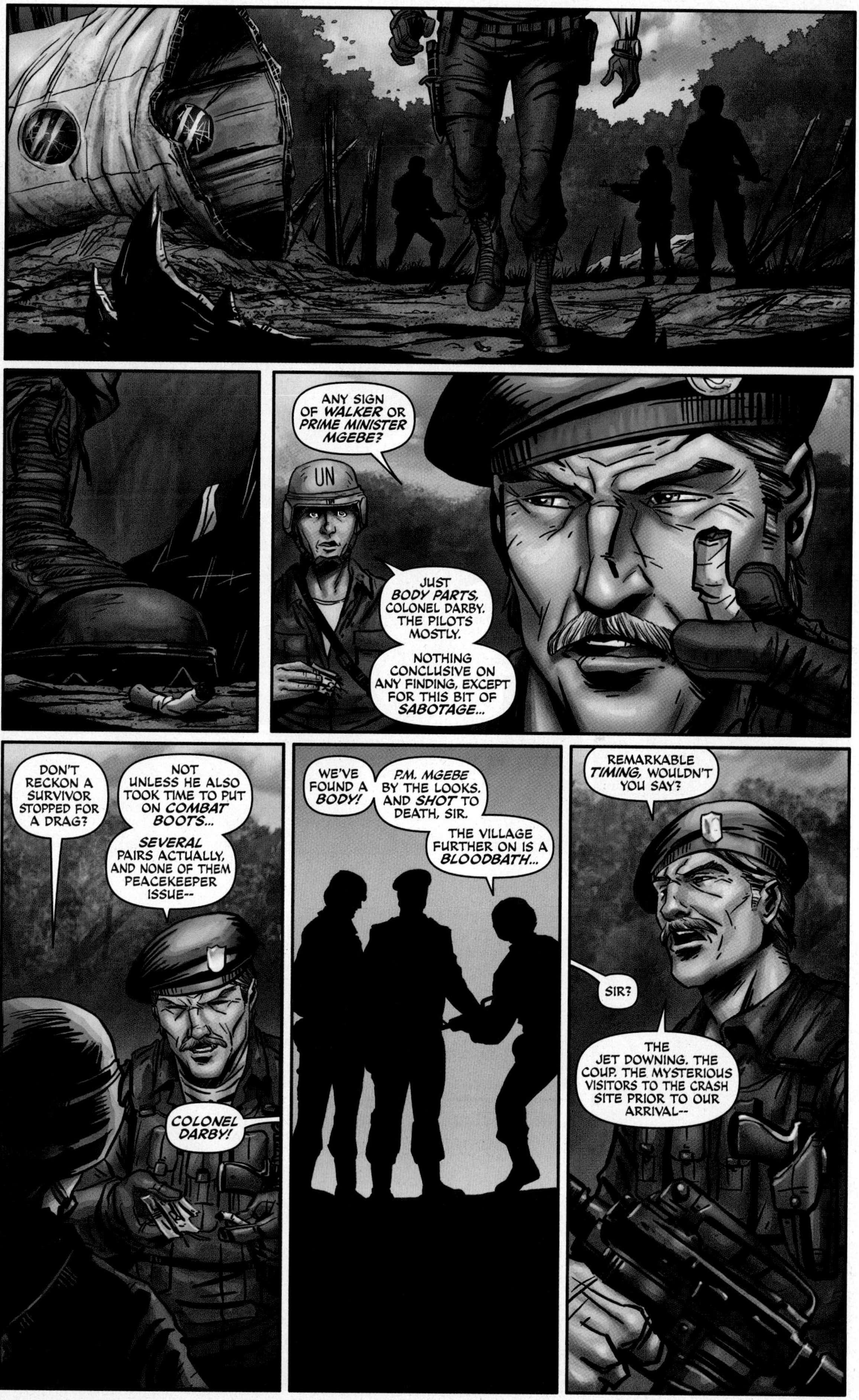
ANY SIGN OF WALKER OR PRIME MINISTER MGEBE?
JUST BODY PARTS, COLONEL DARBY. THE PILOTS MOSTLY.
NOTHING CONCLUSIVE ON ANY FINDING, EXCEPT FOR THIS BIT OF SABOTAGE...
DON'T RECKON A SURVIVOR STOPPED FOR A DRAG?
NOT UNLESS HE ALSO TOOK TIME TO PUT ON COMBAT BOOTS...
SEVERAL PAIRS ACTUALLY, AND NONE OF THEM PEACEKEEPER ISSUE--
COLONEL DARBY!
WE'VE FOUND A BODY!
P.M. MGEBE BY THE LOOKS. AND SHOT TO DEATH, SIR.
THE VILLAGE FURTHER ON IS A BLOODBATH...
REMARKABLE TIMING, WOULDN'T YOU SAY?
SIR?
THE JET DOWNING. THE COUP. THE MYSTERIOUS VISITORS TO THE CRASH SITE PRIOR TO OUR ARRIVAL--

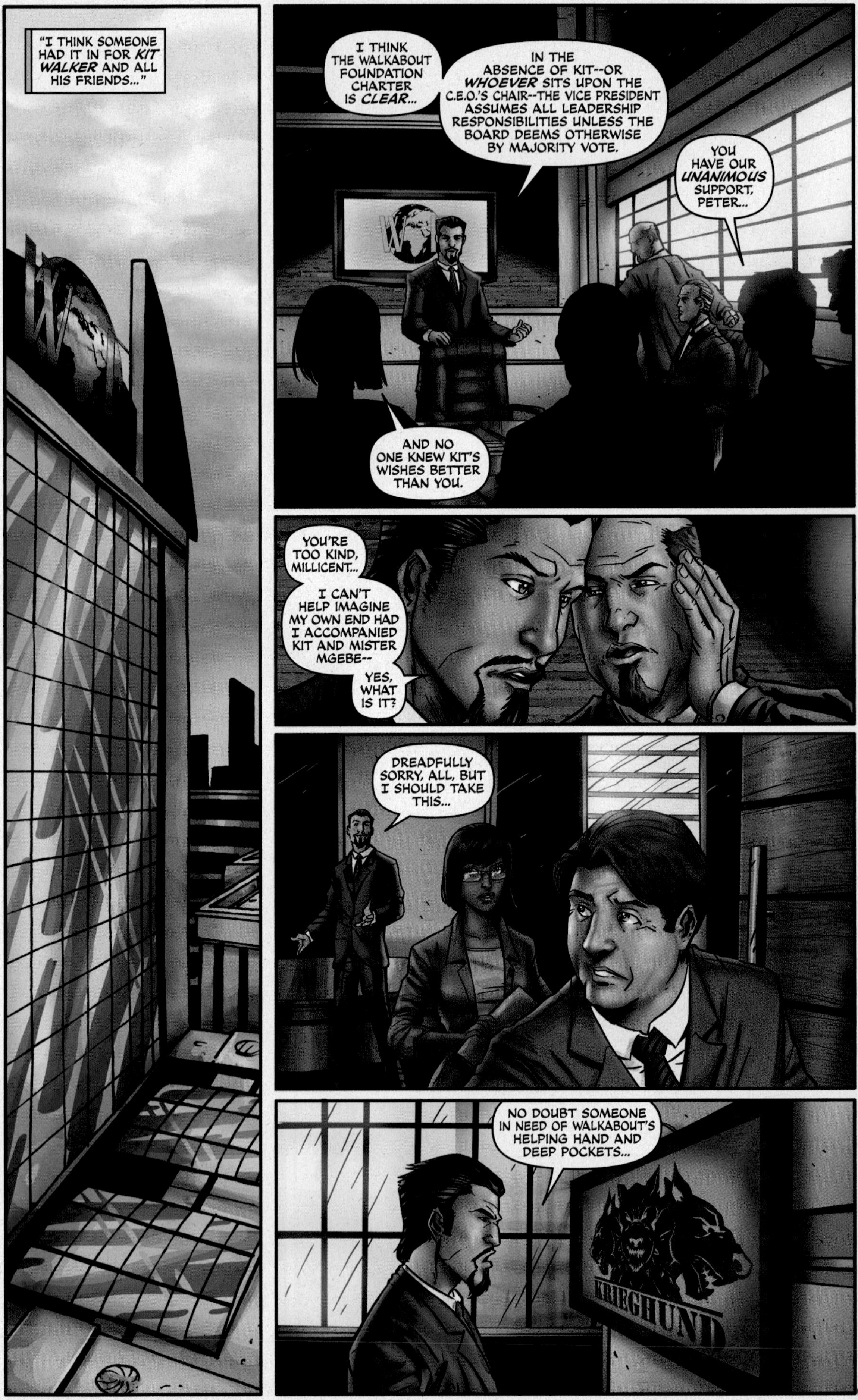
"I THINK SOMEONE HAD IT IN FOR KIT WALKER AND ALL HIS FRIENDS..."
I THINK THE WALKABOUT FOUNDATION CHARTER IS CLEAR...
IN THE ABSENCE OF KIT--OR WHOEVER SITS UPON THE C.E.O.'S CHAIR--THE VICE PRESIDENT ASSUMES ALL LEADERSHIP RESPONSIBILITIES UNLESS THE BOARD DEEMS OTHERWISE BY MAJORITY VOTE.
YOU HAVE OUR UNANIMOUS SUPPORT, PETER...
AND NO ONE KNEW KIT'S WISHES BETTER THAN YOU.
YOU'RE TOO KIND, MILLICENT...
I CAN'T HELP IMAGINE MY OWN END HAD I ACCOMPANIED KIT AND MISTER MGEBE--
YES, WHAT IS IT?
DREADFULLY SORRY, ALL, BUT I SHOULD TAKE THIS...
NO DOUBT SOMEONE IN NEED OF WALKABOUT'S HELPING HAND AND DEEP POCKETS...
KRIEGHUND

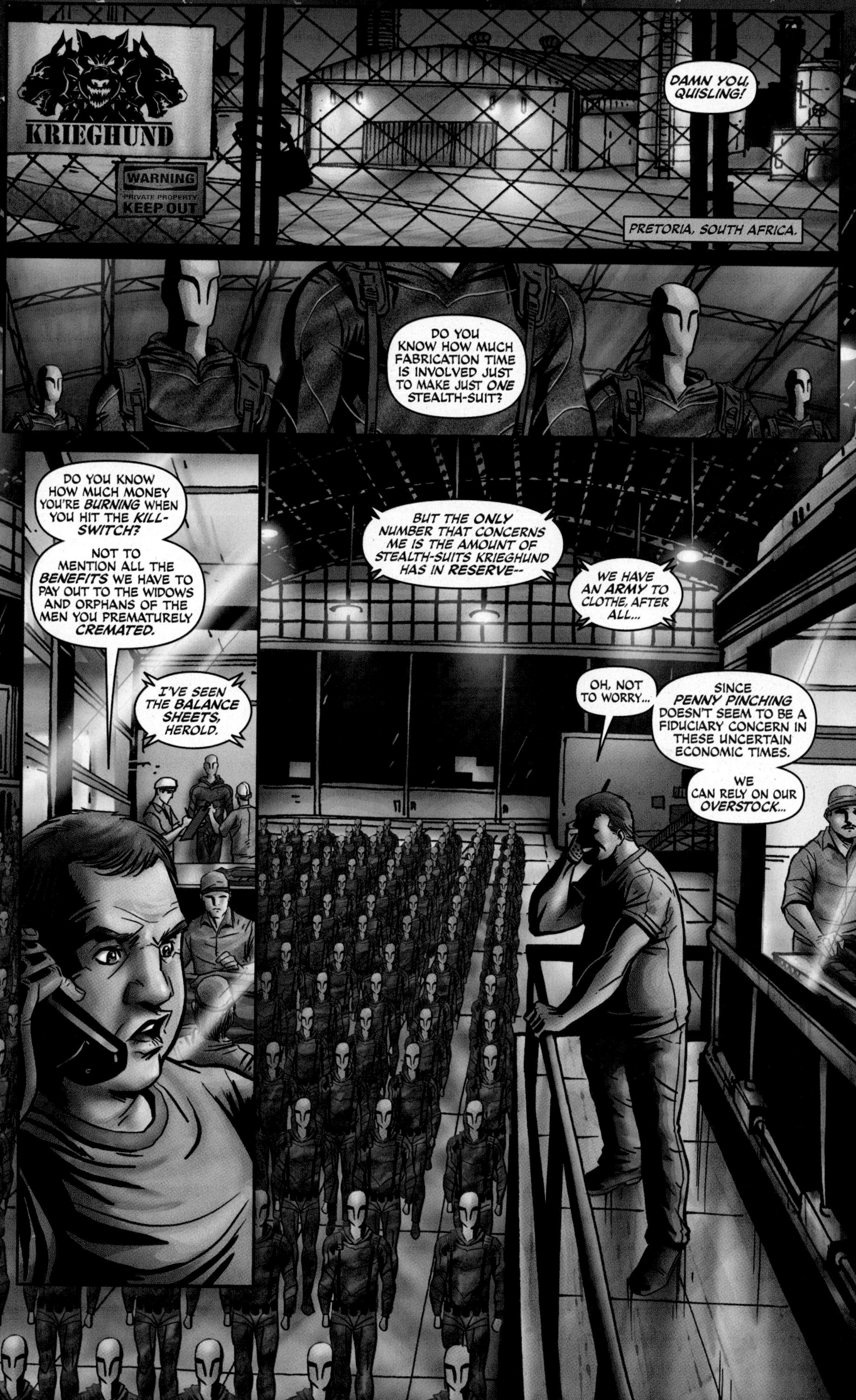
KRIEGHUND
WARNING
PRIVATE PROPERTY
KEEP OUT
DAMN YOU, QUISLING!
PRETORIA, SOUTH AFRICA.
DO YOU KNOW HOW MUCH FABRICATION TIME IS INVOLVED JUST TO MAKE JUST ONE STEALTH-SUIT?
DO YOU KNOW HOW MUCH MONEY YOU'RE BURNING WHEN YOU HIT THE KILL-SWITCH?
NOT TO MENTION ALL THE BENEFITS WE HAVE TO PAY OUT TO THE WIDOWS AND ORPHANS OF THE MEN YOU PREMATURELY CREMATED.
I'VE SEEN THE BALANCE SHEETS, HEROLD.
BUT THE ONLY NUMBER THAT CONCERNS ME IS THE AMOUNT OF STEALTH-SUITS KRIEGHUND HAS IN RESERVE--
WE HAVE AN ARMY TO CLOTHE, AFTER ALL...
OH, NOT TO WORRY...
SINCE PENNY PINCHING DOESN'T SEEM TO BE A FIDUCIARY CONCERN IN THESE UNCERTAIN ECONOMIC TIMES.
WE CAN RELY ON OUR OVERSTOCK...

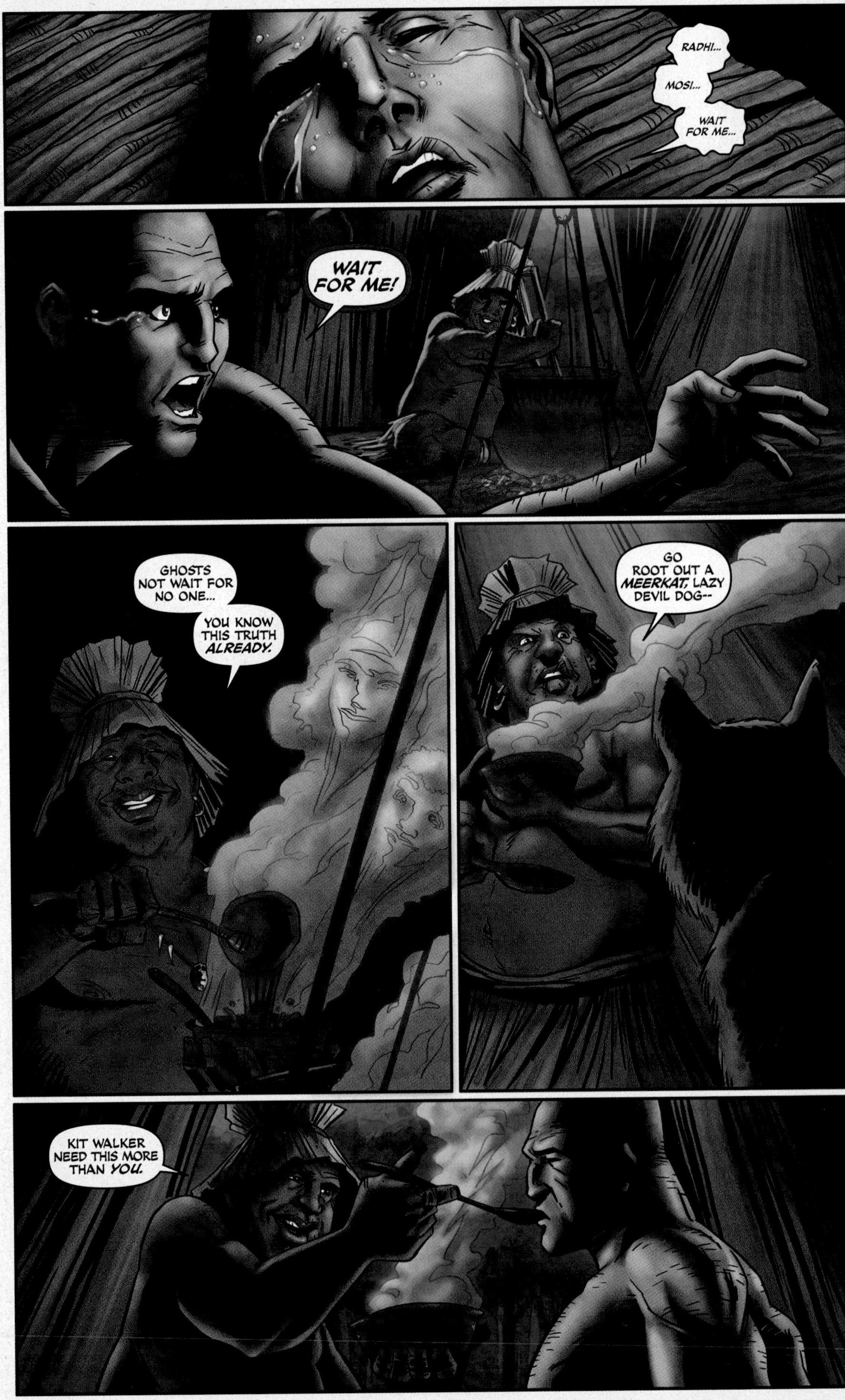
RADHI...
MOSI...
WAIT FOR ME...
WAIT FOR ME!
GHOSTS NOT WAIT FOR NO ONE...
YOU KNOW THIS TRUTH ALREADY.
GO ROOT OUT A MEERKAT, LAZY DEVIL DOG--
KIT WALKER NEED THIS MORE THAN YOU.

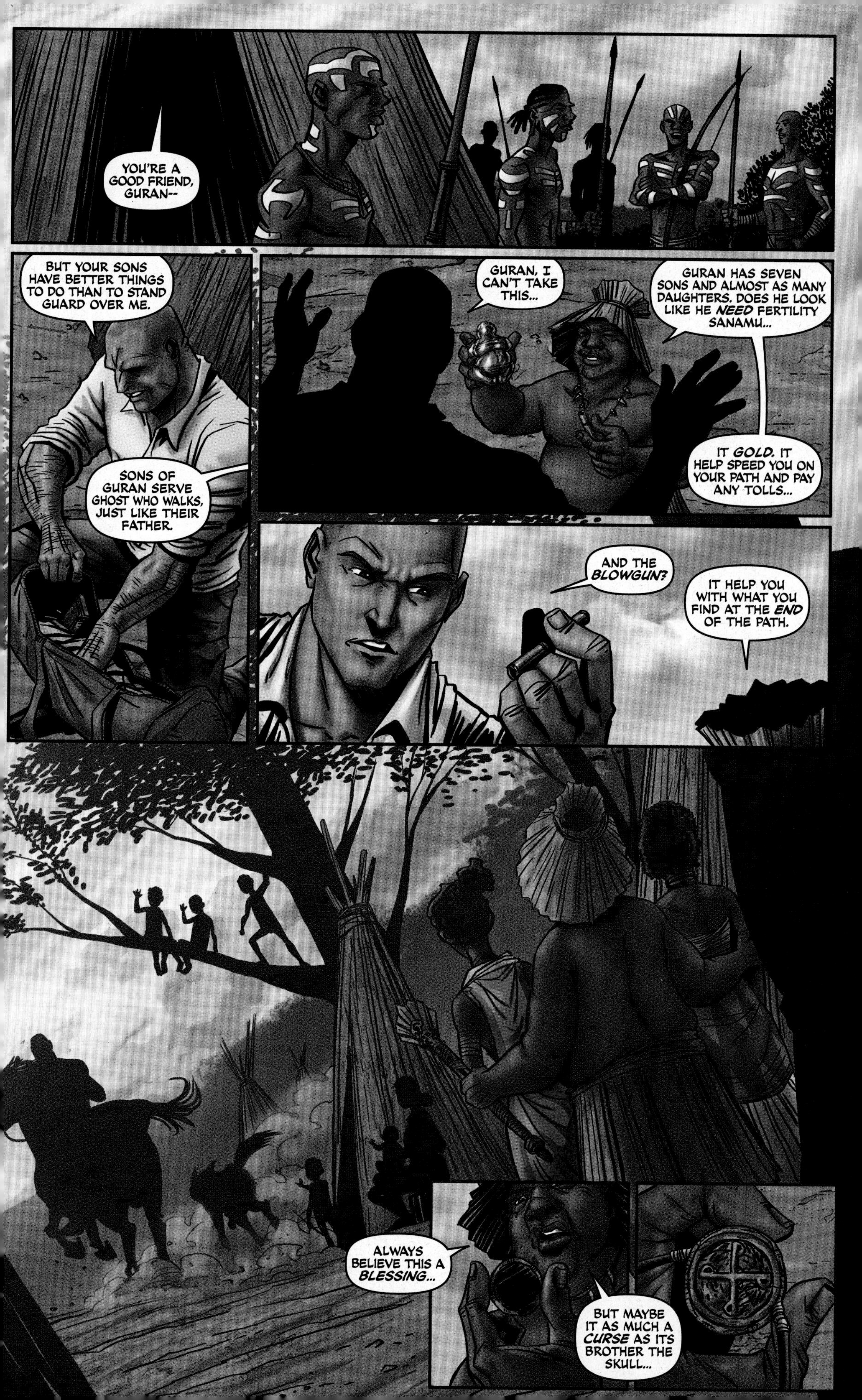

YOU'RE A GOOD FRIEND, GURAN--
BUT YOUR SONS HAVE BETTER THINGS TO DO THAN TO STAND GUARD OVER ME.
SONS OF GURAN SERVE GHOST WHO WALKS, JUST LIKE THEIR FATHER.
GURAN, I CAN'T TAKE THIS...
GURAN HAS SEVEN SONS AND ALMOST AS MANY DAUGHTERS. DOES HE LOOK LIKE HE NEED FERTILITY SANAMU...
IT GOLD. IT HELP SPEED YOU ON YOUR PATH AND PAY ANY TOLLS...
AND THE BLOWGUN?
IT HELP YOU WITH WHAT YOU FIND AT THE END OF THE PATH.
ALWAYS BELIEVE THIS A BLESSING...
BUT MAYBE IT AS MUCH A CURSE AS ITS BROTHER THE SKULL...

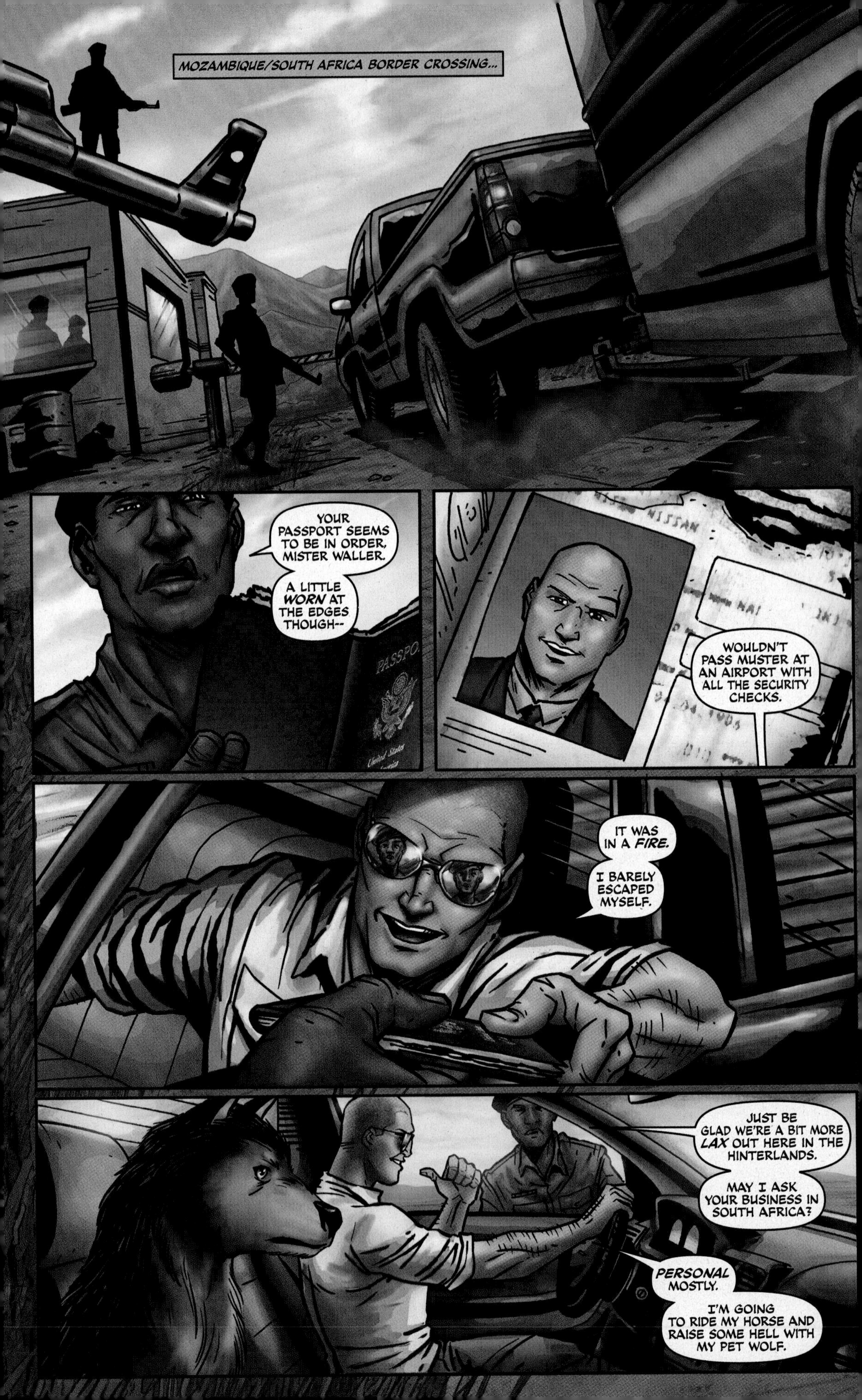
MOZAMBIQUE/SOUTH AFRICA BORDER CROSSING...
YOUR PASSPORT SEEMS TO BE IN ORDER, MISTER WALLER.
A LITTLE WORN AT THE EDGES THOUGH--
PASSPORT
WOULDN'T PASS MUSTER AT AN AIRPORT WITH ALL THE SECURITY CHECKS.
IT WAS IN A FIRE.
I BARELY ESCAPED MYSELF.
JUST BE GLAD WE'RE A BIT MORE LAX OUT HERE IN THE HINTERLANDS.
MAY I ASK YOUR BUSINESS IN SOUTH AFRICA?
PERSONAL MOSTLY.
I'M GOING TO RIDE MY HORSE AND RAISE SOME HELL WITH MY PET WOLF.

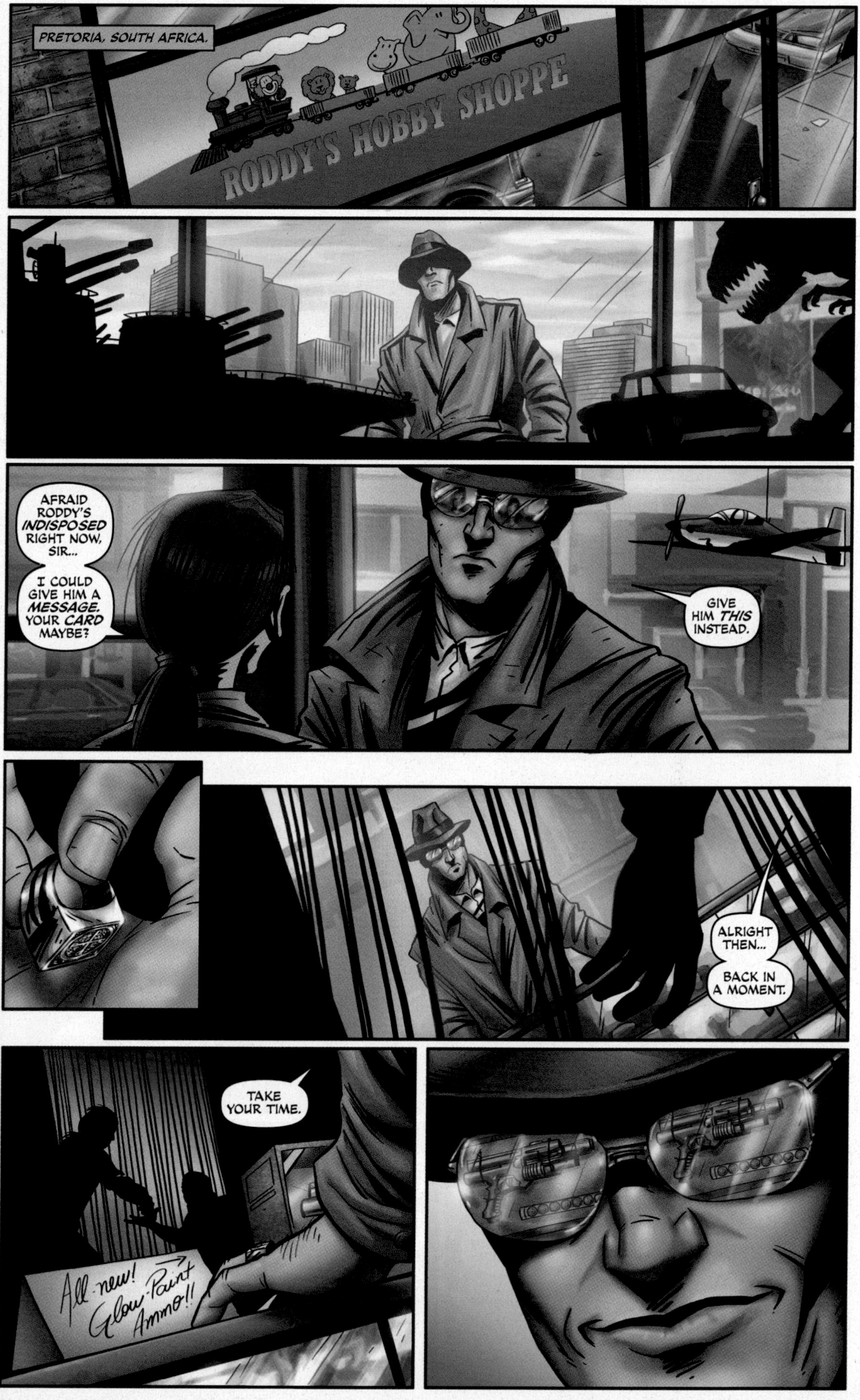
PRETORIA, SOUTH AFRICA.
RODDY'S HOBBY SHOPPE
AFRAID RODDY'S *INDISPOSED* RIGHT NOW, SIR...
I COULD GIVE HIM A *MESSAGE*. YOUR *CARD* MAYBE?
GIVE HIM *THIS* INSTEAD.
ALRIGHT THEN...
BACK IN A MOMENT.
TAKE YOUR TIME.
All-new! Glow-Paint Ammo!!

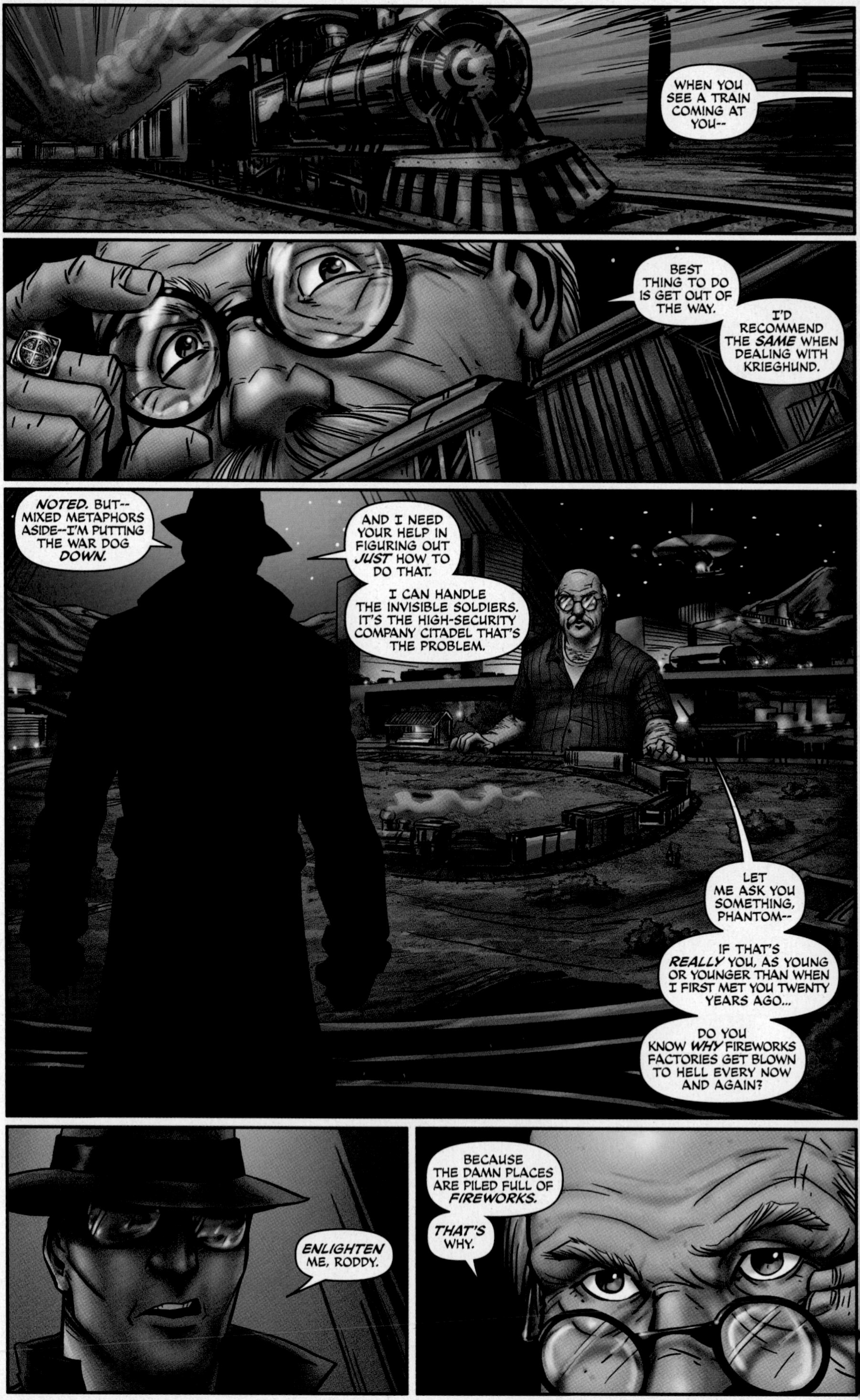
WHEN YOU SEE A TRAIN COMING AT YOU--
BEST THING TO DO IS GET OUT OF THE WAY.
I'D RECOMMEND THE SAME WHEN DEALING WITH KRIEGHUND.
NOTED. BUT--MIXED METAPHORS ASIDE--I'M PUTTING THE WAR DOG DOWN.
AND I NEED YOUR HELP IN FIGURING OUT JUST HOW TO DO THAT.
I CAN HANDLE THE INVISIBLE SOLDIERS. IT'S THE HIGH-SECURITY COMPANY CITADEL THAT'S THE PROBLEM.
LET ME ASK YOU SOMETHING, PHANTOM--
IF THAT'S REALLY YOU, AS YOUNG OR YOUNGER THAN WHEN I FIRST MET YOU TWENTY YEARS AGO...
DO YOU KNOW WHY FIREWORKS FACTORIES GET BLOWN TO HELL EVERY NOW AND AGAIN?
ENLIGHTEN ME, RODDY.
BECAUSE THE DAMN PLACES ARE PILED FULL OF FIREWORKS.
THAT'S WHY.

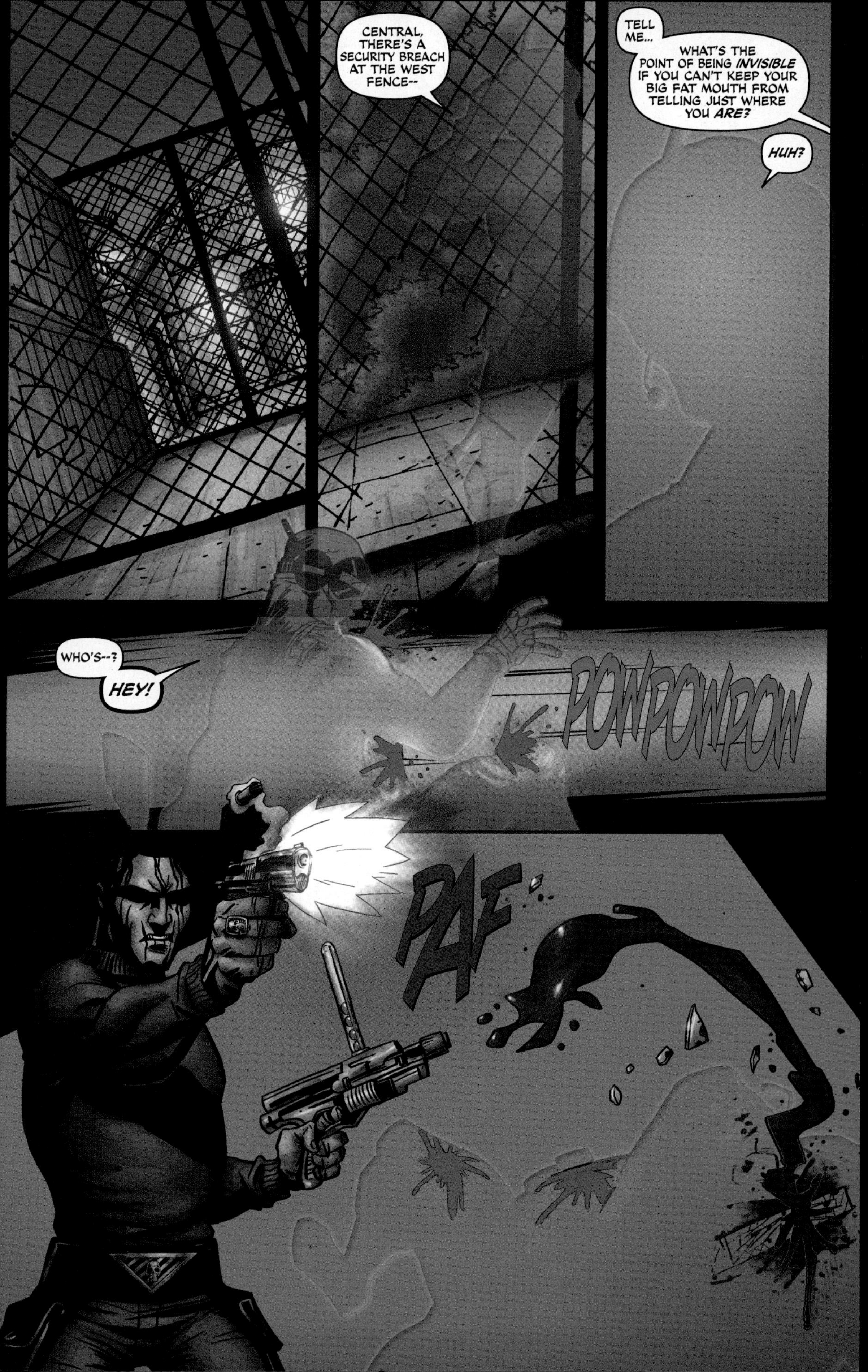

CENTRAL, THERE'S A SECURITY BREACH AT THE WEST FENCE--
TELL ME...
WHAT'S THE POINT OF BEING *INVISIBLE* IF YOU CAN'T KEEP YOUR BIG FAT MOUTH FROM TELLING JUST WHERE YOU *ARE?*
HUH?
WHO'S--?
HEY!
POWPOWPOW
PAF

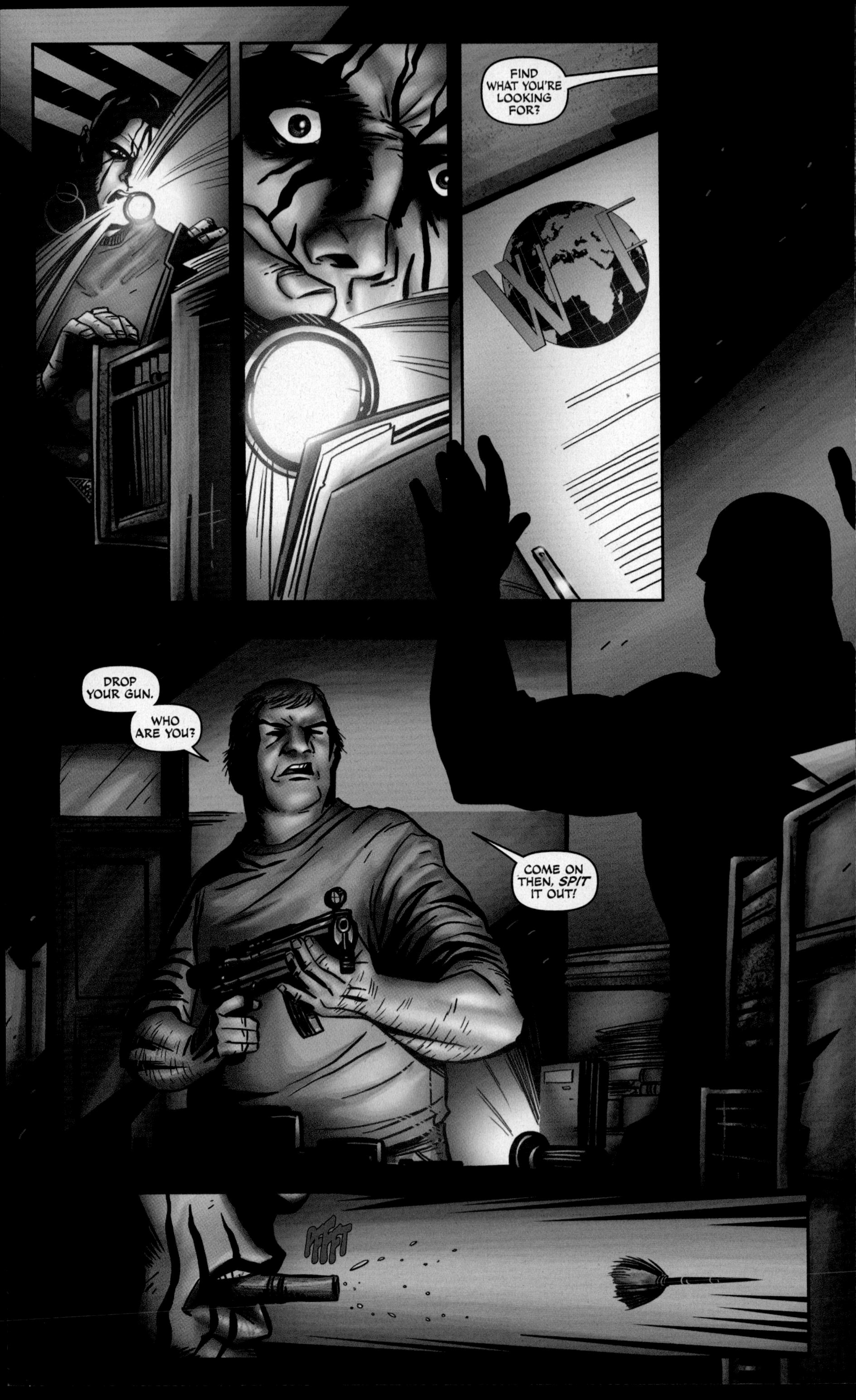
FIND WHAT YOU'RE LOOKING FOR?
DROP YOUR GUN.
WHO ARE YOU?
COME ON THEN, *SPIT* IT OUT!
PTFFT

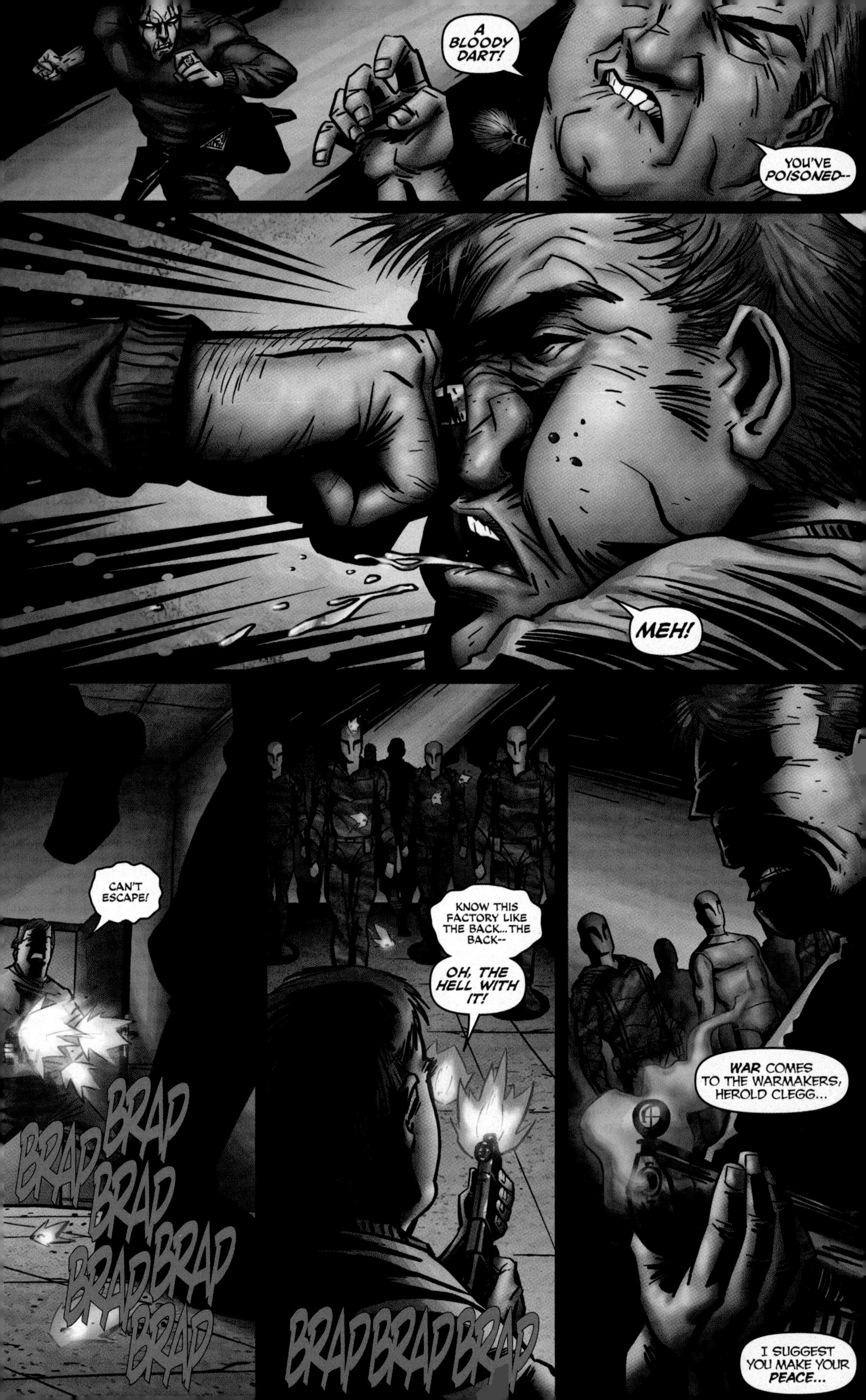
A BLOODY DART!
YOU'VE POISONED--
MEH!
CAN'T ESCAPE!
BRAP BRAP BRAP BRAP BRAP BRAP
KNOW THIS FACTORY LIKE THE BACK...THE BACK--
OH, THE HELL WITH IT!
BRAP BRAP BRAP
WAR COMES TO THE WARMAKERS, HEROLD CLEGG...
I SUGGEST YOU MAKE YOUR PEACE...

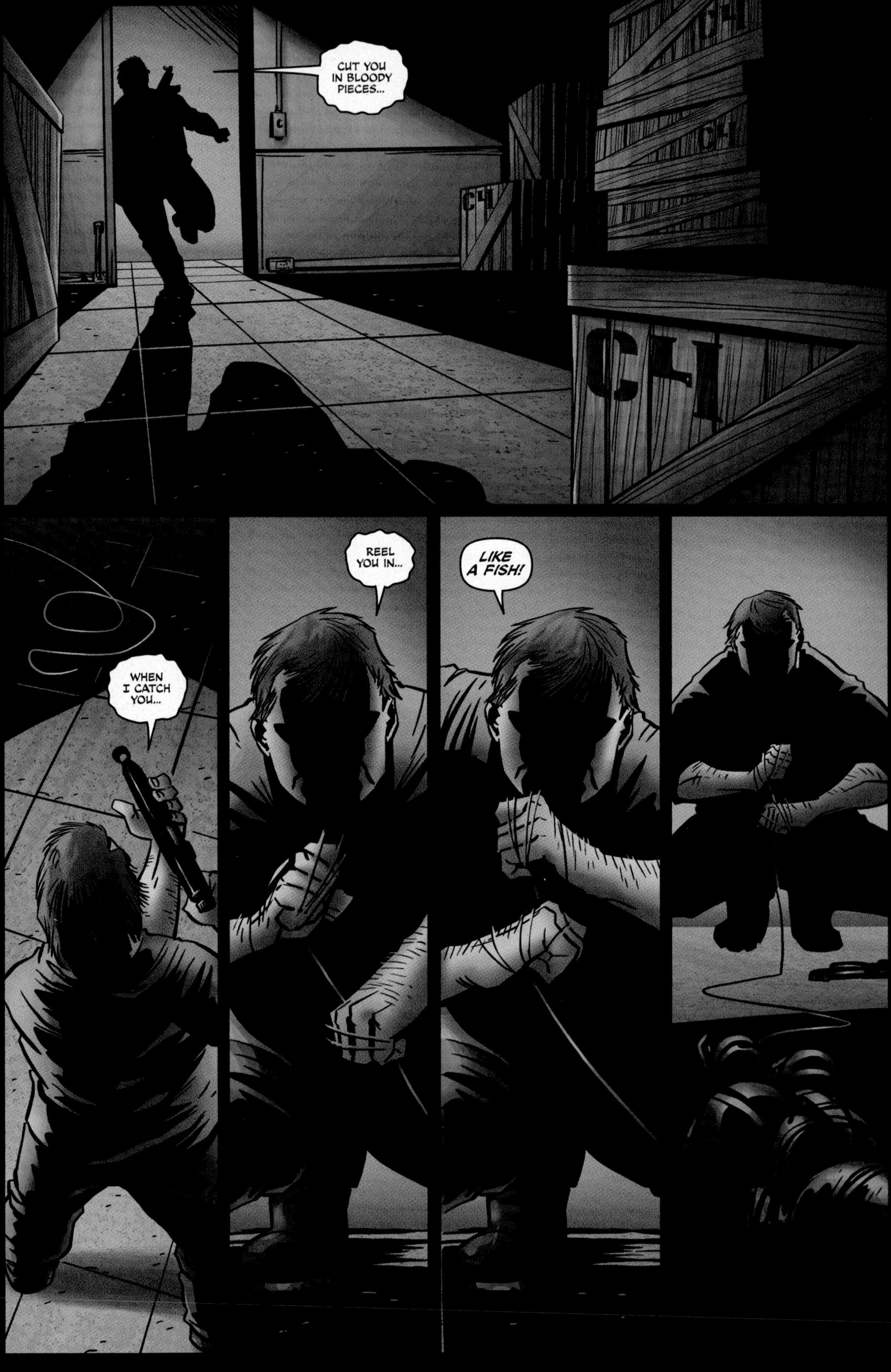
CUT YOU IN BLOODY PIECES...
WHEN I CATCH YOU...
REEL YOU IN...
LIKE A FISH!

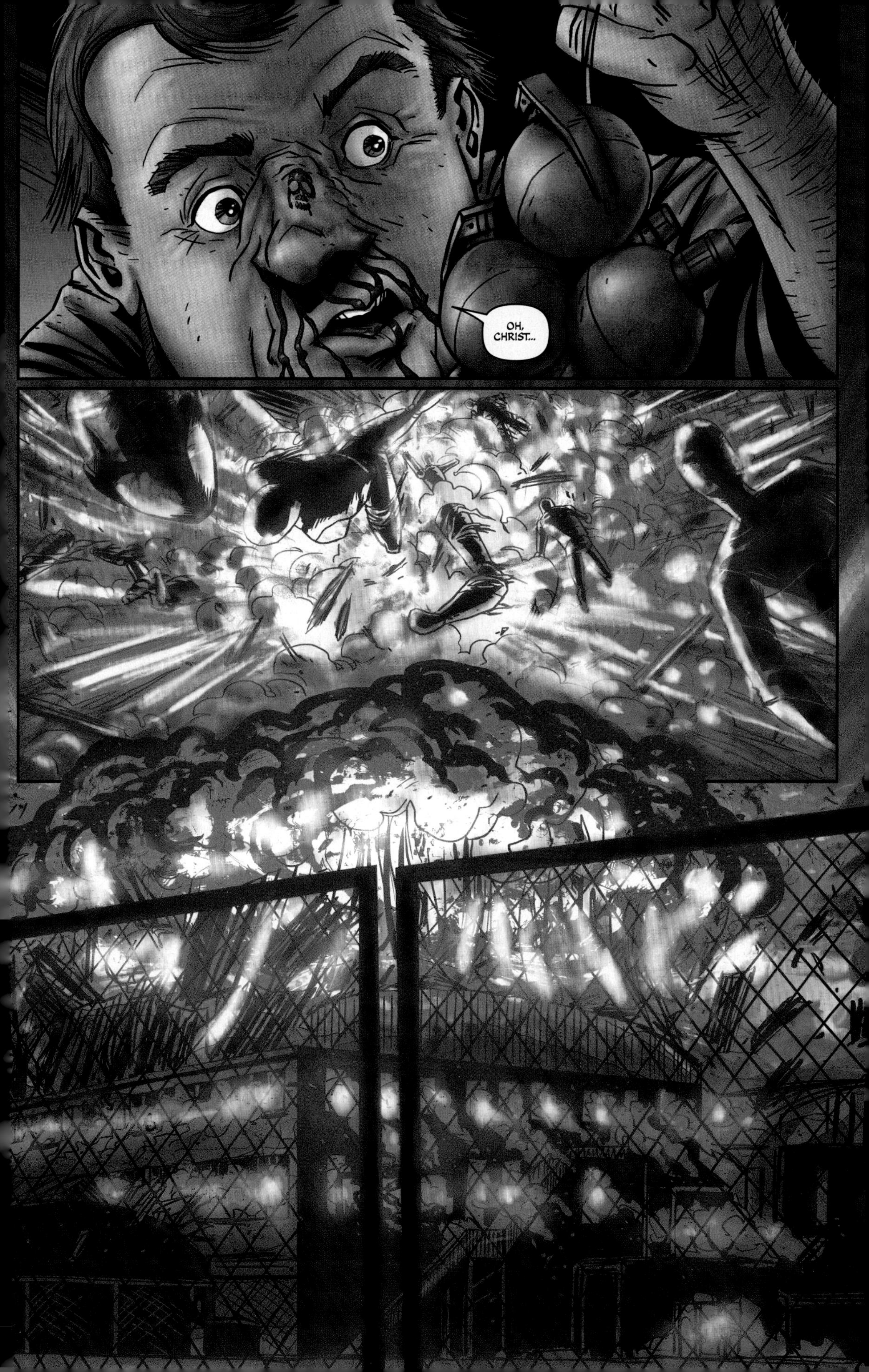
OH, CHRIST...

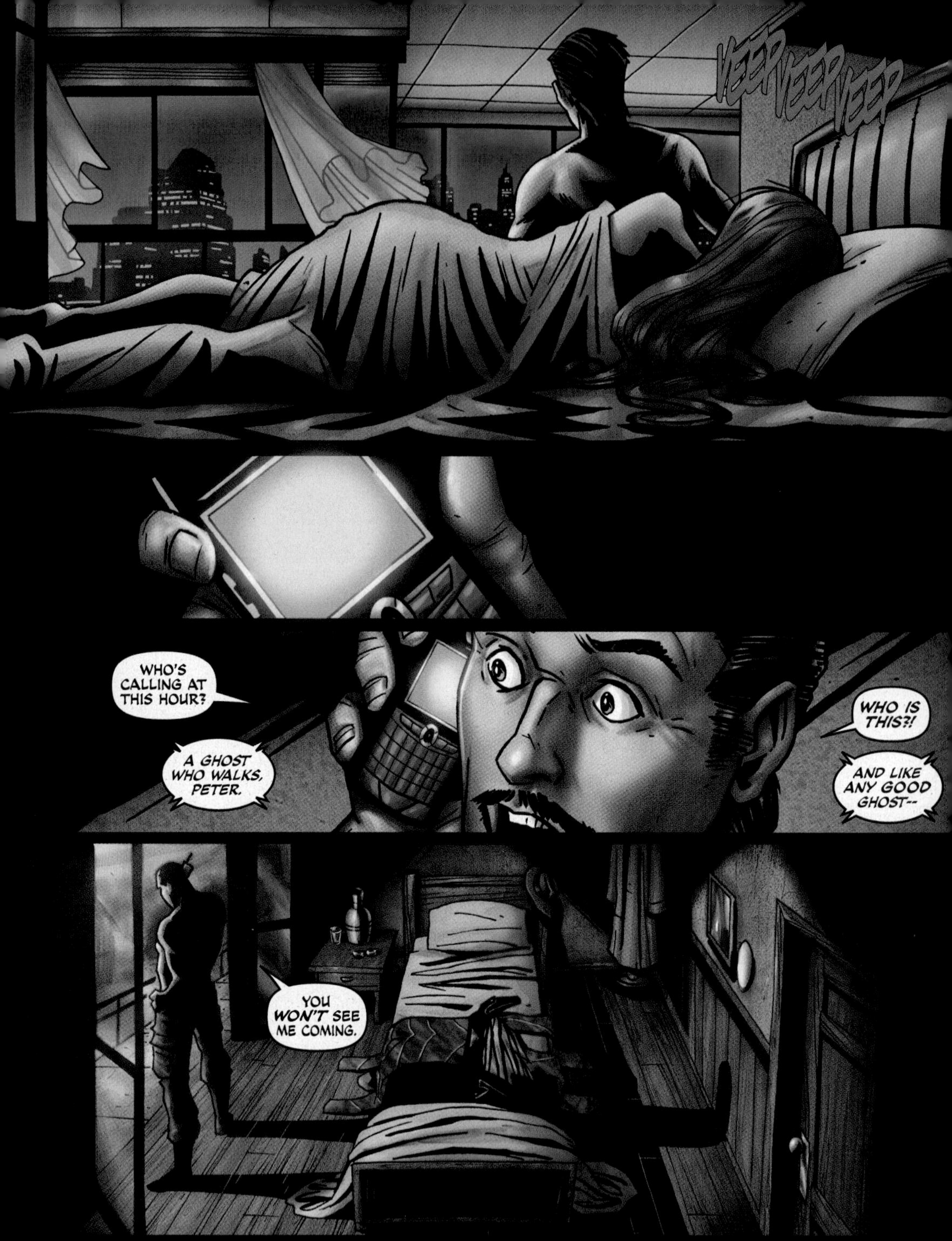
VEEP VEEP VEEP
WHO'S CALLING AT THIS HOUR?
A GHOST WHO WALKS, PETER.
WHO IS THIS?!
AND LIKE ANY GOOD GHOST--
YOU WON'T SEE ME COMING.

GHOSTWALK

chapter three: THE WARMAKERS

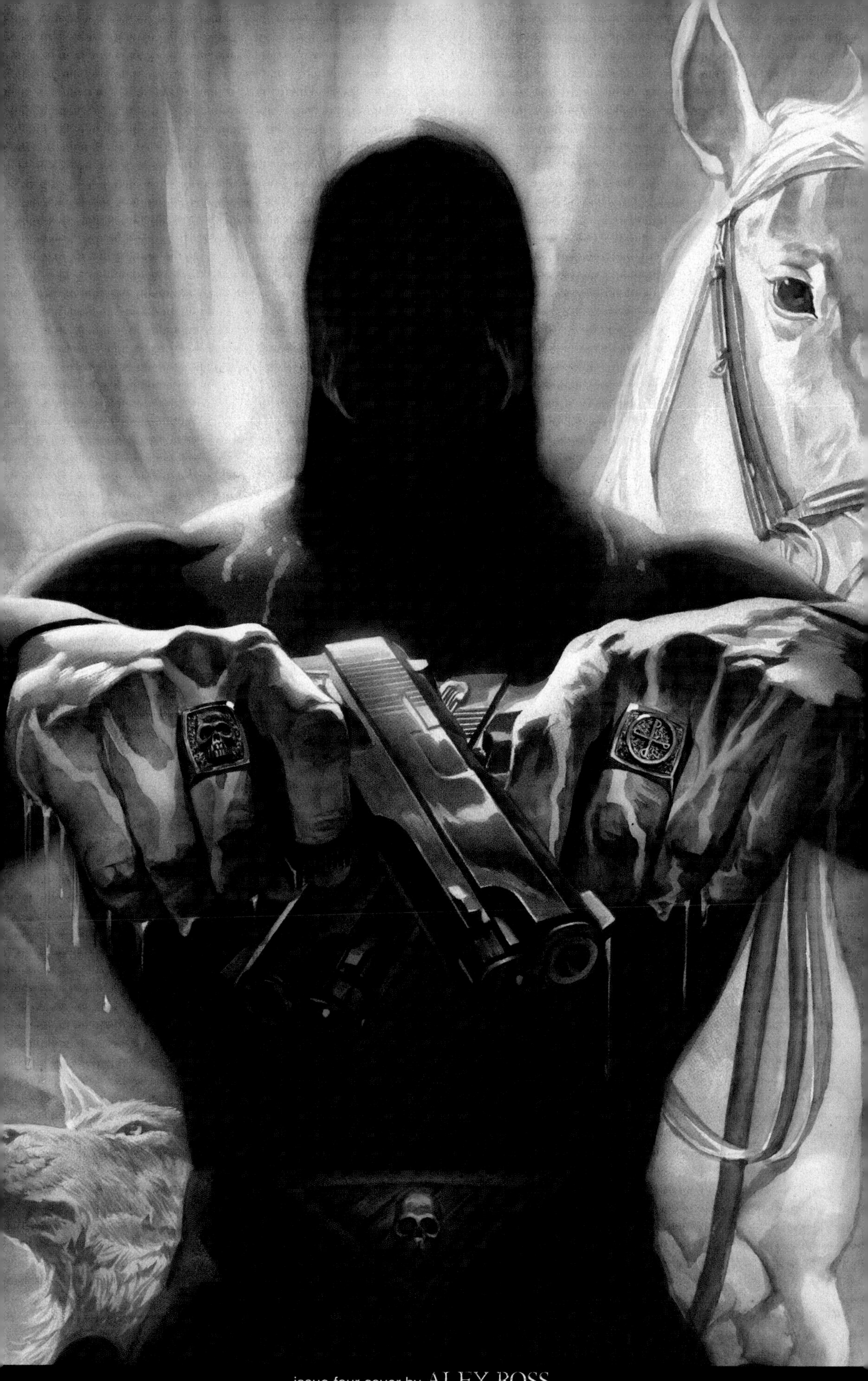

issue four cover by ALEX ROSS

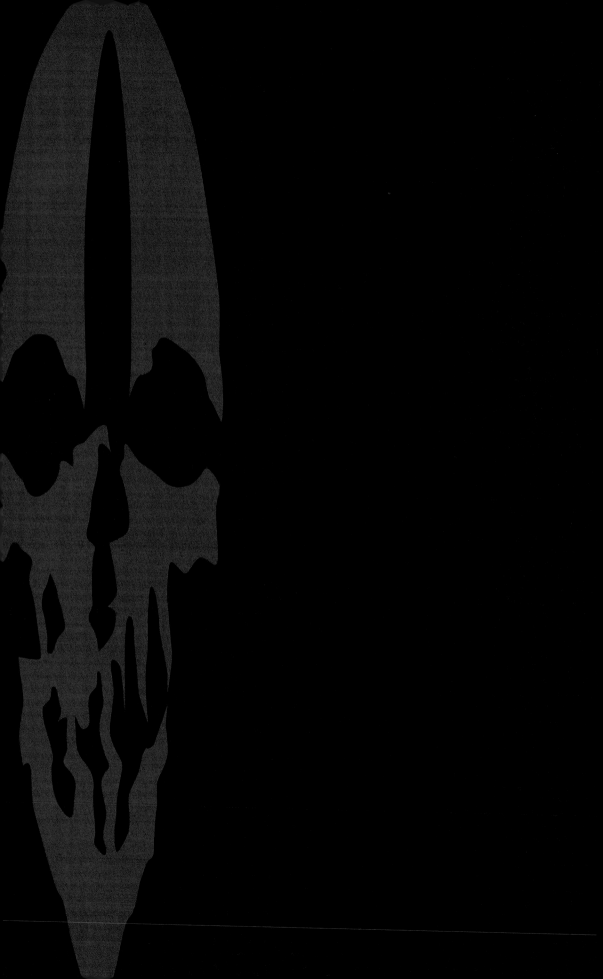

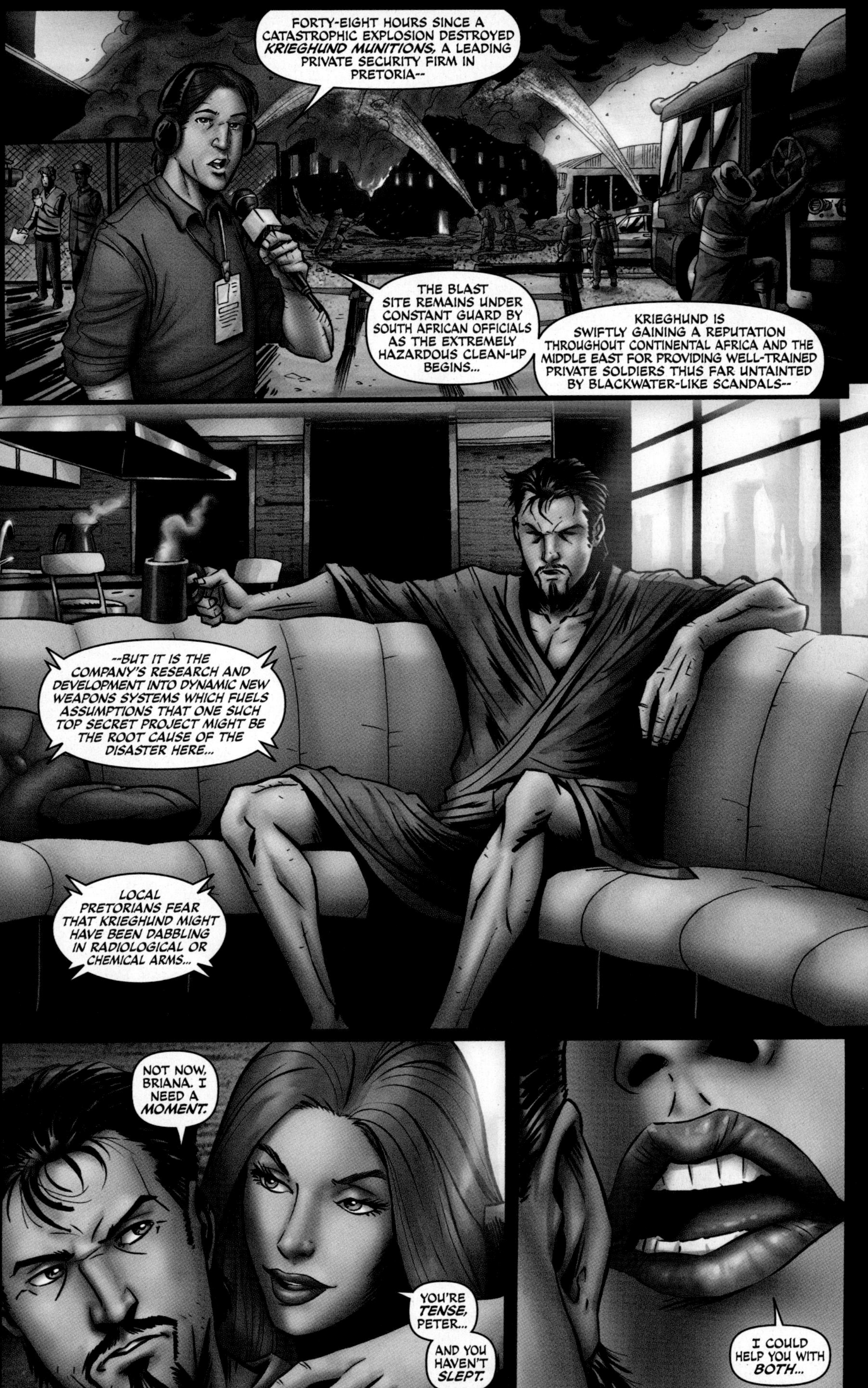
FORTY-EIGHT HOURS SINCE A CATASTROPHIC EXPLOSION DESTROYED KRIEGHUND MUNITIONS, A LEADING PRIVATE SECURITY FIRM IN PRETORIA--
THE BLAST SITE REMAINS UNDER CONSTANT GUARD BY SOUTH AFRICAN OFFICIALS AS THE EXTREMELY HAZARDOUS CLEAN-UP BEGINS...
KRIEGHUND IS SWIFTLY GAINING A REPUTATION THROUGHOUT CONTINENTAL AFRICA AND THE MIDDLE EAST FOR PROVIDING WELL-TRAINED PRIVATE SOLDIERS THUS FAR UNTAINTED BY BLACKWATER-LIKE SCANDALS--
--BUT IT IS THE COMPANY'S RESEARCH AND DEVELOPMENT INTO DYNAMIC NEW WEAPONS SYSTEMS WHICH FUELS ASSUMPTIONS THAT ONE SUCH TOP SECRET PROJECT MIGHT BE THE ROOT CAUSE OF THE DISASTER HERE...
LOCAL PRETORIANS FEAR THAT KRIEGHUND MIGHT HAVE BEEN DABBLING IN RADIOLOGICAL OR CHEMICAL ARMS...
NOT NOW, BRIANA. I NEED A MOMENT.
YOU'RE TENSE, PETER...
AND YOU HAVEN'T SLEPT.
I COULD HELP YOU WITH BOTH...

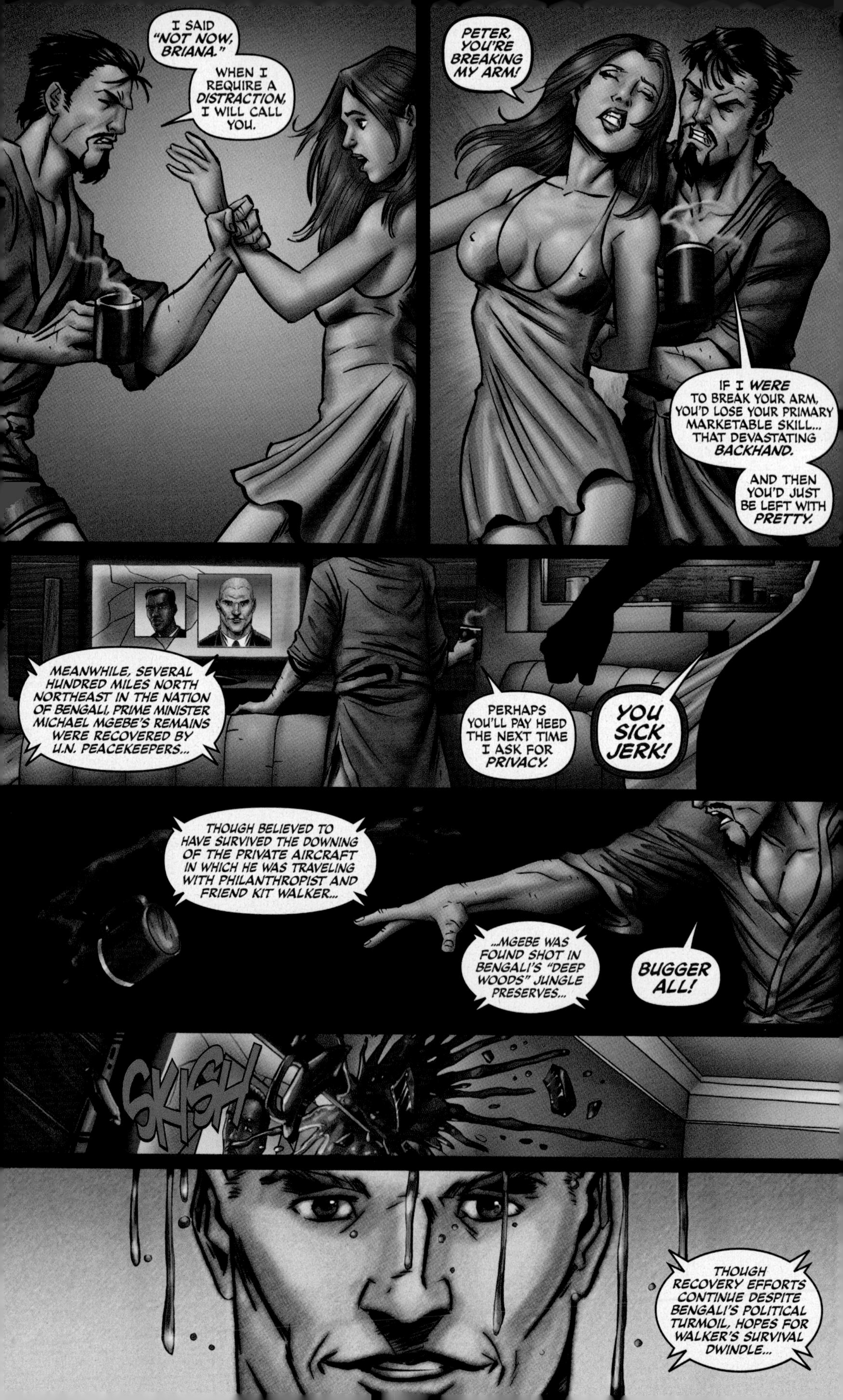

I SAID "NOT NOW, BRIANA."
WHEN I REQUIRE A DISTRACTION, I WILL CALL YOU.
PETER, YOU'RE BREAKING MY ARM!
IF I WERE TO BREAK YOUR ARM, YOU'D LOSE YOUR PRIMARY MARKETABLE SKILL... THAT DEVASTATING BACKHAND.
AND THEN YOU'D JUST BE LEFT WITH PRETTY.
MEANWHILE, SEVERAL HUNDRED MILES NORTH NORTHEAST IN THE NATION OF BENGALI, PRIME MINISTER MICHAEL MGEBE'S REMAINS WERE RECOVERED BY U.N. PEACEKEEPERS...
PERHAPS YOU'LL PAY HEED THE NEXT TIME I ASK FOR PRIVACY.
YOU SICK JERK!
THOUGH BELIEVED TO HAVE SURVIVED THE DOWNING OF THE PRIVATE AIRCRAFT IN WHICH HE WAS TRAVELING WITH PHILANTHROPIST AND FRIEND KIT WALKER...
...MGEBE WAS FOUND SHOT IN BENGALI'S "DEEP WOODS" JUNGLE PRESERVES...
BUGGER ALL!
SKISH
THOUGH RECOVERY EFFORTS CONTINUE DESPITE BENGALI'S POLITICAL TURMOIL, HOPES FOR WALKER'S SURVIVAL DWINDLE...

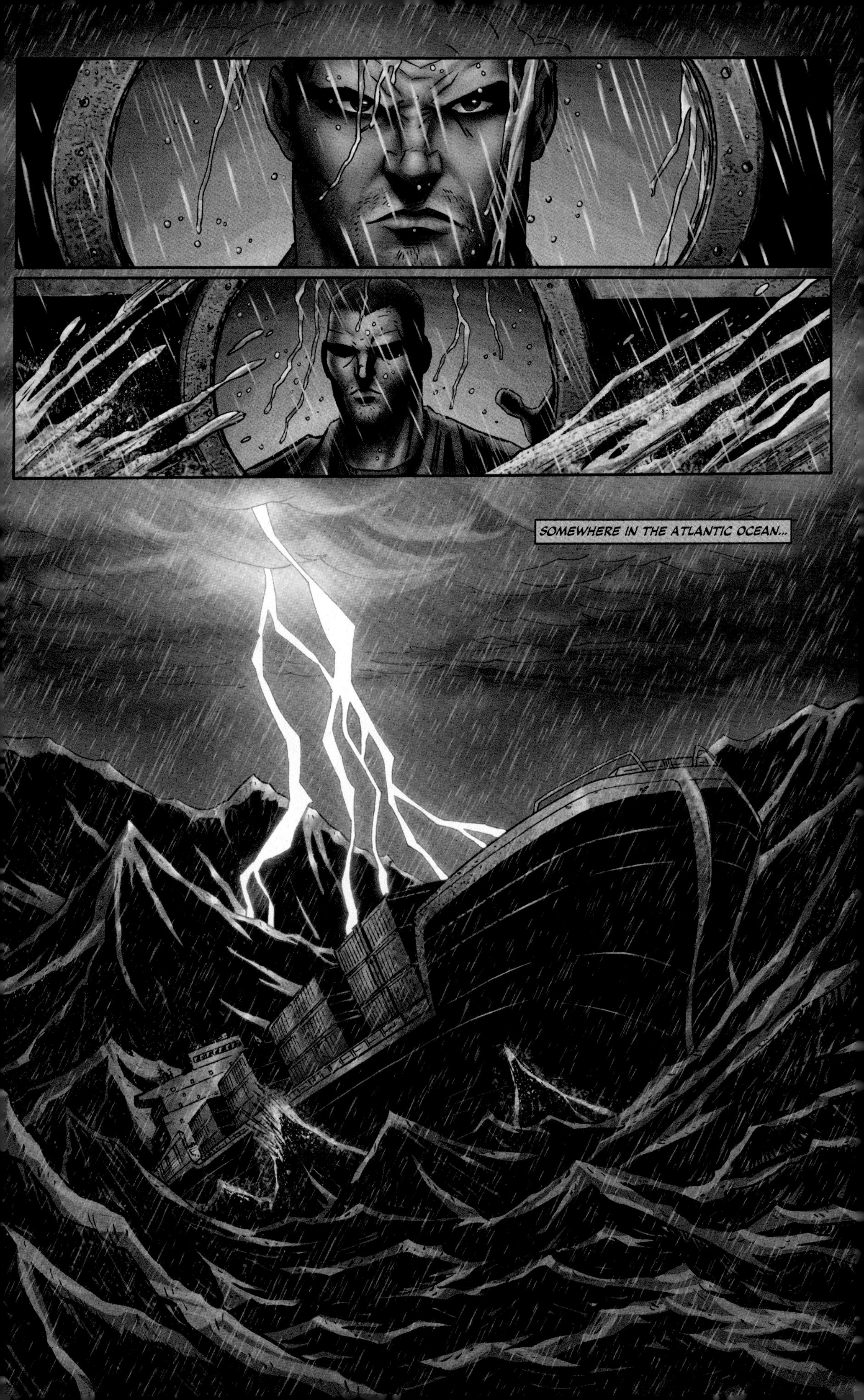
SOMEWHERE IN THE ATLANTIC OCEAN...

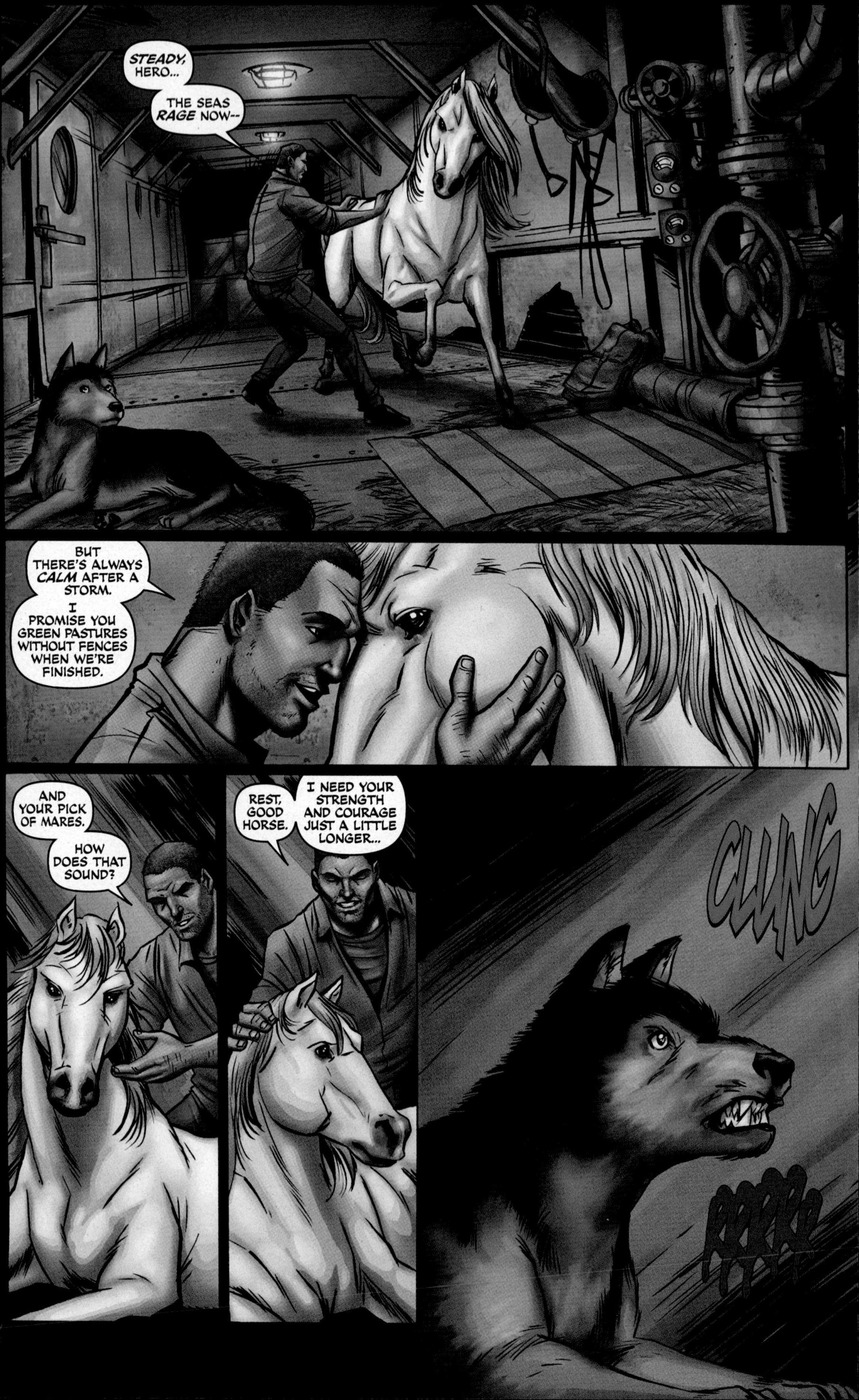
STEADY, HERO...
THE SEAS RAGE NOW--
BUT THERE'S ALWAYS CALM AFTER A STORM.
I PROMISE YOU GREEN PASTURES WITHOUT FENCES WHEN WE'RE FINISHED.
AND YOUR PICK OF MARES.
HOW DOES THAT SOUND?
REST, GOOD HORSE.
I NEED YOUR STRENGTH AND COURAGE JUST A LITTLE LONGER...
CLLING
RRRRR

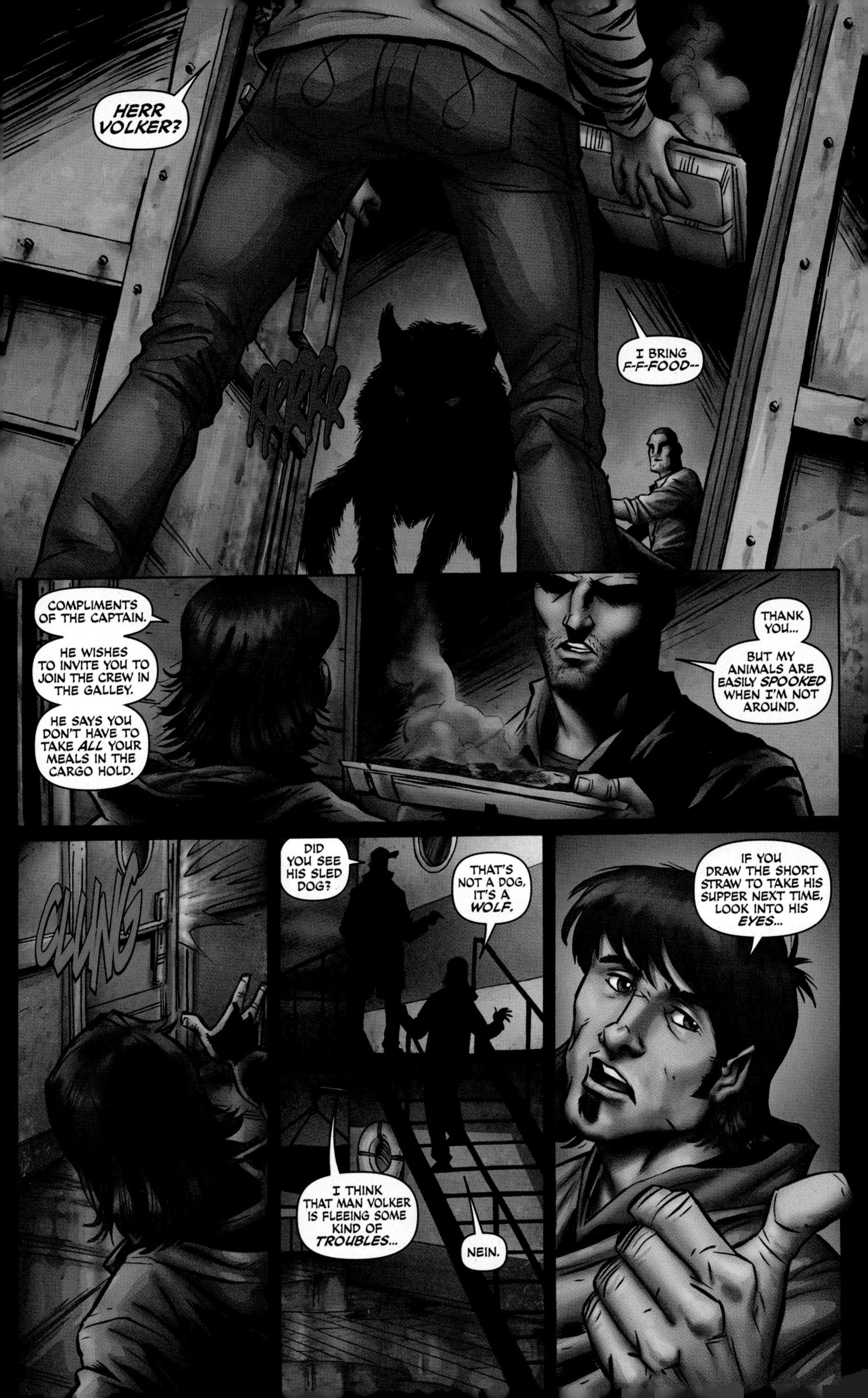
HERR VOLKER?
RRRRR
I BRING F-F-FOOD--
COMPLIMENTS OF THE CAPTAIN.
HE WISHES TO INVITE YOU TO JOIN THE CREW IN THE GALLEY.
HE SAYS YOU DON'T HAVE TO TAKE ALL YOUR MEALS IN THE CARGO HOLD.
THANK YOU...
BUT MY ANIMALS ARE EASILY SPOOKED WHEN I'M NOT AROUND.
CLUNG
DID YOU SEE HIS SLED DOG?
THAT'S NOT A DOG, IT'S A WOLF.
I THINK THAT MAN VOLKER IS FLEEING SOME KIND OF TROUBLES...
NEIN.
IF YOU DRAW THE SHORT STRAW TO TAKE HIS SUPPER NEXT TIME, LOOK INTO HIS EYES...

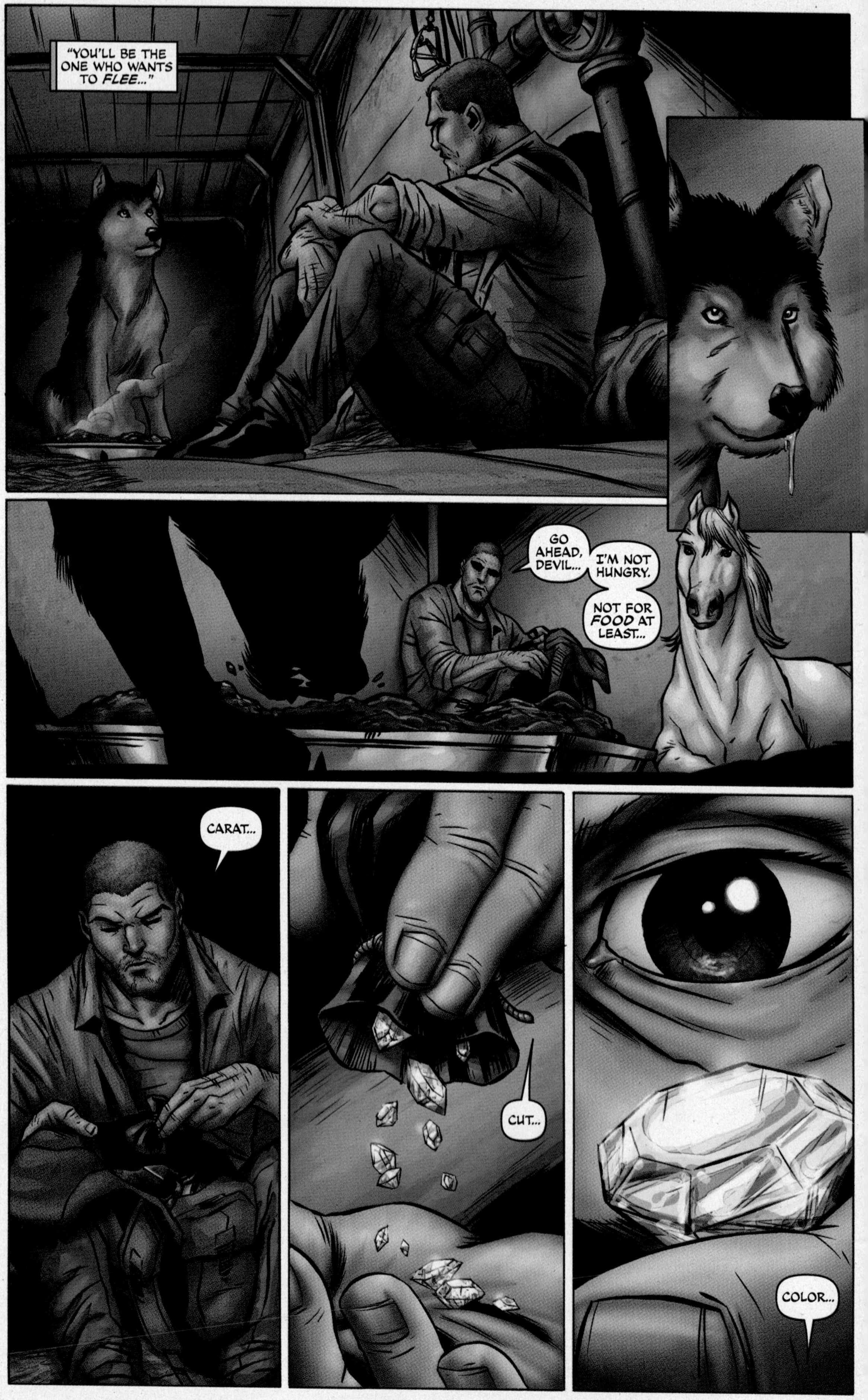
"YOU'LL BE THE ONE WHO WANTS TO FLEE..."
GO AHEAD, DEVIL...
I'M NOT HUNGRY.
NOT FOR FOOD AT LEAST...
CARAT...
CUT...
COLOR...

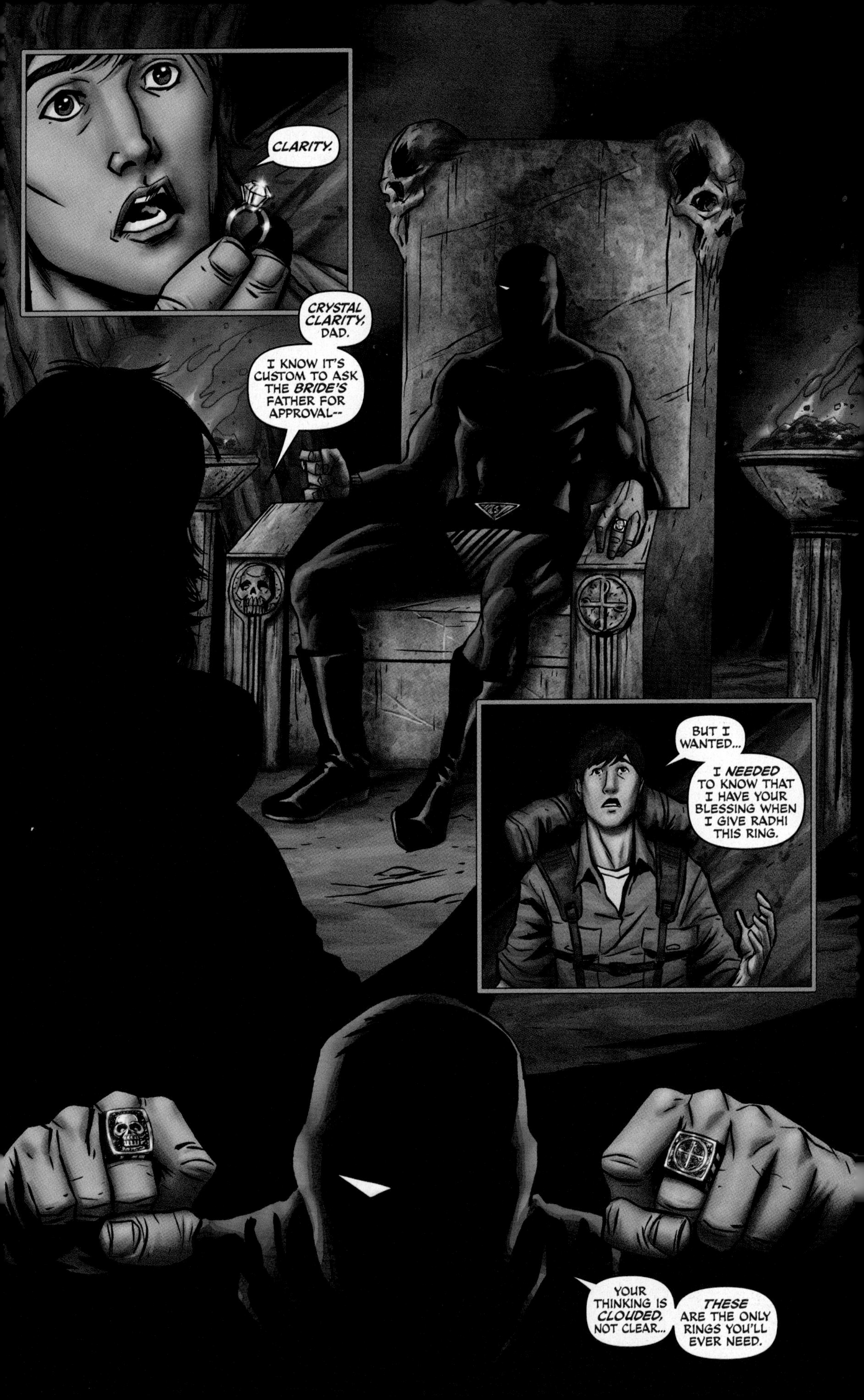
CLARITY.
CRYSTAL CLARITY, DAD.
I KNOW IT'S CUSTOM TO ASK THE BRIDE'S FATHER FOR APPROVAL--
BUT I WANTED...
I NEEDED TO KNOW THAT I HAVE YOUR BLESSING WHEN I GIVE RADHI THIS RING.
YOUR THINKING IS CLOUDED, NOT CLEAR...
THESE ARE THE ONLY RINGS YOU'LL EVER NEED.

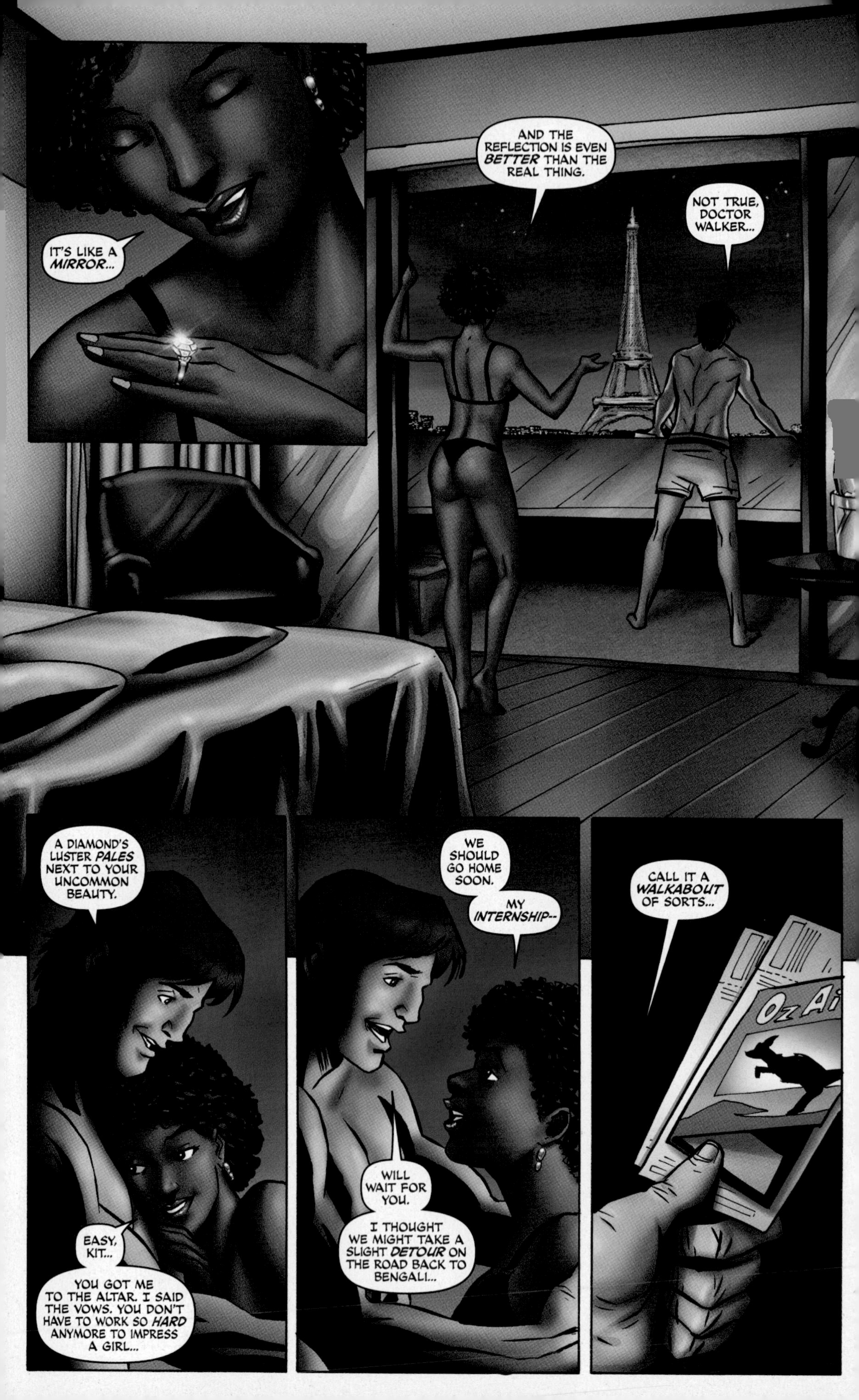
IT'S LIKE A MIRROR...
AND THE REFLECTION IS EVEN BETTER THAN THE REAL THING.
NOT TRUE, DOCTOR WALKER...
A DIAMOND'S LUSTER PALES NEXT TO YOUR UNCOMMON BEAUTY.
EASY, KIT...
YOU GOT ME TO THE ALTAR. I SAID THE VOWS. YOU DON'T HAVE TO WORK SO HARD ANYMORE TO IMPRESS A GIRL...
WE SHOULD GO HOME SOON.
MY INTERNSHIP--
WILL WAIT FOR YOU.
I THOUGHT WE MIGHT TAKE A SLIGHT DETOUR ON THE ROAD BACK TO BENGALI...
CALL IT A WALKABOUT OF SORTS...
Oz Ai

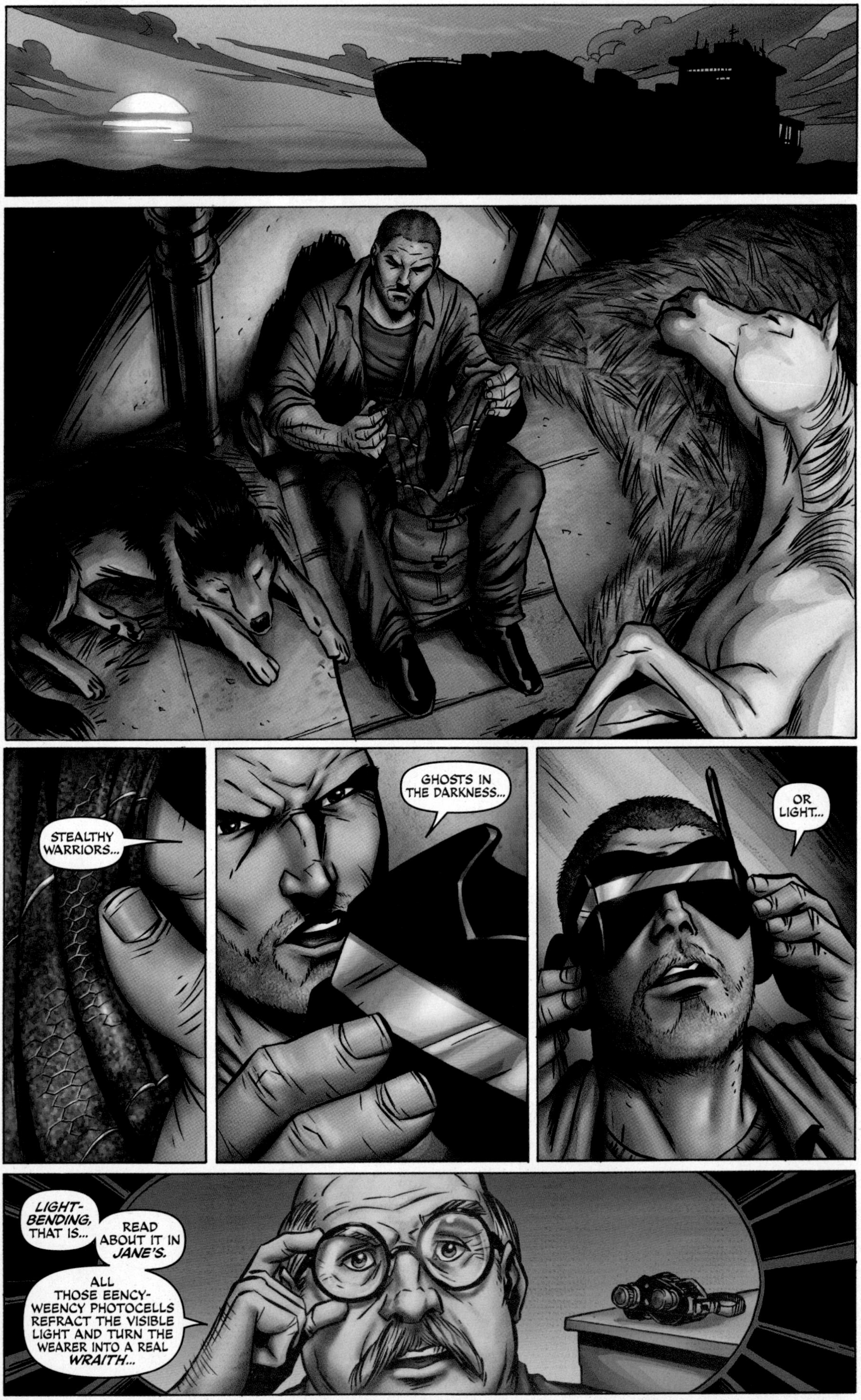
STEALTHY WARRIORS...
GHOSTS IN THE DARKNESS...
OR LIGHT...
LIGHT-BENDING, THAT IS...
READ ABOUT IT IN JANE'S.
ALL THOSE EENCY-WEENCY PHOTOCELLS REFRACT THE VISIBLE LIGHT AND TURN THE WEARER INTO A REAL WRAITH...

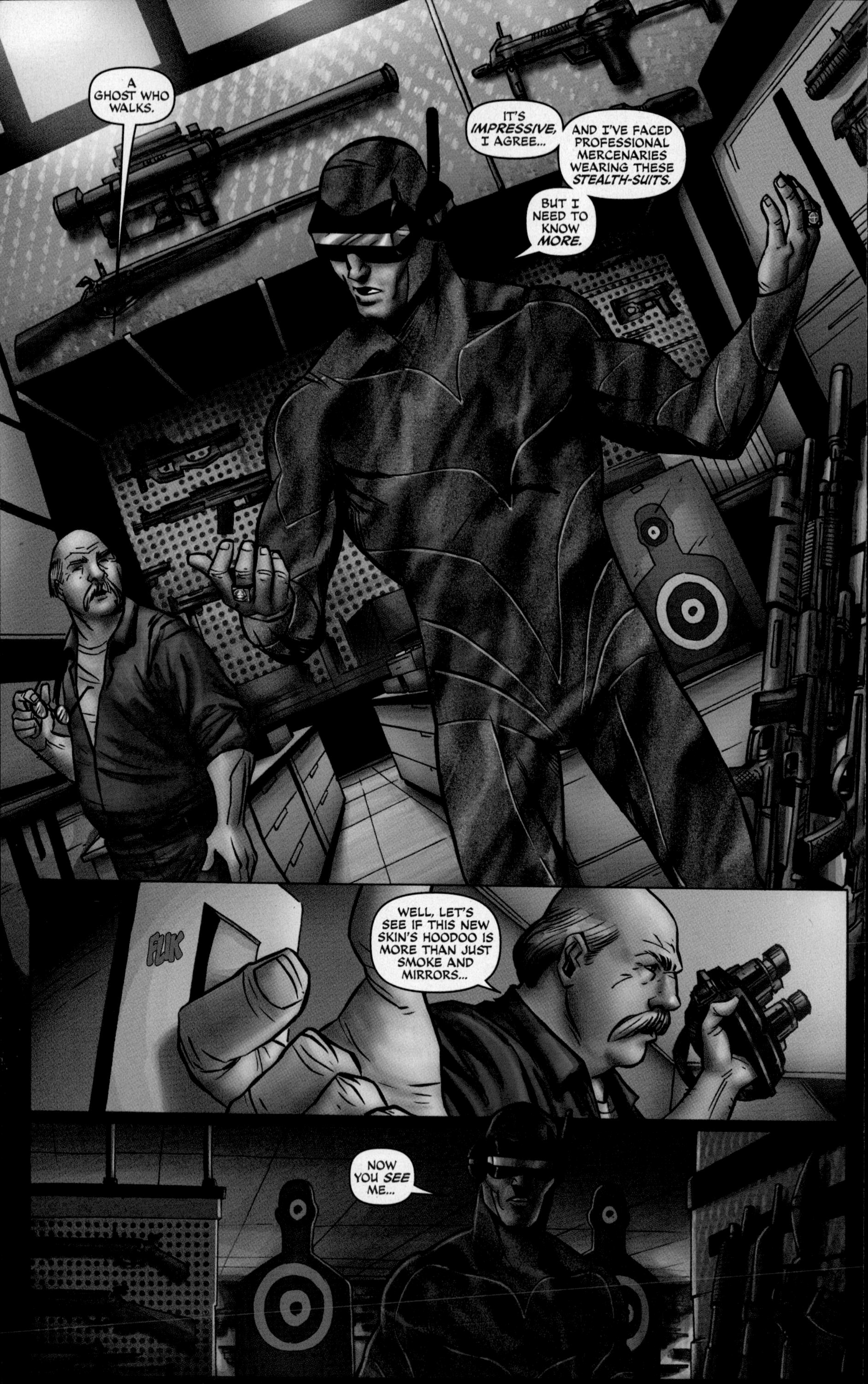
A GHOST WHO WALKS.
IT'S *IMPRESSIVE,* I AGREE...
AND I'VE FACED PROFESSIONAL MERCENARIES WEARING THESE *STEALTH-SUITS.*
BUT I NEED TO KNOW *MORE.*
FLIK
WELL, LET'S SEE IF THIS NEW SKIN'S HOODOO IS MORE THAN JUST SMOKE AND MIRRORS...
NOW YOU *SEE* ME...

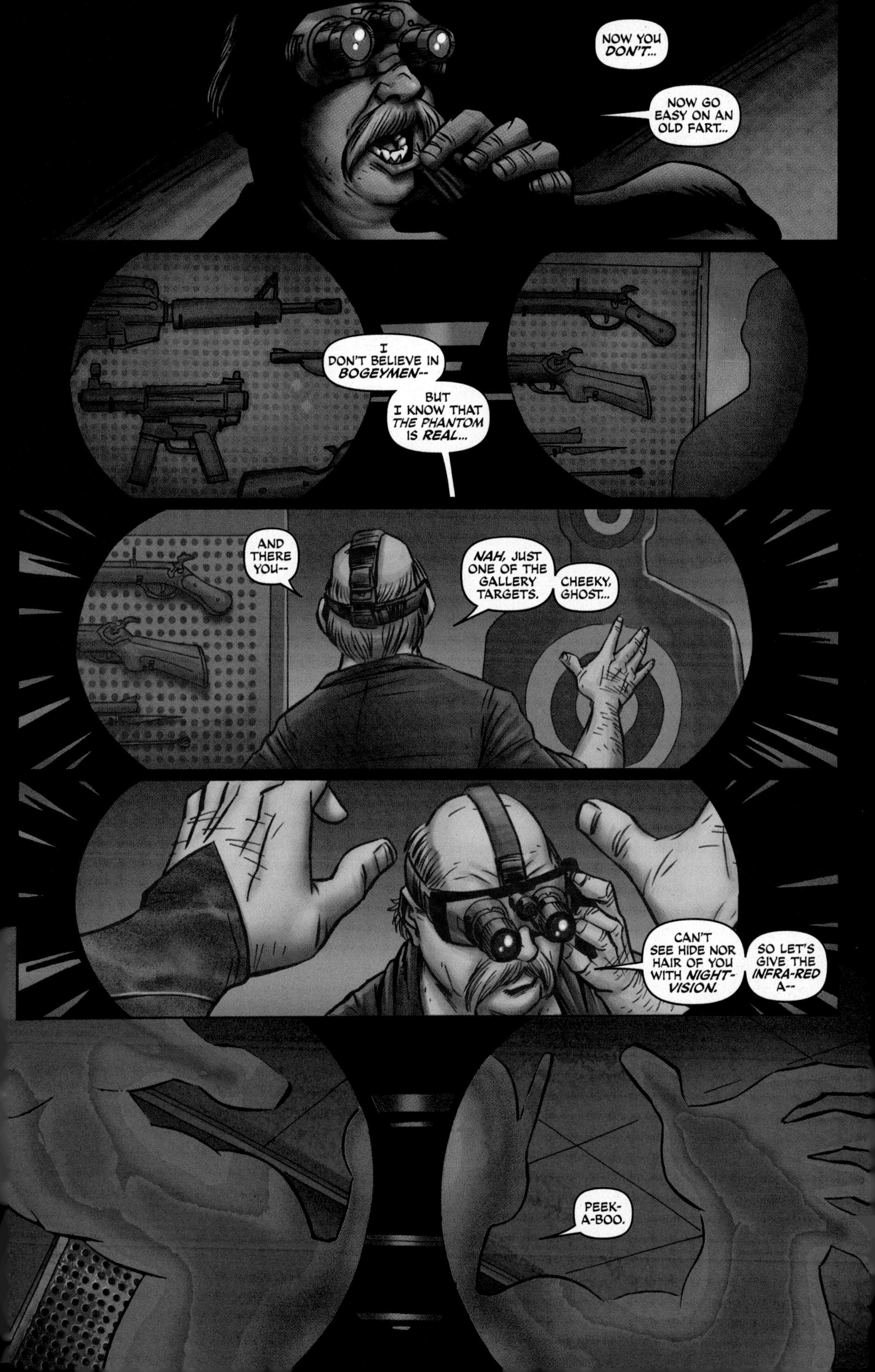
NOW YOU *DON'T*...
NOW GO EASY ON AN OLD FART...
I DON'T BELIEVE IN *BOGEYMEN*--
BUT I KNOW THAT *THE PHANTOM* IS *REAL*...
AND THERE YOU--
NAH, JUST ONE OF THE GALLERY TARGETS.
CHEEKY, GHOST...
CAN'T SEE HIDE NOR HAIR OF YOU WITH *NIGHT-VISION.*
SO LET'S GIVE THE *INFRA-RED* A--
PEEK-A-BOO.

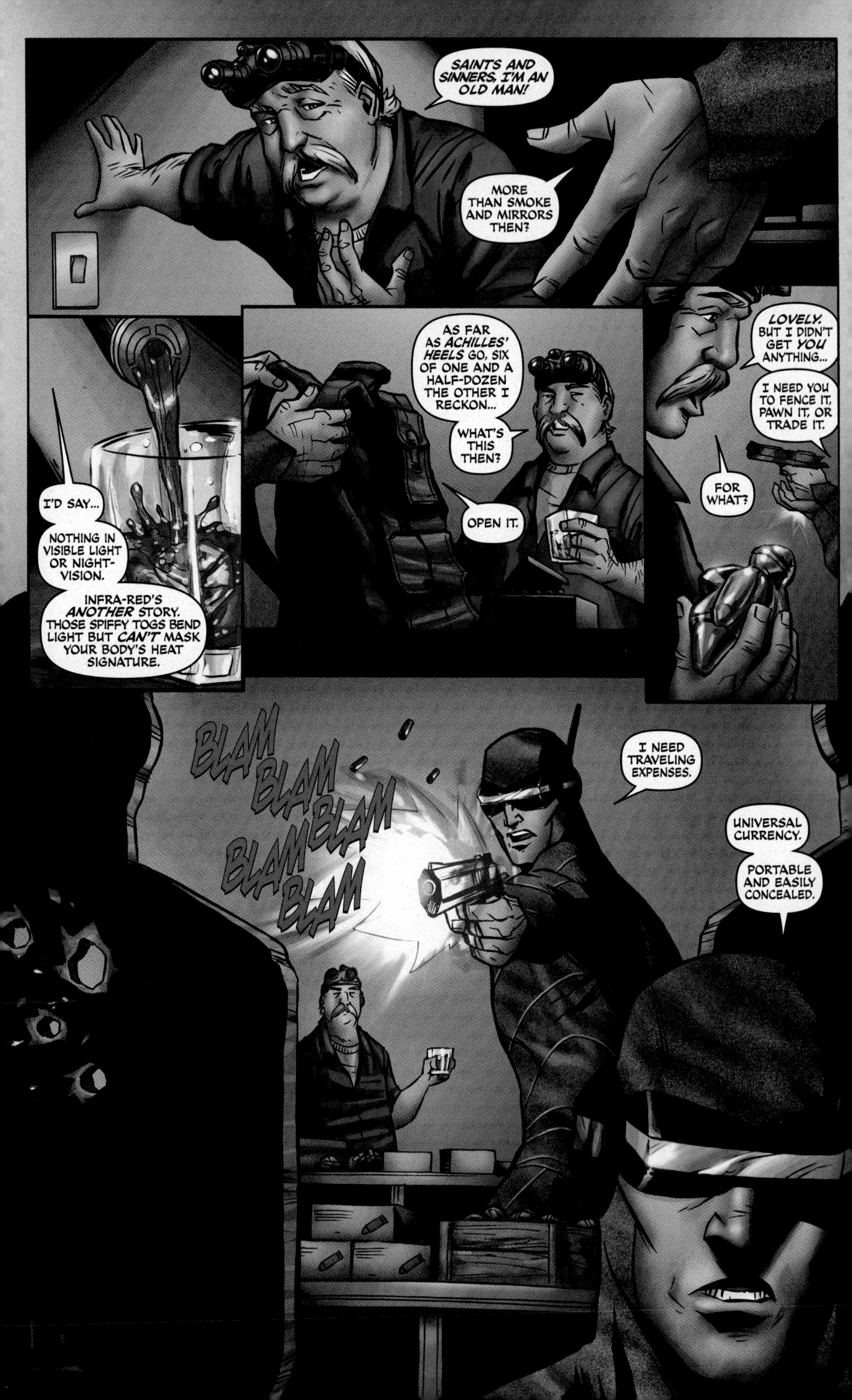
SAINTS AND SINNERS, I'M AN OLD MAN!
MORE THAN SMOKE AND MIRRORS THEN?
I'D SAY...
NOTHING IN VISIBLE LIGHT OR NIGHT-VISION.
INFRA-RED'S ANOTHER STORY. THOSE SPIFFY TOGS BEND LIGHT BUT CAN'T MASK YOUR BODY'S HEAT SIGNATURE.
AS FAR AS ACHILLES' HEELS GO, SIX OF ONE AND A HALF-DOZEN THE OTHER I RECKON...
WHAT'S THIS THEN?
OPEN IT.
LOVELY. BUT I DIDN'T GET YOU ANYTHING...
I NEED YOU TO FENCE IT, PAWN IT, OR TRADE IT.
FOR WHAT?
BLAM BLAM BLAM BLAM BLAM BLAM
I NEED TRAVELING EXPENSES.
UNIVERSAL CURRENCY.
PORTABLE AND EASILY CONCEALED.

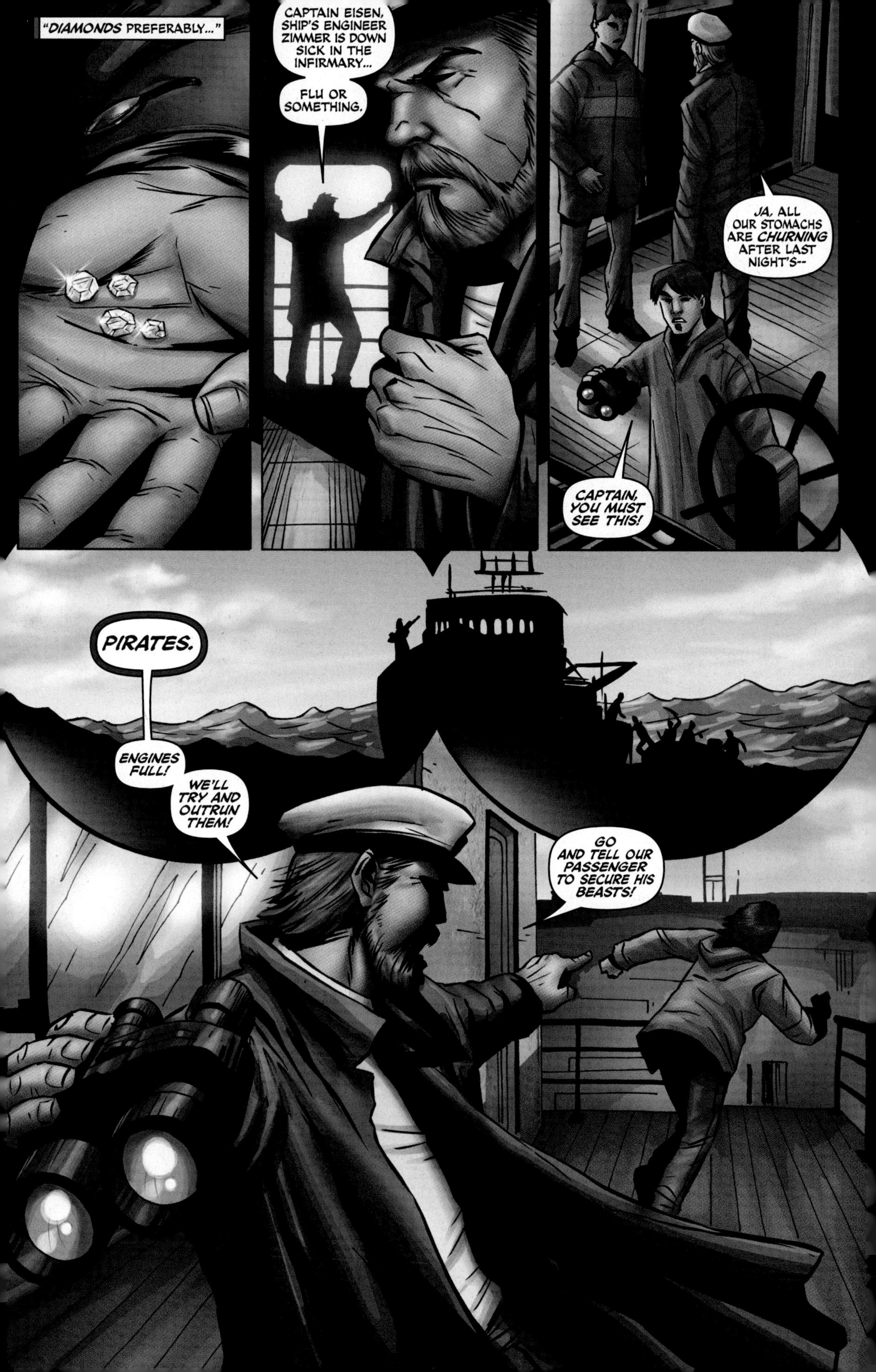
"DIAMONDS PREFERABLY..."
CAPTAIN EISEN, SHIP'S ENGINEER ZIMMER IS DOWN SICK IN THE INFIRMARY...
FLU OR SOMETHING.
JA, ALL OUR STOMACHS ARE CHURNING AFTER LAST NIGHT'S--
CAPTAIN, YOU MUST SEE THIS!
PIRATES.
ENGINES FULL!
WE'LL TRY AND OUTRUN THEM!
GO AND TELL OUR PASSENGER TO SECURE HIS BEASTS!

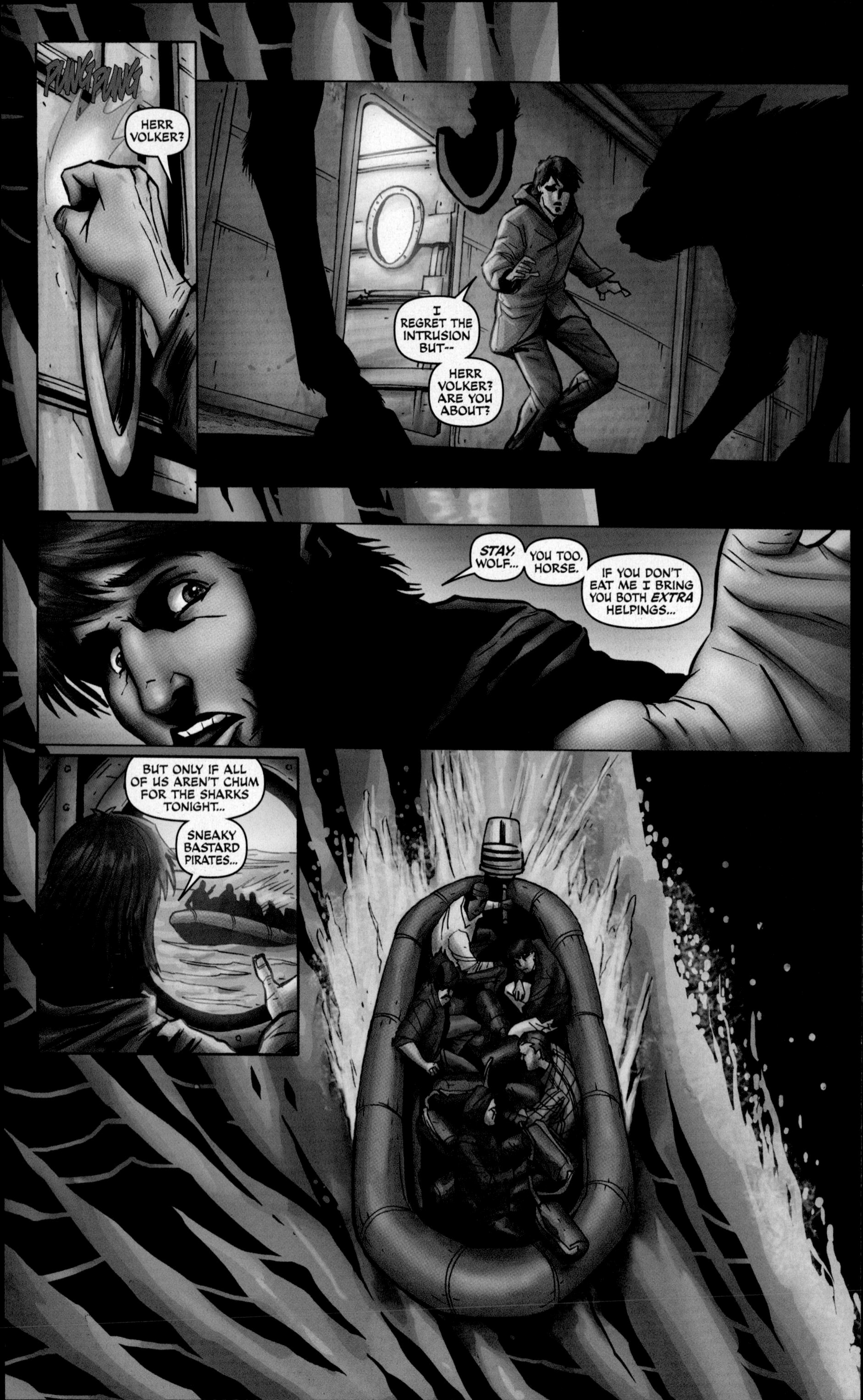
PUNG PUNG
HERR VOLKER?
I REGRET THE INTRUSION BUT--
HERR VOLKER? ARE YOU ABOUT?
STAY, WOLF...
YOU TOO, HORSE.
IF YOU DON'T EAT ME I BRING YOU BOTH EXTRA HELPINGS...
BUT ONLY IF ALL OF US AREN'T CHUM FOR THE SHARKS TONIGHT...
SNEAKY BASTARD PIRATES...

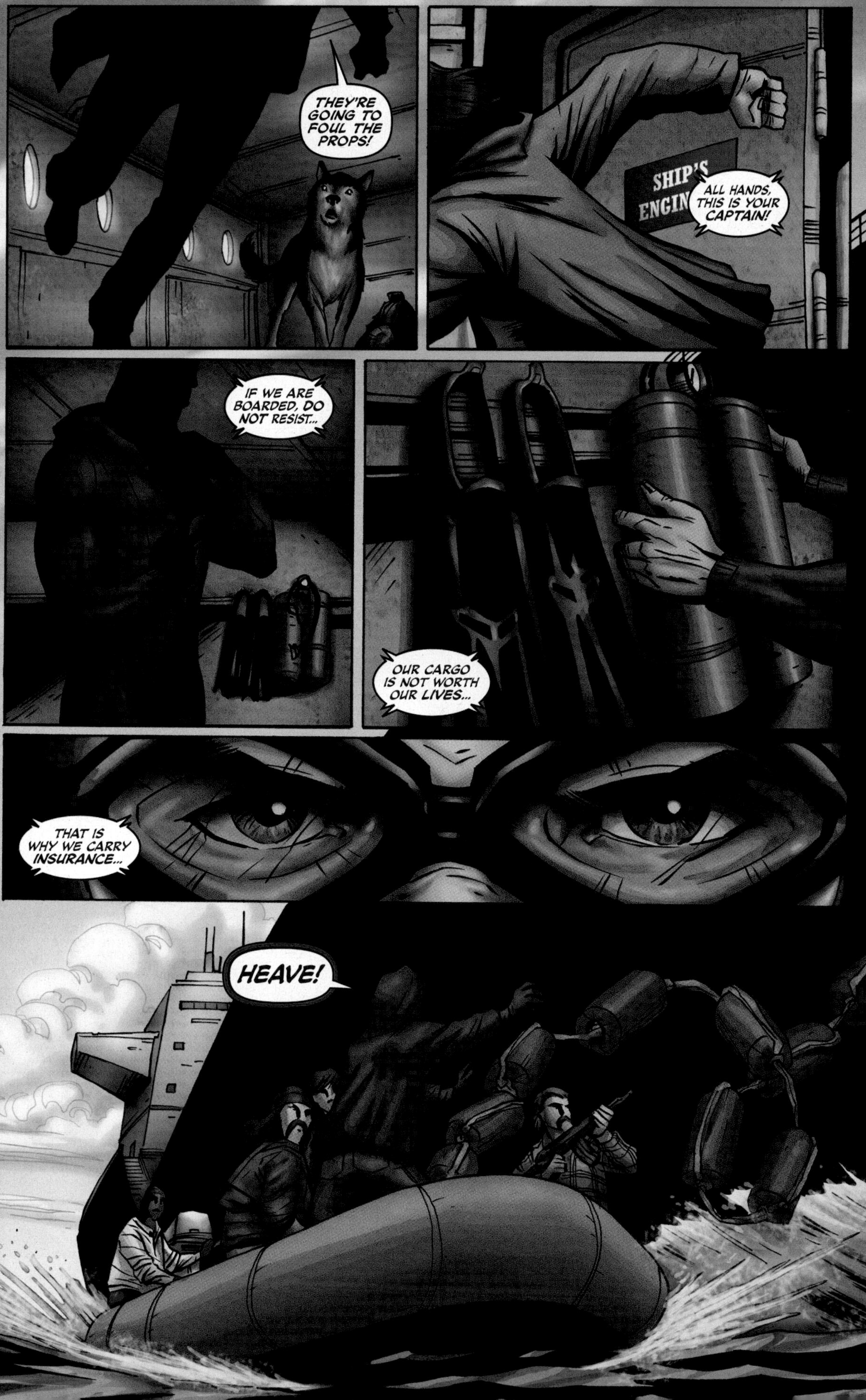
THEY'RE GOING TO FOUL THE PROPS!
SHIP'S ENGIN
ALL HANDS, THIS IS YOUR CAPTAIN!
IF WE ARE BOARDED, DO NOT RESIST...
OUR CARGO IS NOT WORTH OUR LIVES...
THAT IS WHY WE CARRY INSURANCE...
HEAVE!

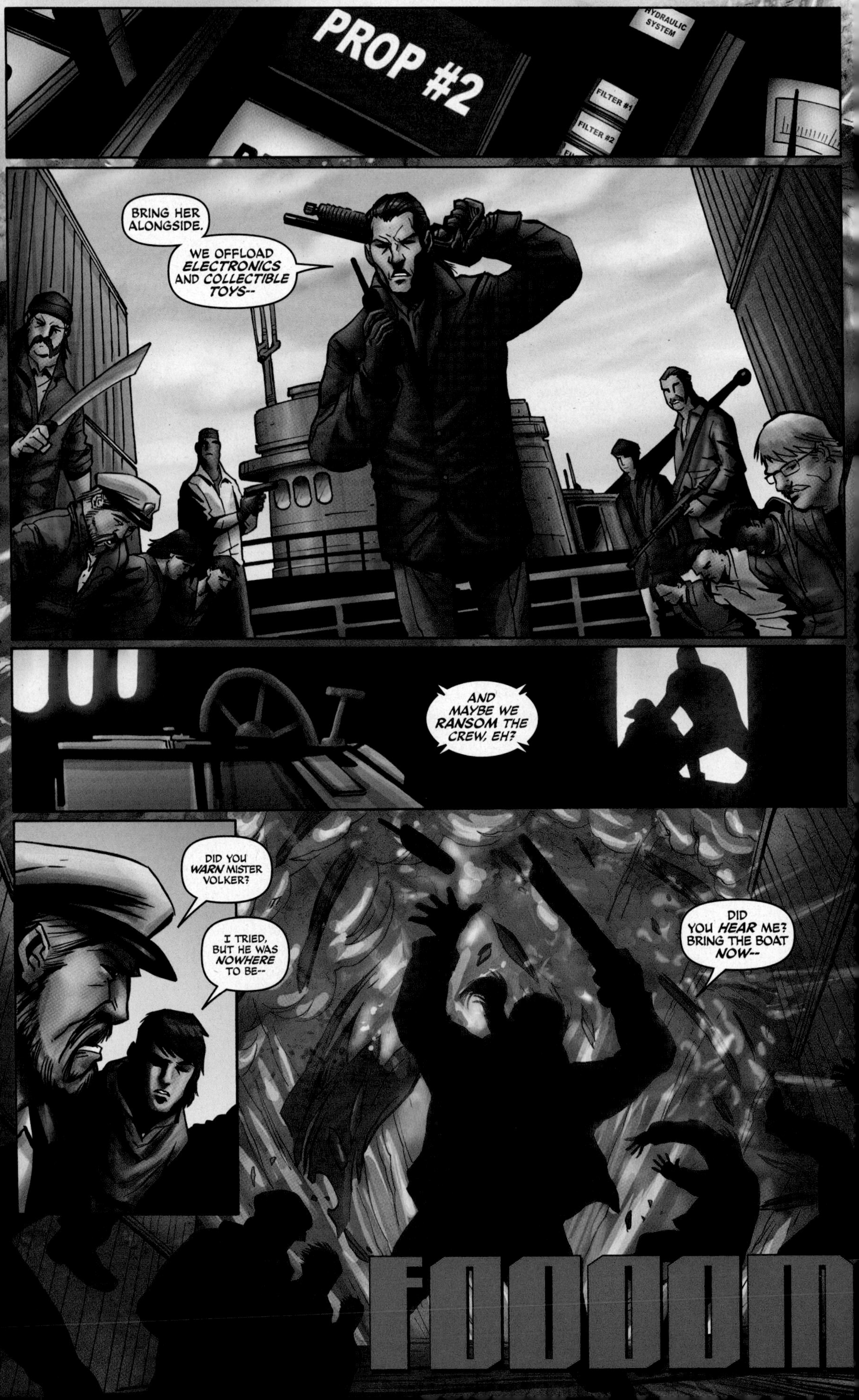
PROP #2
HYDRAULIC SYSTEM
FILTER #1
FILTER #2
BRING HER ALONGSIDE.
WE OFFLOAD *ELECTRONICS* AND *COLLECTIBLE TOYS*--
AND MAYBE WE *RANSOM* THE CREW, EH?
DID YOU *WARN* MISTER VOLKER?
I TRIED, BUT HE WAS *NOWHERE* TO BE--
DID YOU *HEAR* ME? BRING THE BOAT *NOW*--
FOOOOM

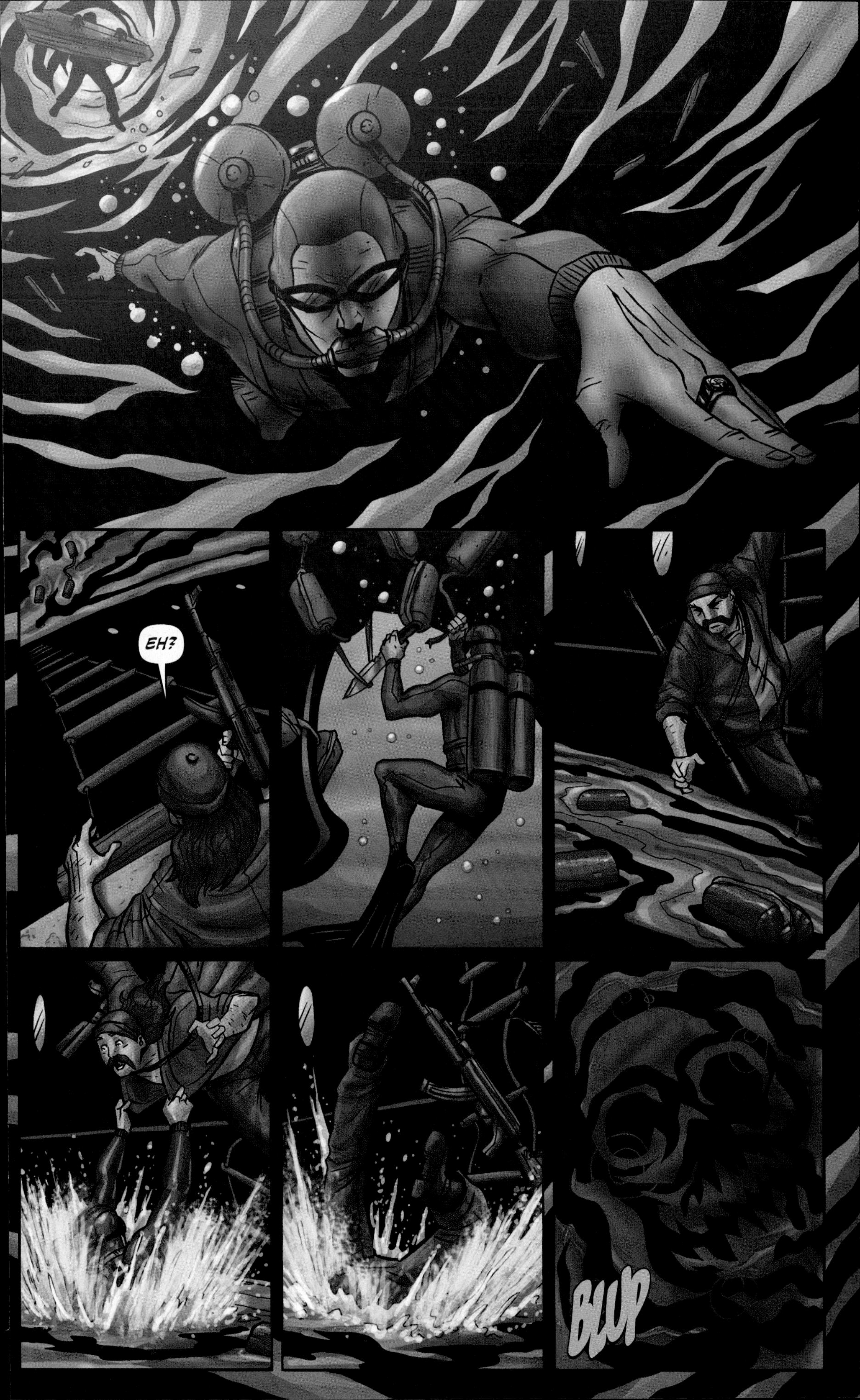
EH?
BLUP

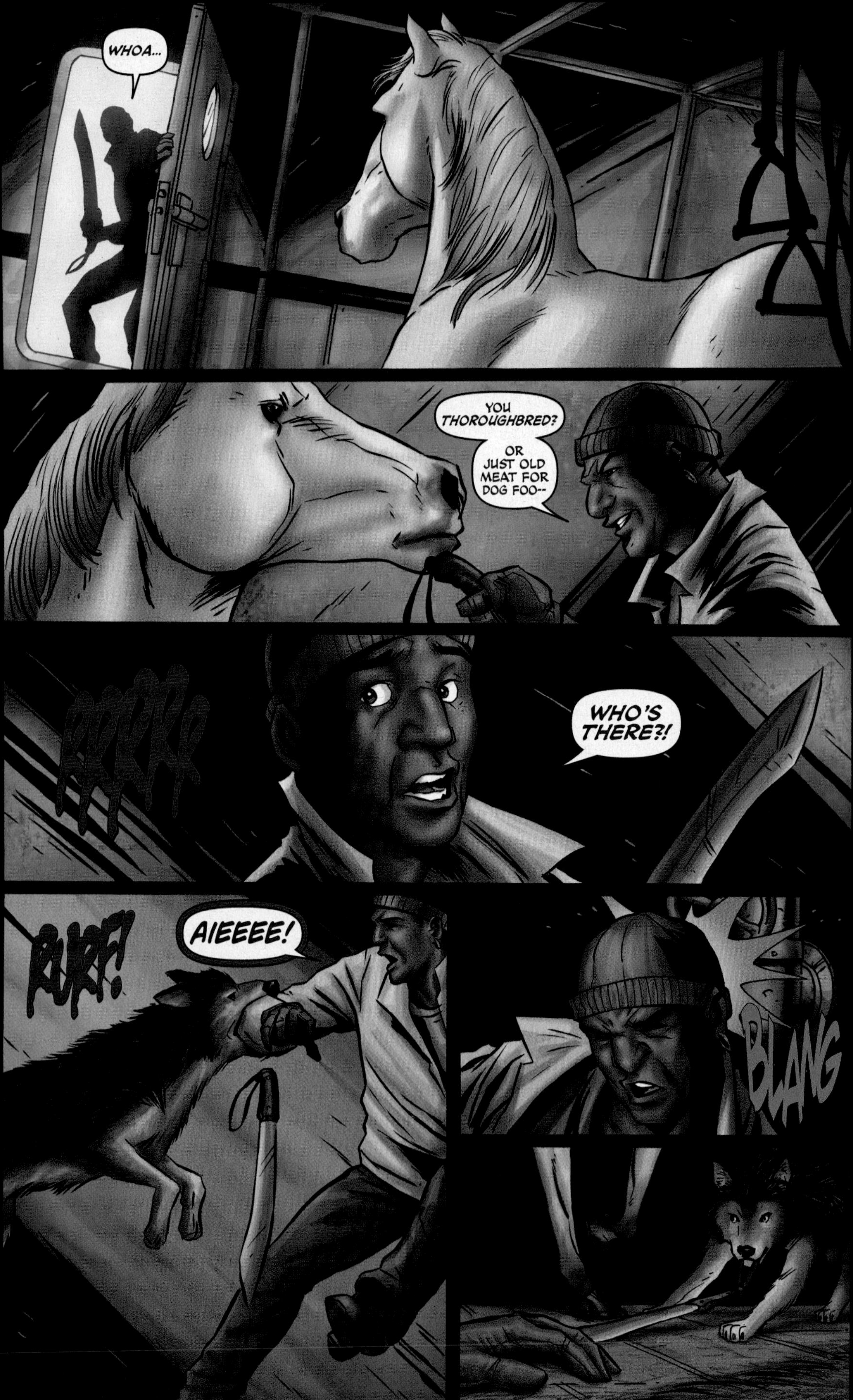
WHOA...
YOU THOROUGHBRED?
OR JUST OLD MEAT FOR DOG FOO--
WHO'S THERE?!
RURF!
AIEEEE!
BLANG

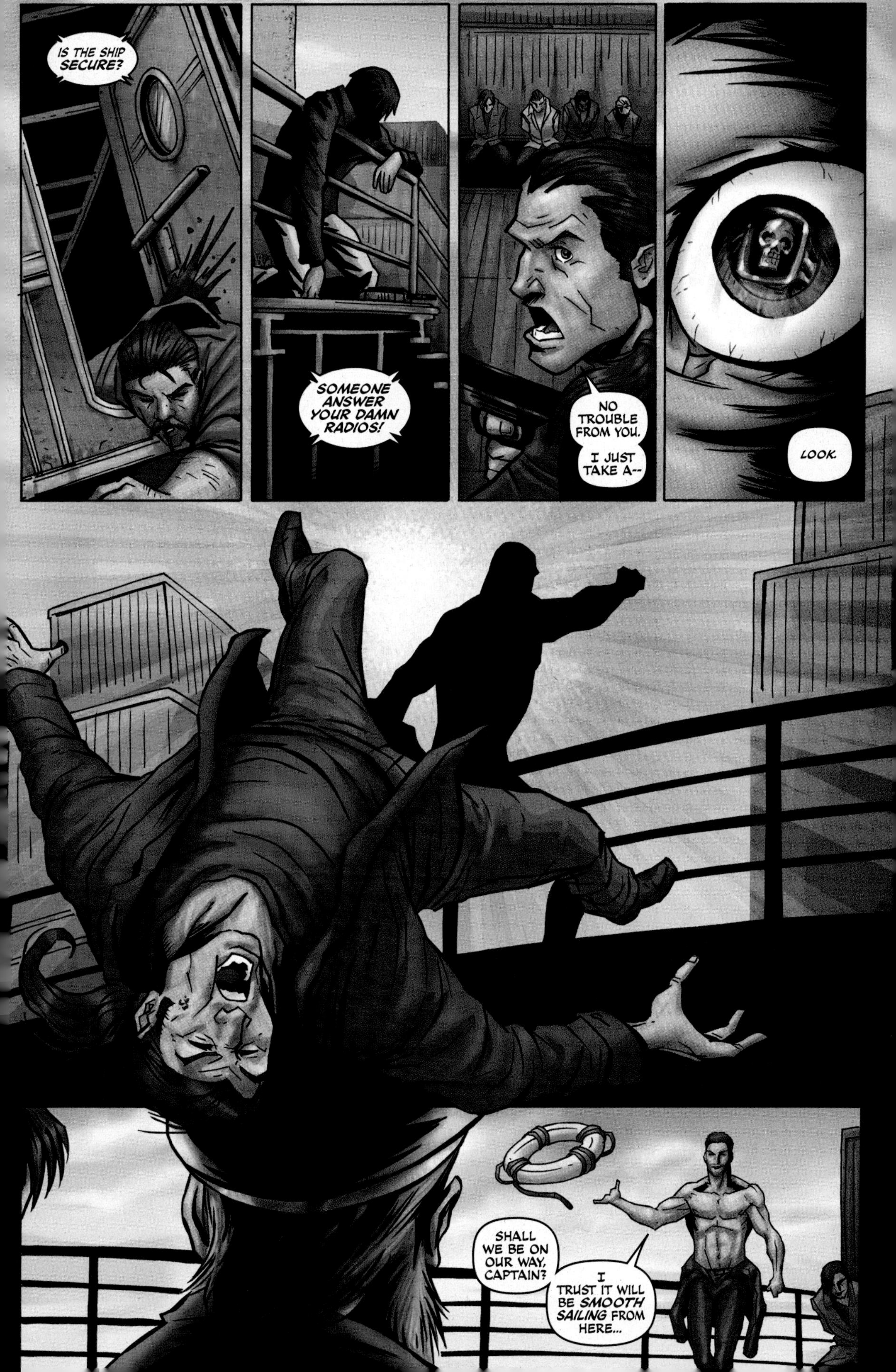
IS THE SHIP SECURE?
SOMEONE ANSWER YOUR DAMN RADIOS!
NO TROUBLE FROM YOU.
I JUST TAKE A--
LOOK.
SHALL WE BE ON OUR WAY, CAPTAIN?
I TRUST IT WILL BE SMOOTH SAILING FROM HERE...

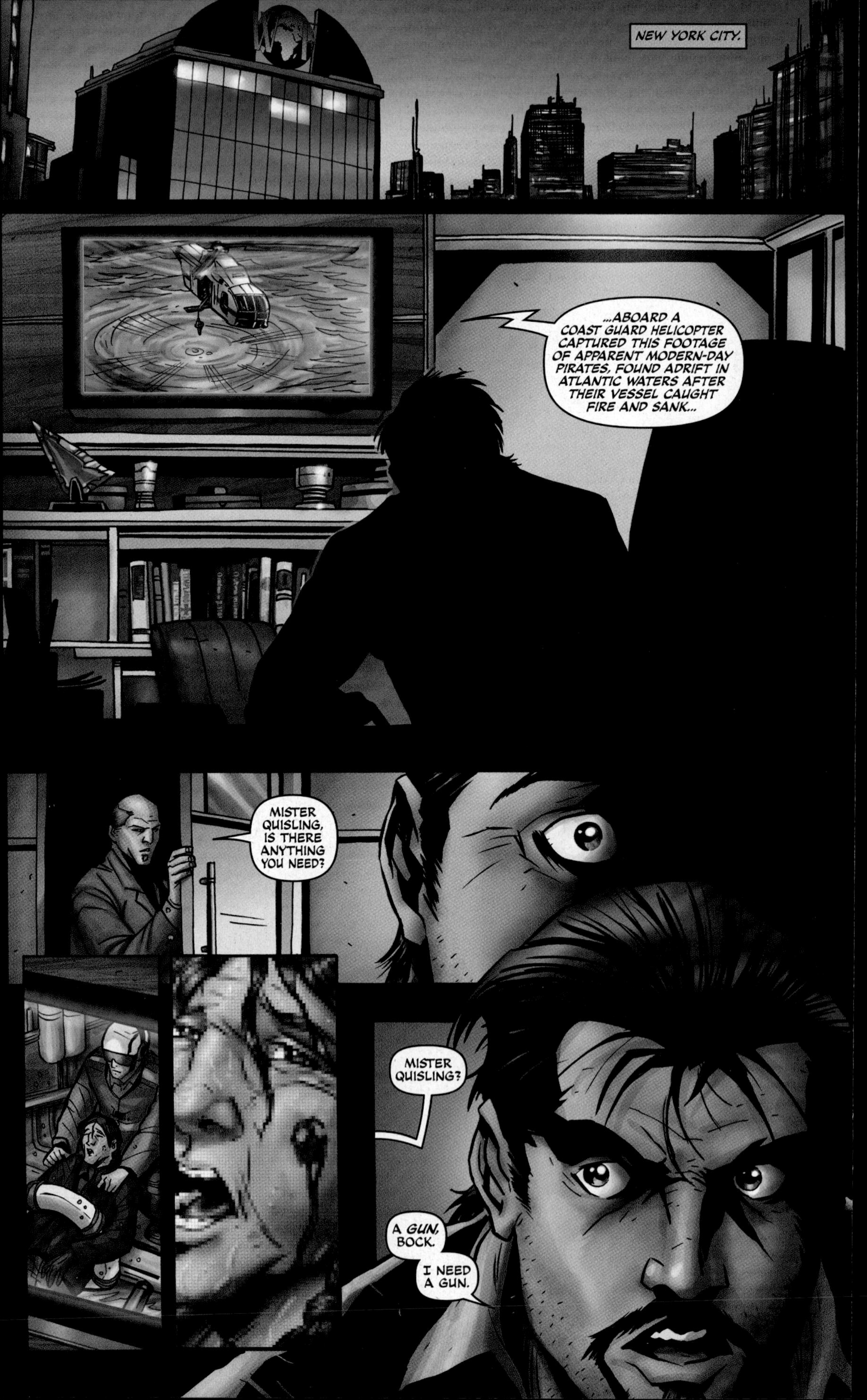
NEW YORK CITY.
...ABOARD A COAST GUARD HELICOPTER CAPTURED THIS FOOTAGE OF APPARENT MODERN-DAY PIRATES, FOUND ADRIFT IN ATLANTIC WATERS AFTER THEIR VESSEL CAUGHT FIRE AND SANK...
MISTER QUISLING, IS THERE ANYTHING YOU NEED?
MISTER QUISLING?
A GUN, BOCK.
I NEED A GUN.

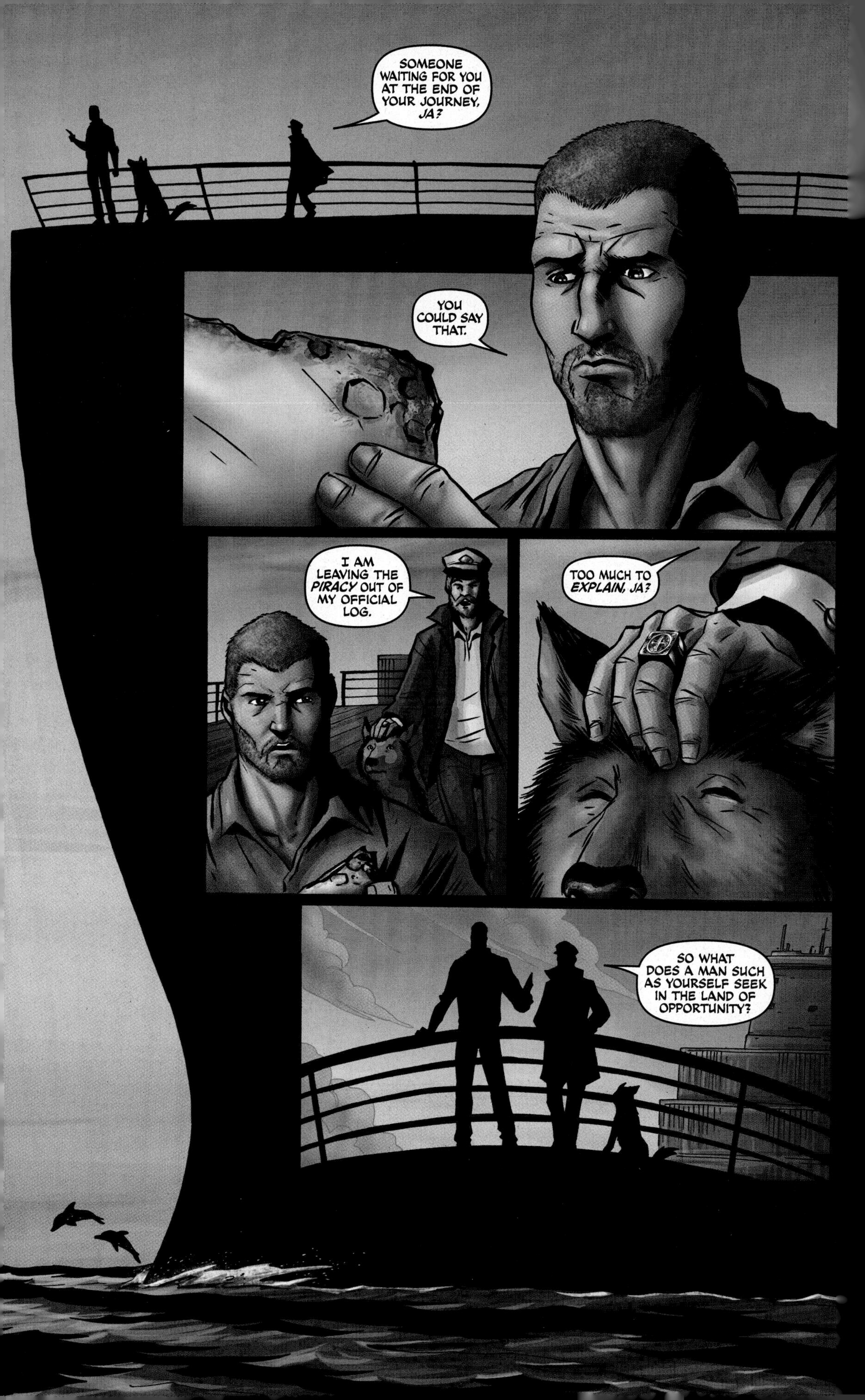
SOMEONE WAITING FOR YOU AT THE END OF YOUR JOURNEY, JA?
YOU COULD SAY THAT.
I AM LEAVING THE PIRACY OUT OF MY OFFICIAL LOG.
TOO MUCH TO EXPLAIN, JA?
SO WHAT DOES A MAN SUCH AS YOURSELF SEEK IN THE LAND OF OPPORTUNITY?

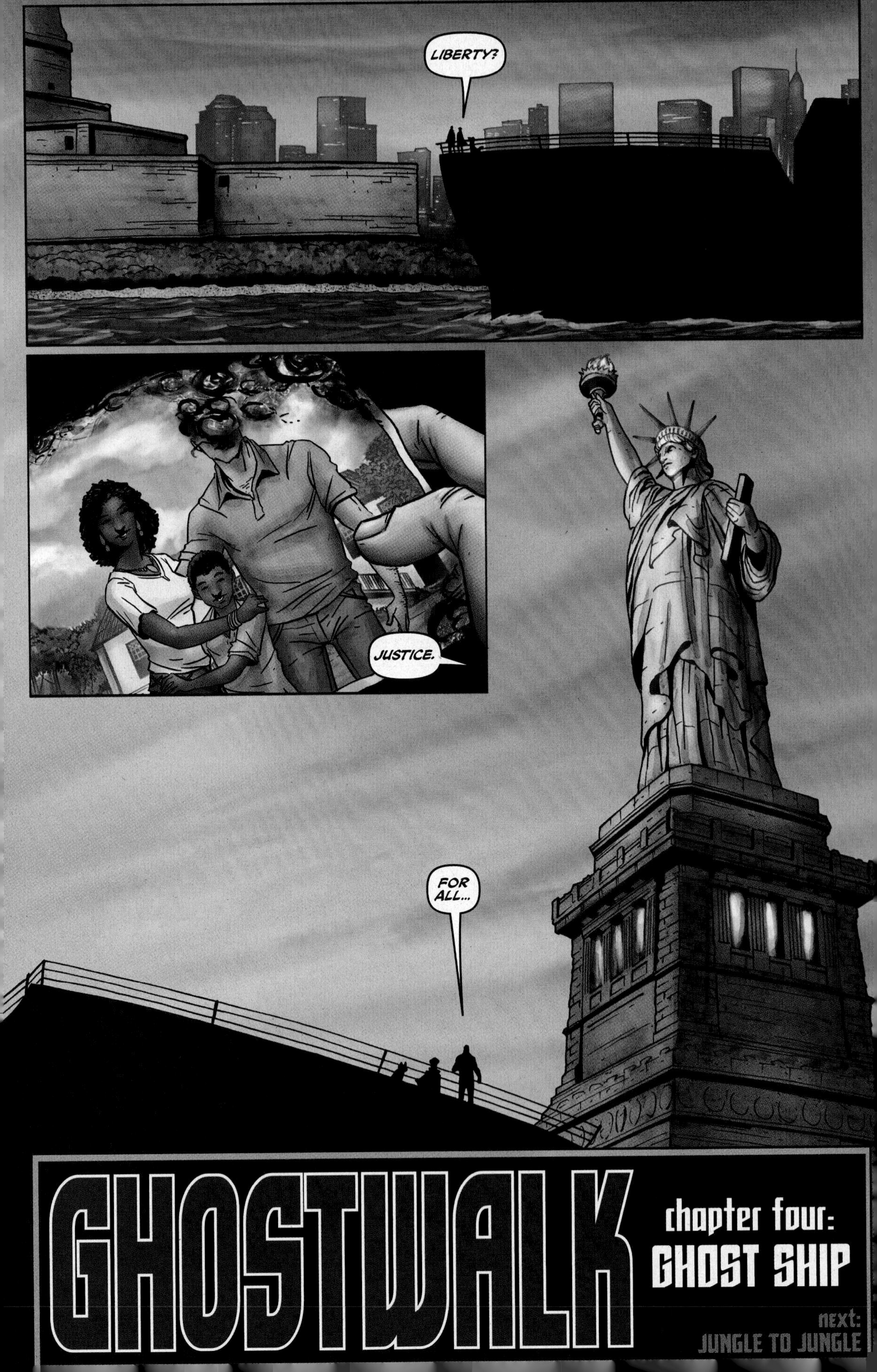
LIBERTY?
JUSTICE.
FOR ALL...
GHOSTWALK
chapter four:
GHOST SHIP
next:
JUNGLE TO JUNGLE

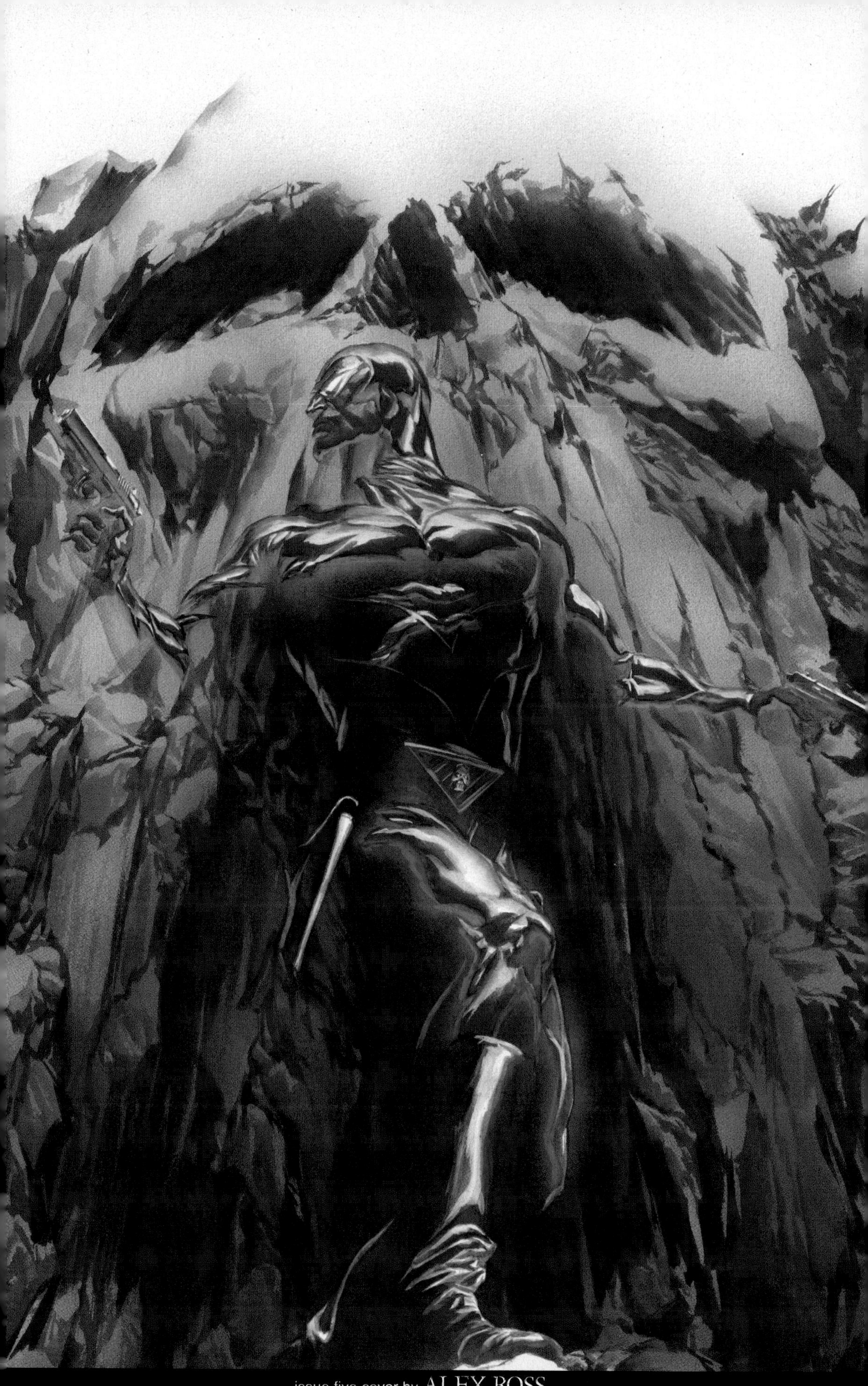

issue five cover by ALEX ROSS

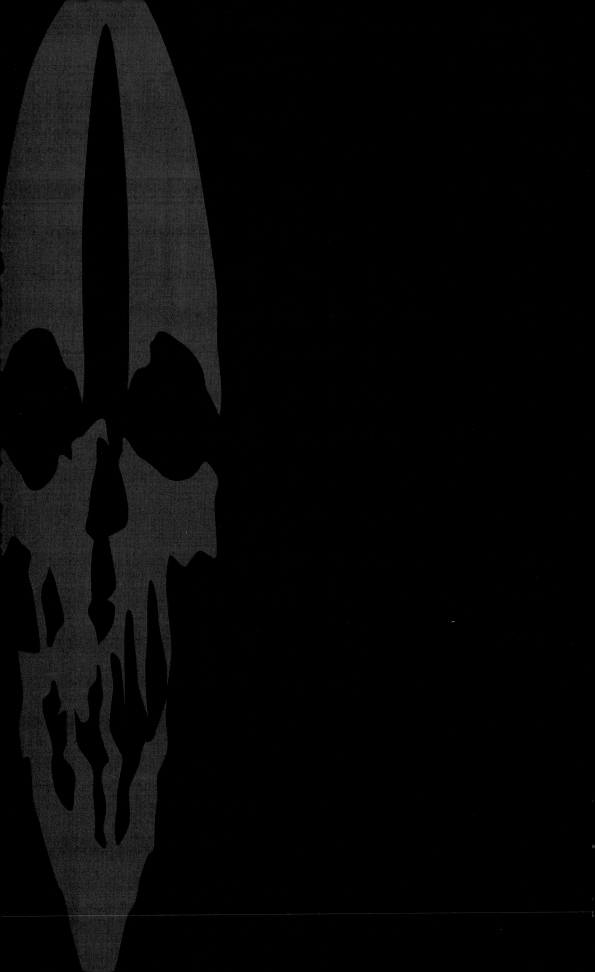

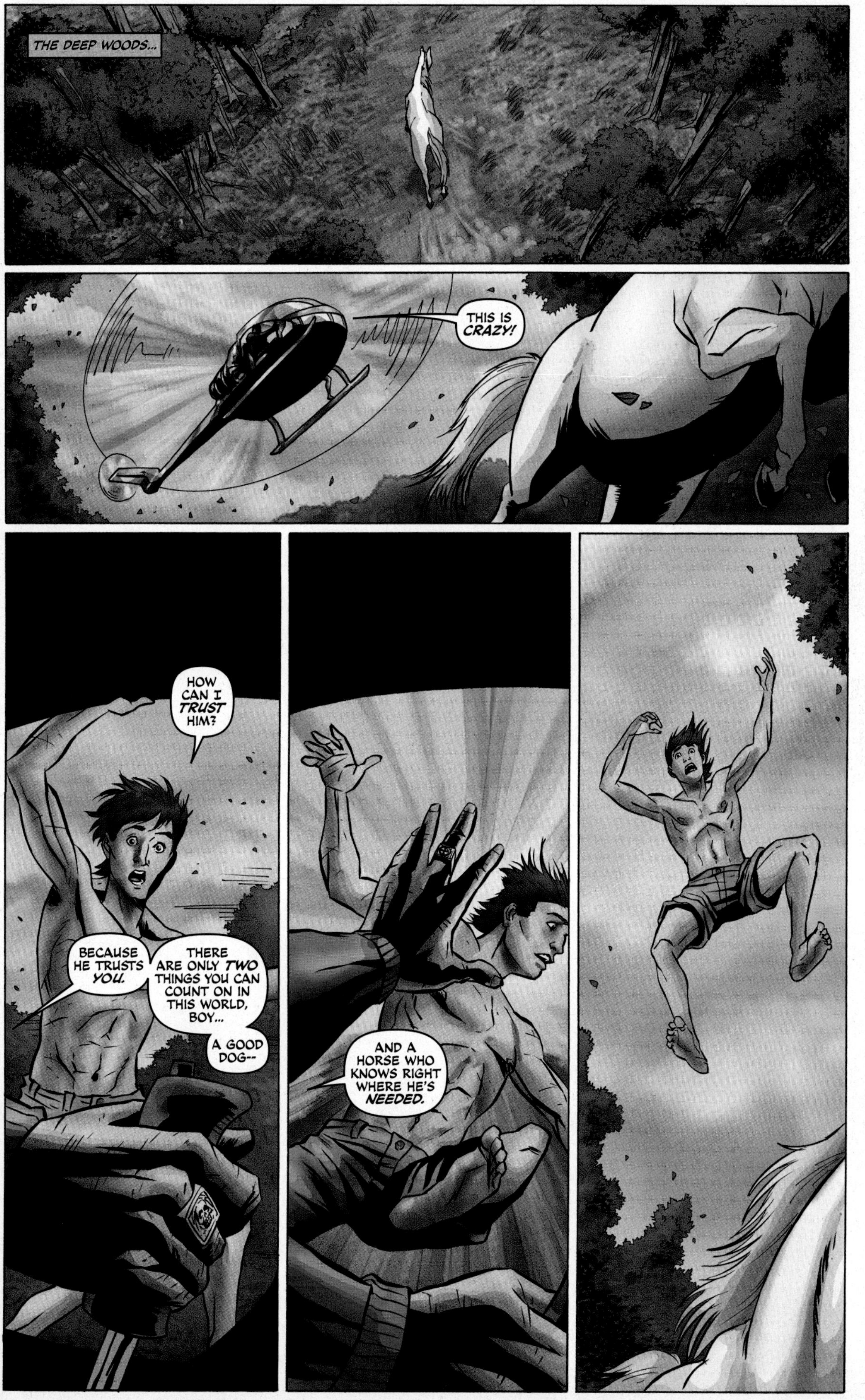
THE DEEP WOODS...
THIS IS CRAZY!
HOW CAN I TRUST HIM?
BECAUSE HE TRUSTS YOU.
THERE ARE ONLY TWO THINGS YOU CAN COUNT ON IN THIS WORLD, BOY...
A GOOD DOG--
AND A HORSE WHO KNOWS RIGHT WHERE HE'S NEEDED.

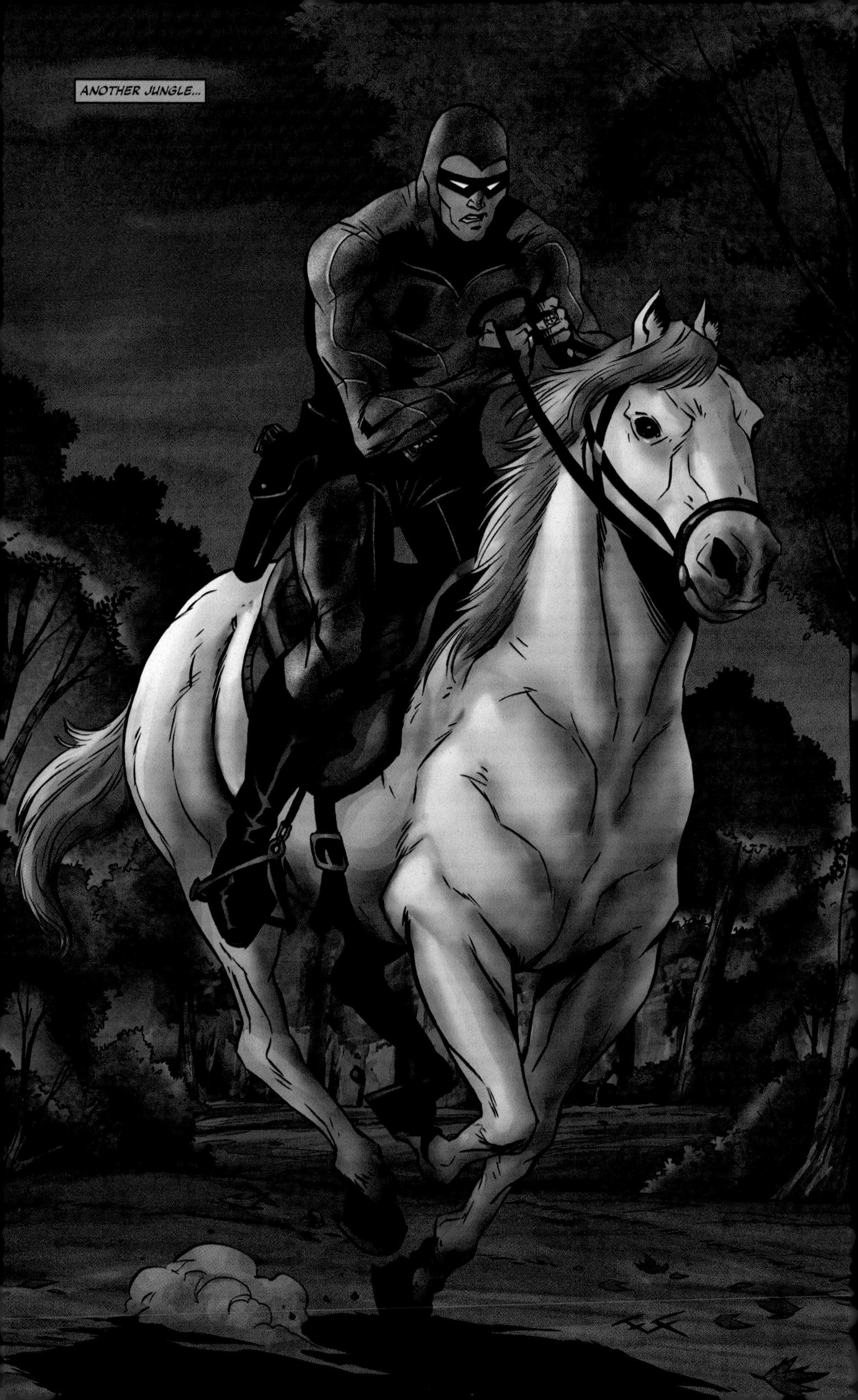
ANOTHER JUNGLE...

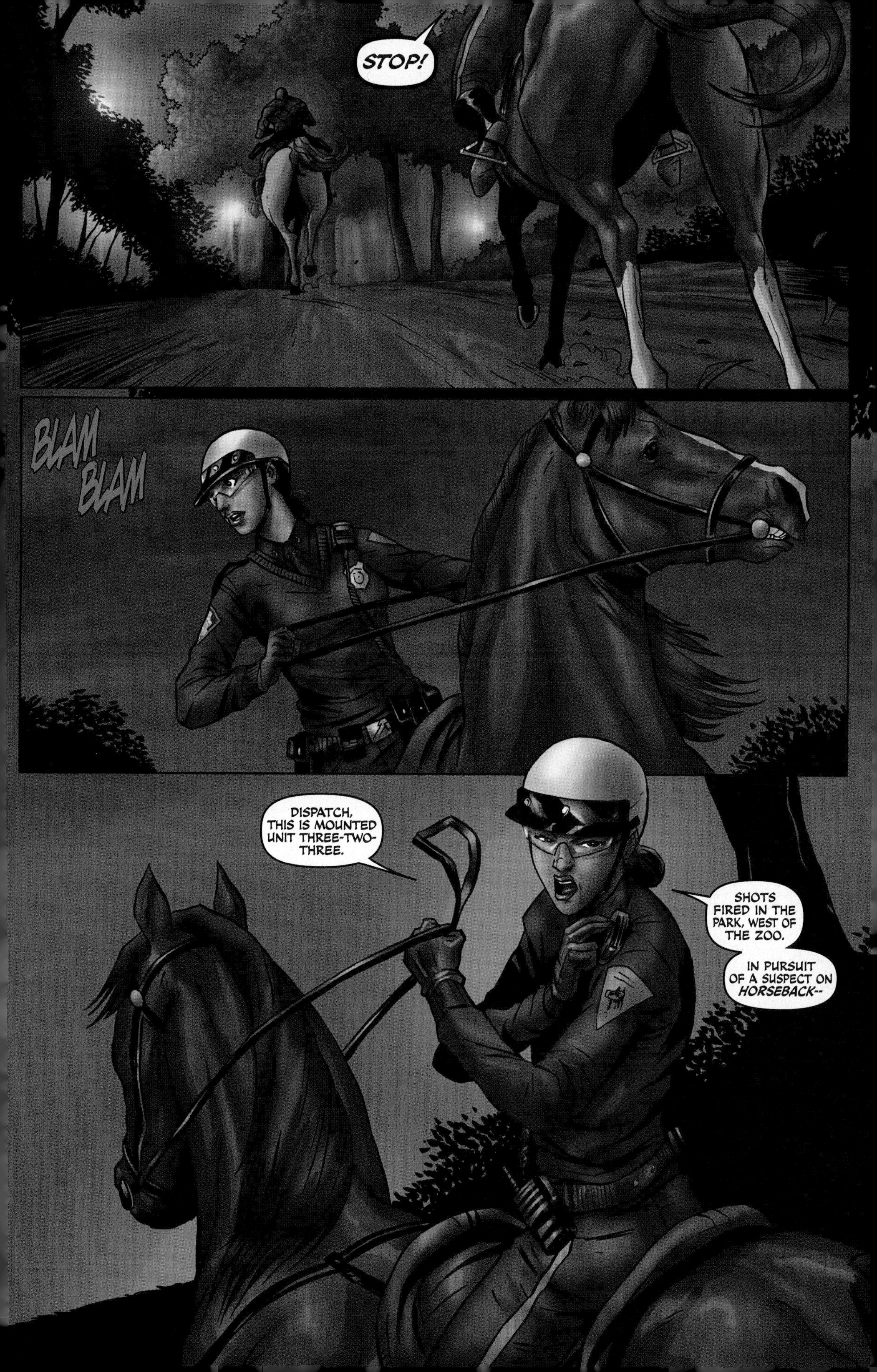
STOP!
BLAM BLAM
DISPATCH, THIS IS MOUNTED UNIT THREE-TWO-THREE.
SHOTS FIRED IN THE PARK, WEST OF THE ZOO.
IN PURSUIT OF A SUSPECT ON *HORSEBACK*--

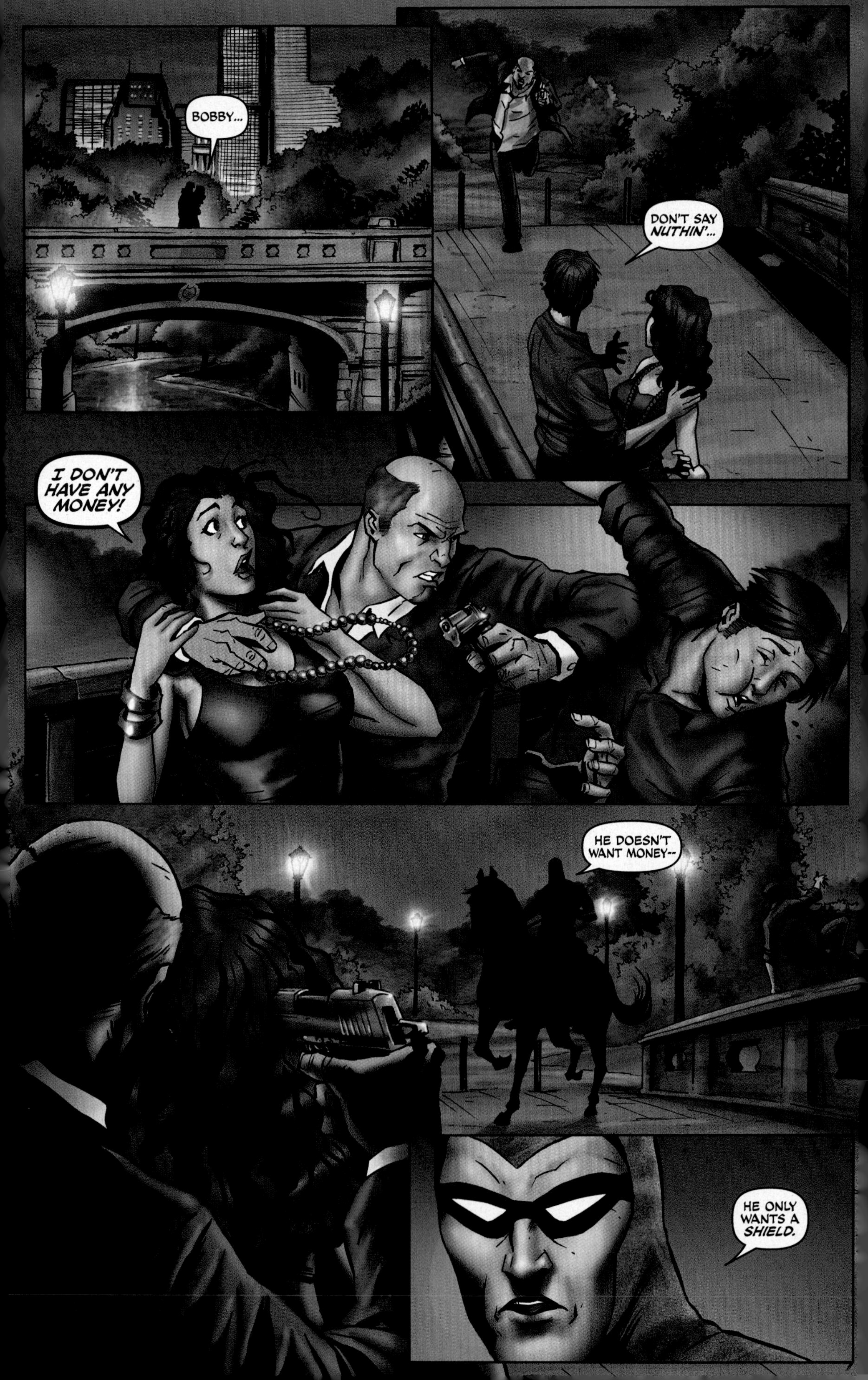
BOBBY...
DON'T SAY NUTHIN'...
I DON'T HAVE ANY MONEY!
HE DOESN'T WANT MONEY--
HE ONLY WANTS A SHIELD.

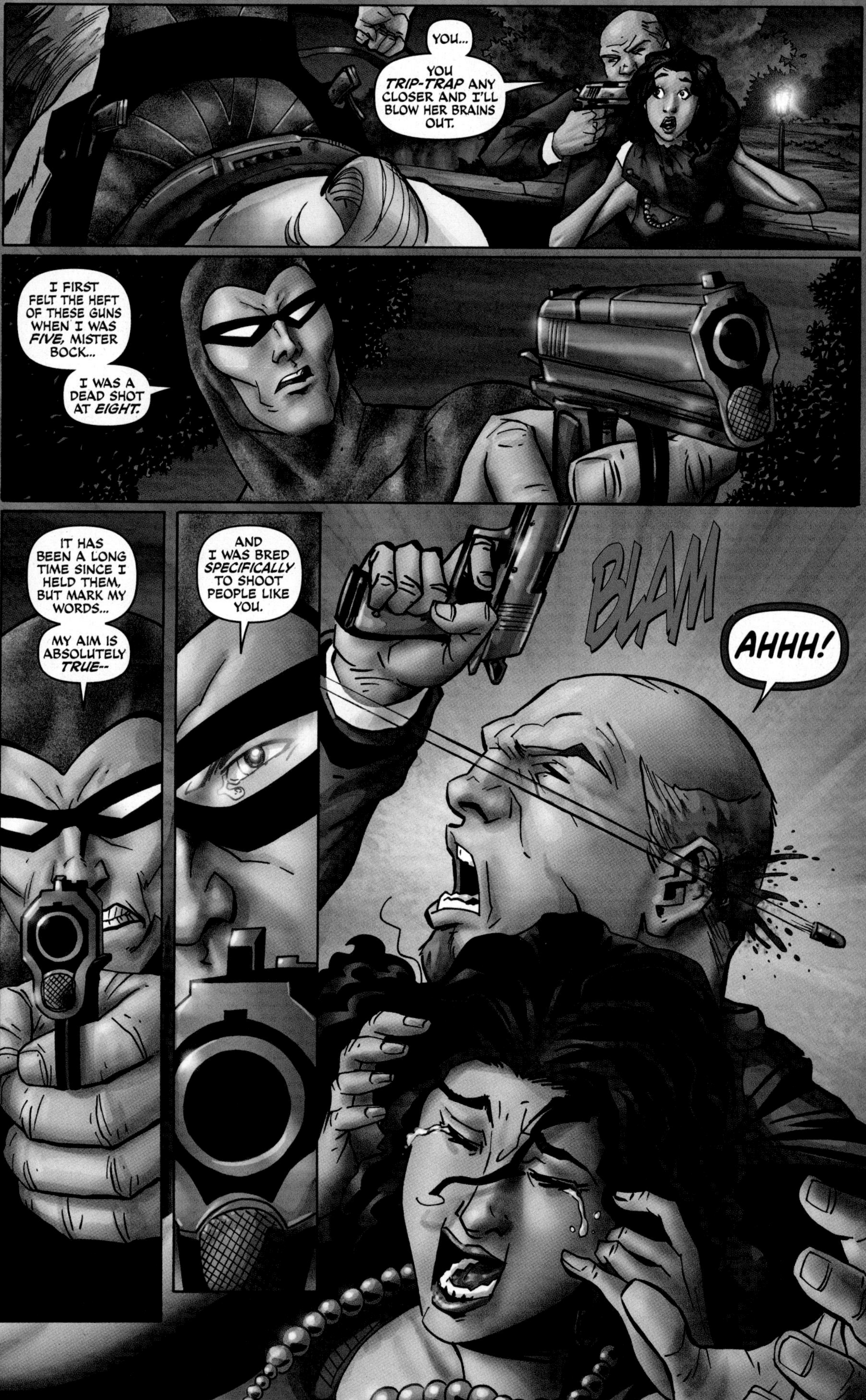

YOU...
YOU *TRIP-TRAP* ANY CLOSER AND I'LL BLOW HER BRAINS OUT.
I FIRST FELT THE HEFT OF THESE GUNS WHEN I WAS *FIVE,* MISTER BOCK...
I WAS A DEAD SHOT AT *EIGHT.*
IT HAS BEEN A LONG TIME SINCE I HELD THEM, BUT MARK MY WORDS...
MY AIM IS ABSOLUTELY *TRUE*--
AND I WAS BRED *SPECIFICALLY* TO SHOOT PEOPLE LIKE YOU.
BLAM
AHHH!

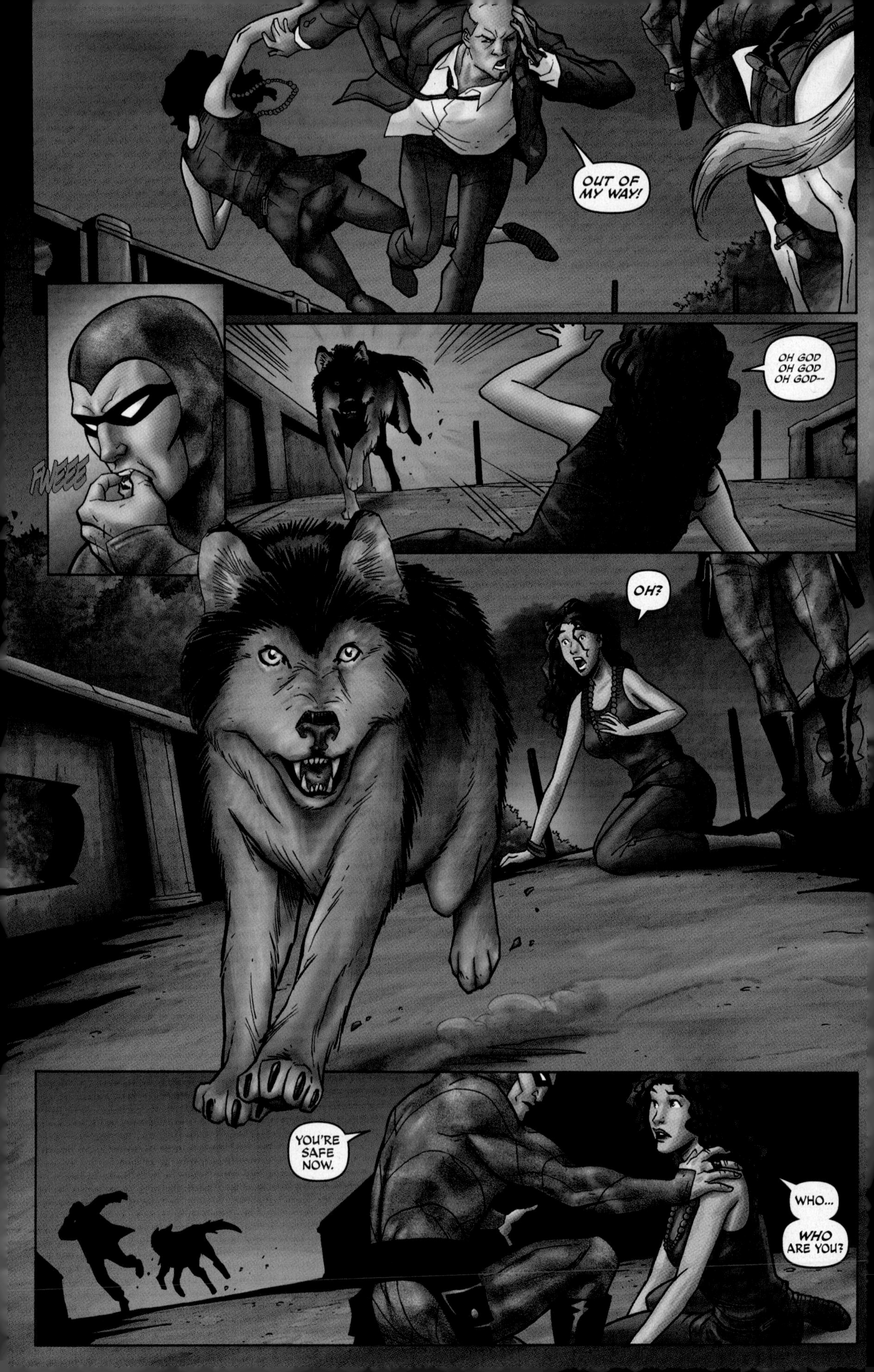
OUT OF MY WAY!
FWEEE
OH GOD OH GOD OH GOD--
OH?
YOU'RE SAFE NOW.
WHO...
WHO ARE YOU?

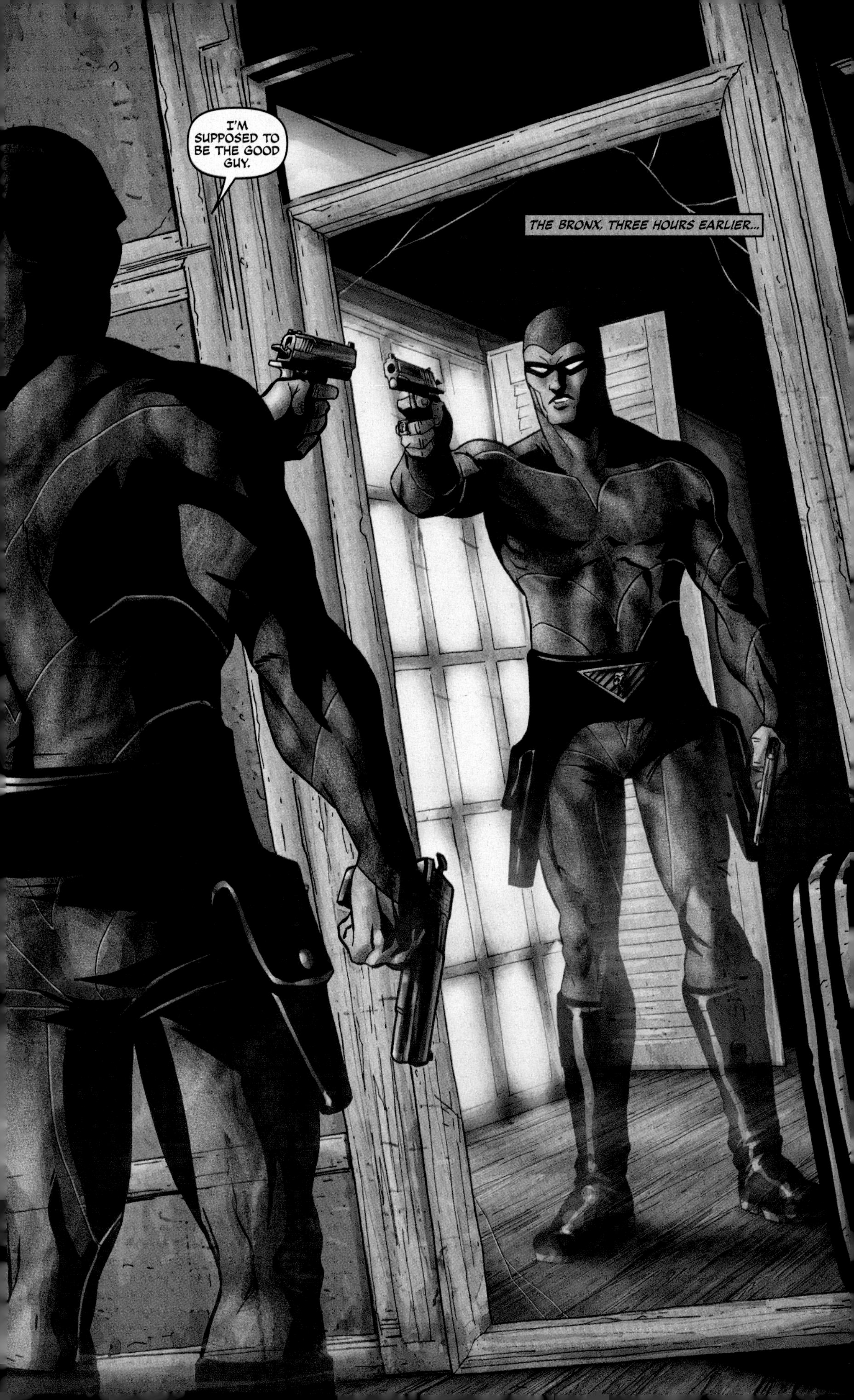
I'M SUPPOSED TO BE THE GOOD GUY.
THE BRONX, THREE HOURS EARLIER...

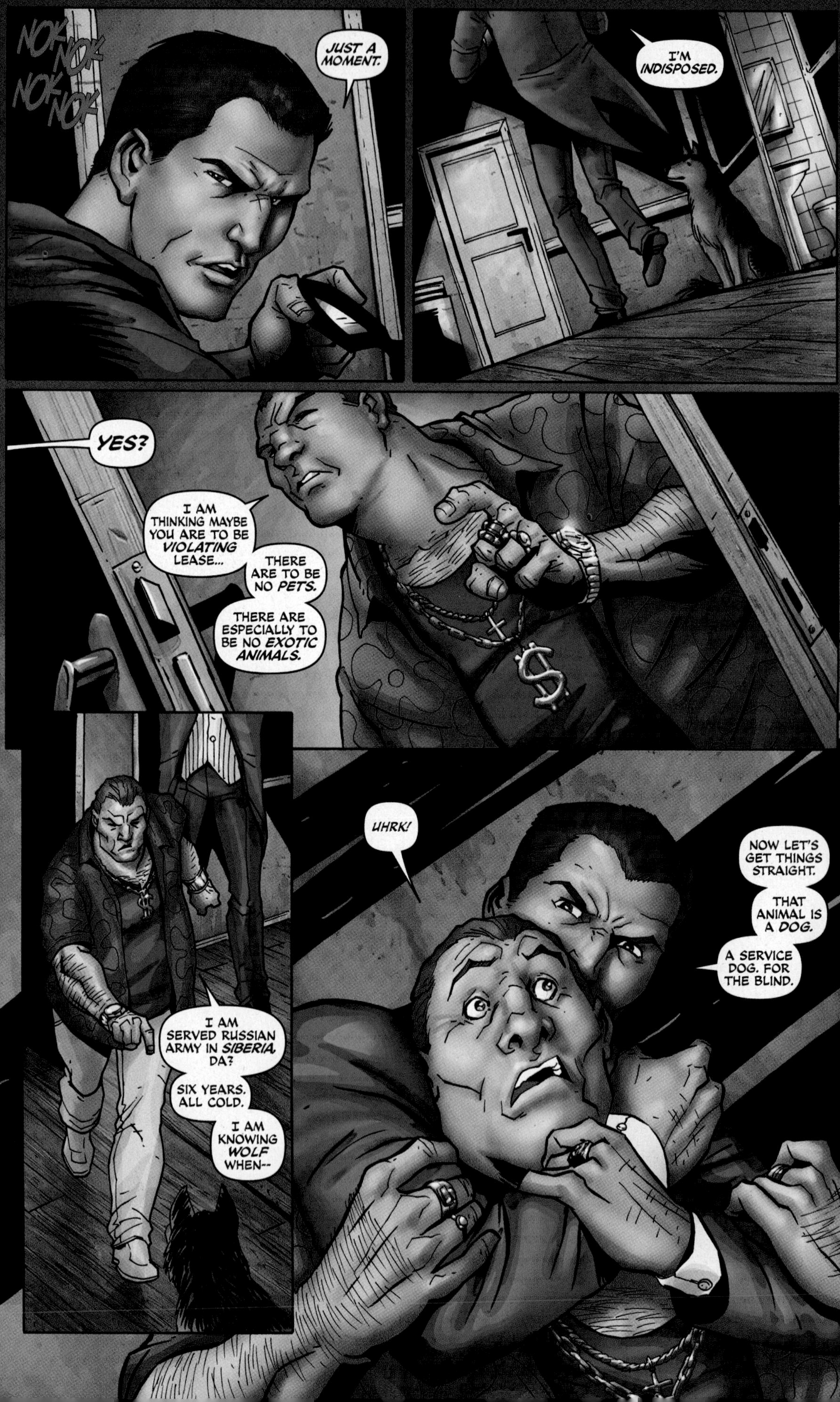
NOK NOK
NOK NOK
JUST A MOMENT.
I'M INDISPOSED.
YES?
I AM THINKING MAYBE YOU ARE TO BE VIOLATING LEASE...
THERE ARE TO BE NO PETS.
THERE ARE ESPECIALLY TO BE NO EXOTIC ANIMALS.
I AM SERVED RUSSIAN ARMY IN SIBERIA, DA?
SIX YEARS. ALL COLD.
I AM KNOWING WOLF WHEN--
UHRK!
NOW LET'S GET THINGS STRAIGHT.
THAT ANIMAL IS A DOG.
A SERVICE DOG. FOR THE BLIND.

HIS HERDING INSTINCT IS *KEEN*.

HE IS INTENSELY *LOYAL*.

AND HE BITES IF *PROVOKED*.

DA?

DA...

AND I AM KNOWING *GHOST* WHEN I SEE ONE...

FOR YOUR *TROUBLES*, FRIEND.

UNITED STATES OF
IN GOD WE TR
ONE HUNDRED

THIS IS YURI. FROM GEORGIA. THE *RUSSIAN* ONE.

TELL ME WHERE I AM TO BE FINDING THE MAN WITH THE *RED BEARD*.

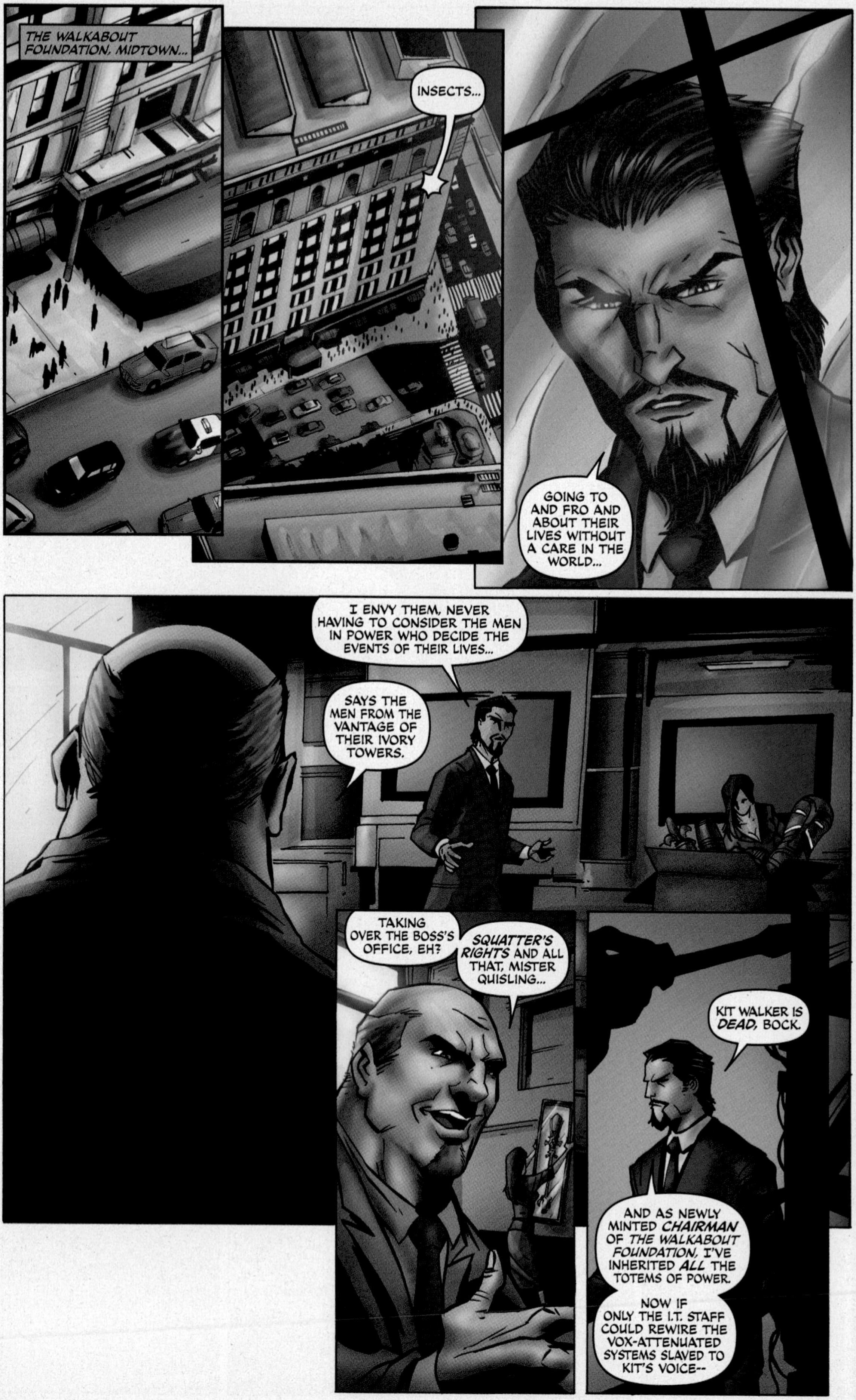

THE WALKABOUT FOUNDATION, MIDTOWN...
INSECTS...
GOING TO AND FRO AND ABOUT THEIR LIVES WITHOUT A CARE IN THE WORLD...
I ENVY THEM, NEVER HAVING TO CONSIDER THE MEN IN POWER WHO DECIDE THE EVENTS OF THEIR LIVES...
SAYS THE MEN FROM THE VANTAGE OF THEIR IVORY TOWERS.
TAKING OVER THE BOSS'S OFFICE, EH?
SQUATTER'S RIGHTS AND ALL THAT, MISTER QUISLING...
KIT WALKER IS DEAD, BOCK.
AND AS NEWLY MINTED CHAIRMAN OF THE WALKABOUT FOUNDATION, I'VE INHERITED ALL THE TOTEMS OF POWER.
NOW IF ONLY THE I.T. STAFF COULD REWIRE THE VOX-ATTENUATED SYSTEMS SLAVED TO KIT'S VOICE--

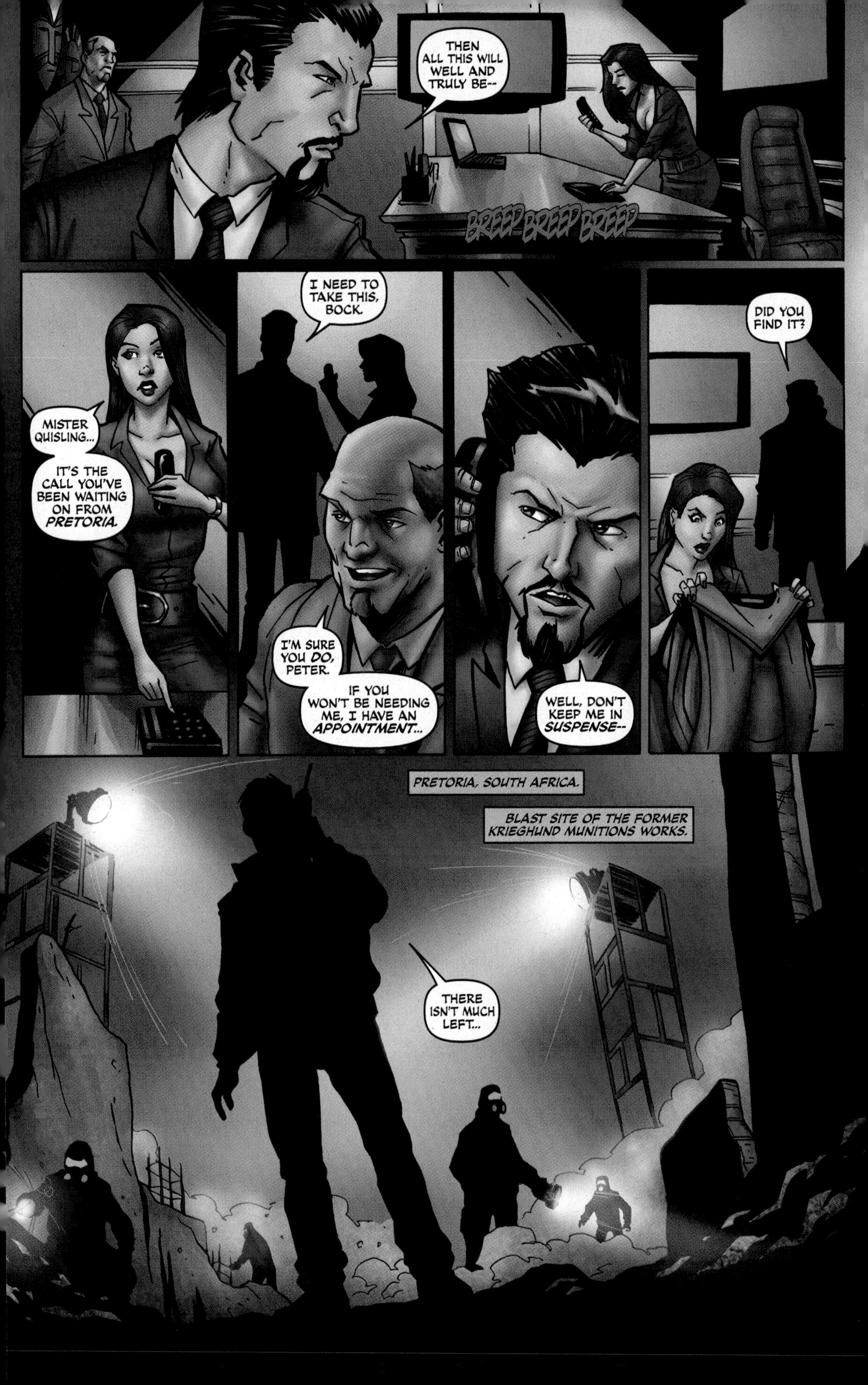
THEN ALL THIS WILL WELL AND TRULY BE--
BREEP BREEP BREEP
MISTER QUISLING...
IT'S THE CALL YOU'VE BEEN WAITING ON FROM *PRETORIA.*
I NEED TO TAKE THIS, BOCK.
I'M SURE YOU *DO,* PETER.
IF YOU WON'T BE NEEDING ME, I HAVE AN *APPOINTMENT...*
WELL, DON'T KEEP ME IN *SUSPENSE--*
DID YOU FIND IT?
PRETORIA, SOUTH AFRICA.
BLAST SITE OF THE FORMER KRIEGHUND MUNITIONS WORKS.
THERE ISN'T MUCH LEFT...

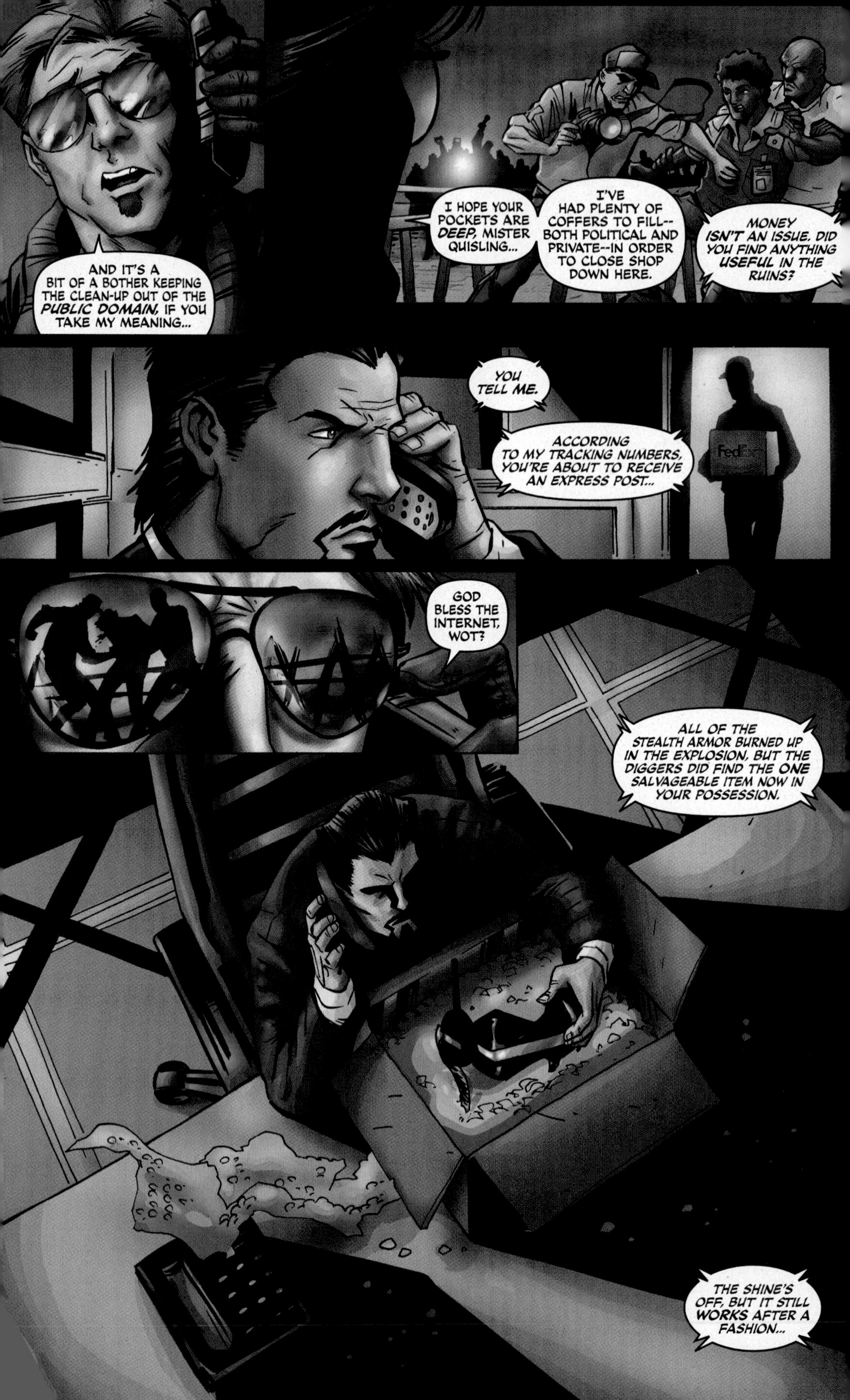
AND IT'S A BIT OF A BOTHER KEEPING THE CLEAN-UP OUT OF THE PUBLIC DOMAIN, IF YOU TAKE MY MEANING...
I HOPE YOUR POCKETS ARE DEEP, MISTER QUISLING...
I'VE HAD PLENTY OF COFFERS TO FILL--BOTH POLITICAL AND PRIVATE--IN ORDER TO CLOSE SHOP DOWN HERE.
MONEY ISN'T AN ISSUE. DID YOU FIND ANYTHING USEFUL IN THE RUINS?
YOU TELL ME.
ACCORDING TO MY TRACKING NUMBERS, YOU'RE ABOUT TO RECEIVE AN EXPRESS POST...
FedEx
GOD BLESS THE INTERNET, WOT?
ALL OF THE STEALTH ARMOR BURNED UP IN THE EXPLOSION, BUT THE DIGGERS DID FIND THE ONE SALVAGEABLE ITEM NOW IN YOUR POSSESSION.
THE SHINE'S OFF, BUT IT STILL WORKS AFTER A FASHION...

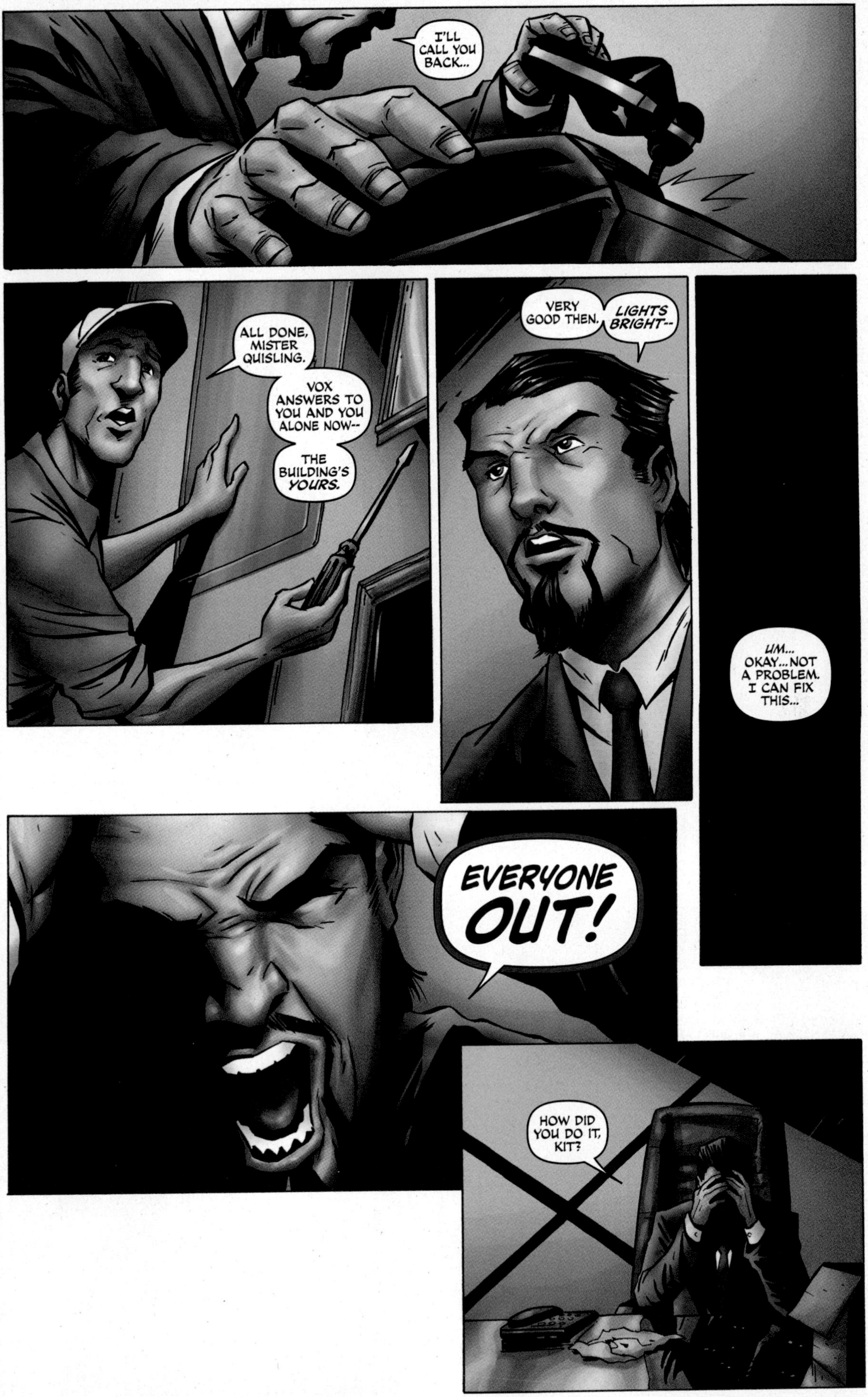
I'LL CALL YOU BACK...
ALL DONE, MISTER QUISLING.
VOX ANSWERS TO YOU AND YOU ALONE NOW--
THE BUILDING'S *YOURS.*
VERY GOOD THEN.
LIGHTS BRIGHT--
UM... OKAY...NOT A PROBLEM. I CAN FIX THIS...
EVERYONE OUT!
HOW DID YOU DO IT, KIT?

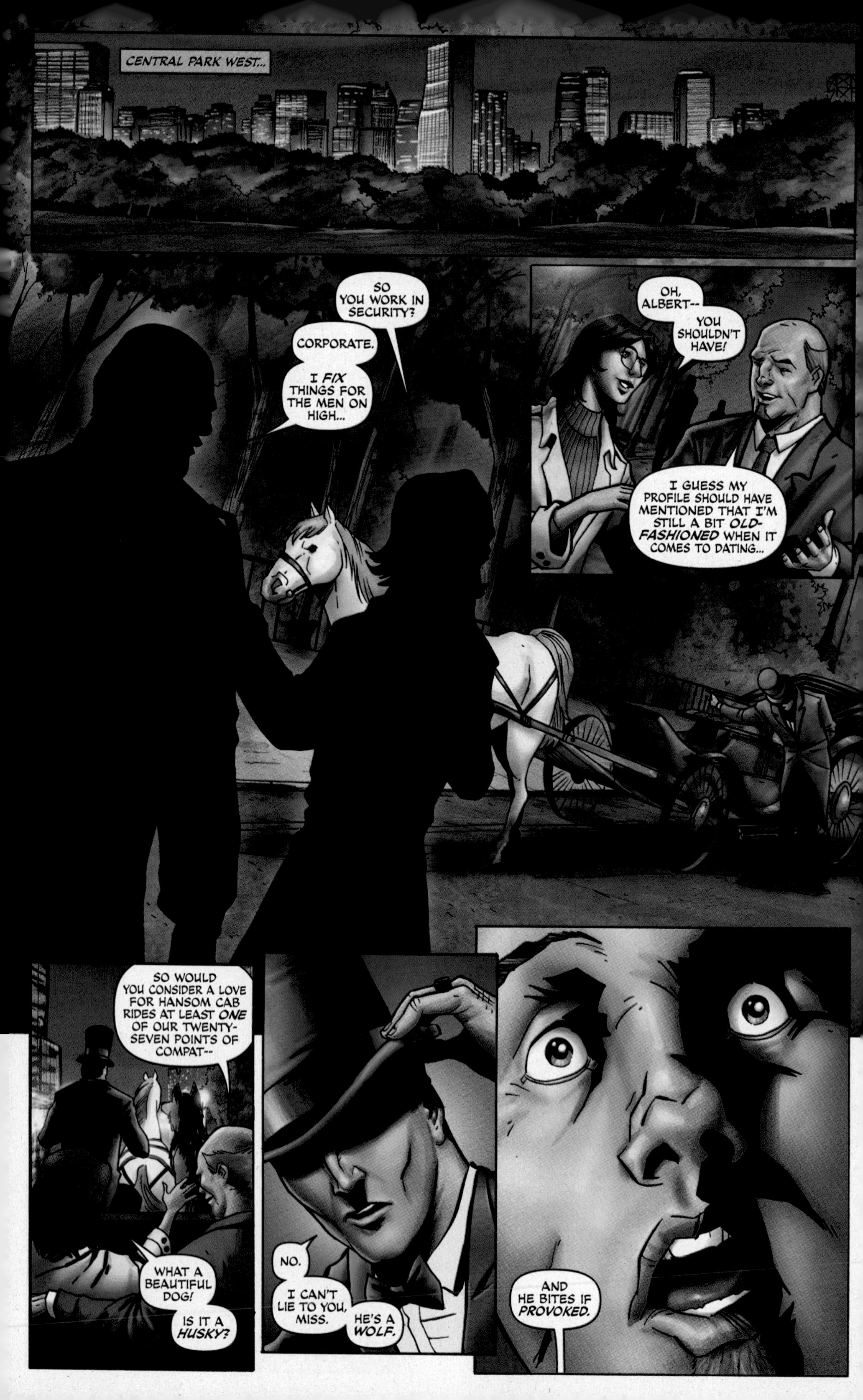
CENTRAL PARK WEST...
SO YOU WORK IN SECURITY?
CORPORATE.
I FIX THINGS FOR THE MEN ON HIGH...
OH, ALBERT--
YOU SHOULDN'T HAVE!
I GUESS MY PROFILE SHOULD HAVE MENTIONED THAT I'M STILL A BIT OLD-FASHIONED WHEN IT COMES TO DATING...
SO WOULD YOU CONSIDER A LOVE FOR HANSOM CAB RIDES AT LEAST ONE OF OUR TWENTY-SEVEN POINTS OF COMPAT--
WHAT A BEAUTIFUL DOG!
IS IT A HUSKY?
NO.
I CAN'T LIE TO YOU, MISS.
HE'S A WOLF.
AND HE BITES IF PROVOKED.

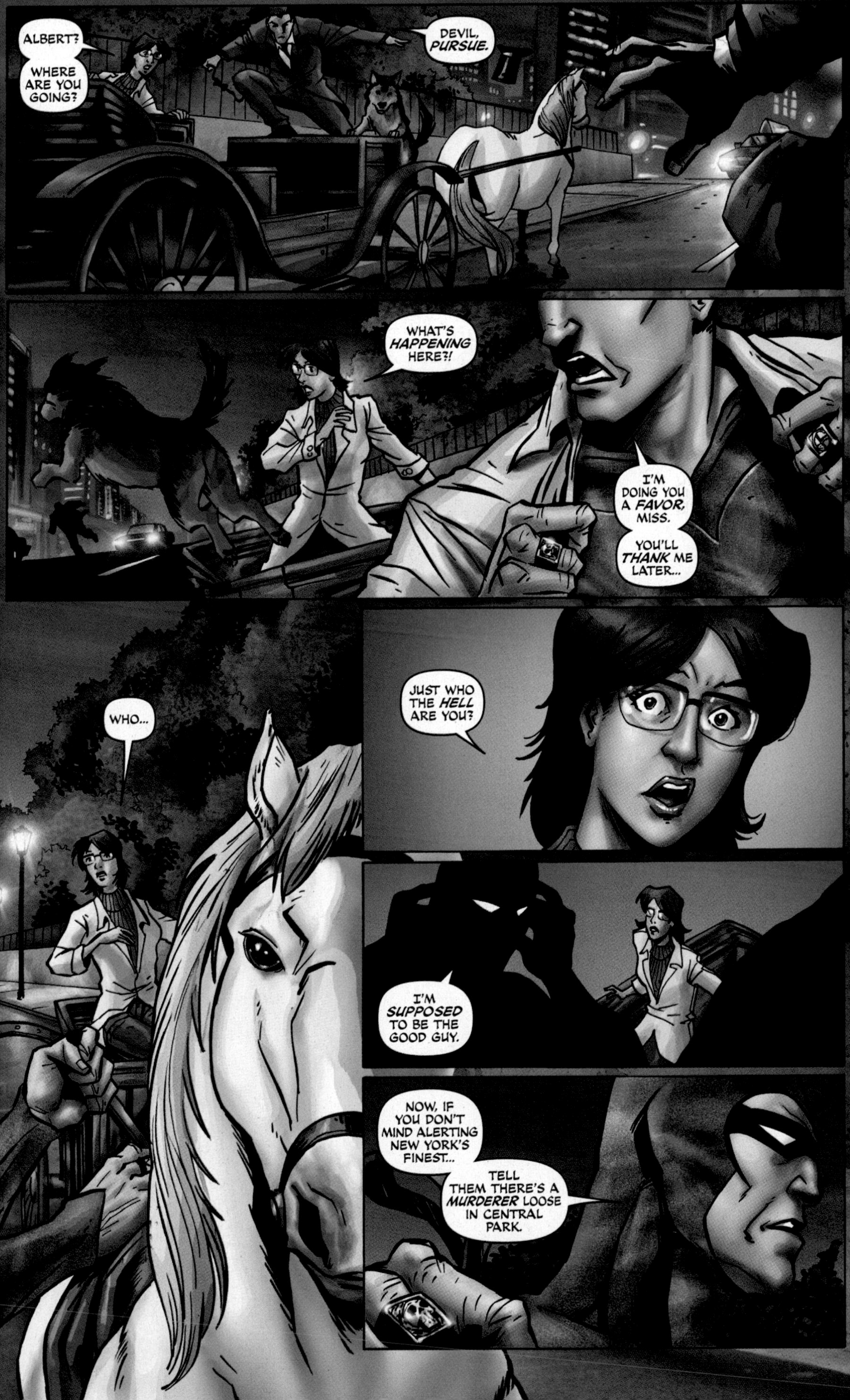
ALBERT?
WHERE ARE YOU GOING?
DEVIL, PURSUE.
WHAT'S HAPPENING HERE?!
I'M DOING YOU A FAVOR, MISS.
YOU'LL THANK ME LATER...
WHO...
JUST WHO THE HELL ARE YOU?
I'M SUPPOSED TO BE THE GOOD GUY.
NOW, IF YOU DON'T MIND ALERTING NEW YORK'S FINEST...
TELL THEM THERE'S A MURDERER LOOSE IN CENTRAL PARK.

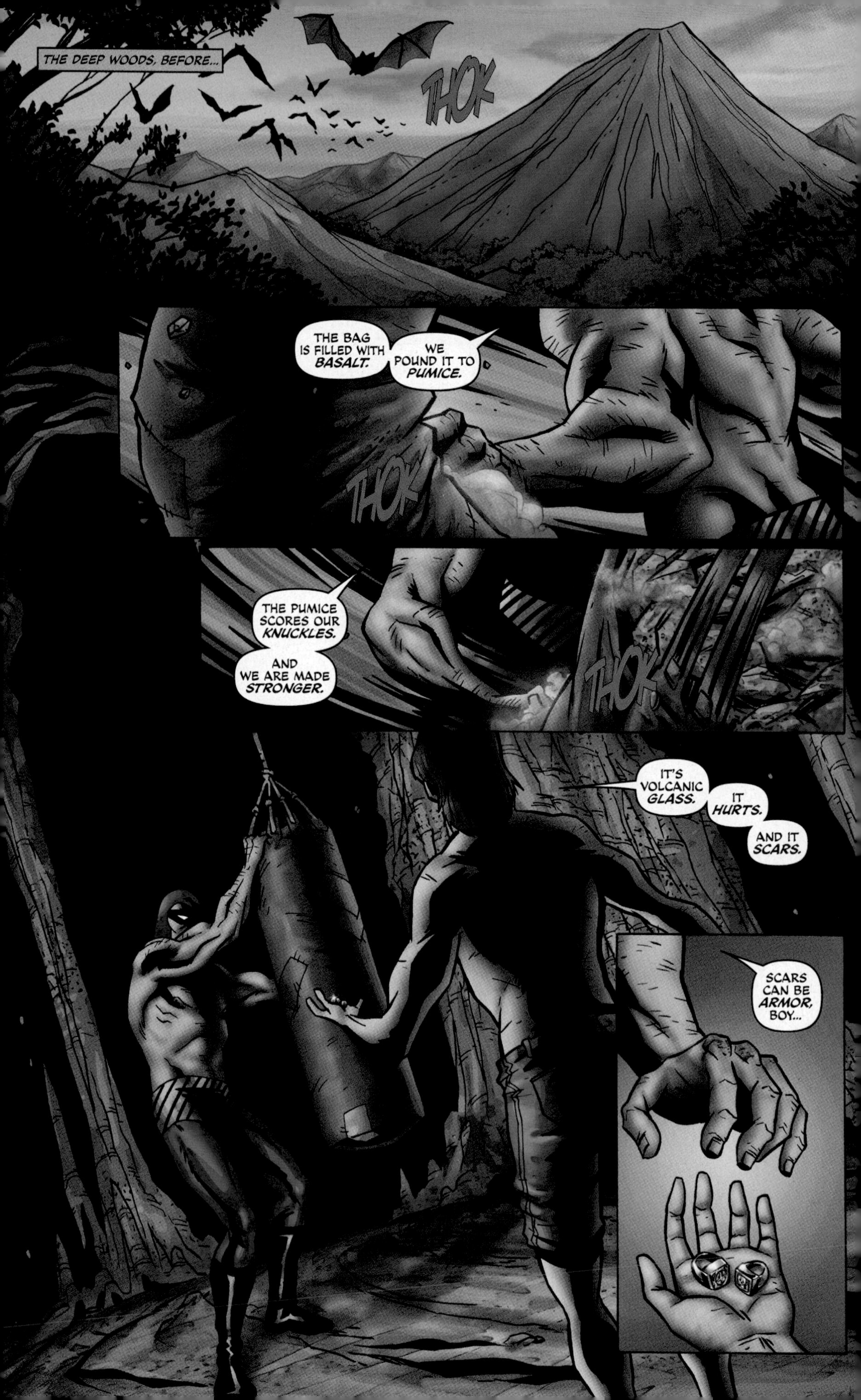
THE DEEP WOODS, BEFORE...
THOK
THE BAG IS FILLED WITH BASALT.
WE POUND IT TO PUMICE.
THOK
THE PUMICE SCORES OUR KNUCKLES.
AND WE ARE MADE STRONGER.
THOK
IT'S VOLCANIC GLASS.
IT HURTS.
AND IT SCARS.
SCARS CAN BE ARMOR, BOY...

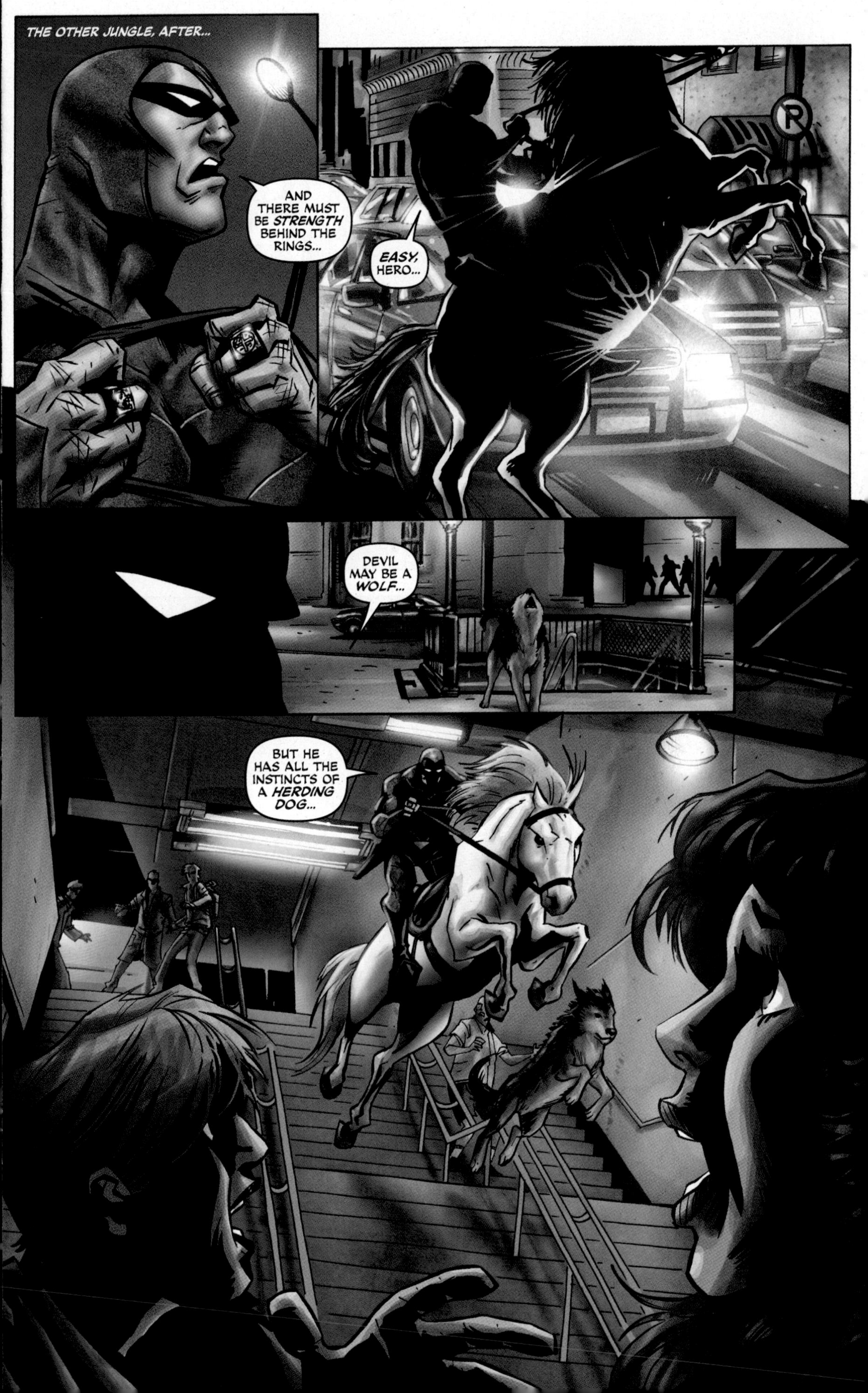
THE OTHER JUNGLE, AFTER...
AND THERE MUST BE STRENGTH BEHIND THE RINGS...
EASY, HERO...
DEVIL MAY BE A WOLF...
BUT HE HAS ALL THE INSTINCTS OF A HERDING DOG...

I'M *HERE,* SIR...

THE *JUNGLE PATROL* STANDS READY TO ASSIST YOU.

WE REMAIN THE *ELITE.*

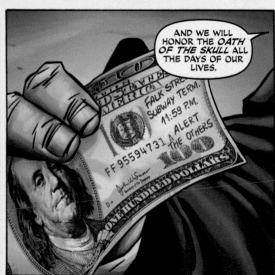

AND WE WILL HONOR THE *OATH OF THE SKULL* ALL THE DAYS OF OUR LIVES.

FALK STR... SUBWAY TERM. 11:59 P.M. ALERT THE OTHERS

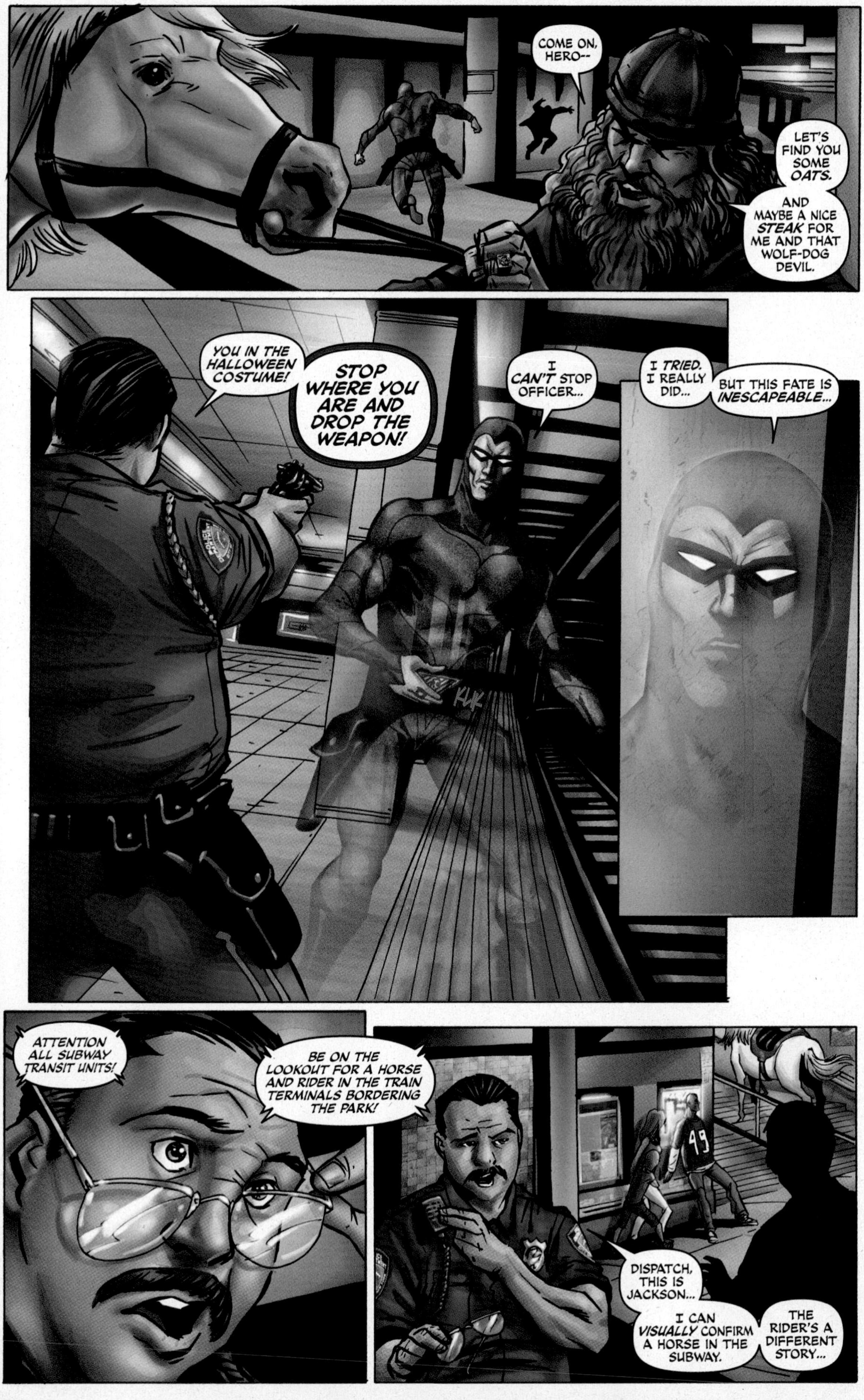
COME ON, HERO--
LET'S FIND YOU SOME OATS.
AND MAYBE A NICE STEAK FOR ME AND THAT WOLF-DOG DEVIL.
YOU IN THE HALLOWEEN COSTUME!
STOP WHERE YOU ARE AND DROP THE WEAPON!
I CAN'T STOP OFFICER...
I TRIED. I REALLY DID...
BUT THIS FATE IS INESCAPEABLE...
ATTENTION ALL SUBWAY TRANSIT UNITS!
BE ON THE LOOKOUT FOR A HORSE AND RIDER IN THE TRAIN TERMINALS BORDERING THE PARK!
DISPATCH, THIS IS JACKSON...
I CAN VISUALLY CONFIRM A HORSE IN THE SUBWAY.
THE RIDER'S A DIFFERENT STORY...

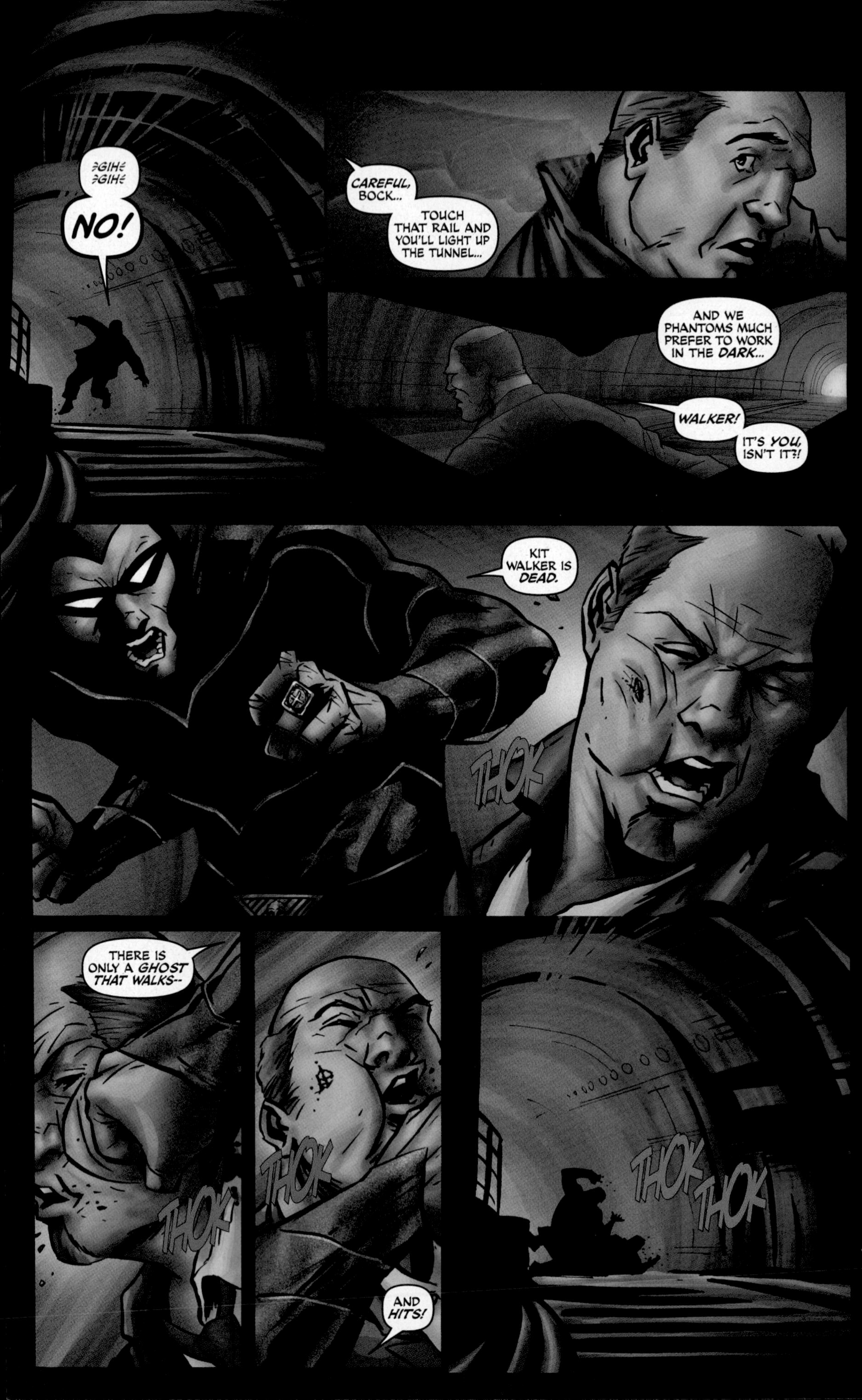

ƎGIHƐ ƎGIHƐ
NO!
CAREFUL, BOCK...
TOUCH THAT RAIL AND YOU'LL LIGHT UP THE TUNNEL...
AND WE PHANTOMS MUCH PREFER TO WORK IN THE DARK...
WALKER!
IT'S YOU, ISN'T IT?!
KIT WALKER IS DEAD.
THOK
THERE IS ONLY A GHOST THAT WALKS--
THOK
THOK
AND HITS!
THOK
THOK

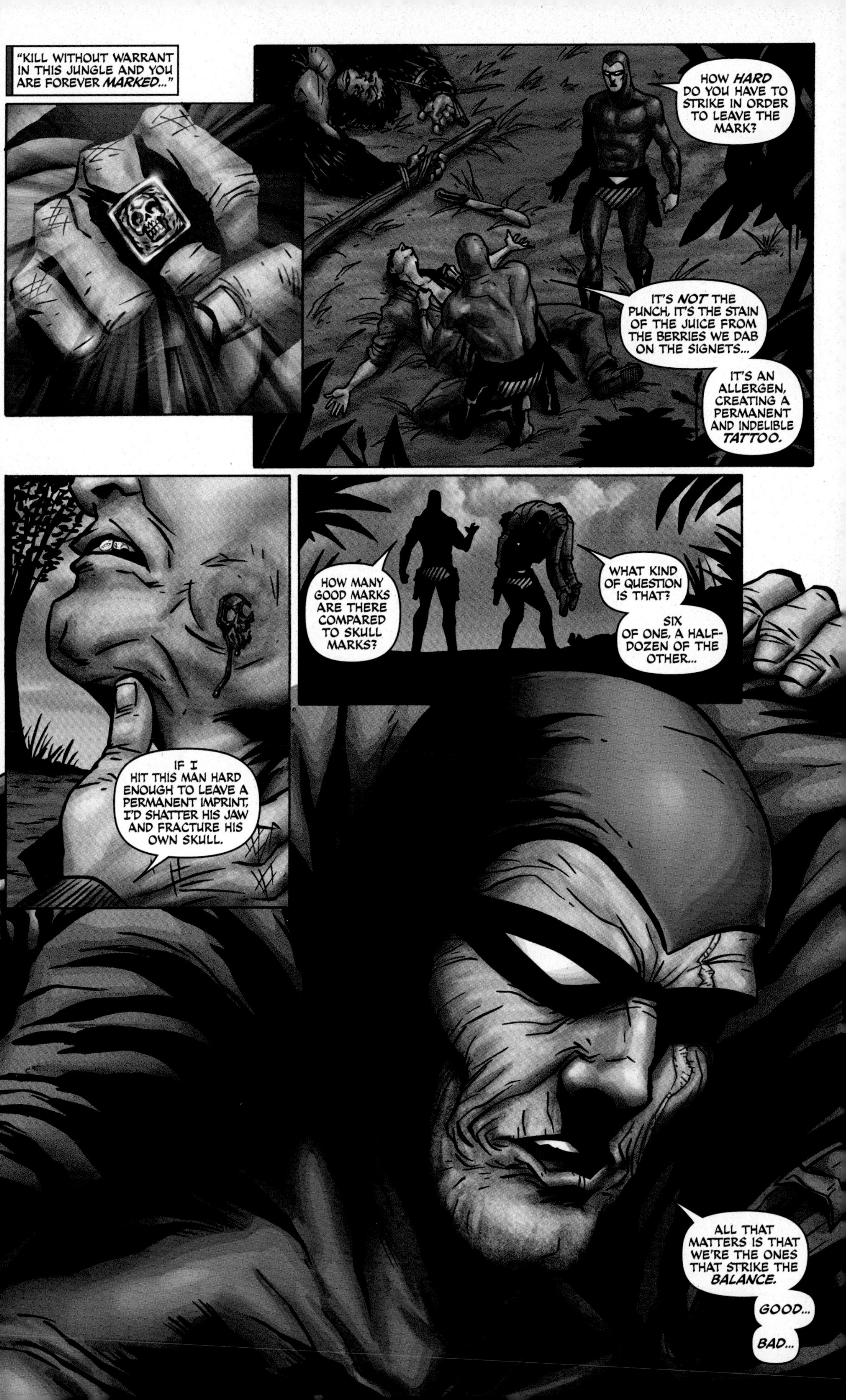
"KILL WITHOUT WARRANT IN THIS JUNGLE AND YOU ARE FOREVER *MARKED*..."
HOW *HARD* DO YOU HAVE TO STRIKE IN ORDER TO LEAVE THE MARK?
IT'S *NOT* THE PUNCH, IT'S THE STAIN OF THE JUICE FROM THE BERRIES WE DAB ON THE SIGNETS...
IT'S AN ALLERGEN, CREATING A PERMANENT AND INDELIBLE *TATTOO.*
IF I HIT THIS MAN HARD ENOUGH TO LEAVE A PERMANENT IMPRINT, I'D SHATTER HIS JAW AND FRACTURE HIS OWN SKULL.
HOW MANY GOOD MARKS ARE THERE COMPARED TO SKULL MARKS?
WHAT KIND OF QUESTION IS THAT?
SIX OF ONE, A HALF-DOZEN OF THE OTHER...
ALL THAT MATTERS IS THAT WE'RE THE ONES THAT STRIKE THE *BALANCE.*
GOOD...
BAD...

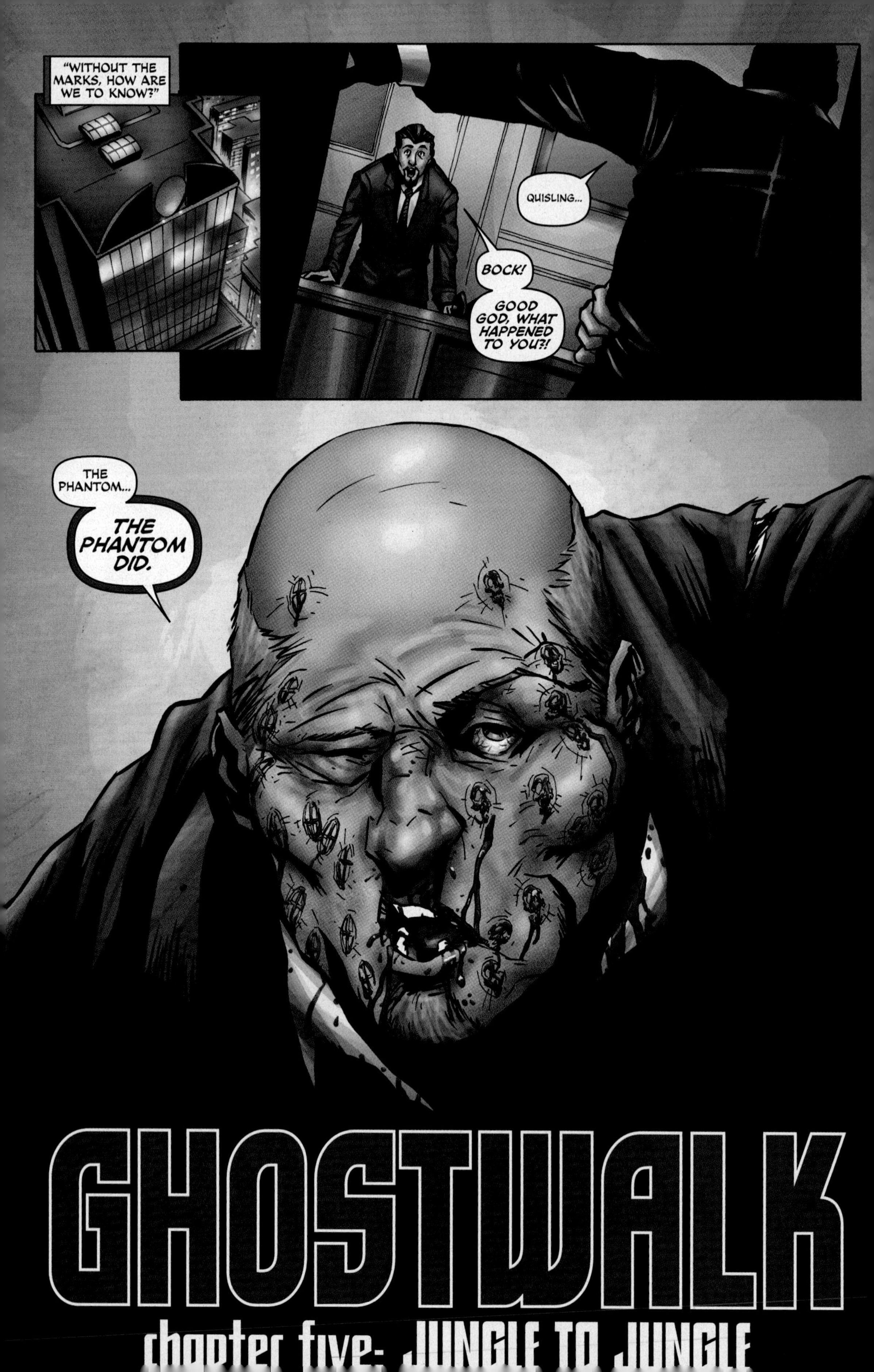
"WITHOUT THE MARKS, HOW ARE WE TO KNOW?"
QUISLING...
BOCK!
GOOD GOD, WHAT HAPPENED TO YOU?!
THE PHANTOM...
THE PHANTOM DID.
GHOSTWALK
chapter five: JUNGLE TO JUNGLE

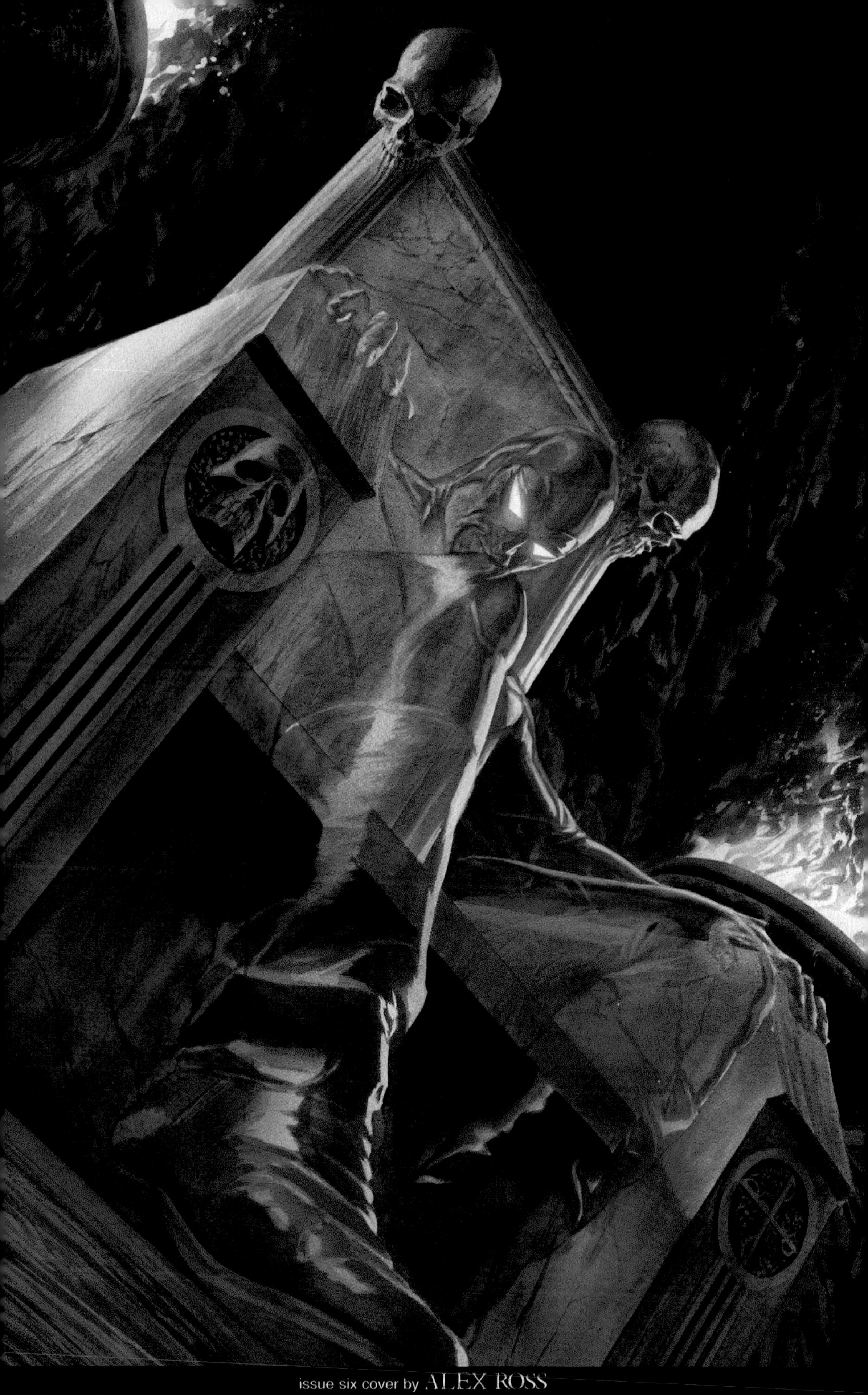

issue six cover by ALEX ROSS

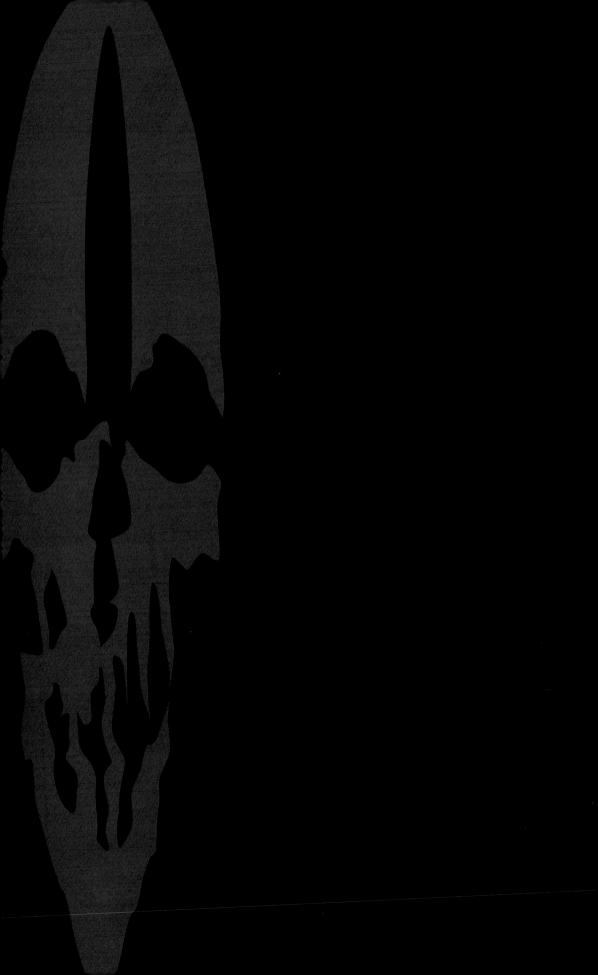

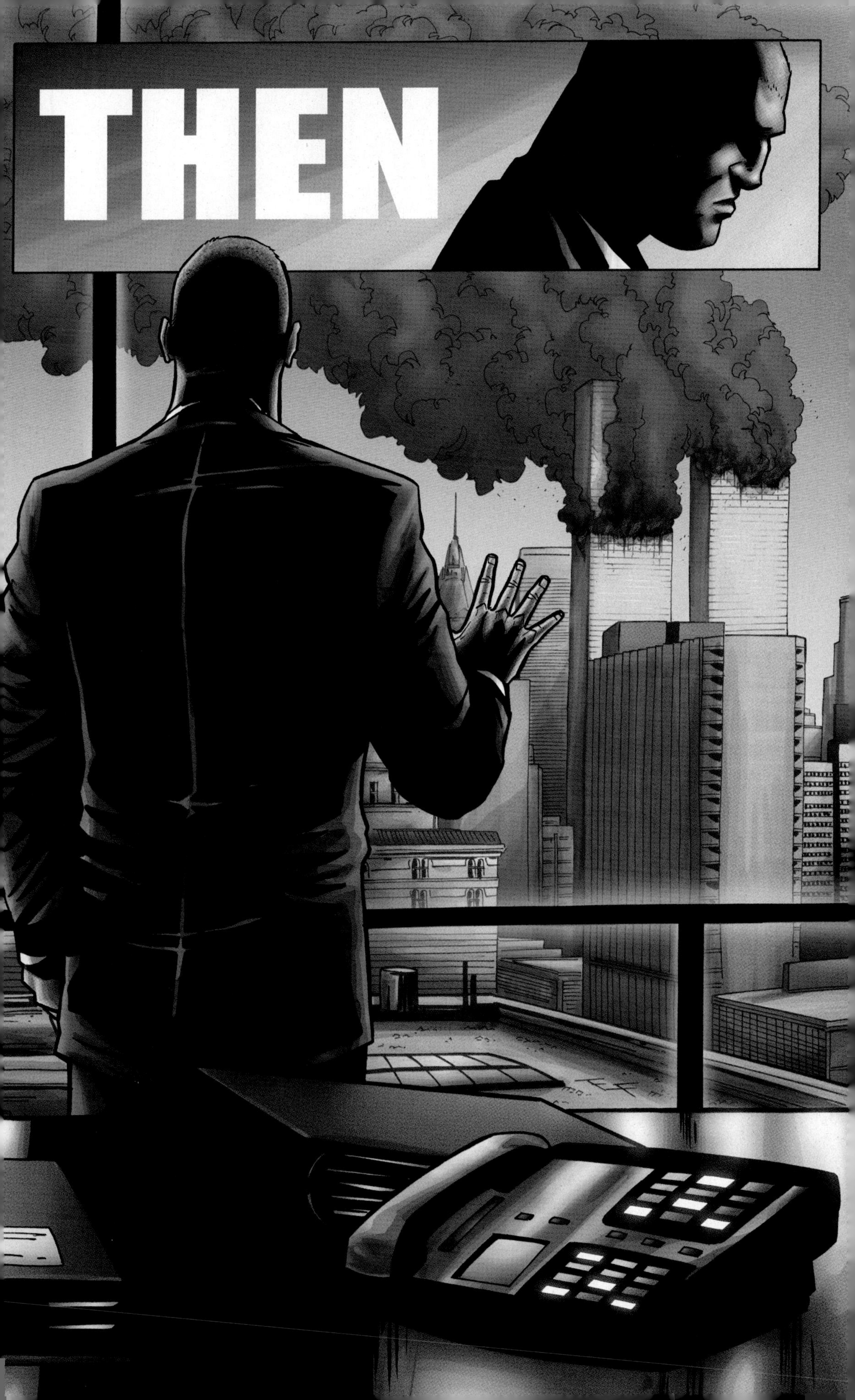
THEN

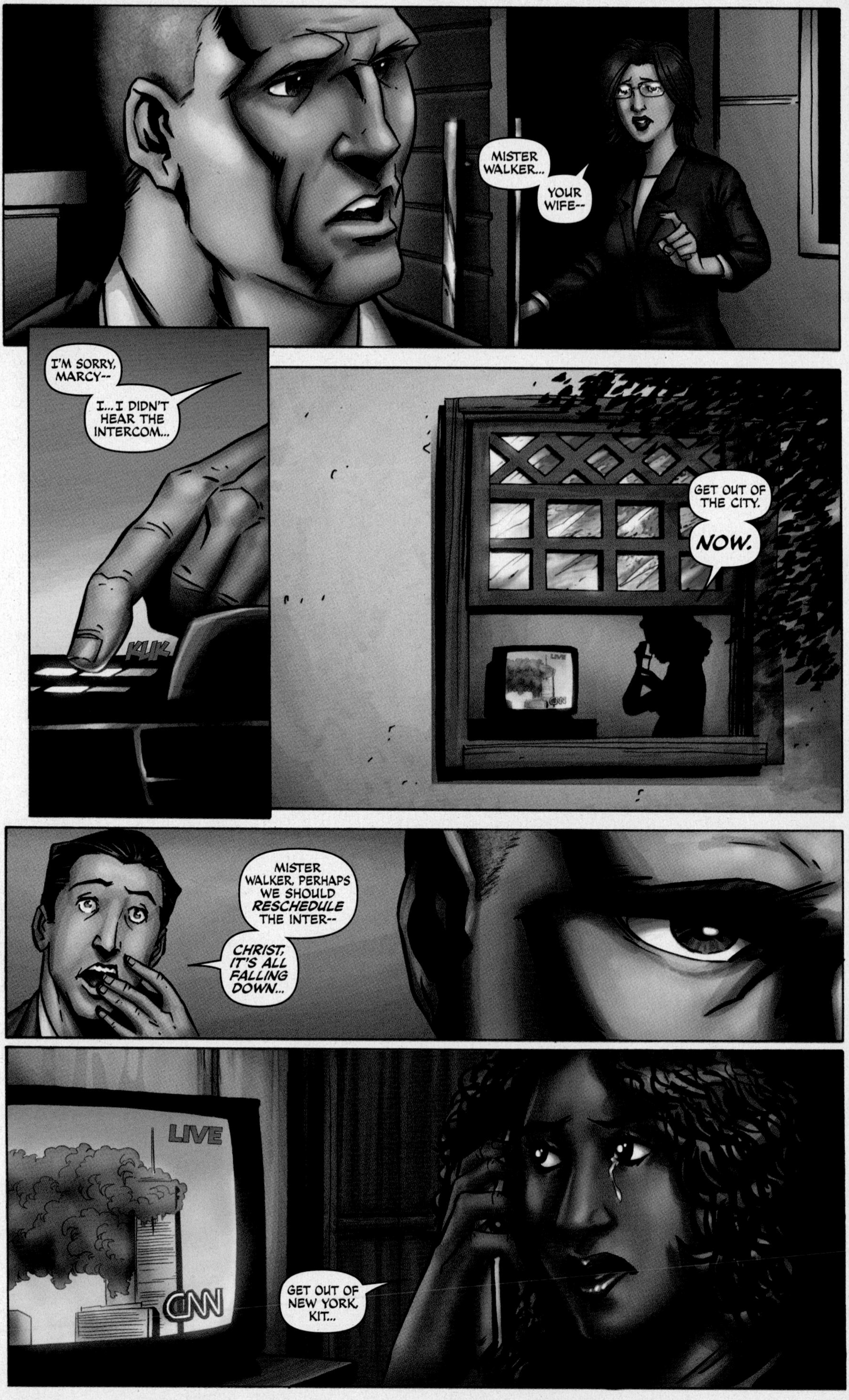
MISTER WALKER...
YOUR WIFE--
I'M SORRY, MARCY--
I... I DIDN'T HEAR THE INTERCOM...
KLIK
GET OUT OF THE CITY.
NOW.
LIVE
CNN
MISTER WALKER, PERHAPS WE SHOULD RESCHEDULE THE INTER--
CHRIST, IT'S ALL FALLING DOWN...
LIVE
CNN
GET OUT OF NEW YORK, KIT...

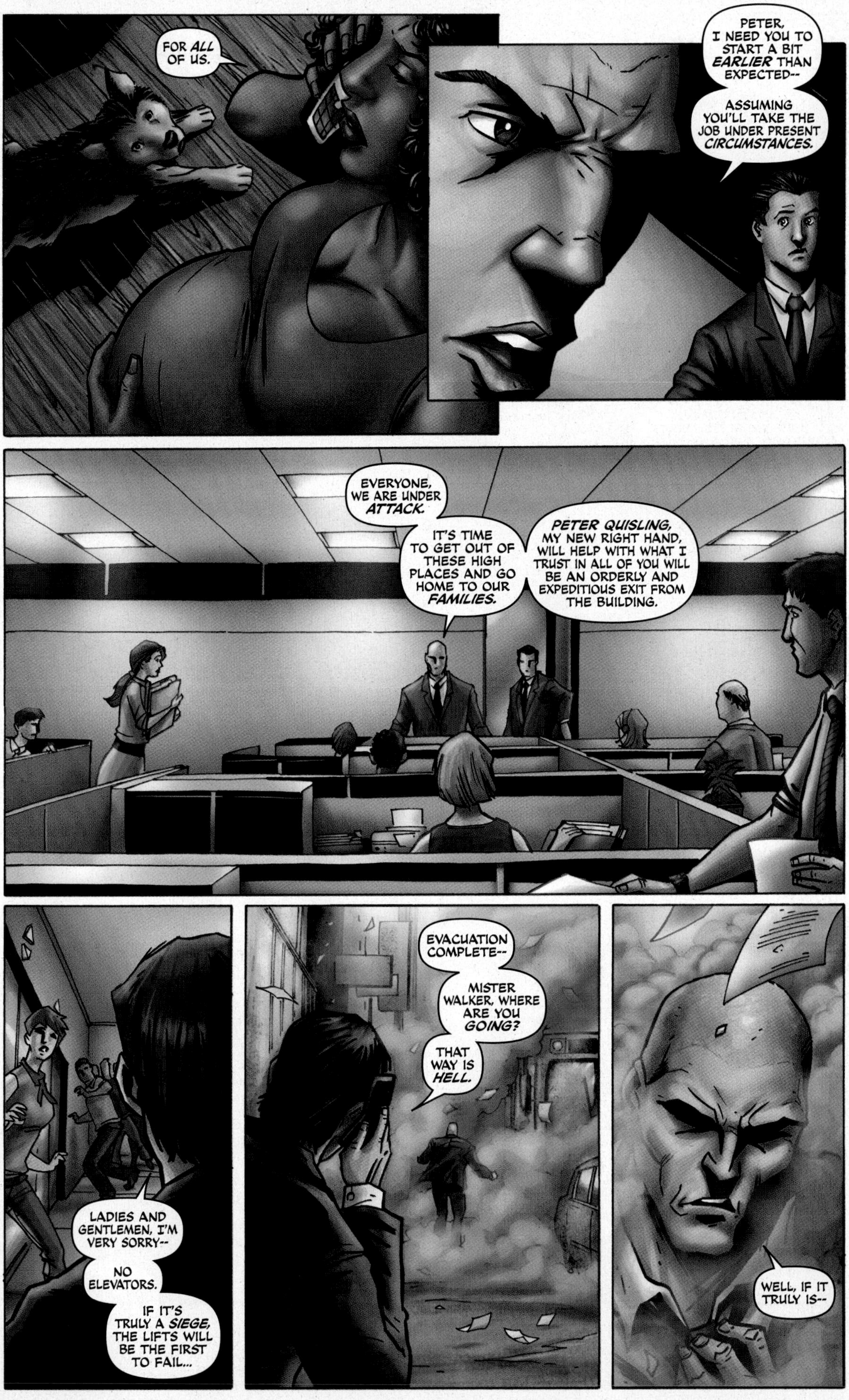
FOR *ALL* OF US.
PETER, I NEED YOU TO START A BIT *EARLIER* THAN EXPECTED--
ASSUMING YOU'LL TAKE THE JOB UNDER PRESENT *CIRCUMSTANCES.*
EVERYONE, WE ARE UNDER *ATTACK.*
IT'S TIME TO GET OUT OF THESE HIGH PLACES AND GO HOME TO OUR *FAMILIES.*
PETER QUISLING, MY NEW RIGHT HAND, WILL HELP WITH WHAT I TRUST IN ALL OF YOU WILL BE AN ORDERLY AND EXPEDITIOUS EXIT FROM THE BUILDING.
LADIES AND GENTLEMEN, I'M VERY SORRY--
NO ELEVATORS.
IF IT'S TRULY A *SIEGE,* THE LIFTS WILL BE THE FIRST TO FAIL...
EVACUATION COMPLETE--
MISTER WALKER, WHERE ARE YOU *GOING?*
THAT WAY IS *HELL.*
WELL, IF IT TRULY IS--

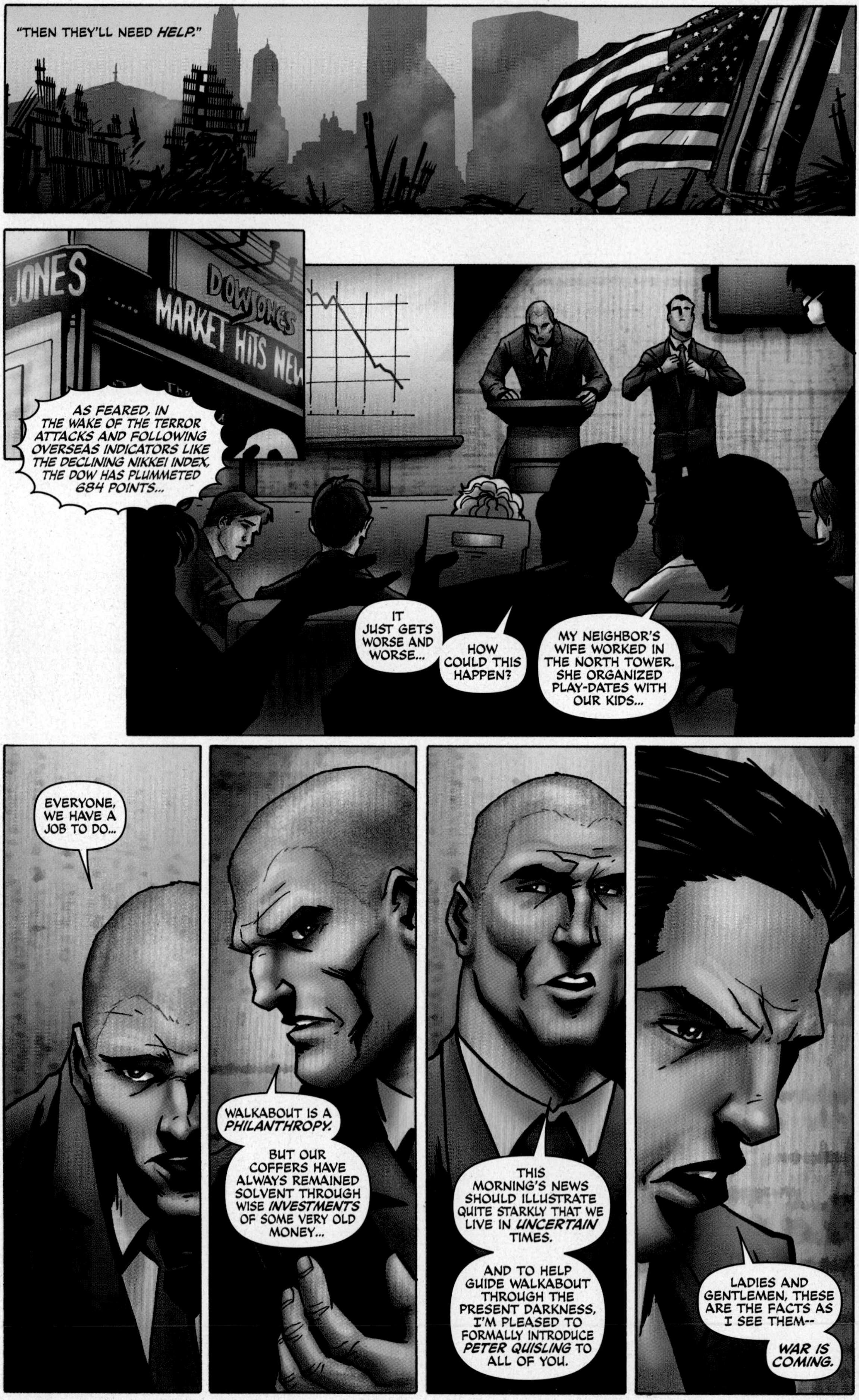
"THEN THEY'LL NEED *HELP*."
JONES
DOW JONES
MARKET HITS NEW
AS FEARED, IN THE WAKE OF THE TERROR ATTACKS AND FOLLOWING OVERSEAS INDICATORS LIKE THE DECLINING NIKKEI INDEX, THE DOW HAS PLUMMETED 684 POINTS...
IT JUST GETS WORSE AND WORSE...
HOW COULD THIS HAPPEN?
MY NEIGHBOR'S WIFE WORKED IN THE NORTH TOWER. SHE ORGANIZED PLAY-DATES WITH OUR KIDS...
EVERYONE, WE HAVE A JOB TO DO...
WALKABOUT IS A *PHILANTHROPY.*
BUT OUR COFFERS HAVE ALWAYS REMAINED SOLVENT THROUGH WISE *INVESTMENTS* OF SOME VERY OLD MONEY...
THIS MORNING'S NEWS SHOULD ILLUSTRATE QUITE STARKLY THAT WE LIVE IN *UNCERTAIN* TIMES.
AND TO HELP GUIDE WALKABOUT THROUGH THE PRESENT DARKNESS, I'M PLEASED TO FORMALLY INTRODUCE *PETER QUISLING* TO ALL OF YOU.
LADIES AND GENTLEMEN, THESE ARE THE FACTS AS I SEE THEM--
WAR IS COMING.

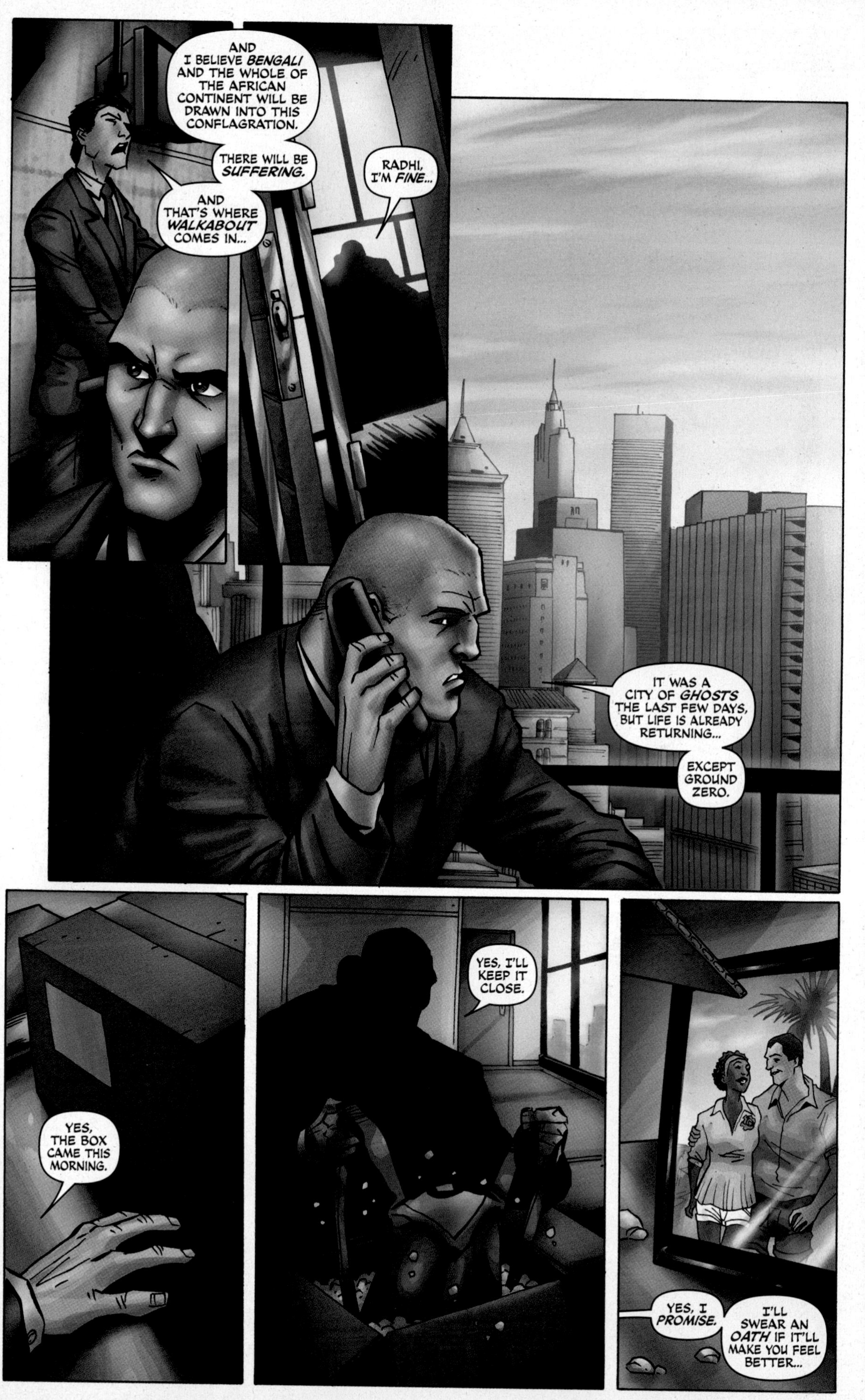
AND I BELIEVE *BENGALI* AND THE WHOLE OF THE AFRICAN CONTINENT WILL BE DRAWN INTO THIS CONFLAGRATION.
THERE WILL BE *SUFFERING.*
AND THAT'S WHERE *WALKABOUT* COMES IN...
RADHI, I'M *FINE*...
IT WAS A CITY OF *GHOSTS* THE LAST FEW DAYS, BUT LIFE IS ALREADY RETURNING...
EXCEPT GROUND ZERO.
YES, THE BOX CAME THIS MORNING.
YES, I'LL KEEP IT CLOSE.
YES, I *PROMISE.*
I'LL SWEAR AN *OATH* IF IT'LL MAKE YOU FEEL BETTER...

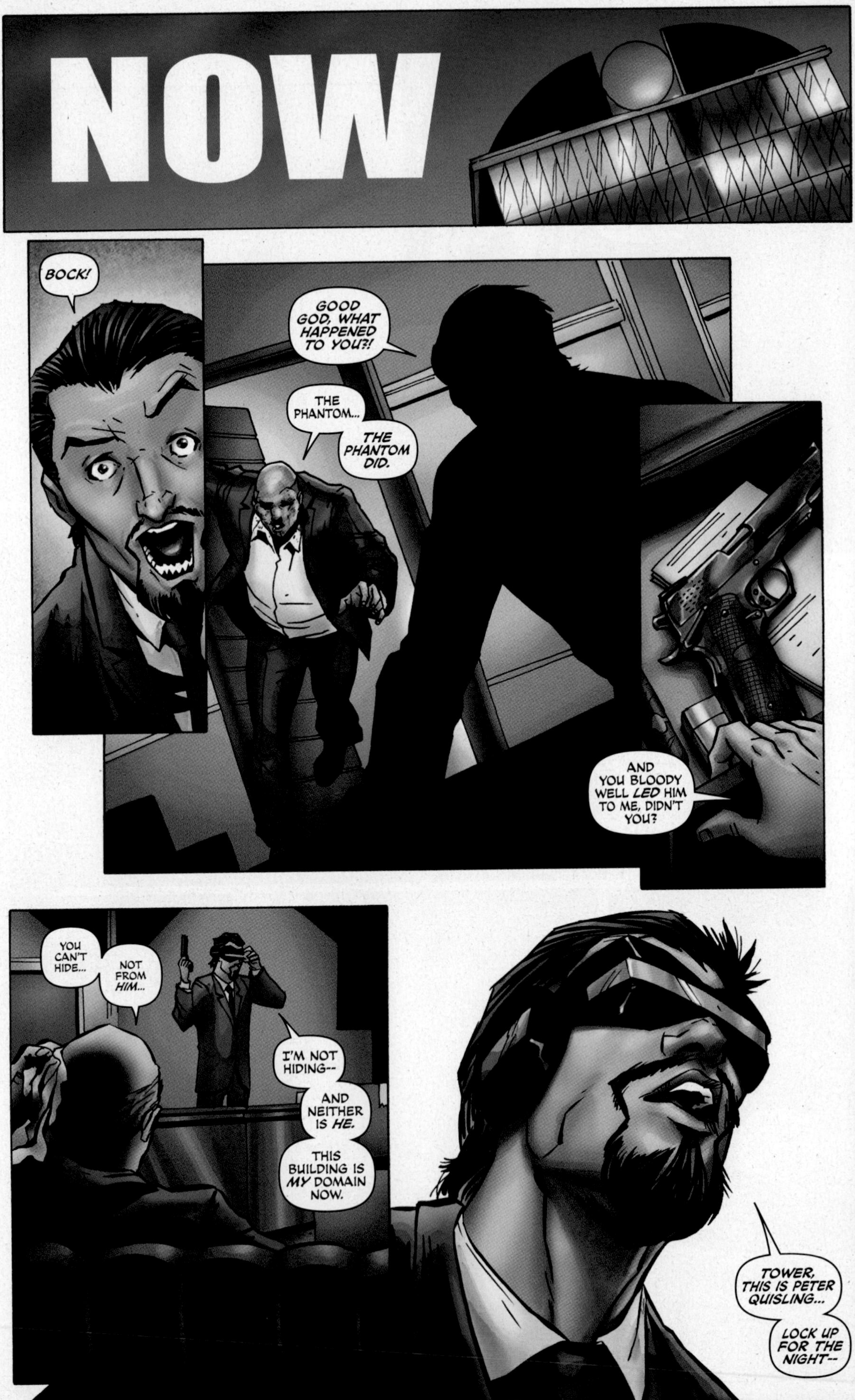
NOW
BOCK!
GOOD GOD, WHAT HAPPENED TO YOU?!
THE PHANTOM...
THE PHANTOM DID.
AND YOU BLOODY WELL LED HIM TO ME, DIDN'T YOU?
YOU CAN'T HIDE...
NOT FROM HIM...
I'M NOT HIDING--
AND NEITHER IS HE.
THIS BUILDING IS MY DOMAIN NOW.
TOWER, THIS IS PETER QUISLING...
LOCK UP FOR THE NIGHT--

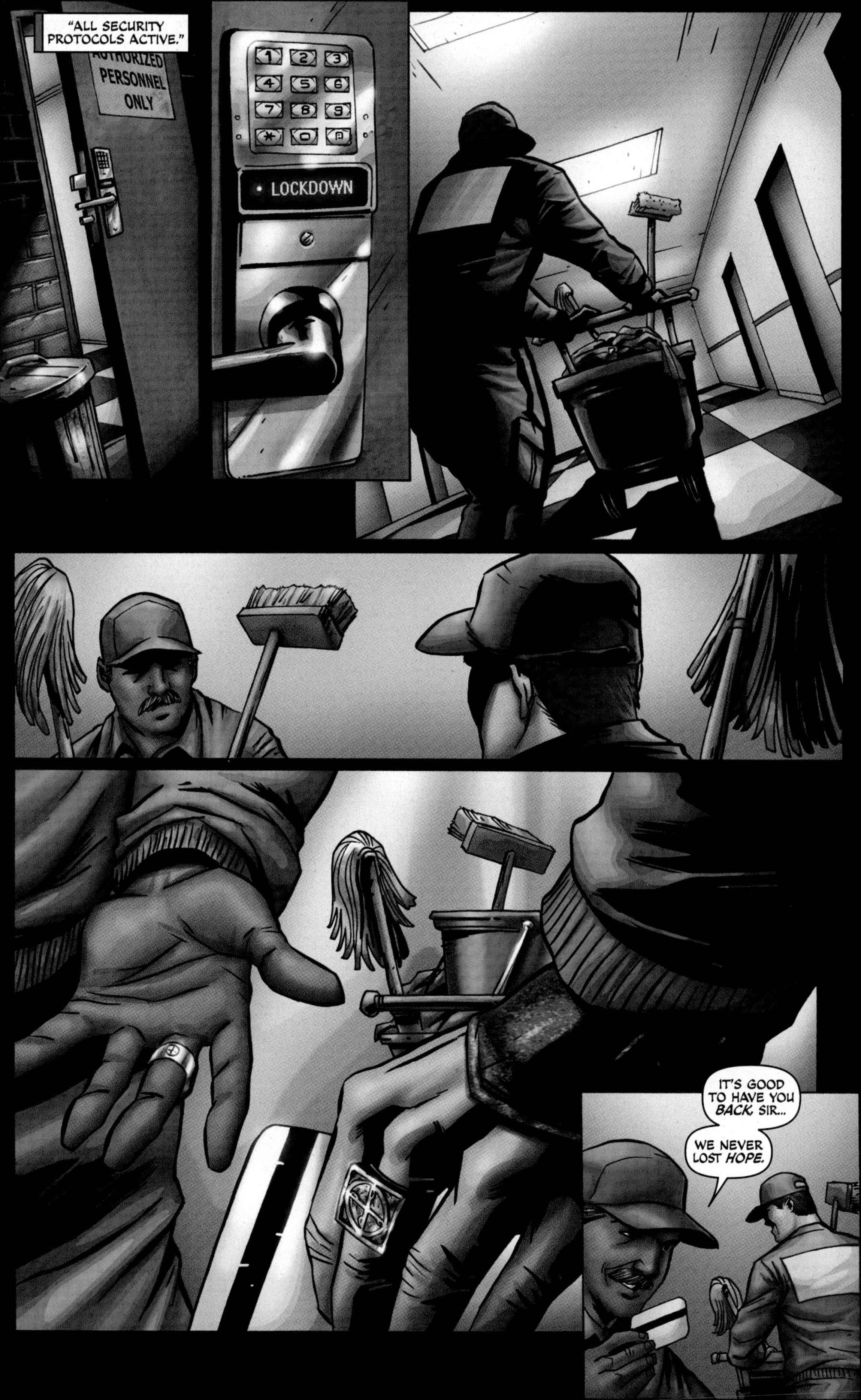
"ALL SECURITY PROTOCOLS ACTIVE."
AUTHORIZED PERSONNEL ONLY
LOCKDOWN
IT'S GOOD TO HAVE YOU *BACK*, SIR...
WE NEVER LOST *HOPE*.

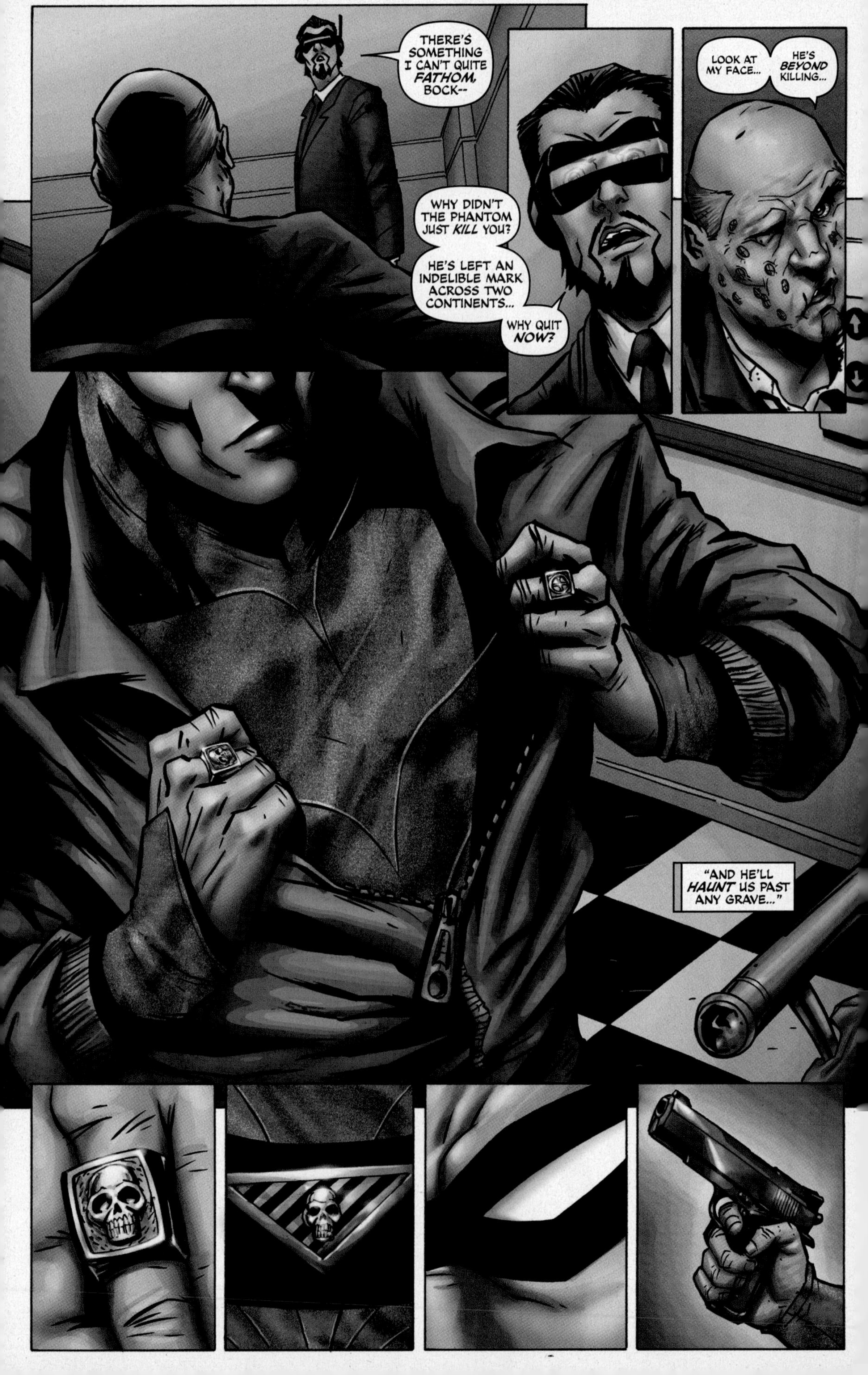
THERE'S SOMETHING I CAN'T QUITE *FATHOM,* BOCK--
WHY DIDN'T THE PHANTOM JUST *KILL* YOU?
HE'S LEFT AN INDELIBLE MARK ACROSS TWO CONTINENTS...
WHY QUIT *NOW?*
LOOK AT MY FACE...
HE'S *BEYOND* KILLING...
"AND HE'LL *HAUNT* US PAST ANY GRAVE..."

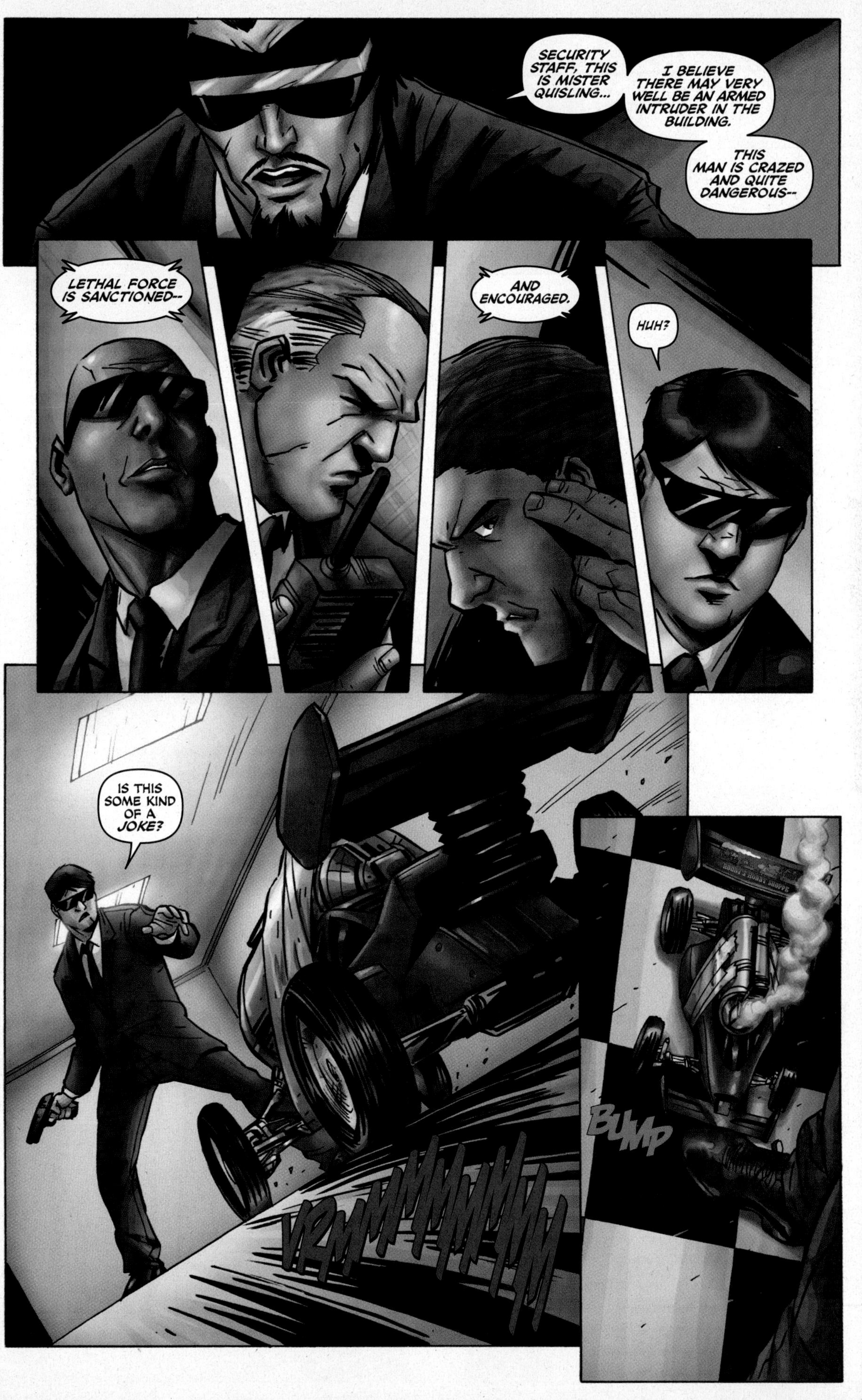
SECURITY STAFF, THIS IS MISTER QUISLING...
I BELIEVE THERE MAY VERY WELL BE AN ARMED INTRUDER IN THE BUILDING.
THIS MAN IS CRAZED AND QUITE DANGEROUS--
LETHAL FORCE IS SANCTIONED--
AND ENCOURAGED.
HUH?
IS THIS SOME KIND OF A JOKE?
BUMP

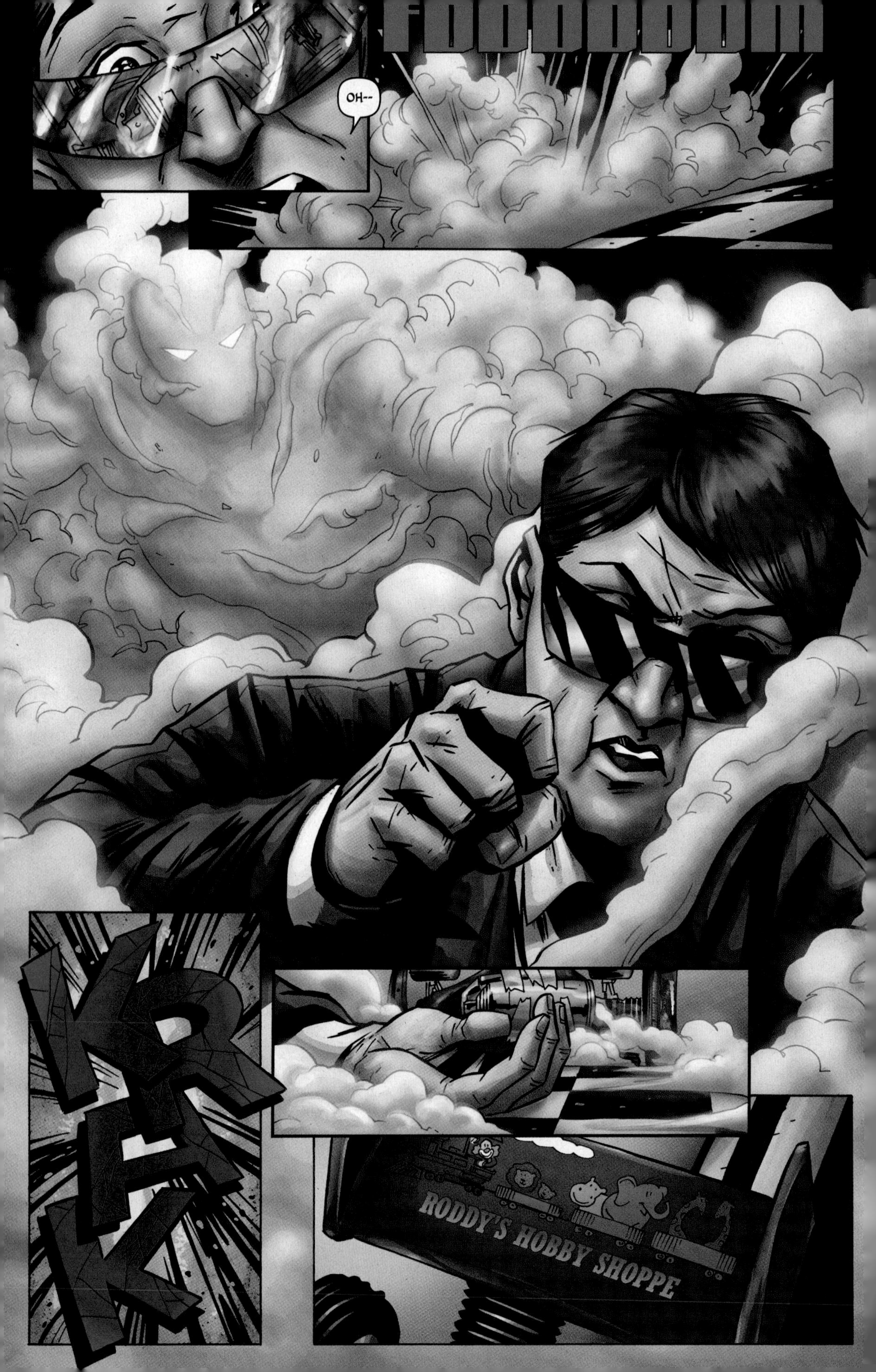
FOOOOOOM
OH--
KRRK
RODDY'S HOBBY SHOPPE

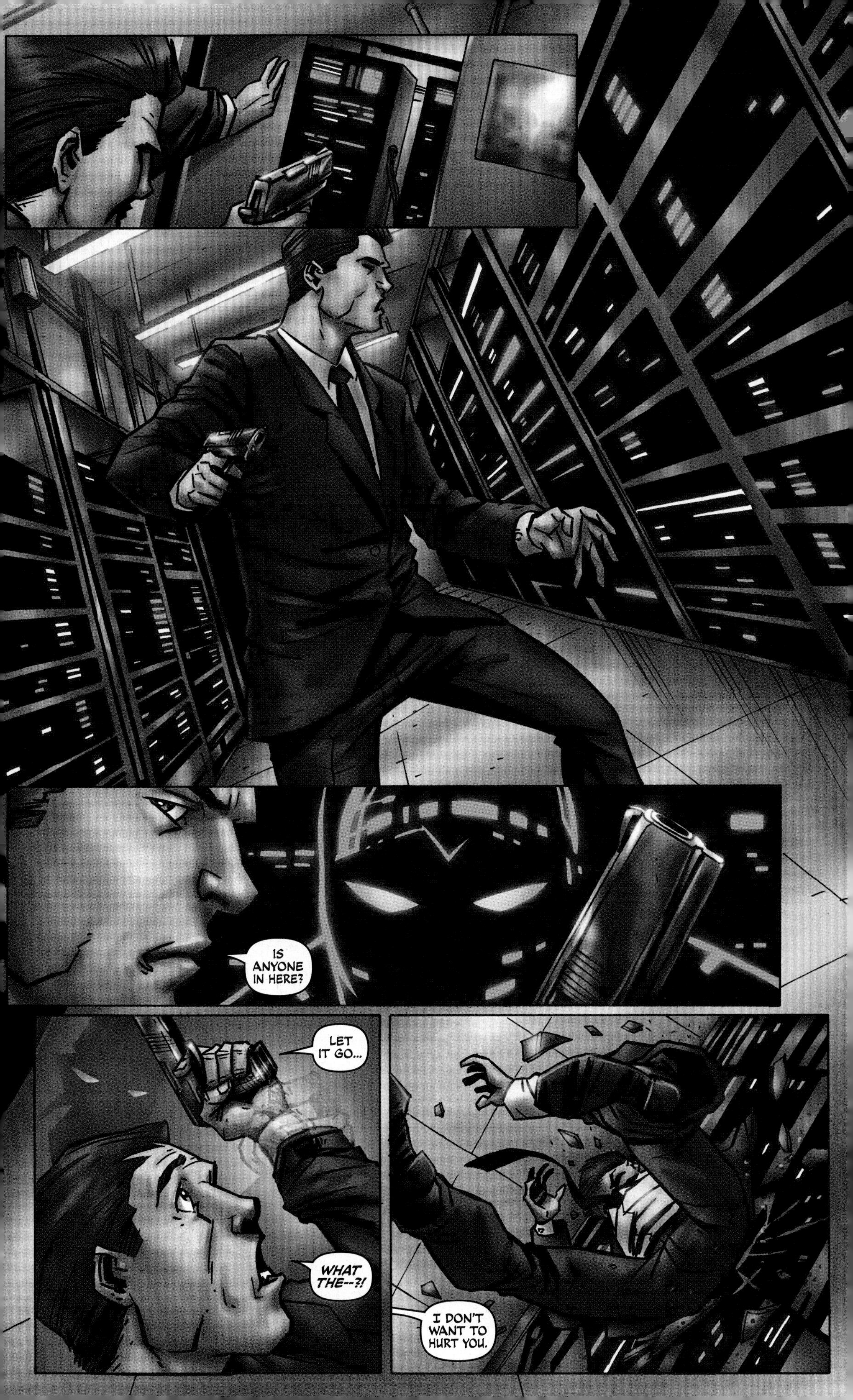
IS ANYONE IN HERE?
LET IT GO...
WHAT THE--?!
I DON'T WANT TO HURT YOU.

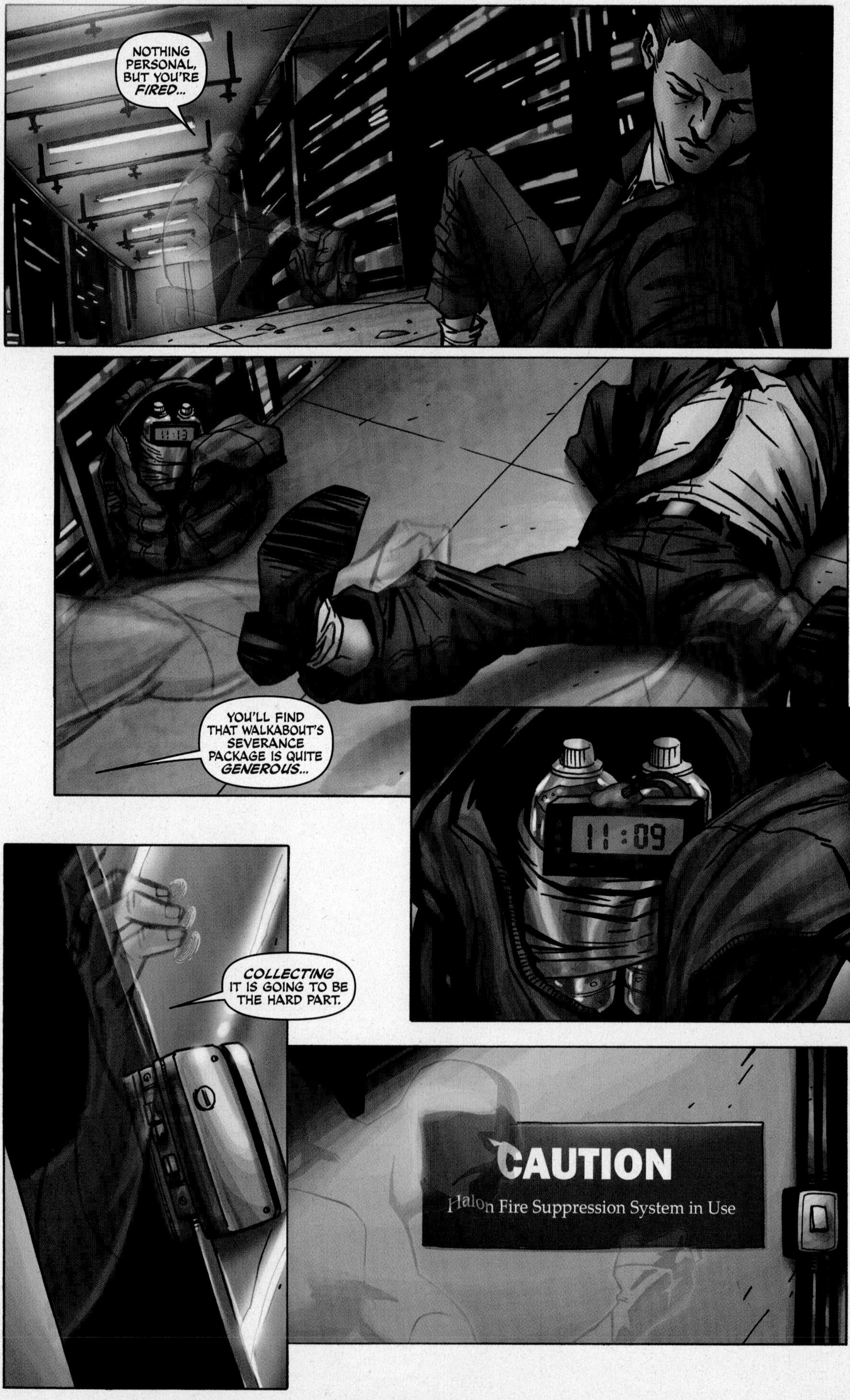
NOTHING PERSONAL, BUT YOU'RE *FIRED*...
YOU'LL FIND THAT WALKABOUT'S SEVERANCE PACKAGE IS QUITE *GENEROUS*...
11:09
COLLECTING IT IS GOING TO BE THE HARD PART.
CAUTION
Halon Fire Suppression System in Use

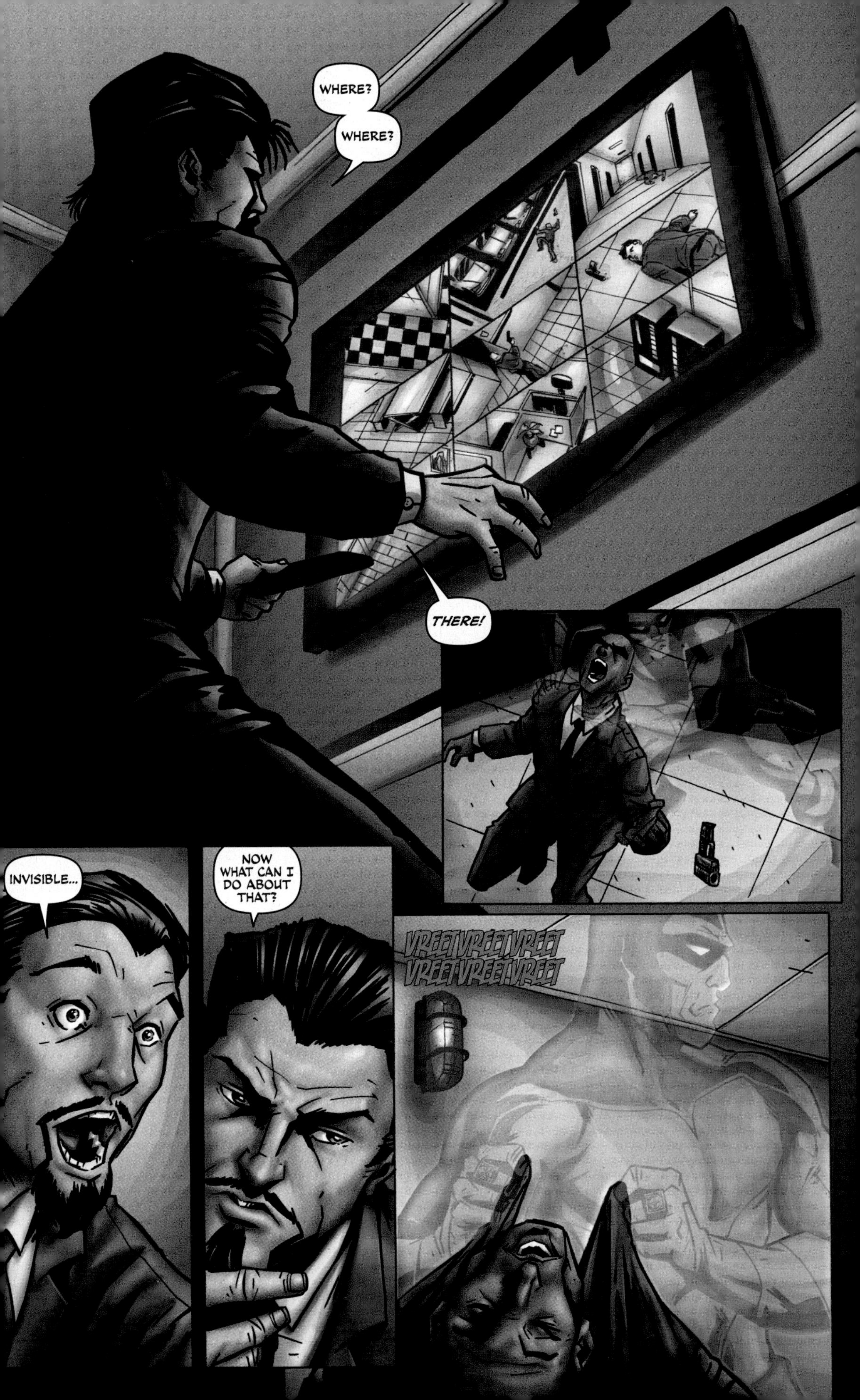

WHERE?
WHERE?
THERE!
INVISIBLE...
NOW WHAT CAN I DO ABOUT THAT?
VREETVREETVREET
VREETVREETVREET

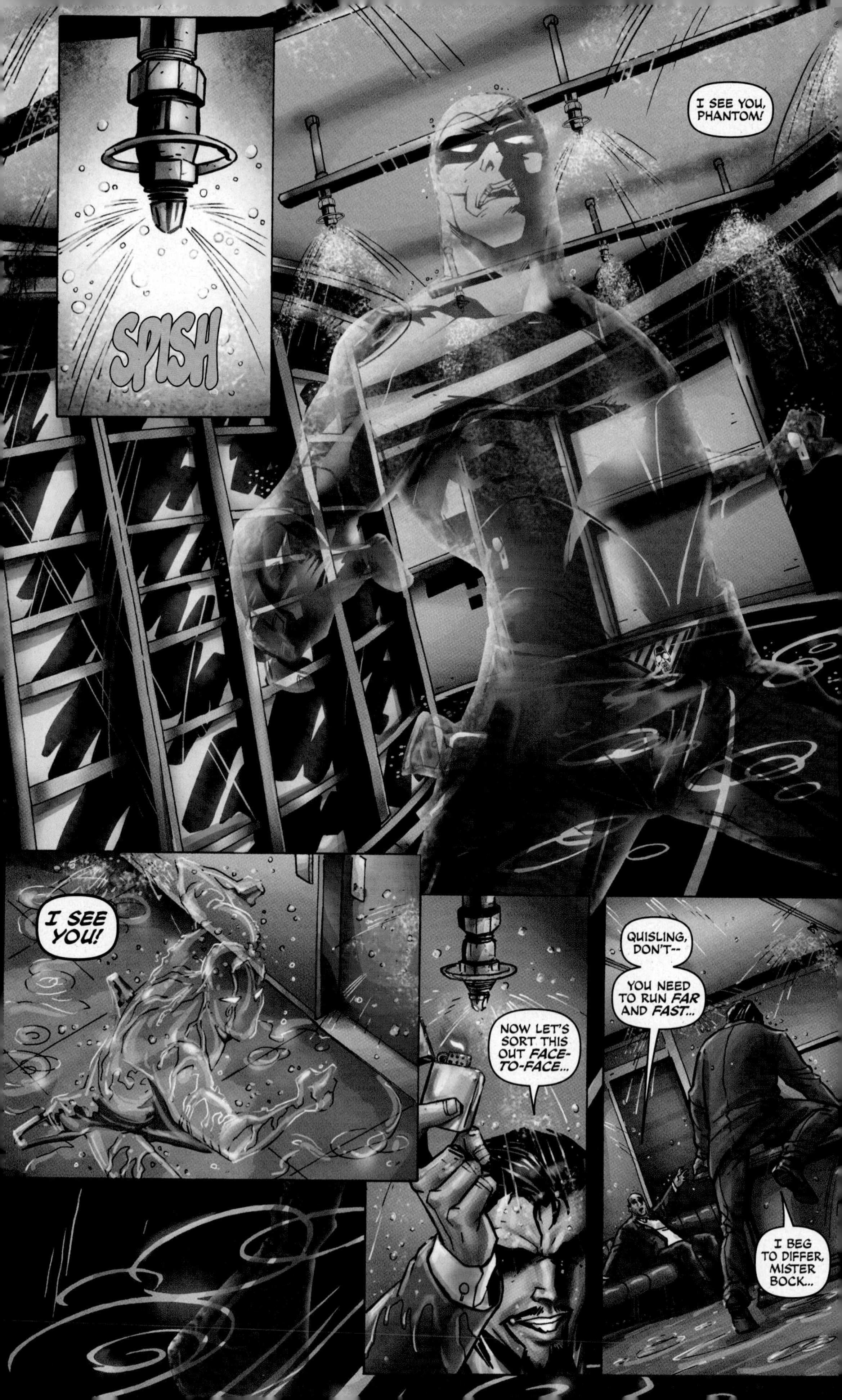
SPISH
I SEE YOU, PHANTOM!
I SEE YOU!
NOW LET'S SORT THIS OUT FACE-TO-FACE...
QUISLING, DON'T--
YOU NEED TO RUN FAR AND FAST...
I BEG TO DIFFER, MISTER BOCK...

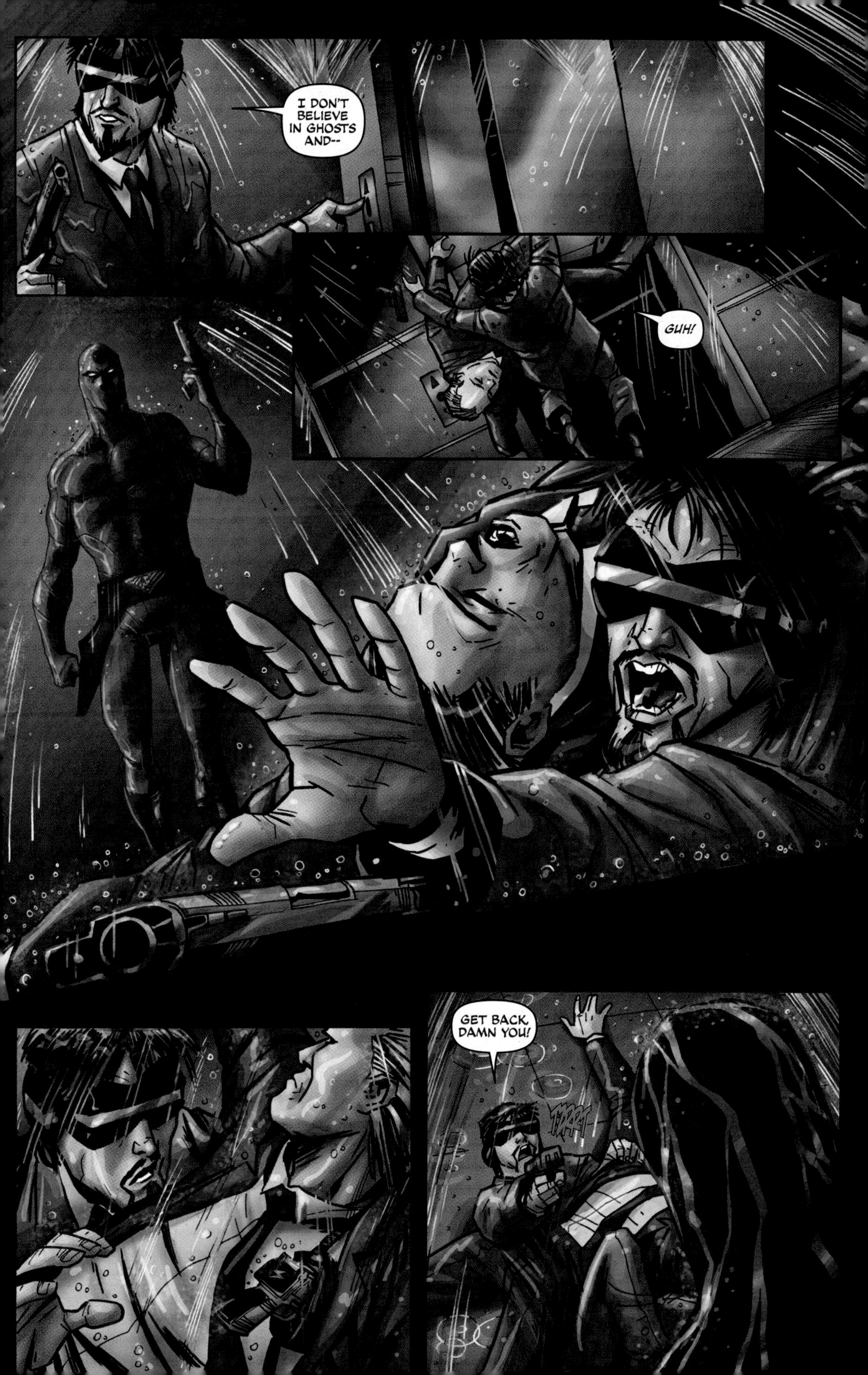
I DON'T BELIEVE IN GHOSTS AND--
GUH!
GET BACK, DAMN YOU!

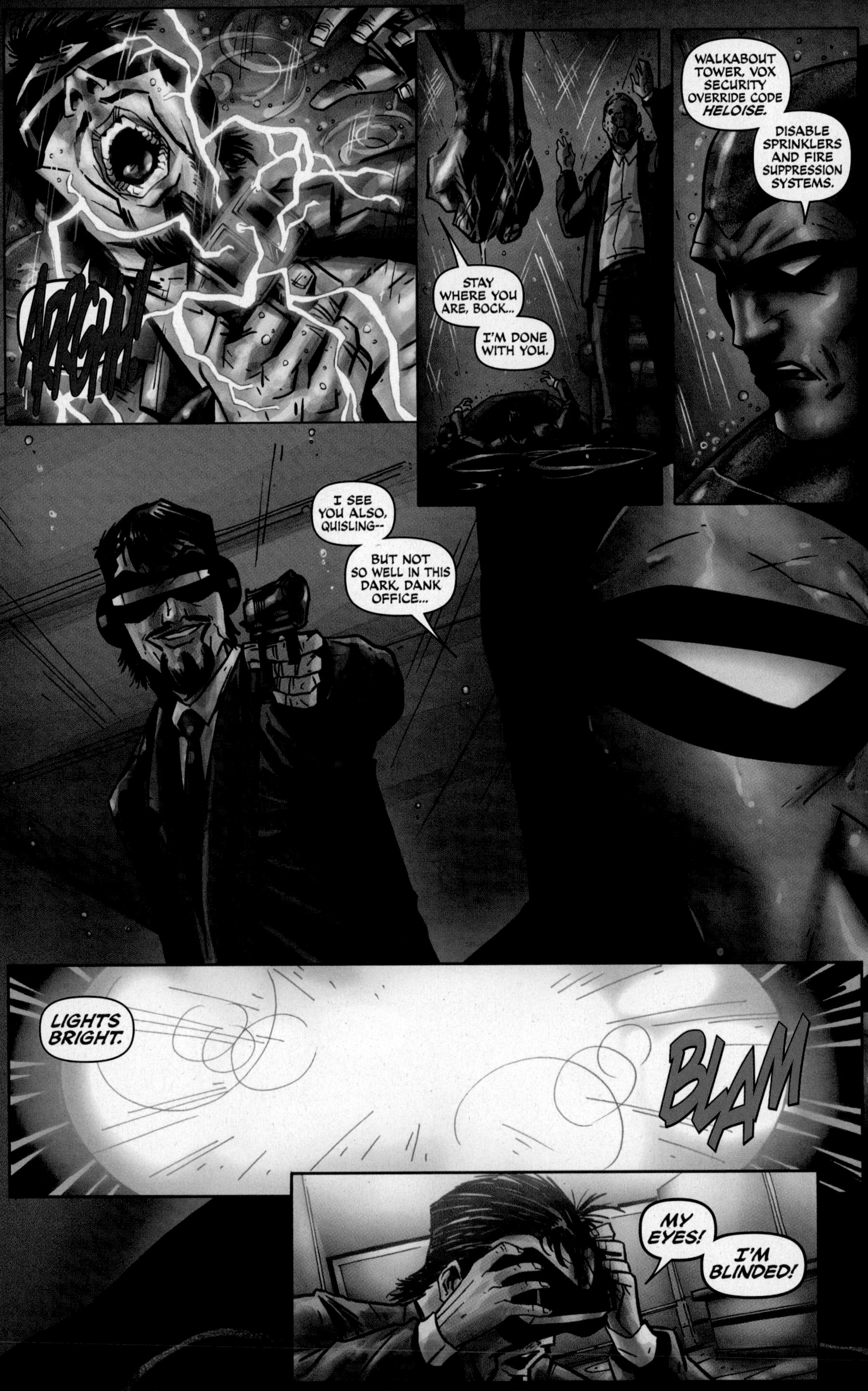
AAAGH!
STAY WHERE YOU ARE, BOCK...
I'M DONE WITH YOU.
WALKABOUT TOWER, VOX SECURITY OVERRIDE CODE HELOISE.
DISABLE SPRINKLERS AND FIRE SUPPRESSION SYSTEMS.
I SEE YOU ALSO, QUISLING--
BUT NOT SO WELL IN THIS DARK, DANK OFFICE...
LIGHTS BRIGHT.
BLAM
MY EYES!
I'M BLINDED!

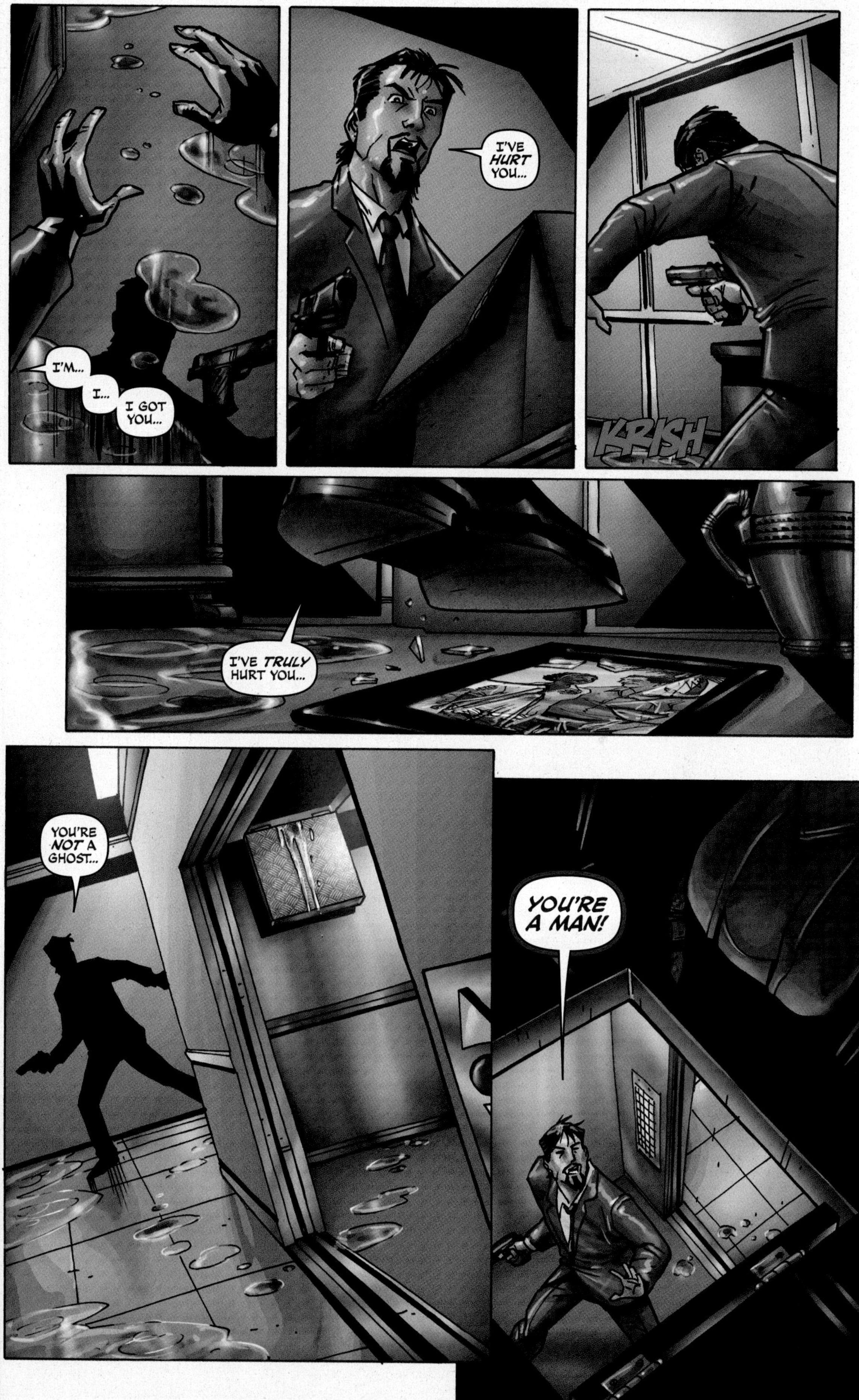
I'M...
I...
I GOT YOU...
I'VE HURT YOU...
KRISH
I'VE TRULY HURT YOU...
YOU'RE NOT A GHOST...
YOU'RE A MAN!

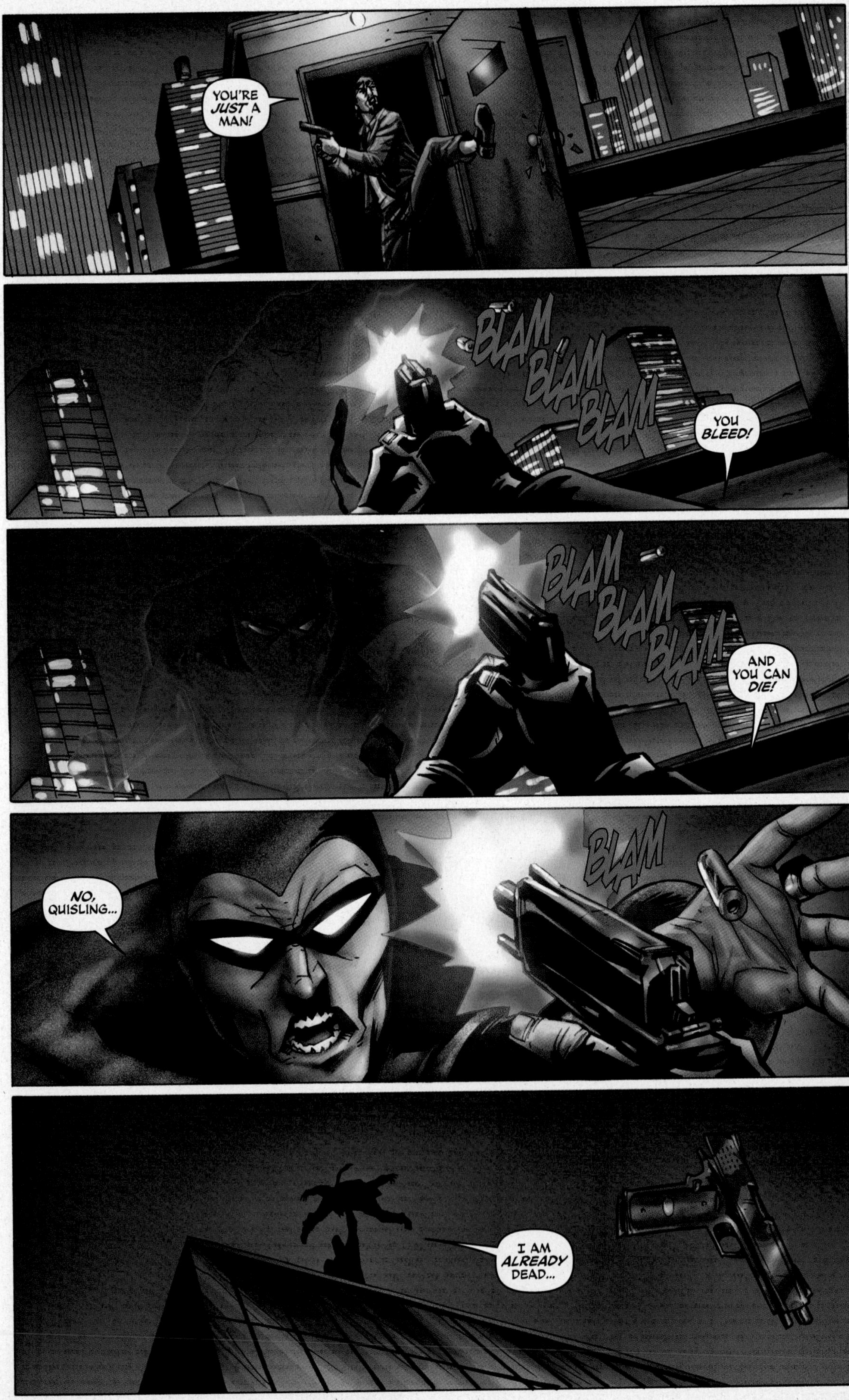
YOU'RE JUST A MAN!
BLAM BLAM BLAM
YOU BLEED!
BLAM BLAM BLAM
AND YOU CAN DIE!
BLAM
NO, QUISLING...
I AM ALREADY DEAD...

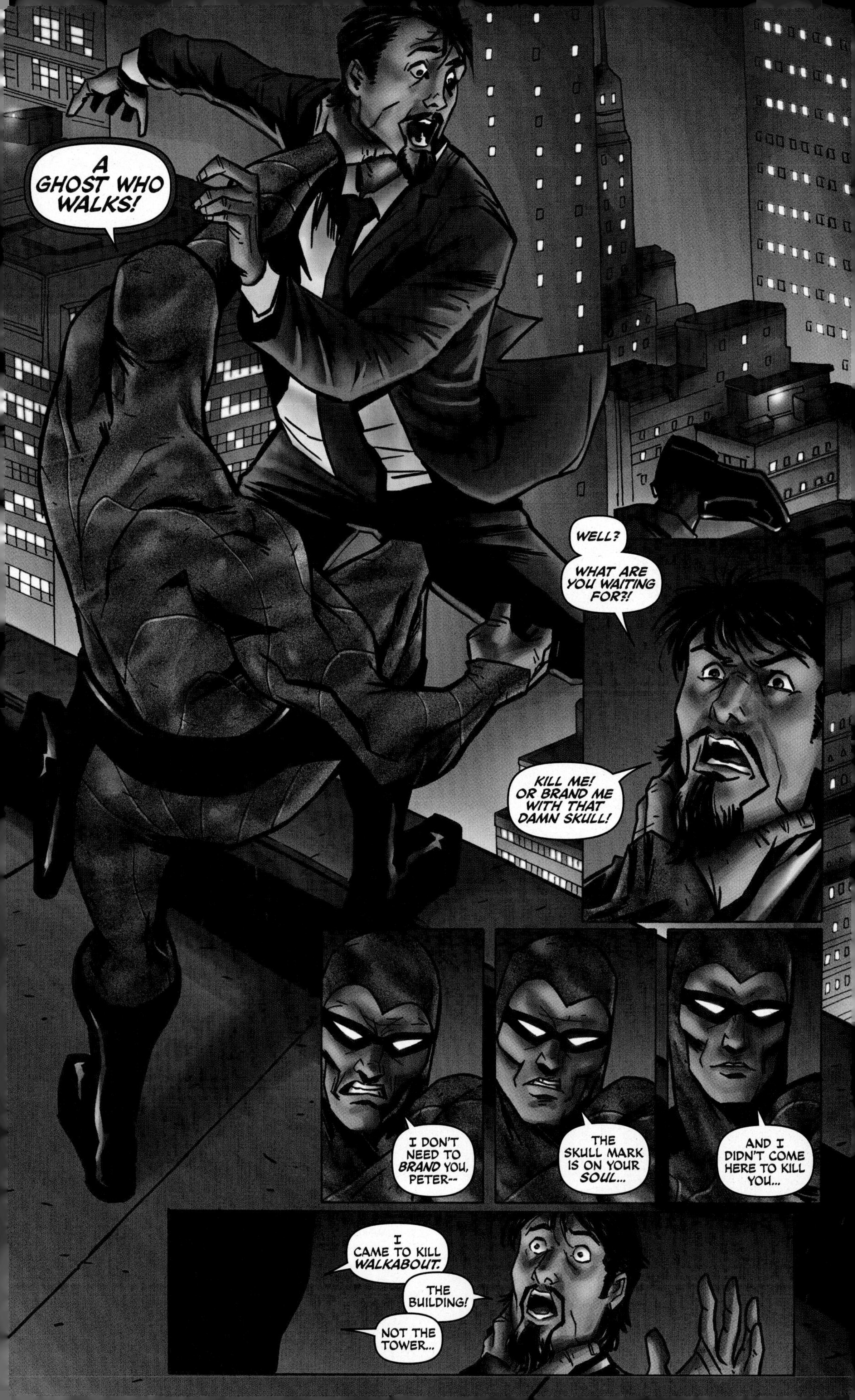
A GHOST WHO WALKS!
WELL?
WHAT ARE YOU WAITING FOR?!
KILL ME! OR BRAND ME WITH THAT DAMN SKULL!
I DON'T NEED TO *BRAND* YOU, PETER--
THE SKULL MARK IS ON YOUR *SOUL*...
AND I DIDN'T COME HERE TO KILL YOU...
I CAME TO KILL *WALKABOUT.*
THE BUILDING!
NOT THE TOWER...

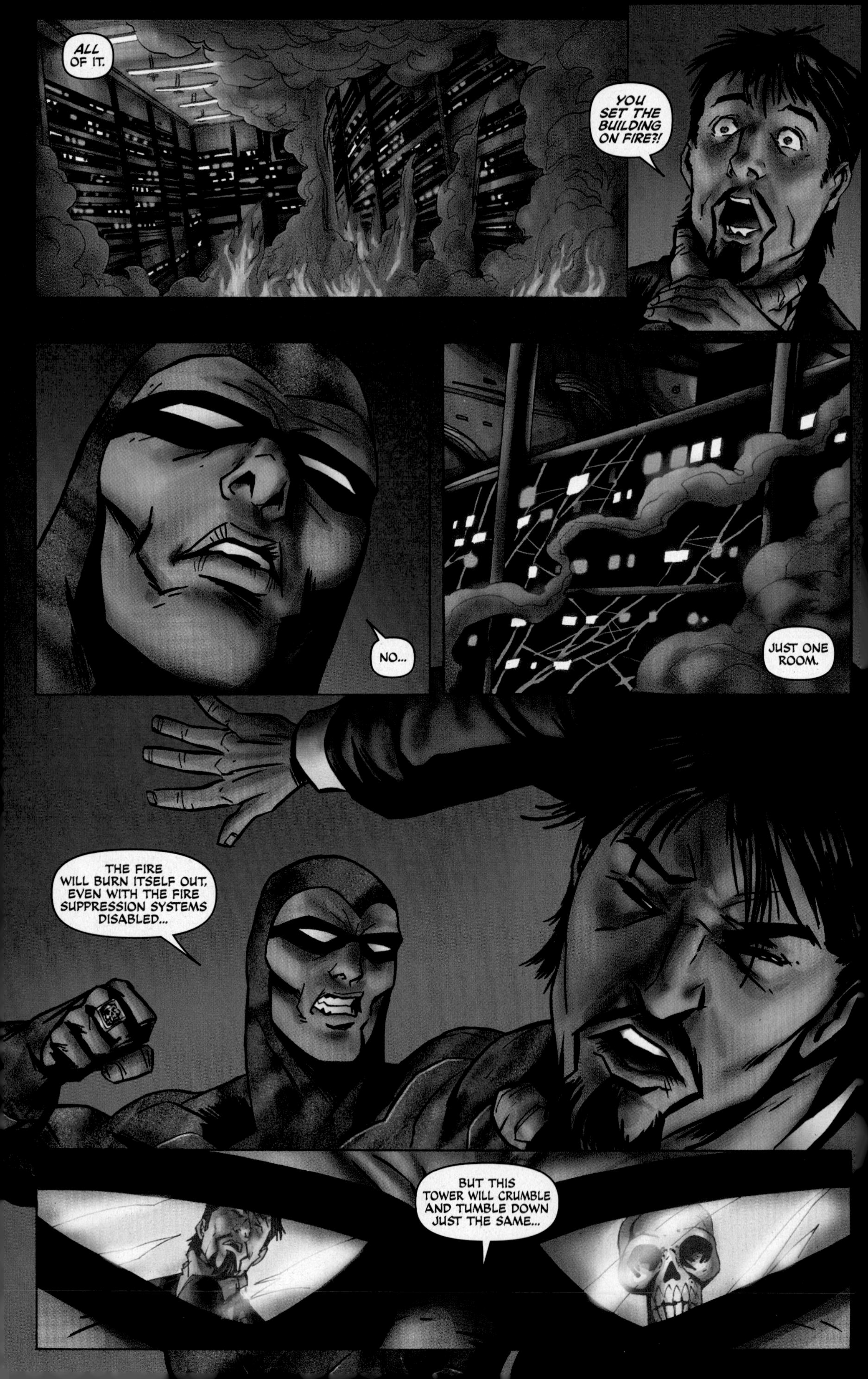
ALL OF IT.
YOU SET THE BUILDING ON FIRE?!
NO...
JUST ONE ROOM.
THE FIRE WILL BURN ITSELF OUT, EVEN WITH THE FIRE SUPPRESSION SYSTEMS DISABLED...
BUT THIS TOWER WILL CRUMBLE AND TUMBLE DOWN JUST THE SAME...

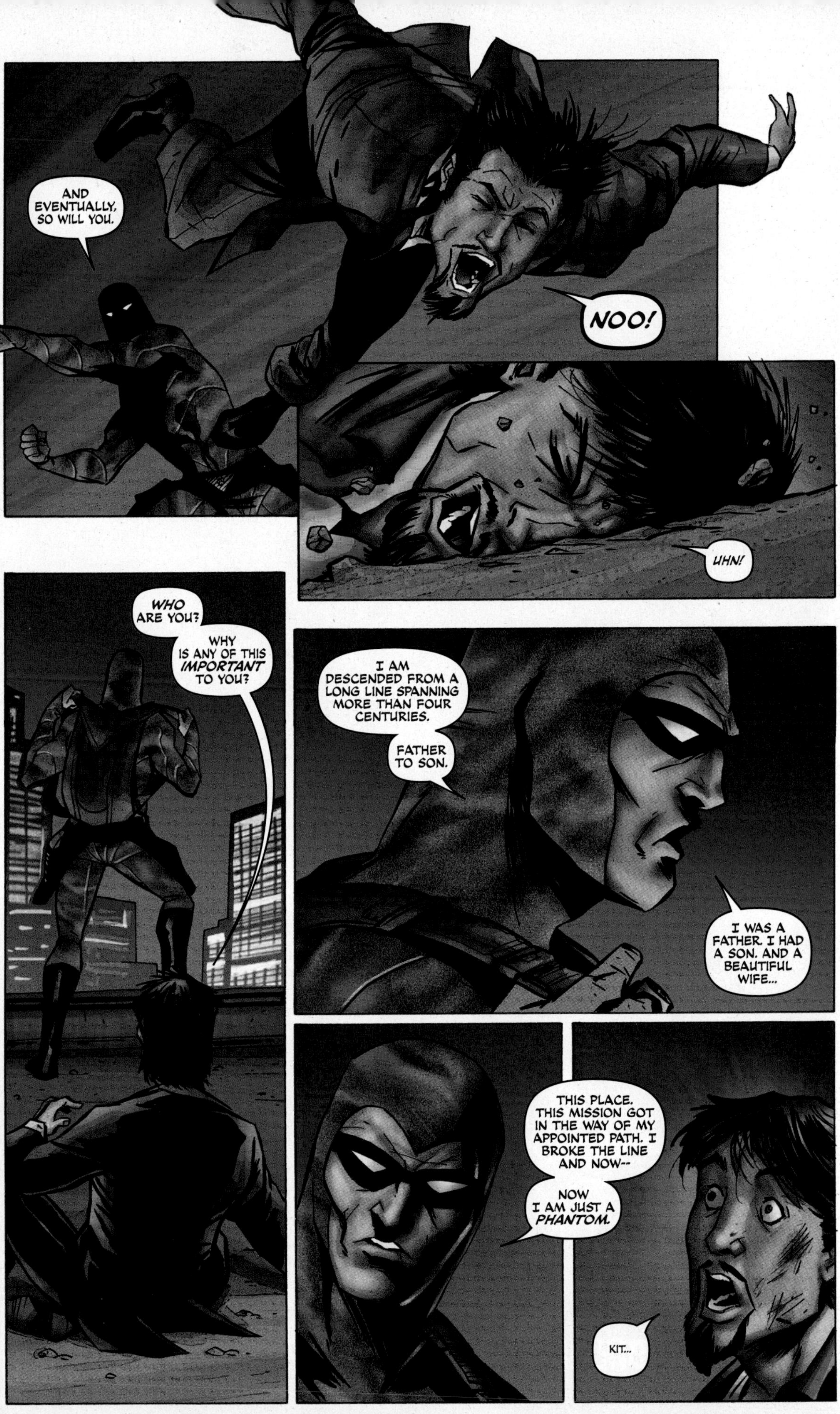
AND EVENTUALLY, SO WILL YOU.
NOO!
UHN!
WHO ARE YOU?
WHY IS ANY OF THIS IMPORTANT TO YOU?
I AM DESCENDED FROM A LONG LINE SPANNING MORE THAN FOUR CENTURIES.
FATHER TO SON.
I WAS A FATHER. I HAD A SON. AND A BEAUTIFUL WIFE...
THIS PLACE. THIS MISSION GOT IN THE WAY OF MY APPOINTED PATH. I BROKE THE LINE AND NOW--
NOW I AM JUST A PHANTOM.
KIT...

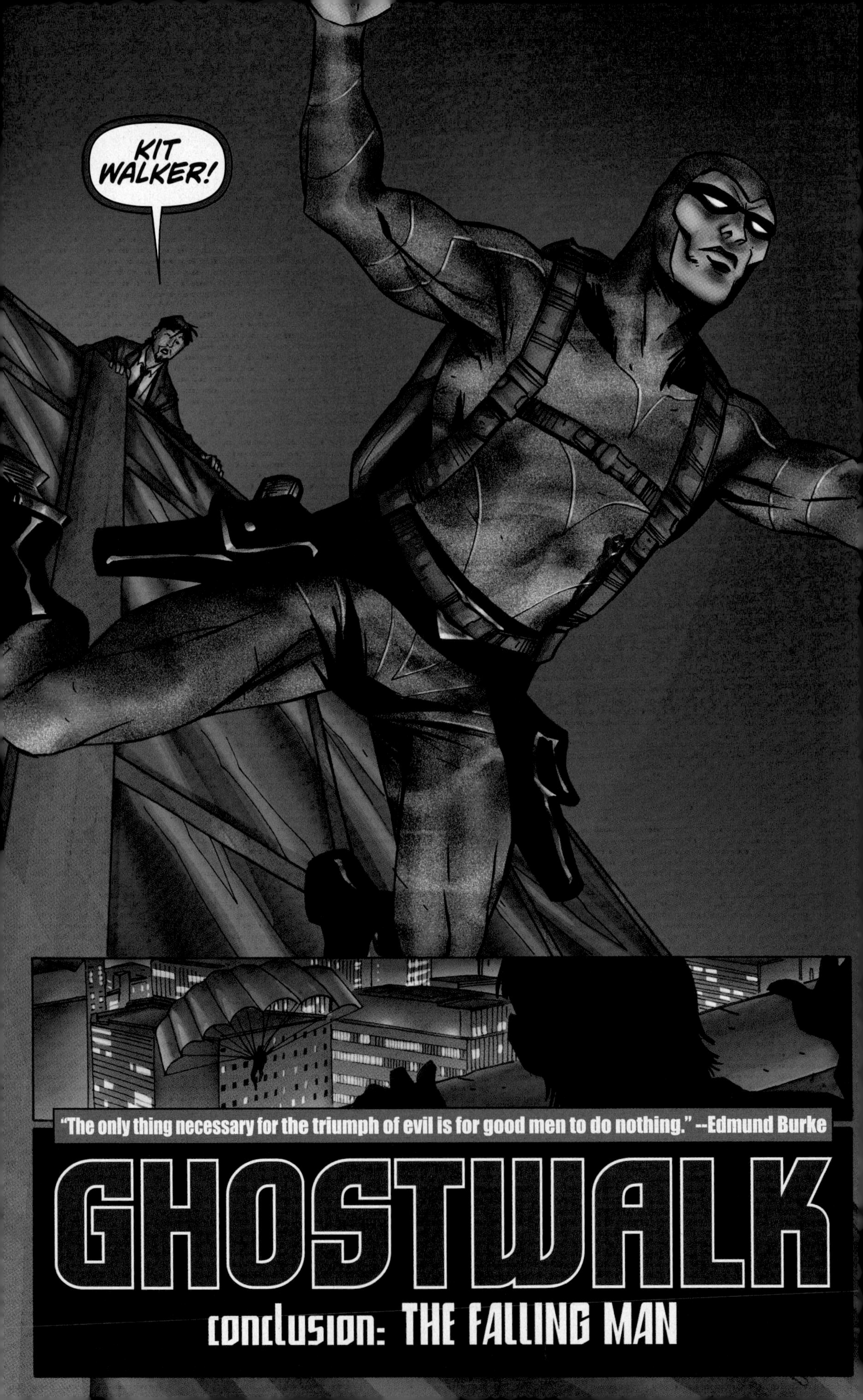
KIT WALKER!
"The only thing necessary for the triumph of evil is for good men to do nothing." --Edmund Burke
GHOSTWALK
conclusion: THE FALLING MAN

ALTERNATE
COVER
GALLERY

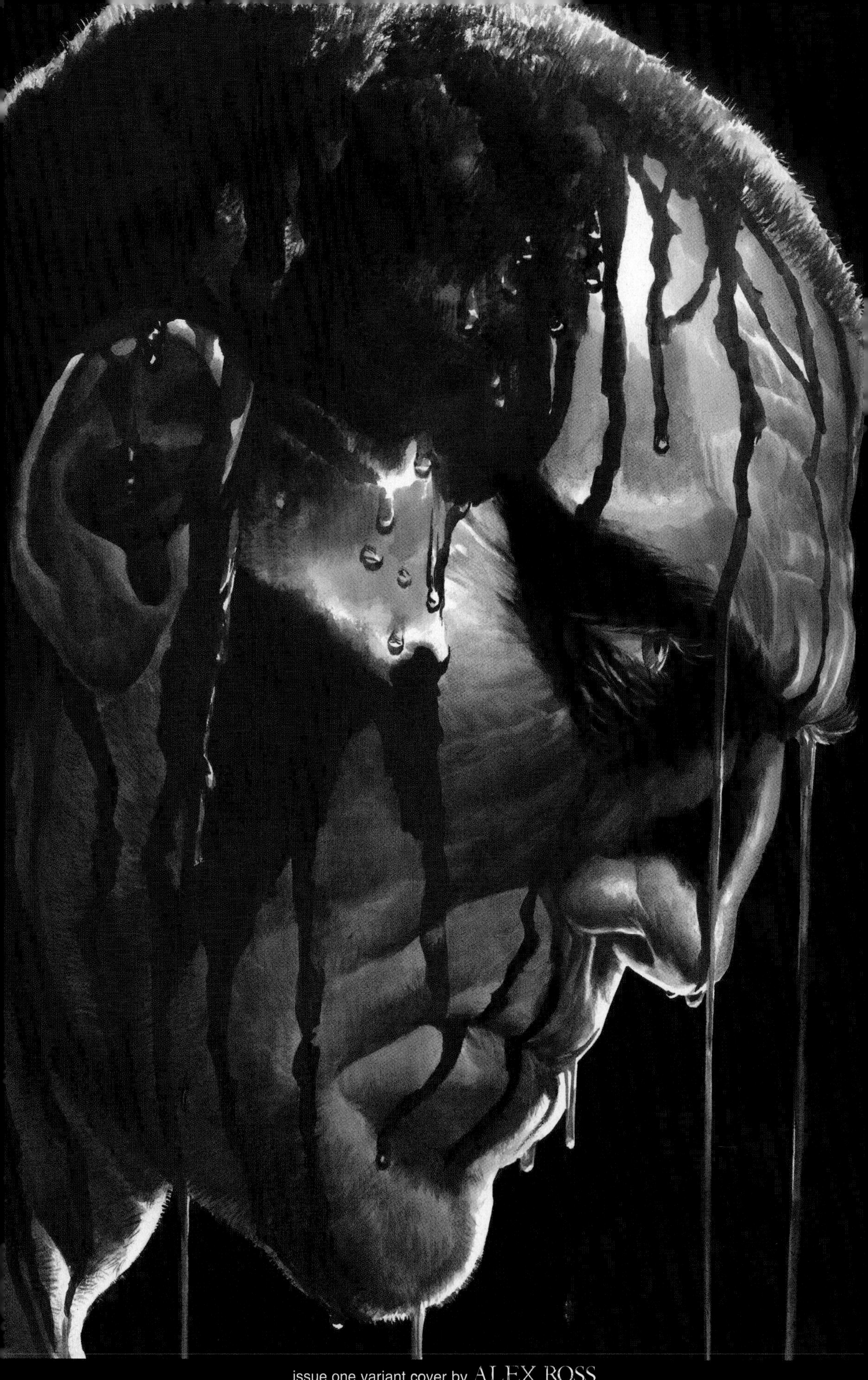

issue one variant cover by ALEX ROSS

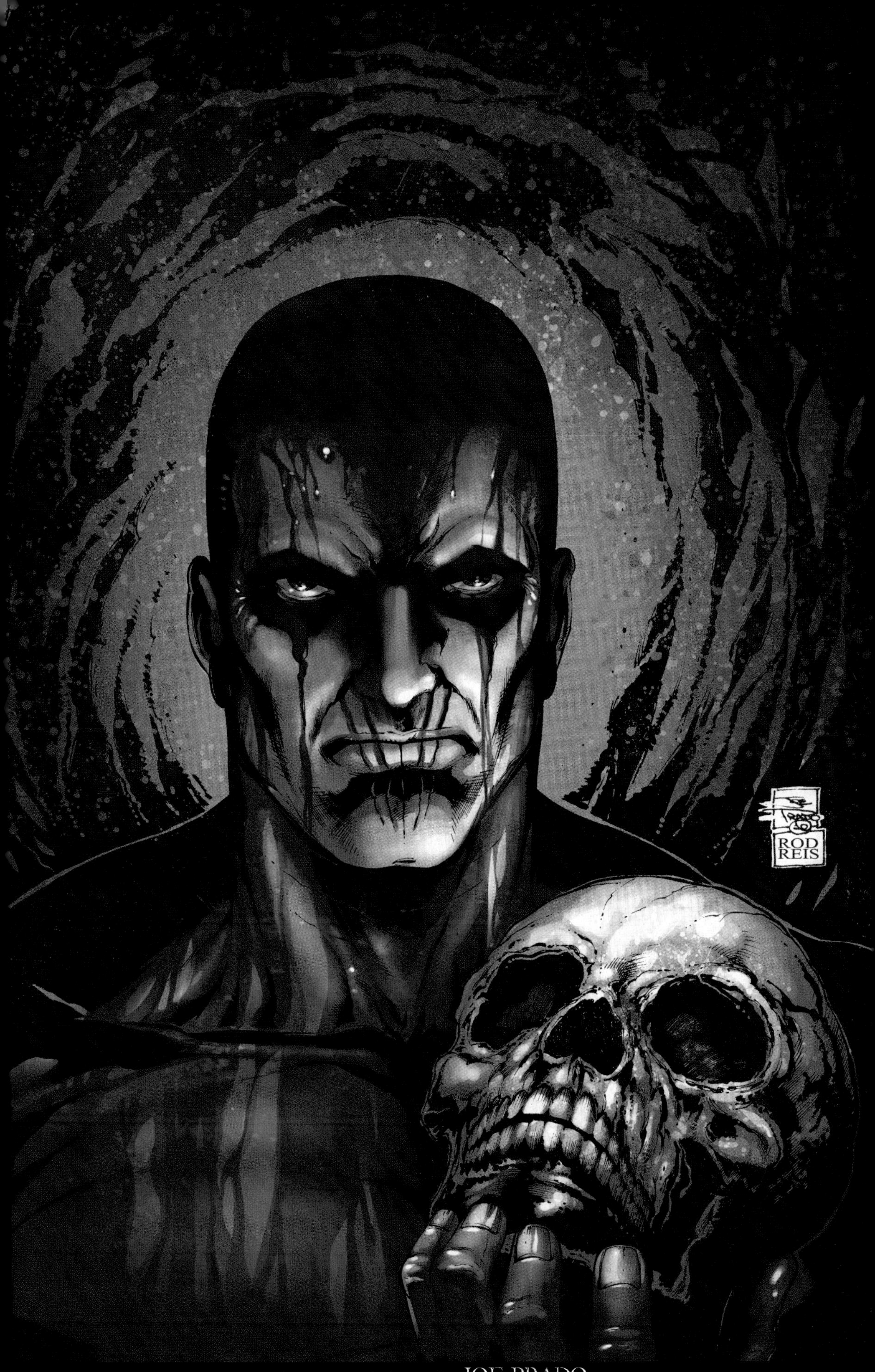
ROD REIS

issue one variant cover by JOE PRADO

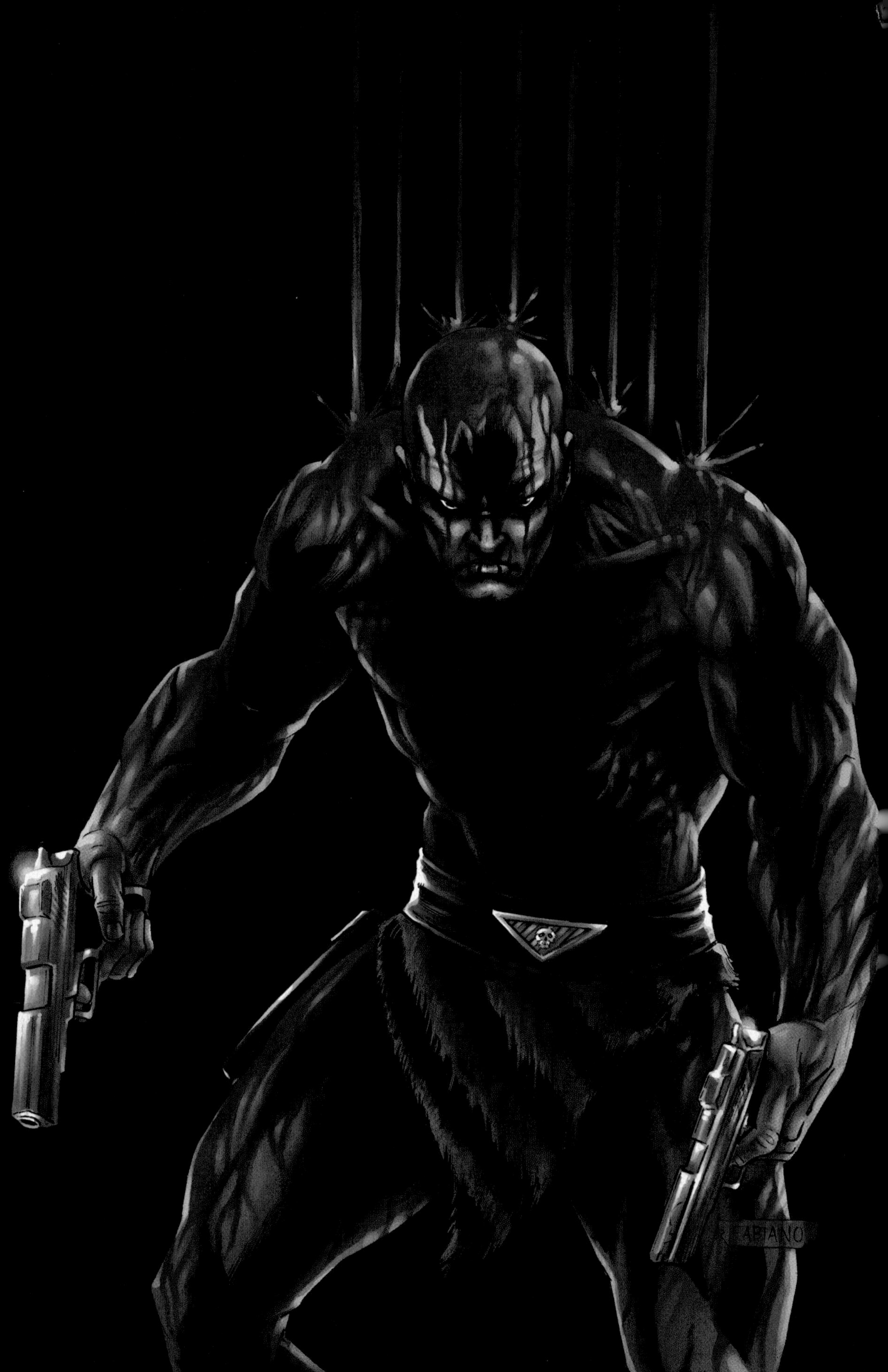
FABIANO

issue one variant cover by FABIANO NEVES

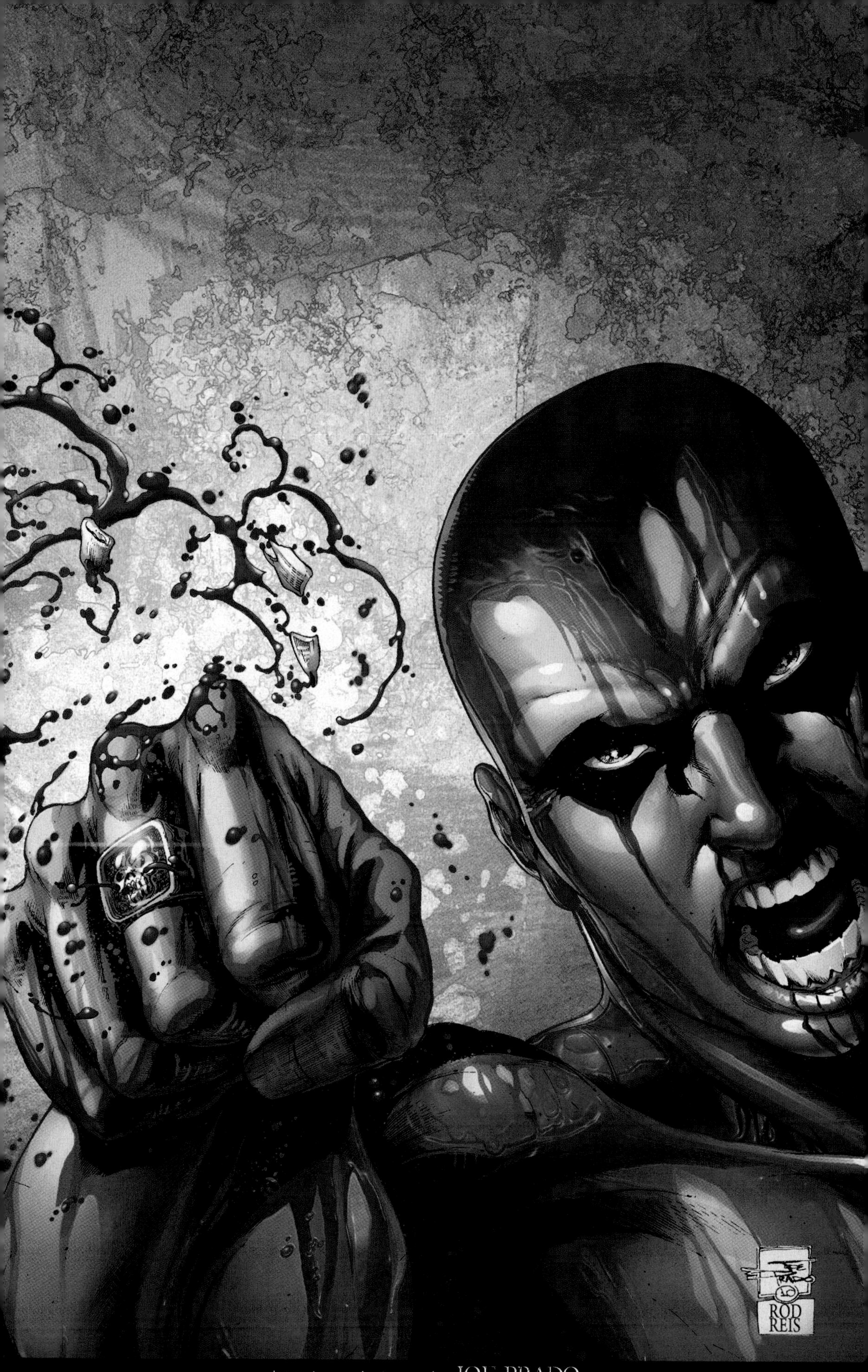
ROD REIS

issue two variant cover by JOE PRADO

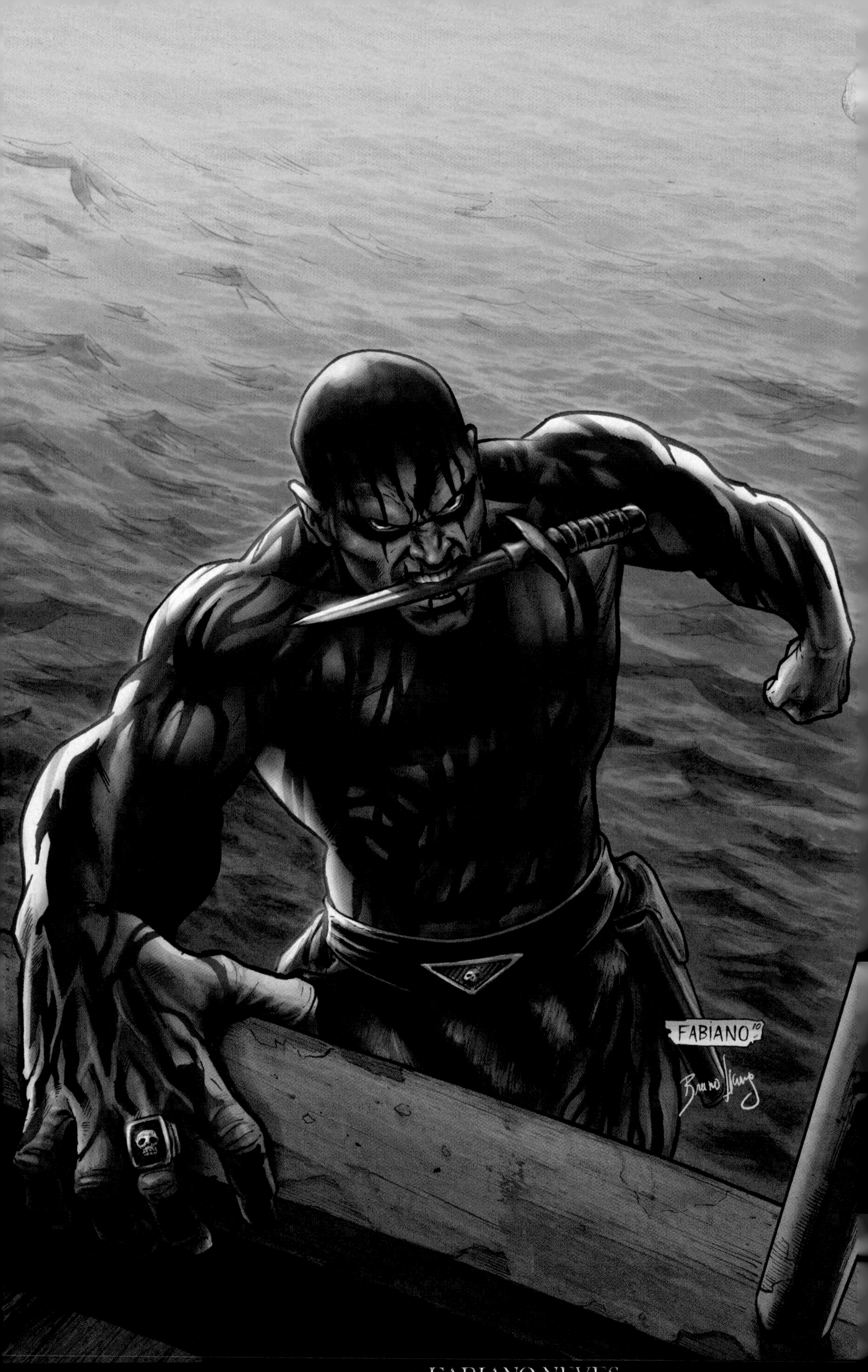
FABIANO '10

issue two variant cover by FABIANO NEVES

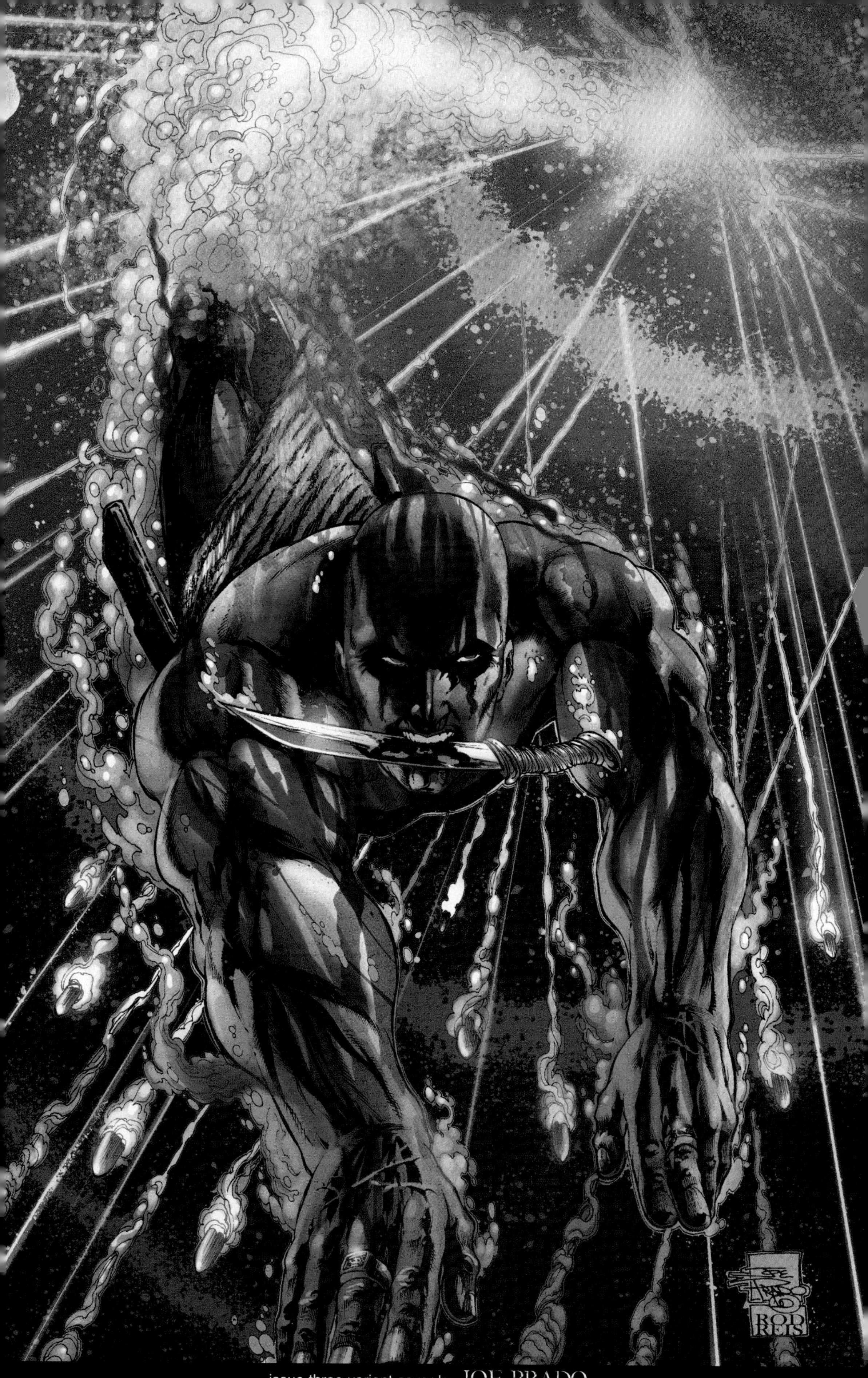
ROD REIS

issue three variant cover by JOE PRADO

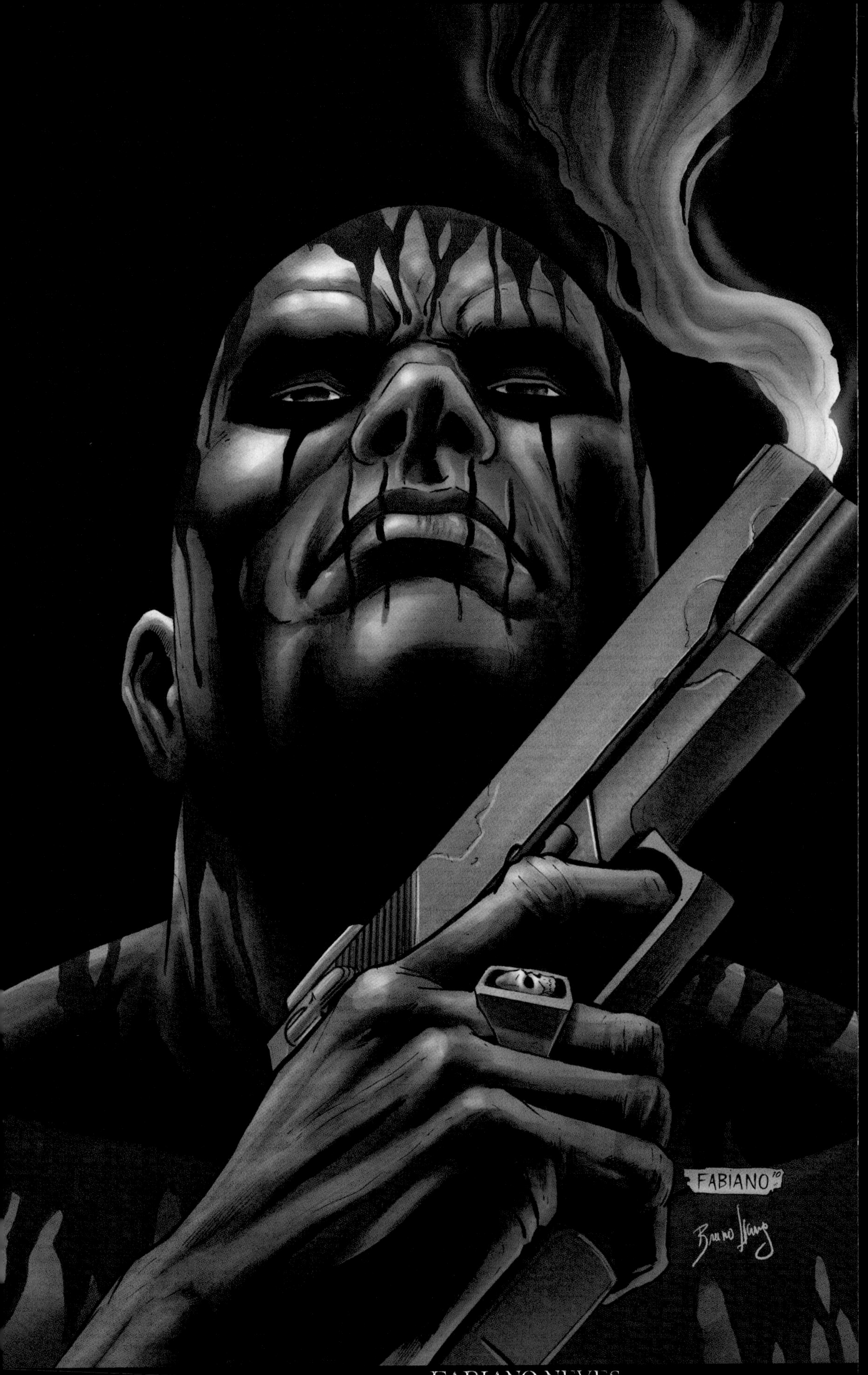
FABIANO

issue three variant cover by FABIANO NEVES

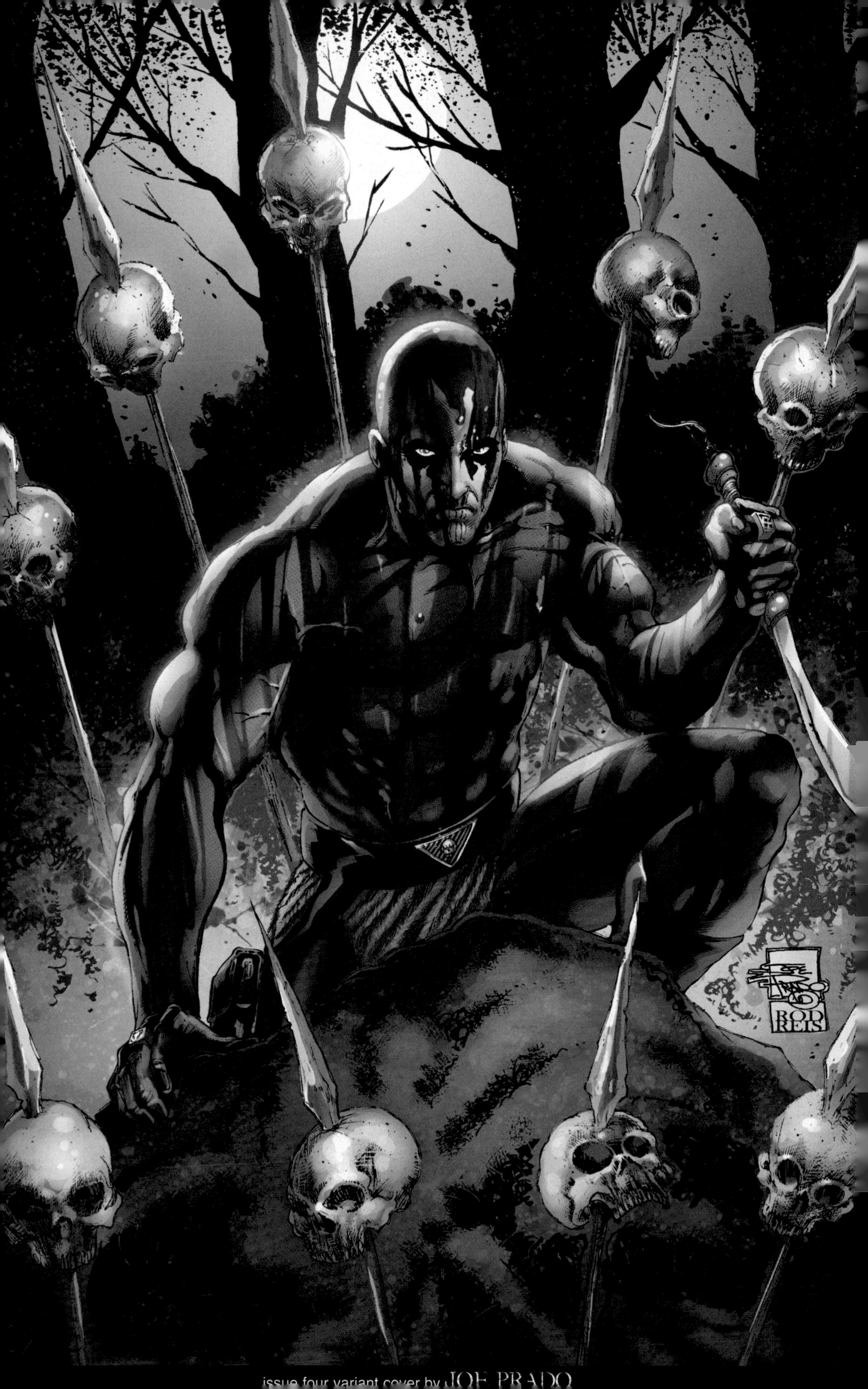
ROD REIS

issue four variant cover by JOE PRADO

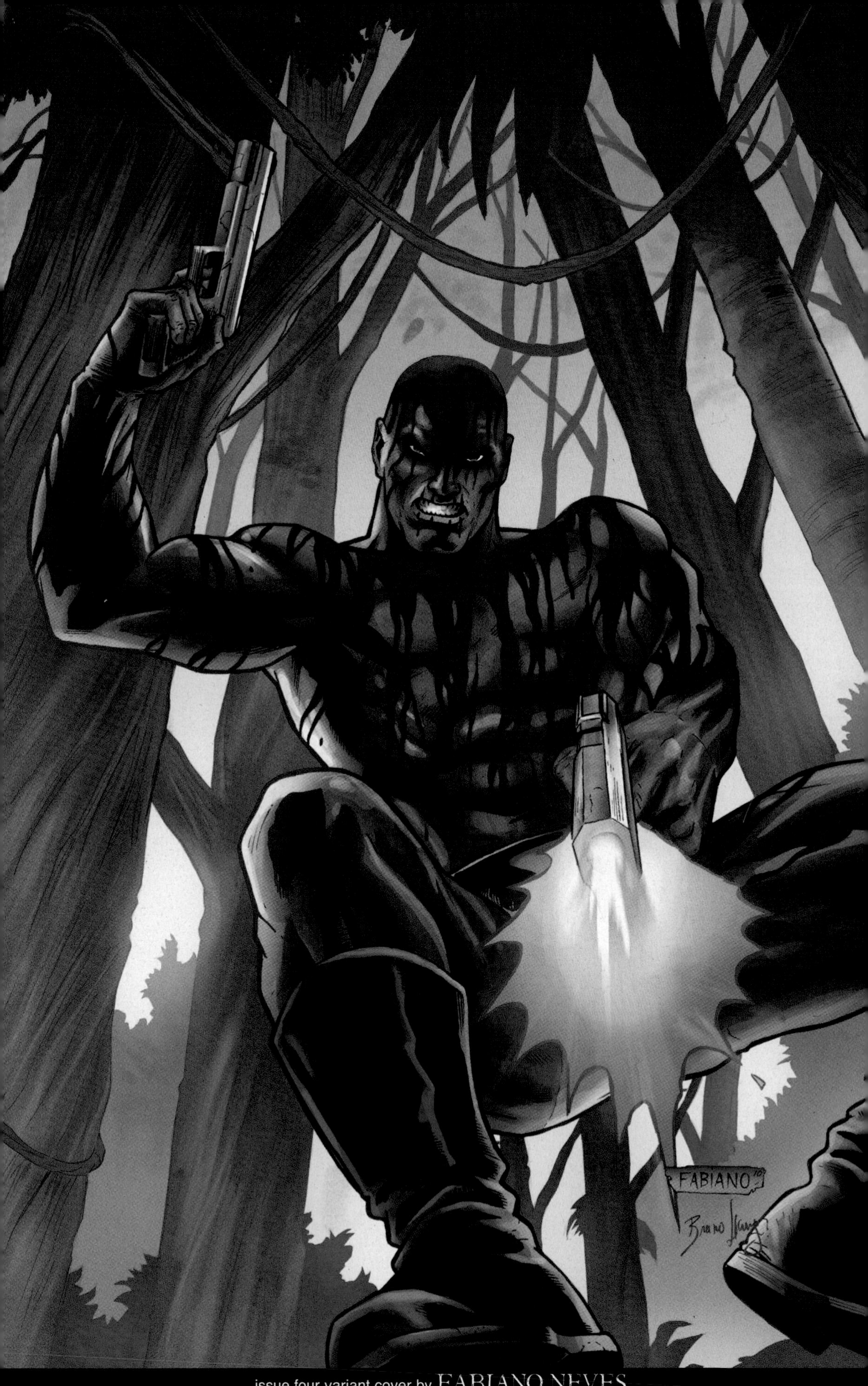
FABIANO

issue four variant cover by FABIANO NEVES

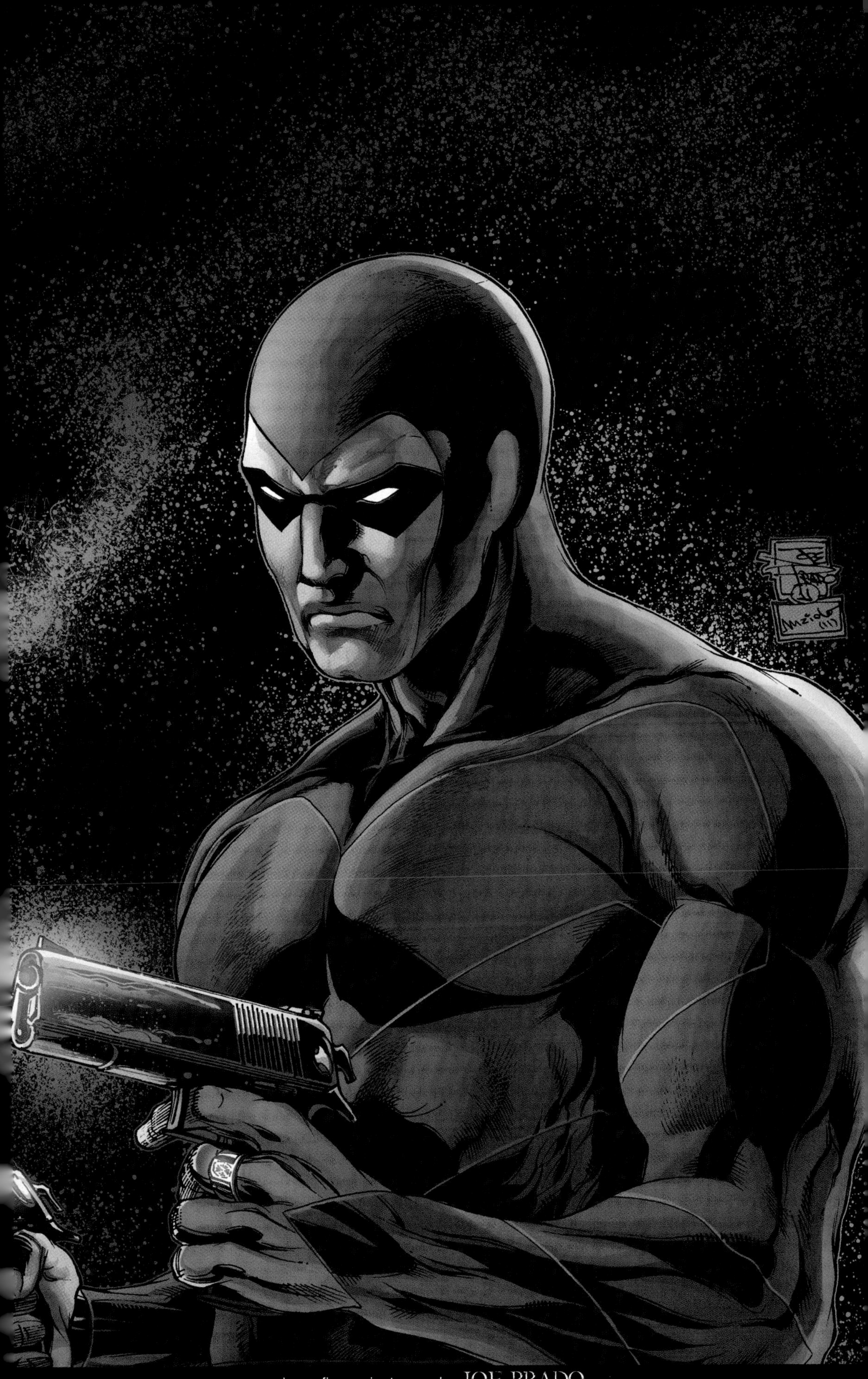

issue five variant cover by JOE PRADO

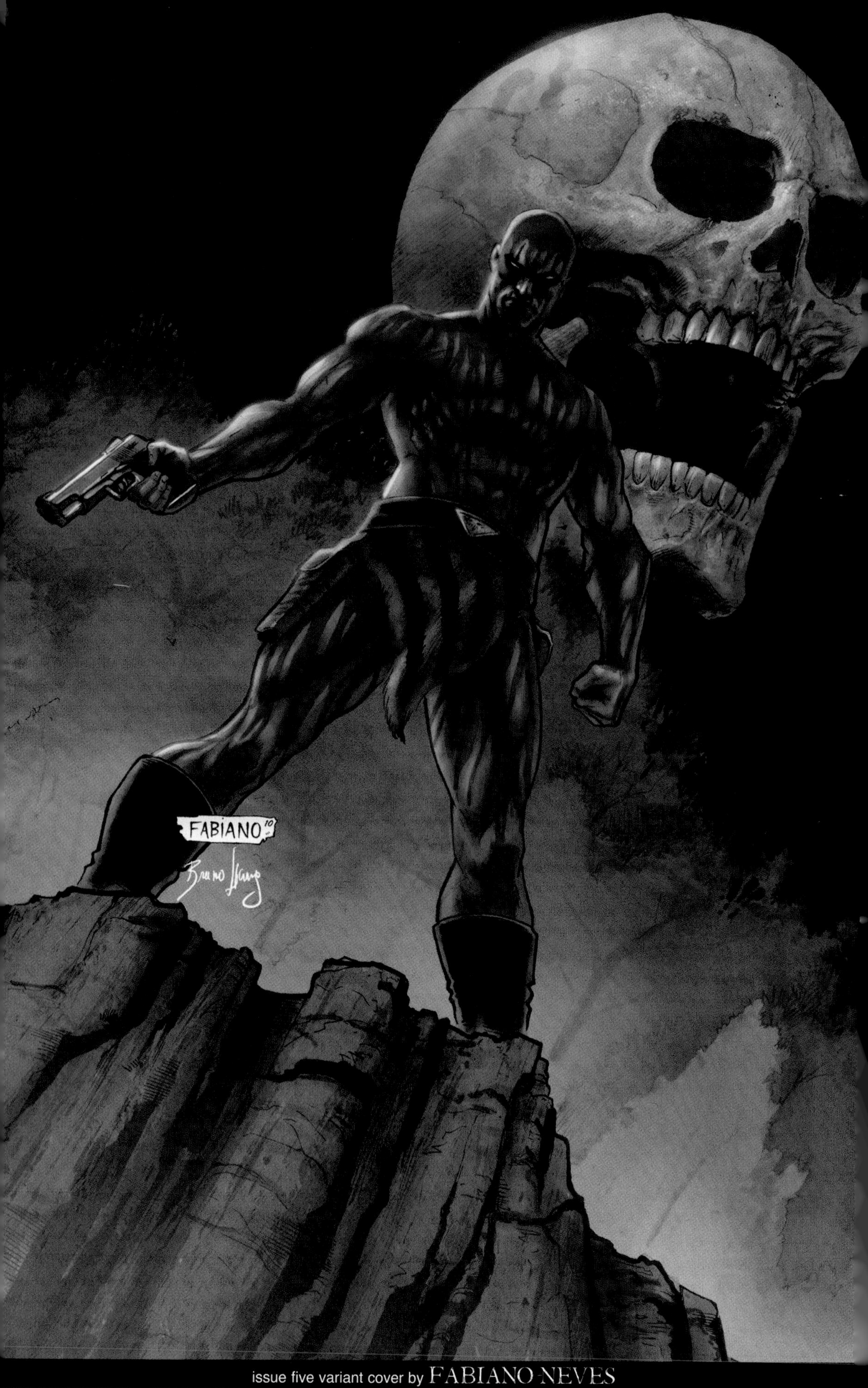
FABIANO

issue five variant cover by FABIANO NEVES

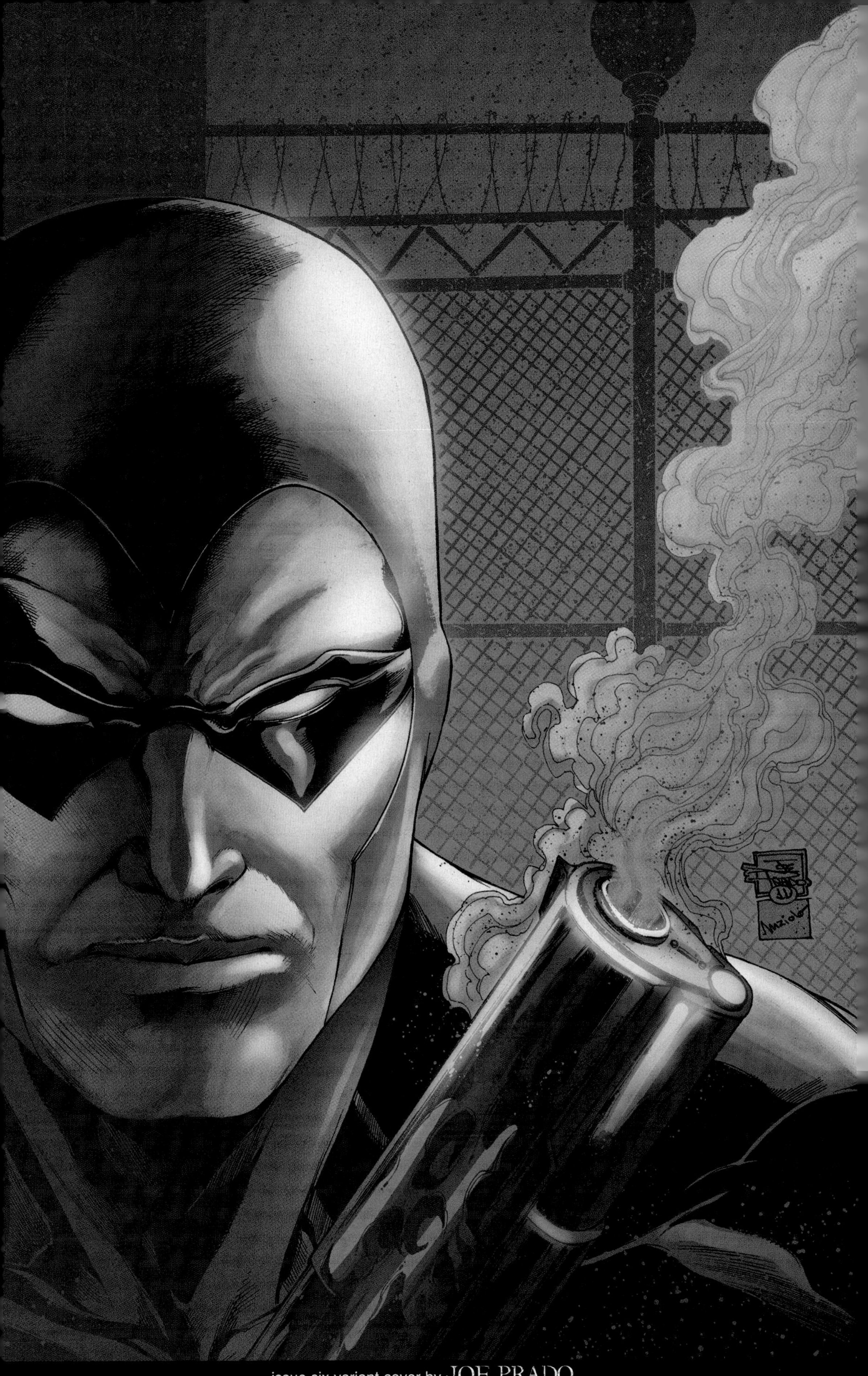

issue six variant cover by JOE PRADO

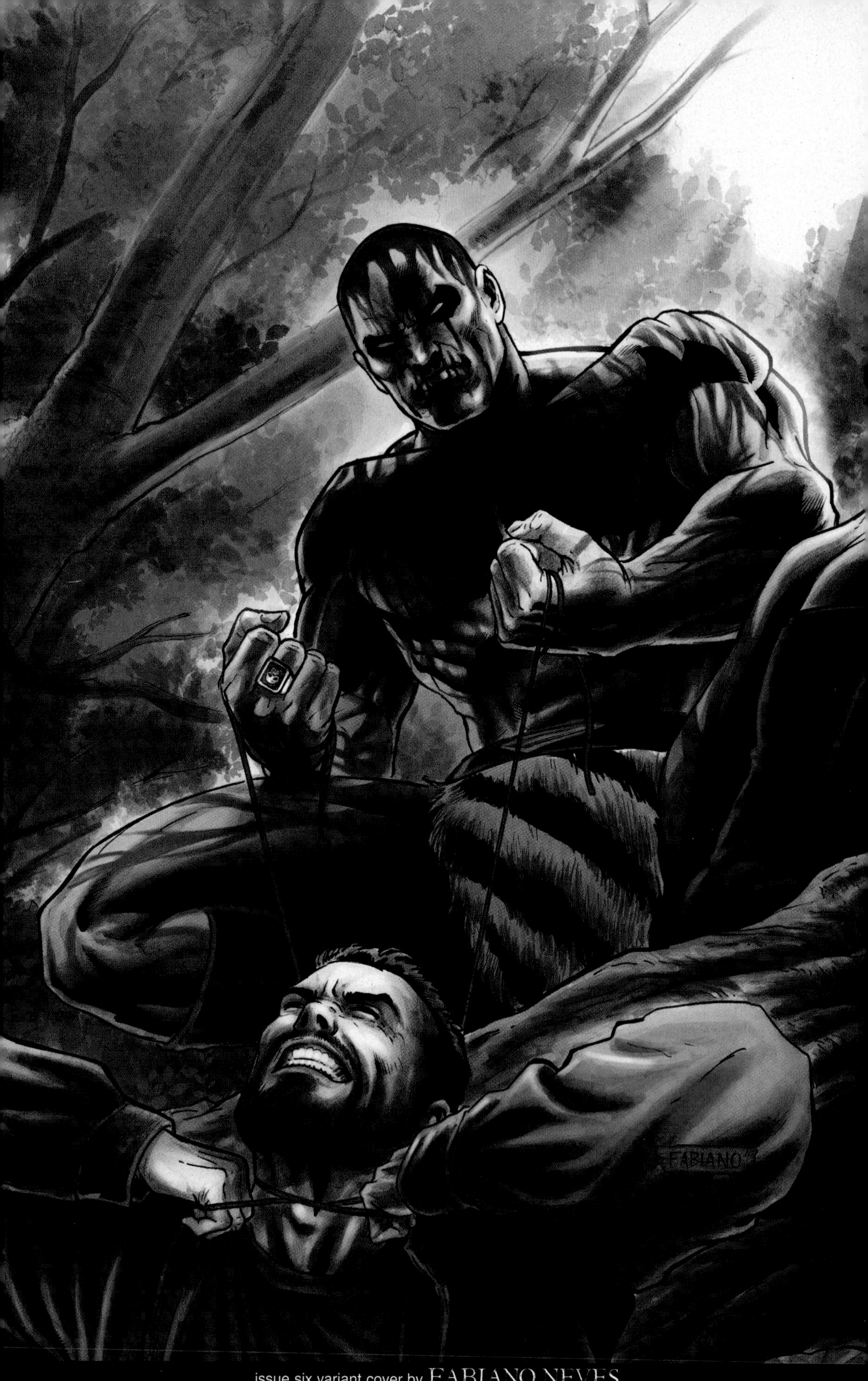
FABIANO

issue six variant cover by FABIANO NEVES

SKETCHES AND
DESIGNS BY
ALEX ROSS

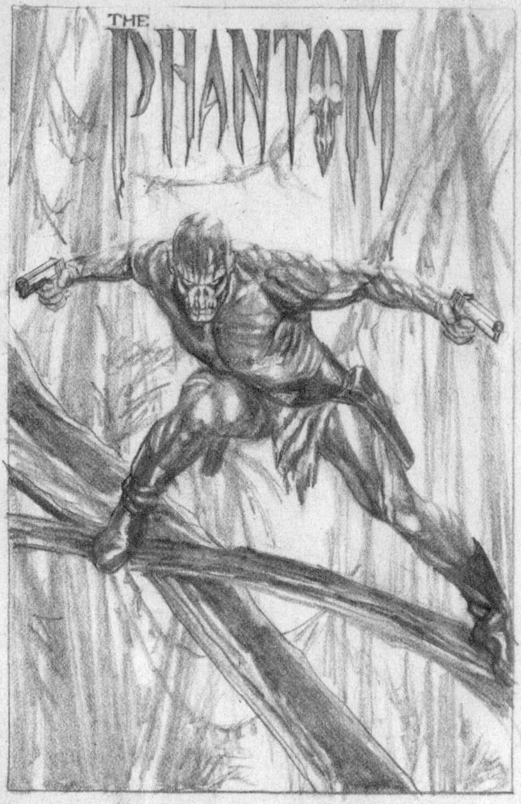
THE
PHANTOM

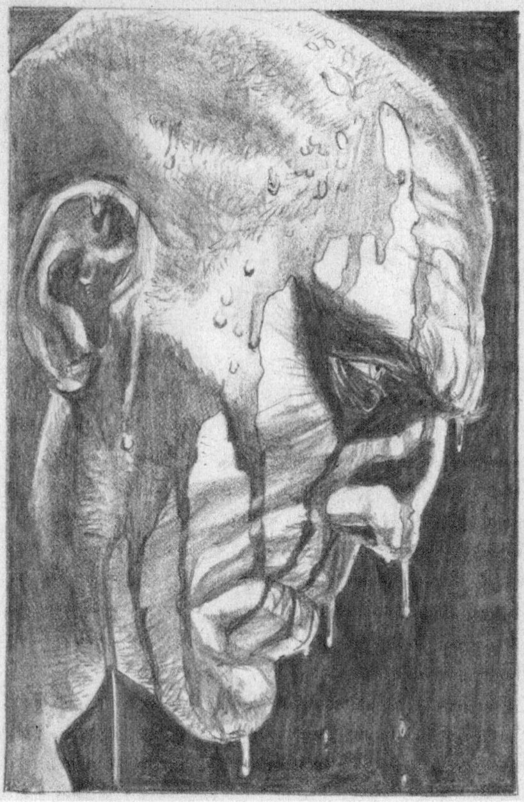

Original thumbnail sketches for the covers to issues 1 through 3 by Alex Ross

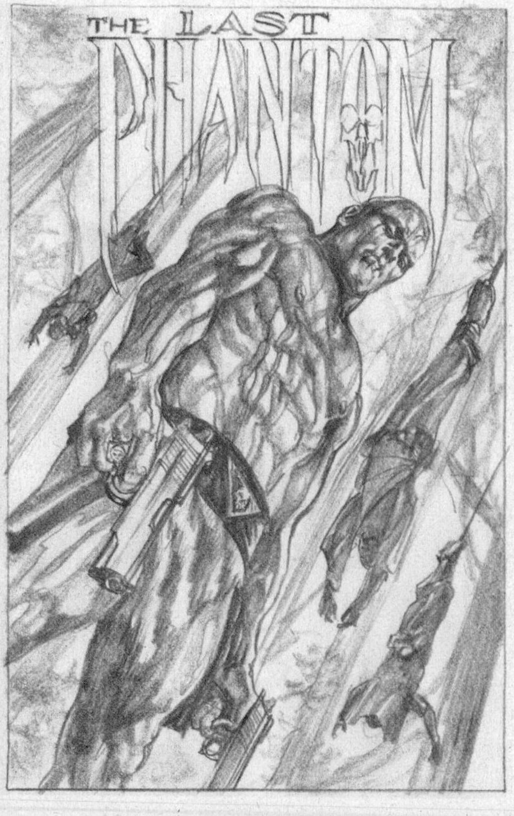
THE LAST
PHANTOM

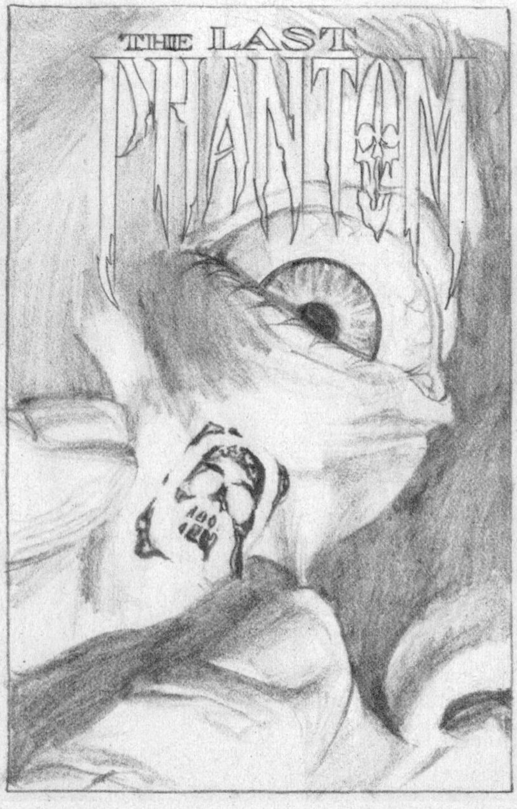
THE LAST
PHANTOM

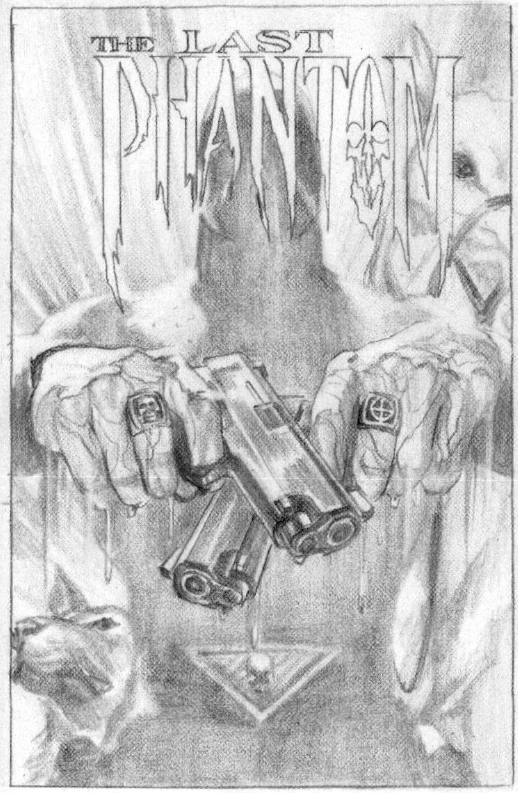
THE LAST
PHANTOM

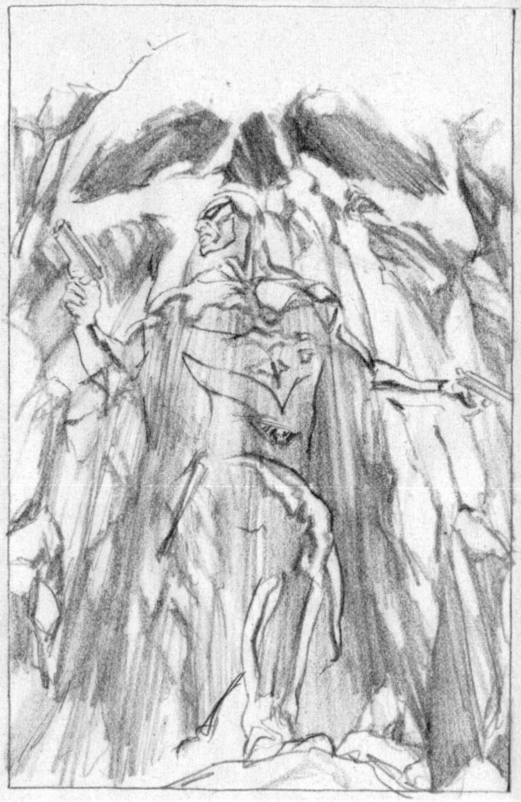

Original thumbnail sketches for the covers to issues 5 through 6 by Alex Ross, including an unused design for the cover to issue 5 (bottom left).

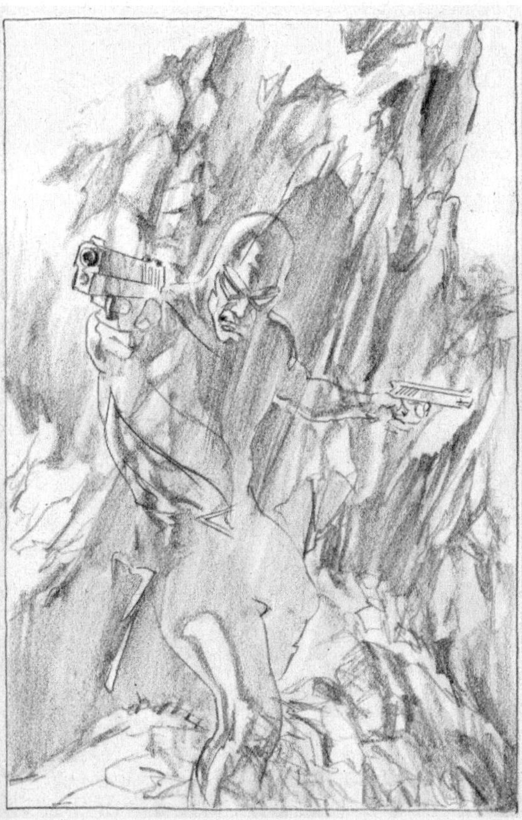

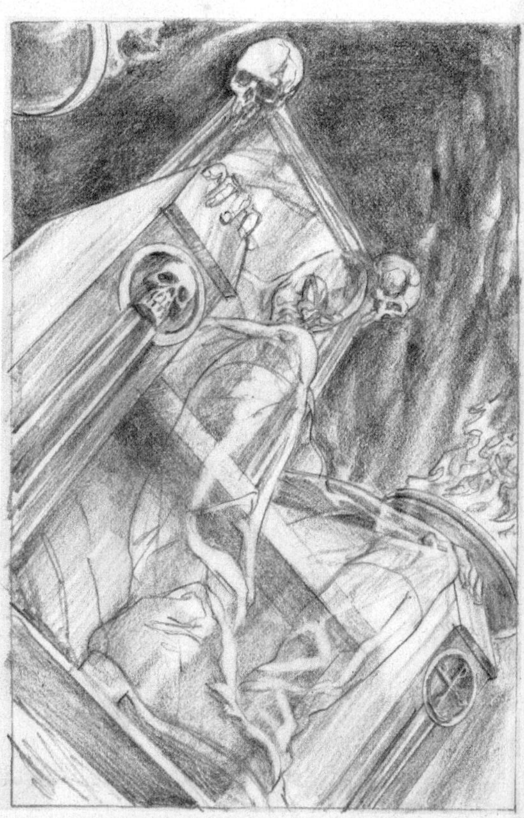

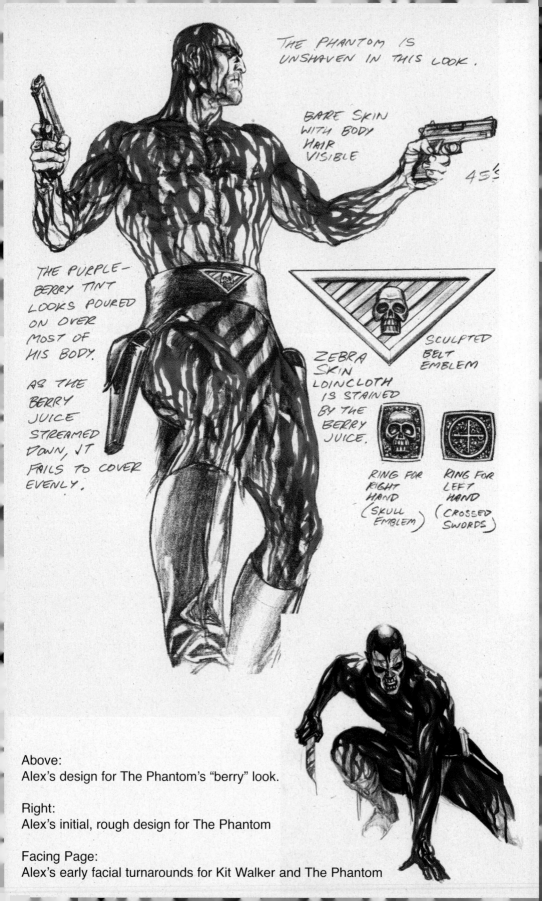

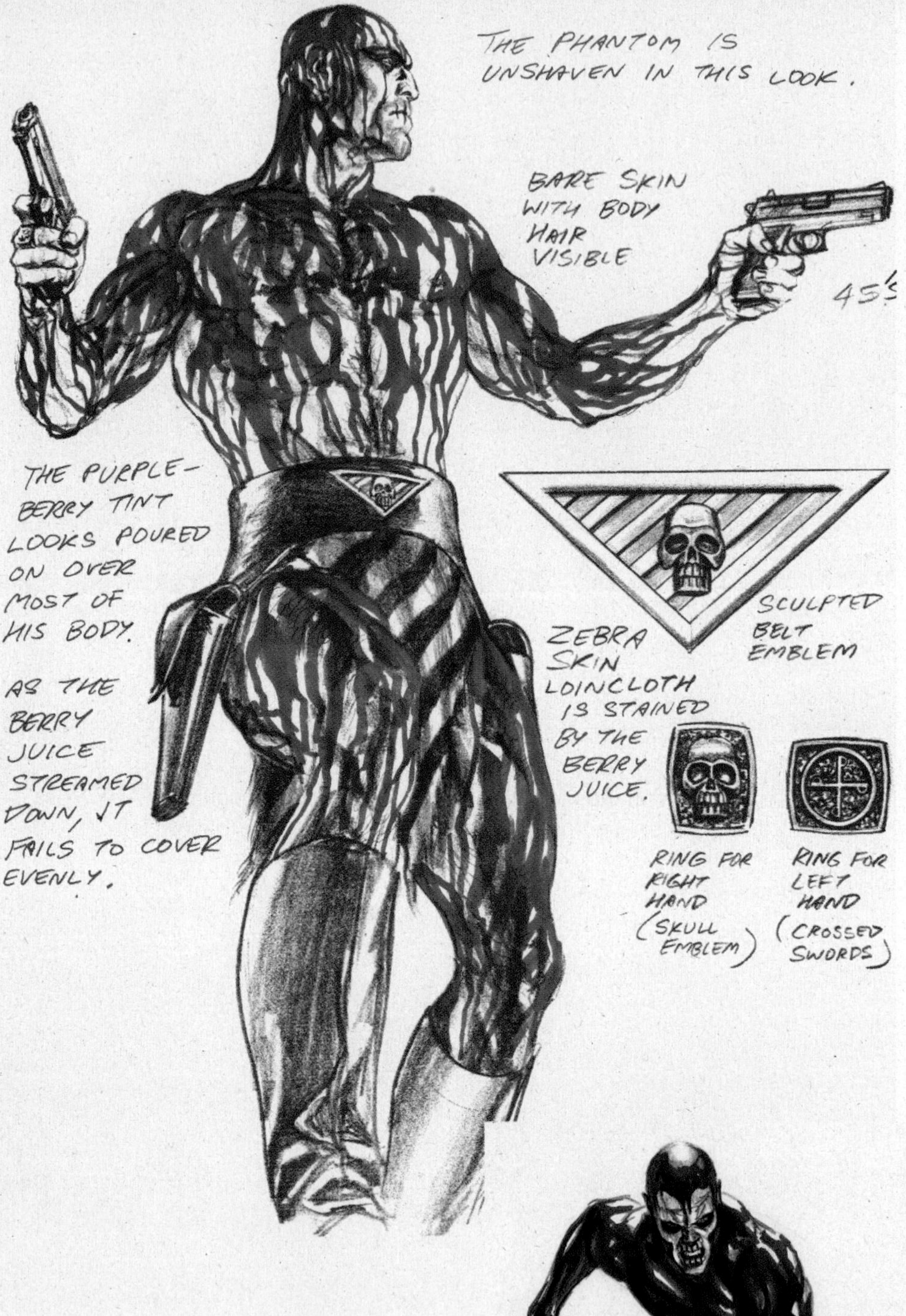
THE PHANTOM IS UNSHAVEN IN THIS LOOK.
BARE SKIN WITH BODY HAIR VISIBLE
45'S
THE PURPLE-BERRY TINT LOOKS POURED ON OVER MOST OF HIS BODY.
AS THE BERRY JUICE STREAMED DOWN, IT FAILS TO COVER EVENLY.
SCULPTED BELT EMBLEM
ZEBRA SKIN LOINCLOTH IS STAINED BY THE BERRY JUICE.
RING FOR RIGHT HAND (SKULL EMBLEM)
RING FOR LEFT HAND (CROSSED SWORDS)

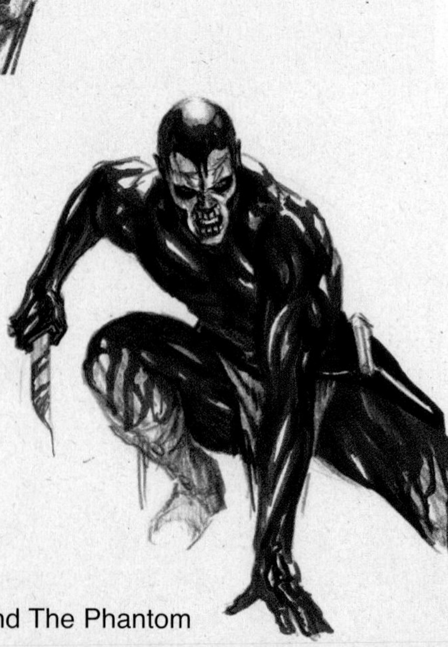

Above:
Alex's design for The Phantom's "berry" look.

Right:
Alex's initial, rough design for The Phantom

Facing Page:
Alex's early facial turnarounds for Kit Walker and The Phantom

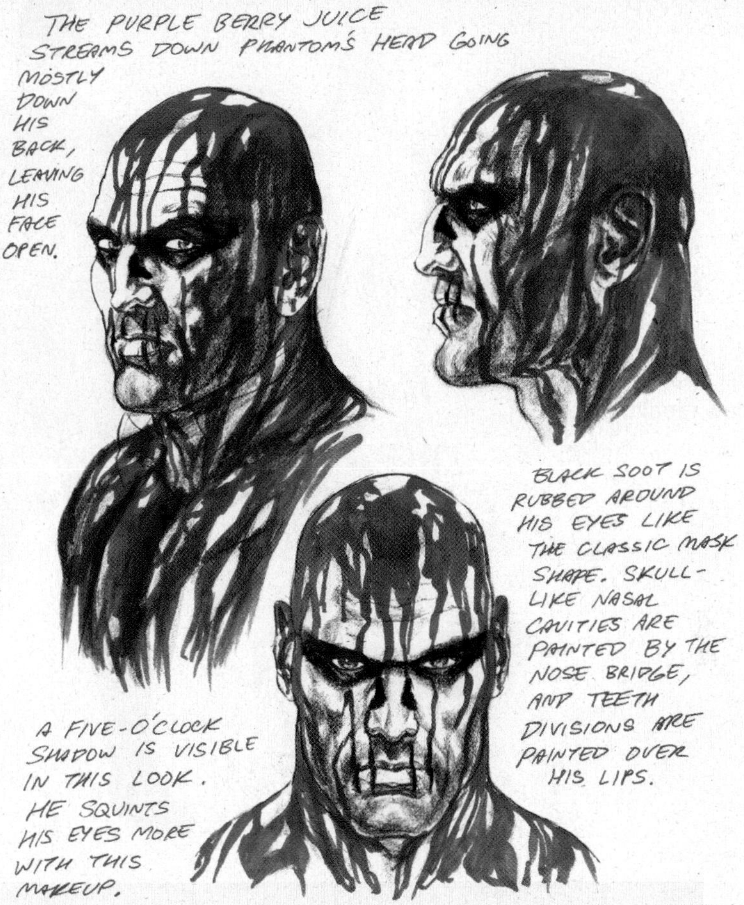
THE PURPLE BERRY JUICE STREAMS DOWN PHANTOM'S HEAD GOING MOSTLY DOWN HIS BACK, LEAVING HIS FACE OPEN.
BLACK SOOT IS RUBBED AROUND HIS EYES LIKE THE CLASSIC MASK SHAPE. SKULL-LIKE NASAL CAVITIES ARE PAINTED BY THE NOSE BRIDGE, AND TEETH DIVISIONS ARE PAINTED OVER HIS LIPS.
A FIVE-O'CLOCK SHADOW IS VISIBLE IN THIS LOOK. HE SQUINTS HIS EYES MORE WITH THIS MAKEUP.

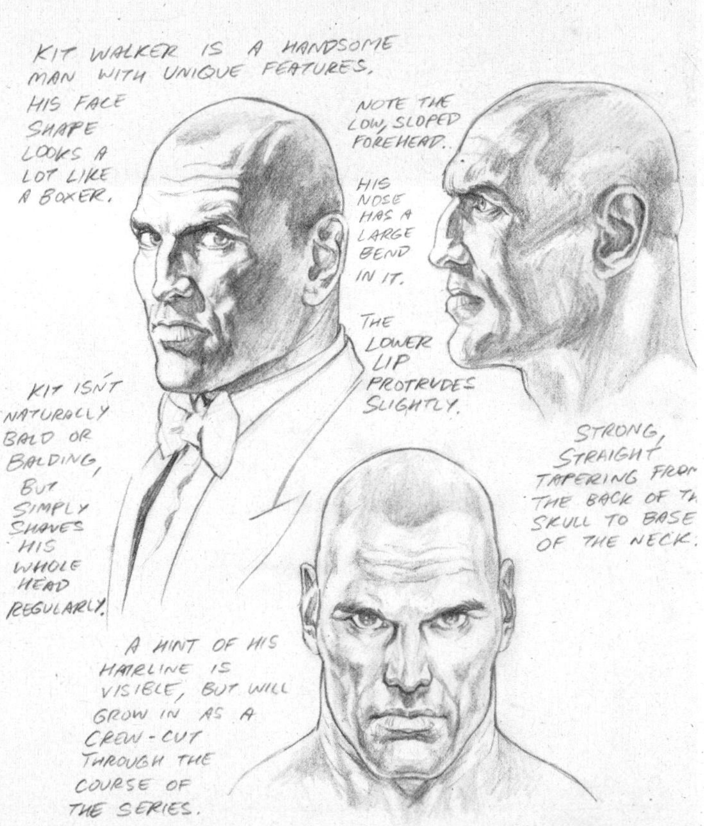
KIT WALKER IS A HANDSOME MAN WITH UNIQUE FEATURES.
HIS FACE SHAPE LOOKS A LOT LIKE A BOXER.
NOTE THE LOW, SLOPED FOREHEAD.
HIS NOSE HAS A LARGE BEND IN IT.
THE LOWER LIP PROTRUDES SLIGHTLY.
KIT ISN'T NATURALLY BALD OR BALDING, BUT SIMPLY SHAVES HIS WHOLE HEAD REGULARLY.
STRONG, STRAIGHT TAPERING FROM THE BACK OF TH SKULL TO BASE OF THE NECK.
A HINT OF HIS HAIRLINE IS VISIBLE, BUT WILL GROW IN AS A CREW-CUT THROUGH THE COURSE OF THE SERIES.

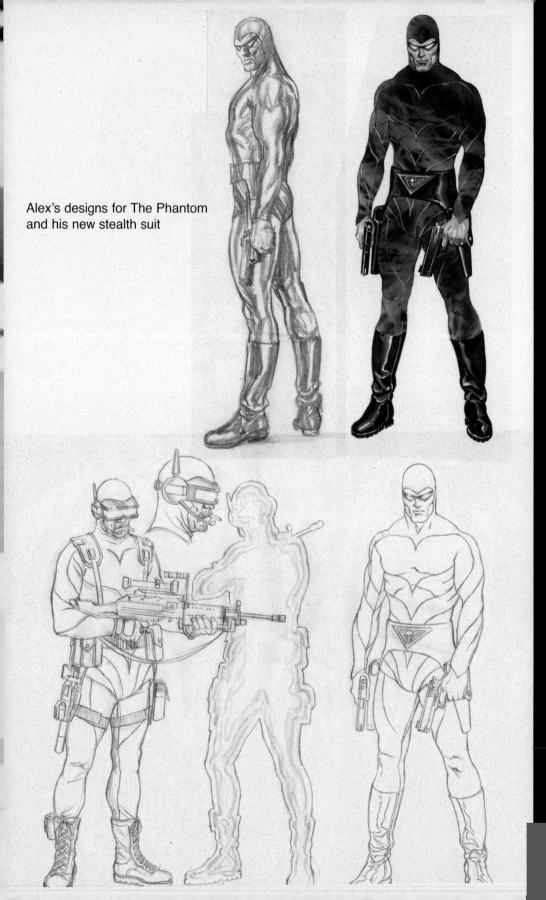

Alex's designs for The Phantom and his new stealth suit

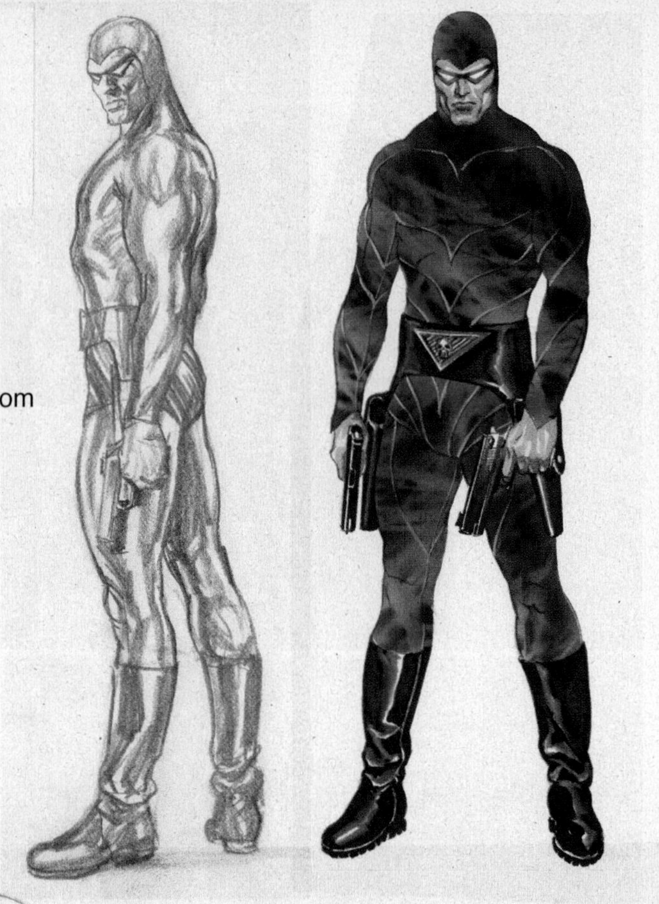

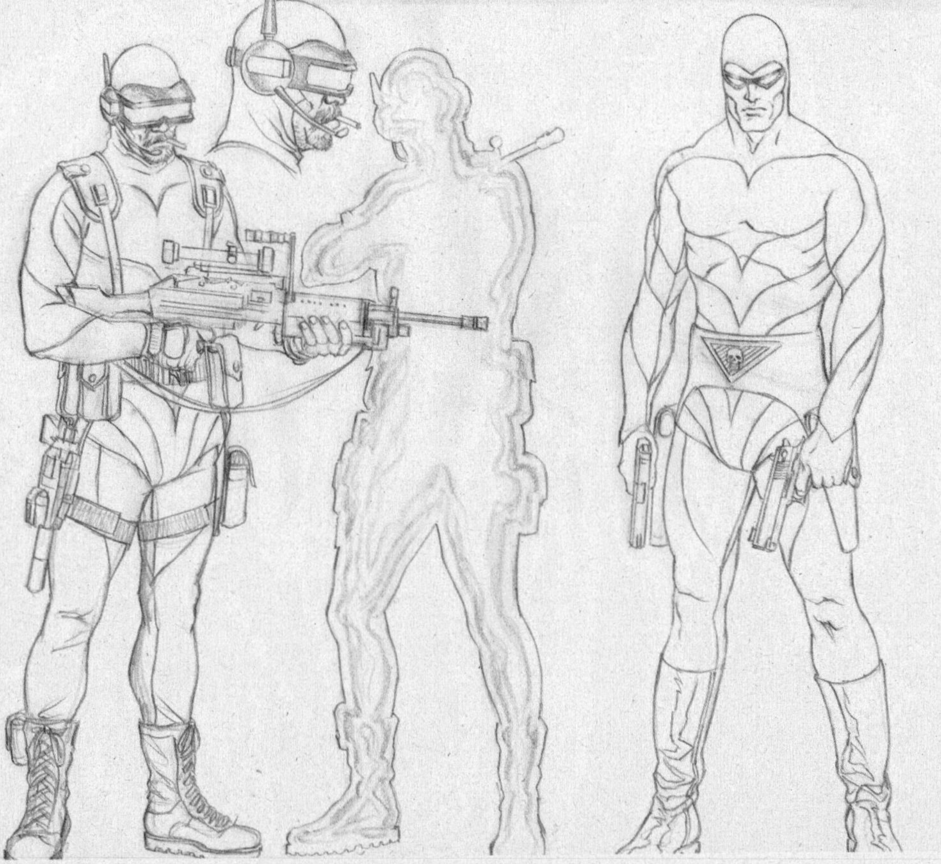

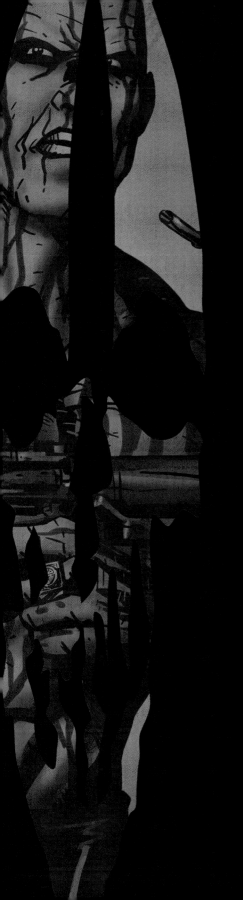

SKETCHES AND
DESIGNS BY
EDUARDO
FERIGATO

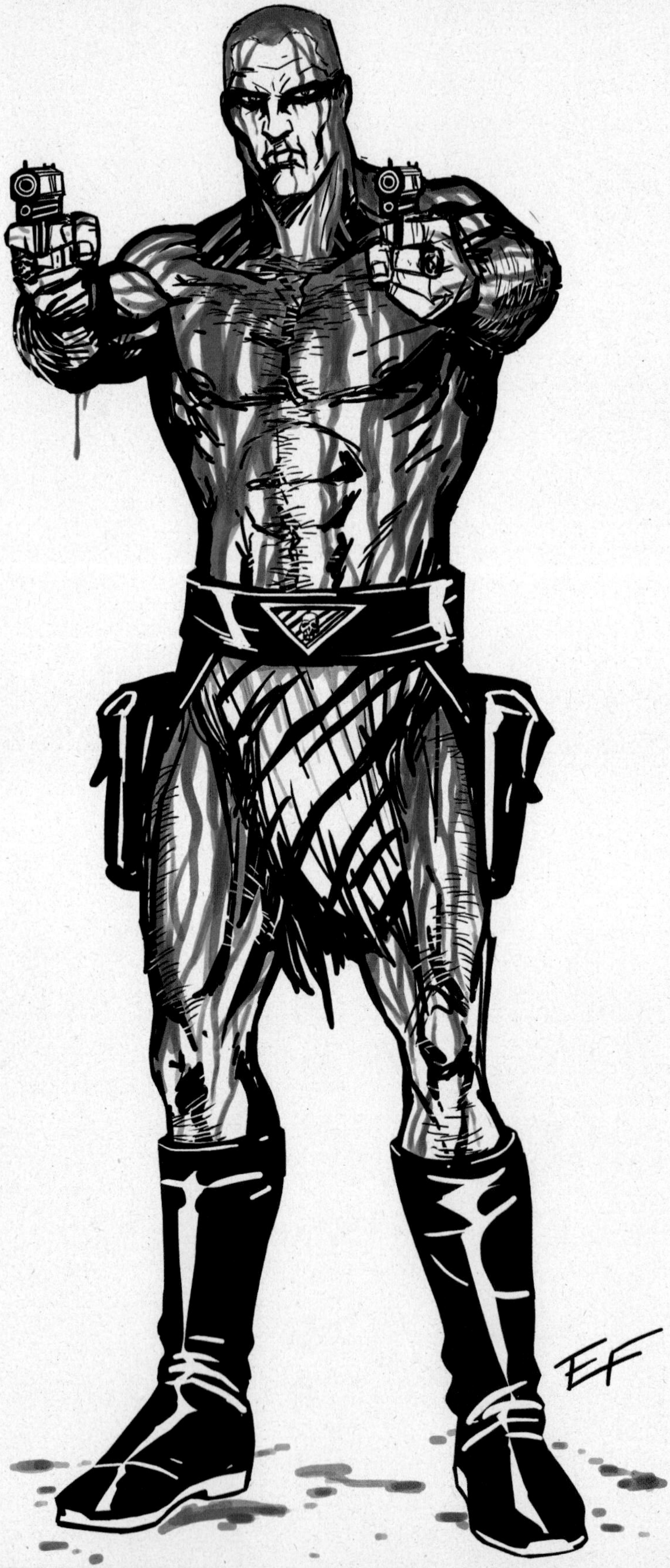
EF

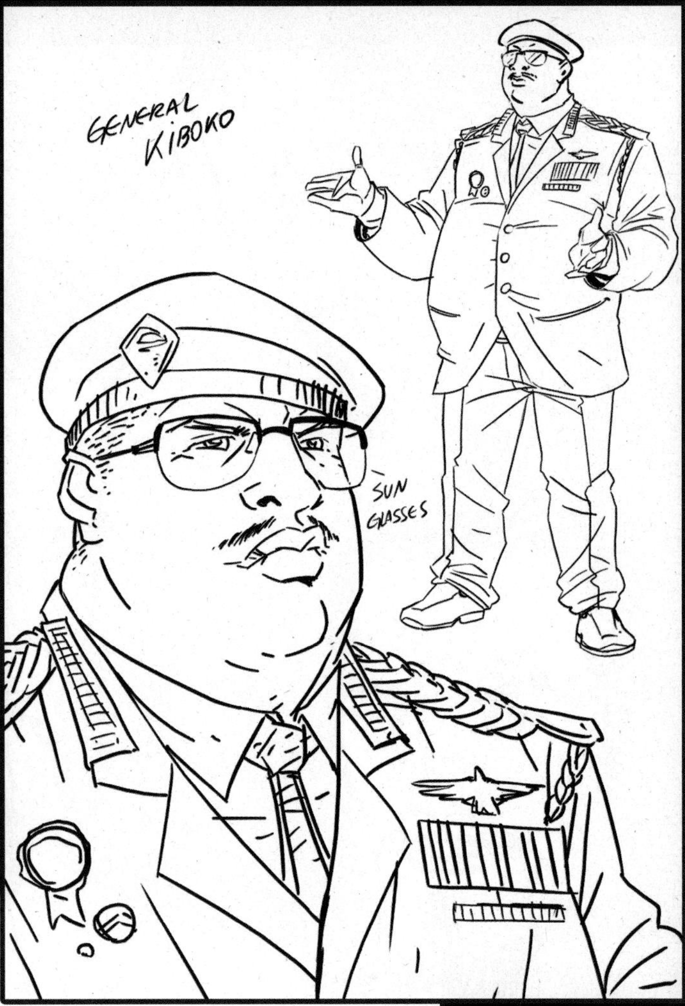
GENERAL KIBOKO
SUN GLASSES

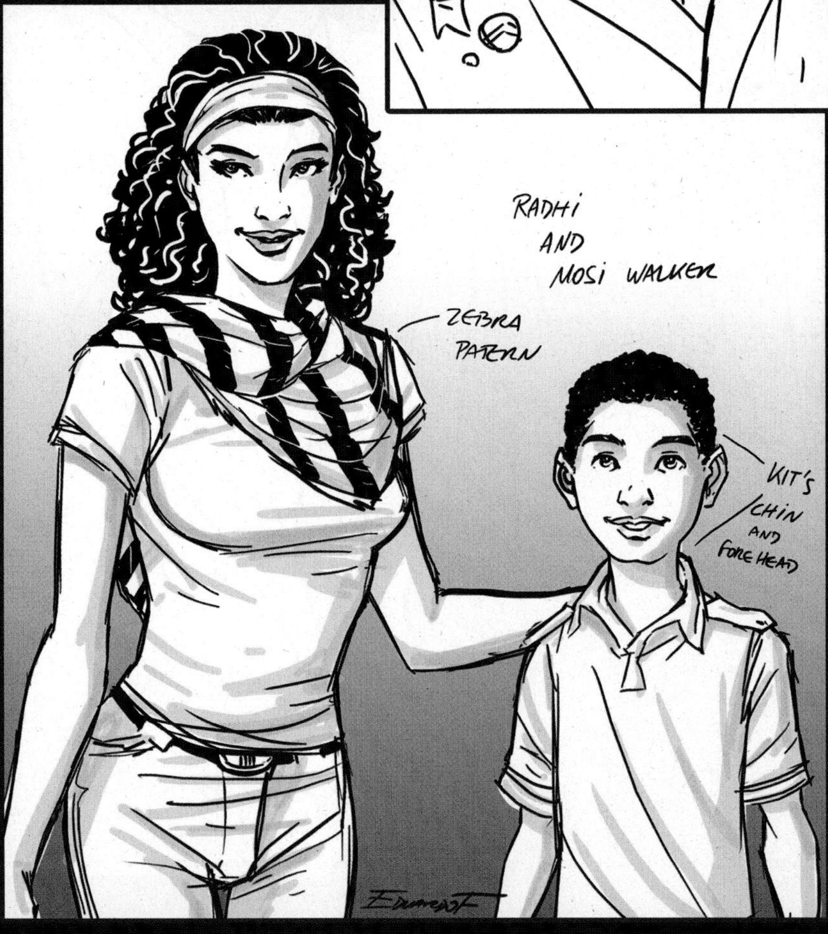
RADHI AND MOSI WALKER
ZEBRA PATTERN
KIT'S CHIN AND FOREHEAD

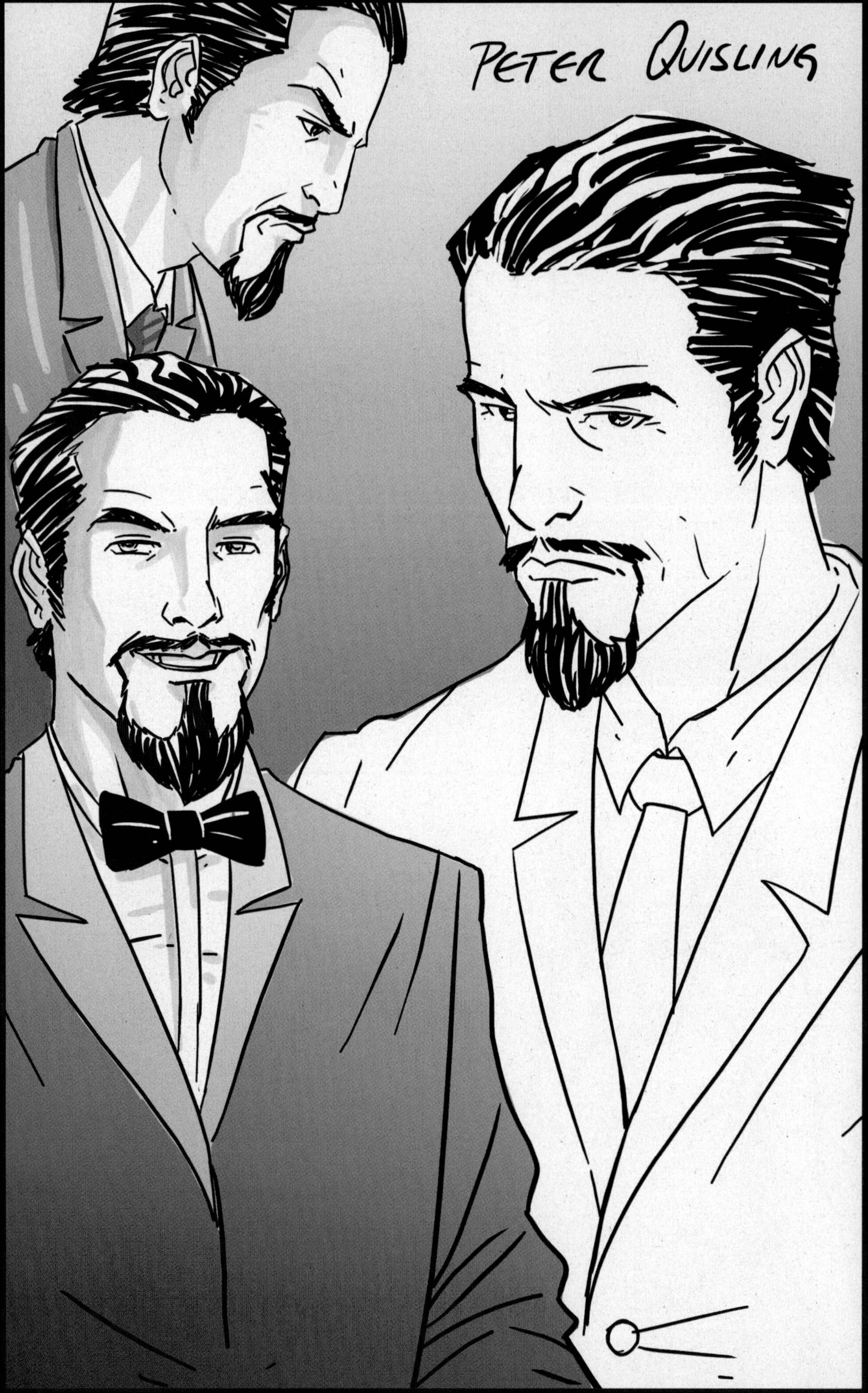
PETER QUISLING

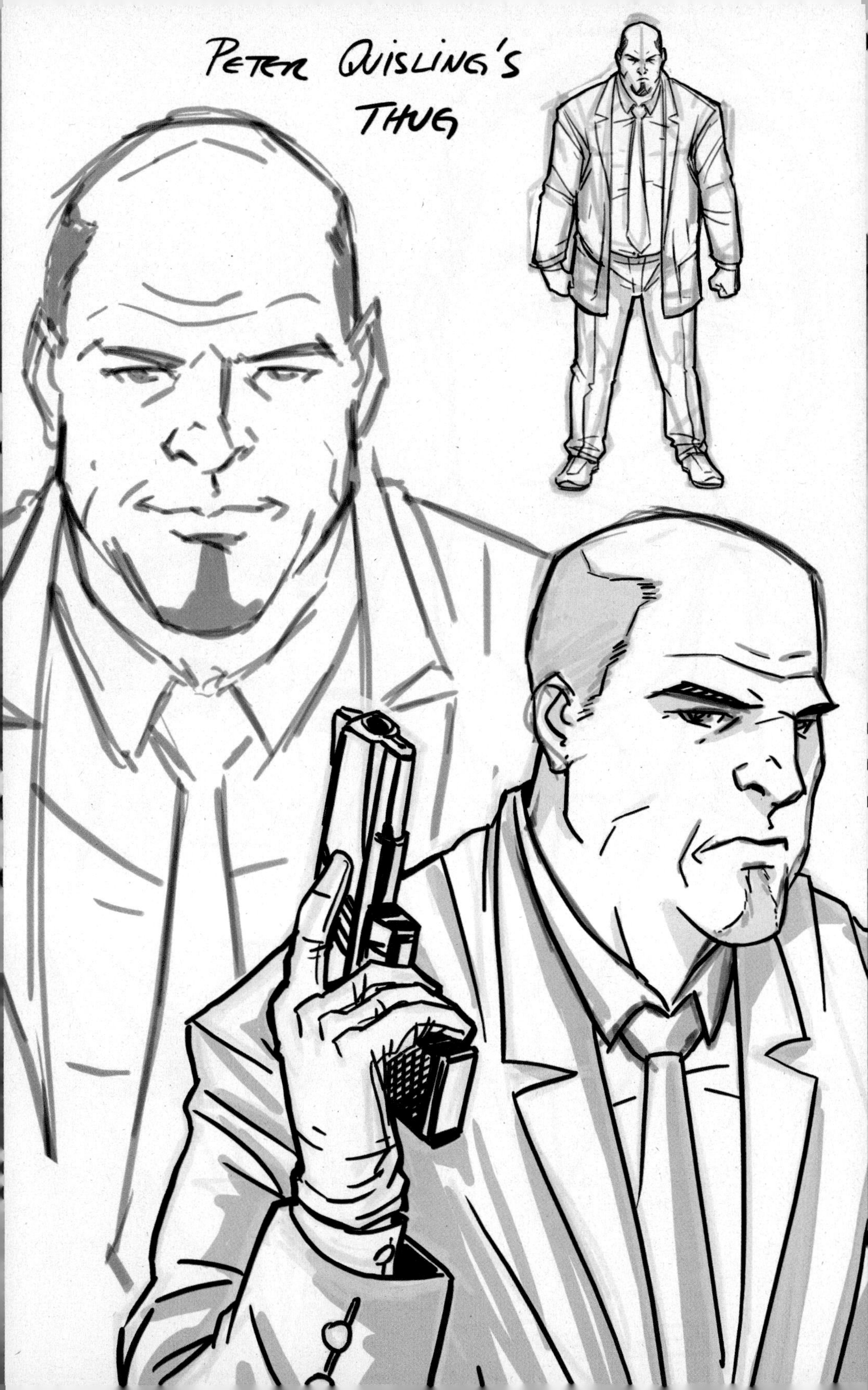
PETER QUISLING'S THUG

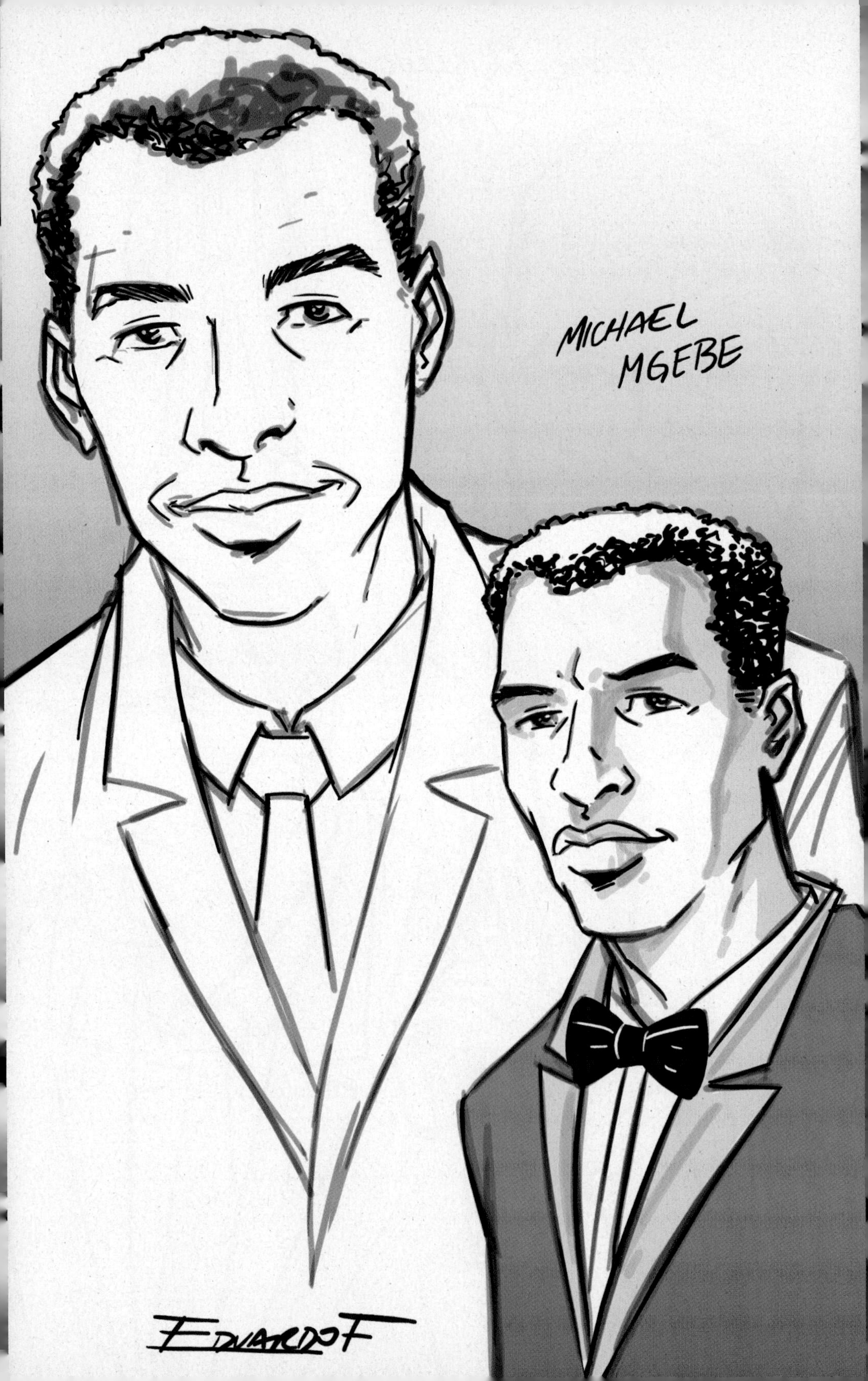
MICHAEL
MGEBE
EDUARDO F

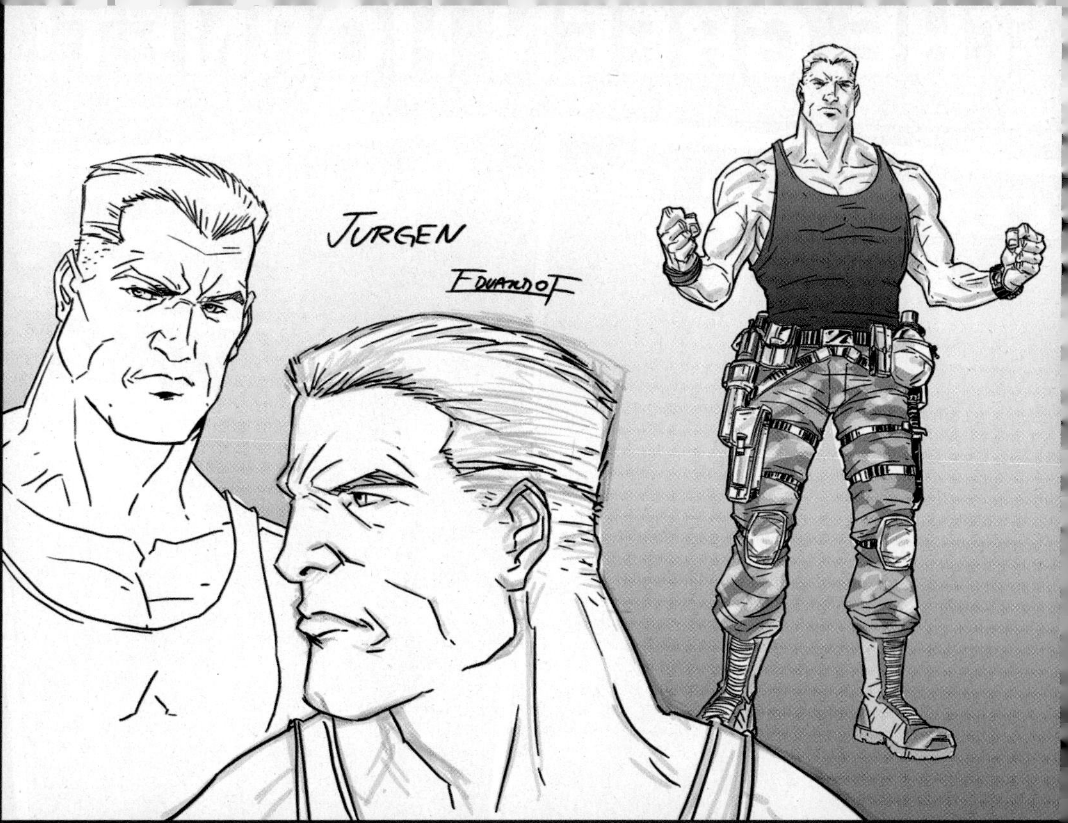
JURGEN

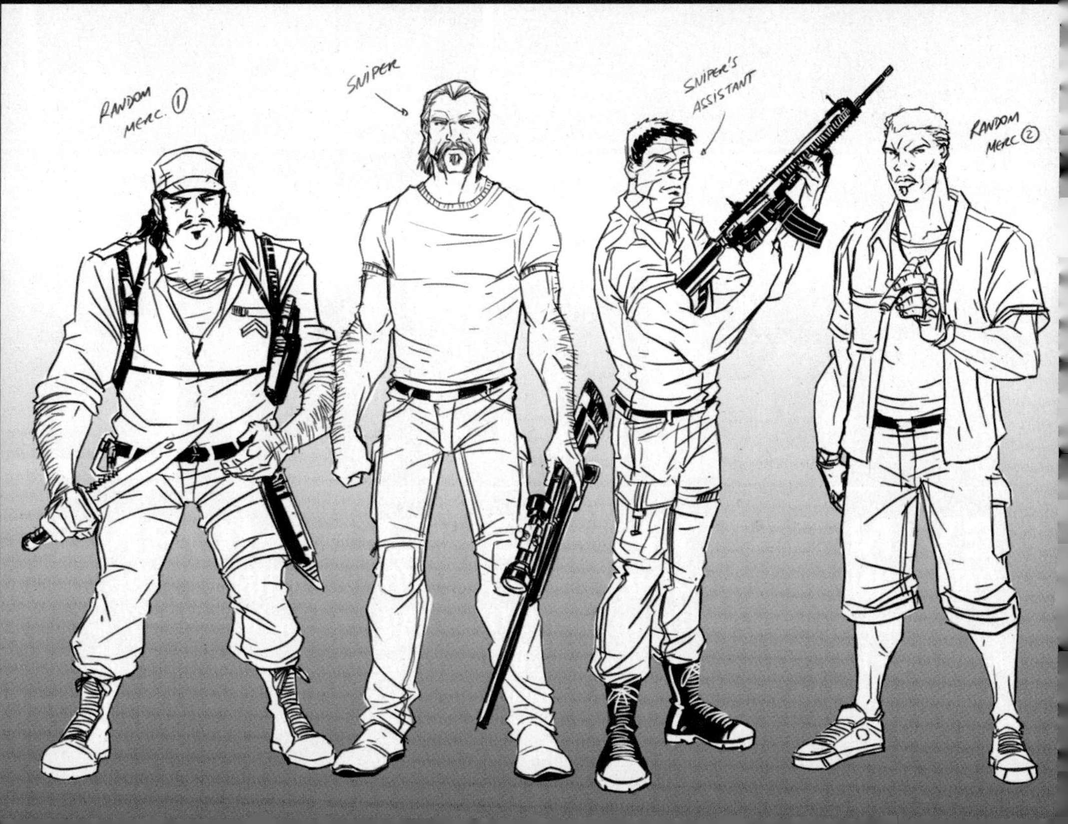
RANDOM MERC. 1
SNIPER
SNIPER'S ASSISTANT
RANDOM MERC 2

KEVIN SMITH presents THE GREEN HORNET!

volume one: SINS OF THE FATHER

volume two: WEARING O' THE GREEN

KEVIN SMITH'S GREEN HORNET
VOL. ONE: "SINS OF THE FATHER" & VOL. TWO "WEARING O' THE GREEN"
written by **KEVIN SMITH**   art by **JONATHAN LAU**   covers by **ALEX ROSS**

Playboy Britt Reid Jr. has lived a frivolous life of luxury. But when a mysterious figure from the past brutally and publicly murders his father, all of that changes. Now, driven by a thirst for vengeance and guided by two generations of Katos, this one time underachiever will find those responsible and take his father's place as Century City's greatest protector – The Green Hornet!

In Stores Now!

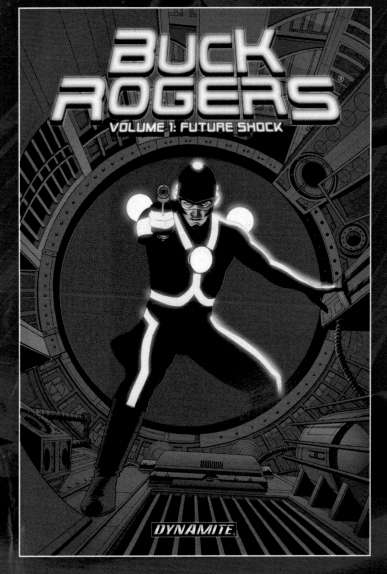

ENTLY AVAILABLE AND UPCOMING COLLECTIONS FROM DYNAMITE ENTERTAINMENT
For a complete list, visit us online at www.dynamiteentertainment.com

RMY OF DARKNESS

Army of Darkness: Movie Adaptation
Raimi, Raimi, Bolton

Army of Darkness: Ashes to Ashes
Hartnell, Bradshaw

Army of Darkness: Shop 'Till You Drop Dead
Kuhoric, Bradshaw, Greene

Army of Darkness vs. Re-Animator
Kuhoric, Bradshaw, Greene

Army of Darkness: Old School & More
Kuhoric, Sharpe

Army of Darkness: Ash vs. The Classic Monsters
Kuhoric, Sharpe, Blanco

Army of Darkness: From The Ashes
Kuhoric, Blanco

Army of Darkness: The Long Road Home
Kuhoric, Raicht, Blanco

Army of Darkness: Home Sweet Hell
Kuhoric, Raicht, Perez

Army of Darkness: Hellbillies & Deadnecks
Kuhoric, Raicht, Cohn

Army of Darkness: League of Light Assemble!
Raicht, Cohn

Army of Darkness Omnibus Vol. 1
Hartnell, Kuhoric, Kirkman, more

Army of Darkness vs. Xena Vol. 1: Why Not?
Layman, Jerwa, Montenegro

Xena vs. Army of Darkness Vol. 2: What...Again?!
Jerwa, Serrano, Montenegro

Darkman vs. Army of Darkness
Busiek, Stern, Fry

BATTLESTAR GALACTICA

Classic Battlestar Galactica Vol. 1
Remender, Rafael

Classic Battlestar Galactica Vol. 2: Cylon Apocalypse
Grillo-Marxuach, Rafael

New Battlestar Galactica Vol. 1
Pak, Raynor

New Battlestar Galactica Vol. 2
Pak, Raynor

New Battlestar Galactica Vol. 3
Pak, Raynor, Lau

New Battlestar Galactica Complete Omnibus V1
Pak, Raynor, Jerwa, Lau

New Battlestar Galactica: Zarek
Jerwa, Batista

New Battlestar Galactica: Season Zero Vol. 1
Jerwa, Herbert

New Battlestar Galactica: Season Zero Vol. 2
Jerwa, Herbert

New Battlestar Galactica Origins: Baltar
Fahey, Lau

New Battlestar Galactica Origins: Adama
Napton, Lau

New Battlestar Galactica Origins: Starbuck & Helo
Fahey, Lau

New Battlestar Galactica: Ghosts
Jerwa, Lau

New Battlestar Galactica: Cylon War
Ortega, Nylund, Raynor

New Battlestar Galactica: The Final Five
Fahey, Reed, Raynor

THE BOYS

The Boys Vol. 1 The Name of the Game
Ennis, Robertson

The Boys Vol. 2 Get Some
Ennis, Robertson, Snejbjerg

The Boys Vol. 3 Good For The Soul
Ennis, Robertson

The Boys Vol. 4 We Gotta Go Now
Ennis, Robertson

The Boys Vol. 5 Herogasm
Ennis, McCrea
Ennis, Robertson

The Boys Vol. 6 The Self-Preservation Society
Ennis, Robertson, Ezquerra

The Boys Vol. 7 The Innocents
Ennis, Robertson, Braun

The Boys Definitive Edition Vol. 1
Ennis, Robertson

The Boys Definitive Edition Vol. 2
Ennis, Robertson

THE GREEN HORNET

Kevin Smith's Green Hornet Vol. 1 Sins of the Father
Smith, Hester, Lau

Kevin Smith's Green Hornet Vol. 2 Wearing o' the Green
Smith, Hester, Lau

Kevin Smith's Kato Vol. 1 Not My Father's Daughter
Parks, Garza, Bernard

The Green Hornet: Year One Vol. 1 The Sting of Justice
Wagner, Campbell, Francavilla

Kato Origins Vol. 1 Way of the Ninja
Nitz, Worley

The Green Hornet Parallel Lives
Nitz, Raynor

THE LONE RANGER

The Lone Ranger Vol. 1: Now & Forever
Matthews, Cariello, Cassaday

The Lone Ranger Vol. 2: Lines Not Crossed
Matthews, Cariello, Cassaday, Pope

The Lone Ranger Vol. 3: Scorched Earth
Matthews, Cariello, Cassaday

The Lone Ranger & Tonto
Matthews, Cariello, More

The Lone Ranger Definitive Edition Vol. 1
Matthews, Cariello, Cassaday

PROJECT SUPERPOWERS

Project Superpowers Chapter 1
Ross, Krueger, Paul, Sadowski

Project Superpowers Chapter 2 Vol. 1
Ross, Krueger, Salazar

Project Superpowers Chapter 2 Vol. 2
Ross, Krueger, Salazar

Project Superpowers: Meet The Bad Guys
Ross, Casey, Lilly, Lau, Paul, Herbert

Black Terror Vol. 1
Ross, Krueger, Lilly

Black Terror Vol. 2
Ross, Hester, Lau, Lilly

The Death-Defying 'Devil Vol. 1
Ross, Casey, Salazar

Masquerade Vol. 1
Ross, Hester, Paul

RED SONJA

Adventures of Red Sonja Vol. 1
Thomas, Thorne, More

Adventures of Red Sonja Vol. 2
Thomas, Thorne, More

Adventures of Red Sonja Vol. 3
Thomas, Thorne, More

Red Sonja She-Devil With a Sword Vol. 1
Oeming, Carey, Rubi

Red Sonja She-Devil With a Sword Vol. 2: Arrowsmiths
Oeming, Rubi, more

Red Sonja She-Devil With a Sword Vol. 3: The Rise of Kulan Gath
Oeming, Rubi, more

Red Sonja She-Devil With a Sword Vol. 4: Animals & More
Oeming, Homs, more

Red Sonja She-Devil With a Sword Vol. 5: World On Fire
Oeming, Reed, Homs

Red Sonja She-Devil With a Sword Vol. 6: Death
Marz, Ortega, Reed, more

Red Sonja She-Devil With a Sword Vol. 7: Born Again
Reed, Geovani

Red Sonja She-Devil With a Sword Vol. 8: Blood Dynasty
Reed, Geovani

Red Sonja She-Devil With a Sword Omnibus Vol. 1
Oeming, Carey, Rubi, more

Red Sonja vs. Thulsa Doom Vol. 1
David, Lieberman, Conrad

Savage Red Sonja: Queen of the Frozen Wastes
Cho, Murray, Homs

Red Sonja: Travels
Marz, Ortega, Thomas, more

Sword of Red Sonja: Doom of the Gods (Red Sonja vs. Thulsa Doom 2)
Lieberman, Antonio

Red Sonja: Wrath of the Gods
Lieberman, Geovani

Queen Sonja Vol. 1
Ortega, Rubi

Savage Tales of Red Sonja
Marz, Gage, Ortega, more

Robert E. Howard Presents: ThulsaDoom Vol. 1
Nelson, Antonio

VAMPIRELLA

Vampirella Masters Series Vol. 1 Grant Morrison & Mark Millar
Morrison, Millar, More

Vampirella Masters Series Vol. 2 Warren Ellis
Ellis, Conner, Palmiotti, More

Vampirella Masters Series Vol. 3 Mark Millar
Millar, Mayhew

Vampirella Archive Vol. 1
Various

Vampirella Archive Vol. 2
Various

Vampirella Archive Vol. 3
Various

ZORRO

Zorro Vol. 1: Year One Trail of the Fox
Wagner, Francavilla

Zorro Vol. 2: Clashing Blades
Wagner, Razek

Zorro: Matanzas
McGregor, Mayhew

MORE FROM GARTH ENNIS!

Dan Dare Omnibus
Ennis, Erskine

Garth Ennis' Battlefields Vol. 1: The Night Witches
Ennis, Braun

Garth Ennis' Battlefields Vol. 2: Dear Billy
Ennis, Snejbjerg

Garth Ennis' Battlefields Vol. 3: The Tankies
Ennis, Ezquerra

Garth Ennis' The Complete Battlefields Vol. 1
Ennis, Braun, Snejbjerg, Ezquerra

Garth Ennis' Battlefields Vol. 4: Happy Valley
Ennis, Holden

Garth Ennis' Battlefields Vol. 5: The Firefly & His Majesty
Ennis, Ezquerra

Garth Ennis' Battlefields Vol. 6: Motherland
Ennis, Braun

Just A Pilgrim
Ennis, Ezquerra

FROM HOWARD CHAYKIN!

American Flagg! Definitive Collection Vol. 1
Chaykin

Black Kiss
Howard Chaykin

Power & Glory
Chaykin

FROM JIM STARLIN!

Dreadstar The Definitive Collection
Starlin

Dreadstar: The Beginning
Starlin

Kid Kosmos: Cosmic Guard
Starlin

Kid Kosmos: Kidnapped
Starlin

AND MANY MORE!

Visit us online at: dynamite.net for a complete listing of Dynamite Entertainment titles!